'The subtitle of this "quietly moving biography" is "the real Charlotte Gray," . . . And it's true that Witherington, like Sebastian Faulks' heroine, joined SOE partly in the hope of re-joining her French boyfriend. But she was "more than a shade superior" to her fictional counterpart.' Book of the Week, The *Week*

'Witherington's loyalty to her French beau feels like a metaphor for her commitment to France. The romance in this story is of a very measured kind: strong, loyal and courageous. What gives Witherington's story an edge is that she not only had all these virtues in spades, she was also extremely effective.'

Claire Mulley, The *Spectator*

'Seymour-Jones's affection for her subject mercifully doesn't mean a sepia-tinted treatment . . . Instead she has served up history through one piercing pair of eyes . . . Also telling the moving story of a spy who loved France, loved a Frenchman and loved justice – enough to risk her life for all three.'

Giles Whittal, *The Times*

'Women were not generally regarded as suitable by SOE's largely Oxbridge recruiters, whose view of the female sex remained mired in Victorian niceties . . . Carole Seymour-Jones shows in *She Landed By Moonlight* [that] the stories of these brave, quixotic, often very young agents have not lost their appeal . . . A gripping tale.'

Caroline Moorehead, *Literary Review*

'This is not the story of a woman who knew no fear, but rather of a woman who overcame fear to serve the countries – England and France – that she loved. Carole Seymour-Jones does full justice to a truly remarkable and little-known woman.'

Country Life

'A thoroughly researched and perceptive biography.' The *Lady*

Also by Carole Seymour-Jones

A Dangerous Liaison (Century, 2008)
Painted Shadow: The Life of Vivienne Eliot, first wife of T. S. Eliot (Constable Robinson, 2001)
Beatrice Webb: a Woman of Conflict (Allison & Busby, 1992)
Journey of Faith: The History of the World YWCA 1945–1994 (Allison & Busby, 1994)
Refugees (Heinemann, 1992)
Homelessness (Heinemann, 1993)
Another Sky: Voices of Conscience from Around the World, co-editor (Profile, 2007)

She Landed by Moonlight: The Story of Secret Agent Pearl Witherington

CAROLE SEYMOUR-JONES

First published in Great Britain in 2013 by
Hodder & Stoughton
An Hachette UK company

First published in paperback in 2014

4

A CIP catalogue record for this title is available from the British Library

ISBN 978 1 444 72462 2

Typeset in Bembo by
Palimpsest Book Production Limited, Falkirk, Stirlingshire

Printed and bound by Clays Ltd, St Ives plc

Hodder & Stoughton Ltd
338 Euston Road
London NW1 3BH

www.hodder.co.uk

To the memory of
M.R.D. Foot
1919–2012
Friend and mentor

Carole Seymour-Jones was born in Wales and educated at Oxford University. She was longlisted for the Samuel Johnson Prize for *Painted Shadow*, her biography of Vivienne Eliot, first wife of TS Eliot. Her biography of Simone de Beauvoir and Jean-Paul Sartre, *A Dangerous Liaison*, was shortlisted for the Marsh Biography Prize. Carole is a Visiting Fellow at the University of Surrey, and former Deputy President and chair of the Writers in Prison Committee of English PEN, the writers' charity.

She has three children and she and her husband divide their time between London and Surrey.

www.caroleseymourjones.co.uk

Contents

CENTRAL FRANCE
ENGLISH CHANNEL
N
Cotentin Peninsula
Cherbourg
OPERATION OVERLORD
Le Havre
Caen
Port-en-Bessin
Paris
ORLEANS
Beaugency
Sologne
Blois
Tours
LOIR
LOIRE
CHER
Saint-Aignan
Romorantin
Selles-sur-Cher
Salbris
Les Tailles De Ruines
Vierzon
Bourges
Nevers
Argenton-sur-Creuse
Valençay
Les Souches
Dun-le-Poëlier
Châteauroux
Tendu
Graçay
Issoudun
La Châtre
DEMARCATION LINE
Montluçon
Limoges
Guéret
Vichy
Oradour-sur-Glane
Clermont-Ferrand
Tulle
A
B
C
D
E
F
DEPARTMENTS
A Loir-et-Cher
B Indre
C Creuse
D Puy-de-Dôme
E Corrèze
F Dordogne
10mi
20km

Map of Former F Circuits

Preface

ONE DAY in May 2012, while following in Pearl's footsteps in France, I hired a car and drove from Châteauroux to Limoges. I took a detour west, to the 'martyr' village of Oradour-sur-Glane. There I walked down the hill in bright sunshine, past the empty, ruined houses into the skeleton of the church in which the women and children of the village were burned alive by the Waffen SS on 10 June 1944.

A shaft of sunlight fell on an altar, and something caught my eye: a pair of calcified clogs, the wooden *sabots* worn by women of the time. They were a mute reminder of their owner, a woman dying, clutching her child to her legs, shielding him in her skirts as the flames crackled around her and the smoke extinguished her breathing.

The image of those clogs stayed with me. They became a symbol of the courage with which Pearl Witherington, a former secretary, faced the terror of the Nazi war machine. '*Avec mes Sabots,*' was her favourite marching song when she was on the road with her *maquisards*, facing the Waffen SS soldiers of the 'Das Reich' division, the same division who had killed the 642 victims of Oradour.

'*Oh, oh, oh, avec mes sabots,*' sang Pearl, as she led her band of Frenchmen into battle. The song she chose, *'Avec mes sabots,'* was also the marching song of Joan of Arc. To Pearl's companions, her lover, Henri Cornioley, Major Clutton of Jedburgh 'Julian', and perhaps to her men, Pearl's visionary leadership in May – September 1944 was reminiscent of Joan's. Pearl never said so. But she fought under the same flag of freedom, the Cross of Lorraine, to rid France, the country she called home, from oppression.

The clogs were crude, wooden footwear, worn by peasant women whose brothers put down their scythes and sickles, left their fields and their cattle to answer Pearl's call to arms in June 1944. It seemed an unequal match: peasants against Nazis. But the men of the Indre, newly armed by Pearl with unfamiliar weapons, Sten guns and rocket launchers, learnt fast. Comrades in arms, the British and the French, and many Commonwealth citizens – Mauritians, Canadians, New Zealanders – took on the Gestapo, the German repression columns and the SS Panzers.

The agents of SOE have, rightly, been called amateurs, brainchild of the greatest 'gentleman amateur' of all, Winston Churchill. The Resistance has been equally maligned, the credit for victory in 1944 solely ascribed to the regular forces. But Eisenhower, the Supreme Commander, said SOE circuits and the *maquis* were worth several divisions. Thanks to them, the Germans lost control of their rear during Overlord, and it was the men and women of the Resistance who liberated France south of the Loire.

This is Pearl's story, but it is also theirs.

Carole Seymour-Jones
March 2013

Note Eisenhower to Major General Gubbins of SOE, 31 May 1945.

1

Into the Field

THE STARS are growing fainter in the night sky as the Halifax bomber approaches the dropping zone. In the belly of the bomber, Secret Agent Pearl Witherington, a.k.a Agent 'Marie', clings to the fuselage, feeling, not for the first time, like Jonah inside the whale. The aircraft banks sharply and she almost loses her balance. They have crossed the Loire and the Cher rivers by the light of the moon, and are circling the landing ground at Les Tailles de Ruines, north-east of Valençay, in central France. The roar of the four engines is deafening, the smell of oil and petrol from the spare cans overpowering. Pearl has lost all feeling in her feet, for it is icy cold and her ankles are tightly bandaged to prevent them breaking on the impact of landing. She crouches beside the exit hole, ready for her parachute drop, and glances at the despatcher who will give her the signal to jump.

Her heart beats furiously. Any moment now he will shout 'Action stations!', the light will turn red, then green, and he will tell her 'Go!' She takes a deep breath. This is the culmination of all her dreams of returning to Occupied France, the fulfilment of hours of training ever since she, a twenty-nine-year-old British secretary, volunteered to join the Special Operations Executive in the spring of that year, 1943.

The black bomber is losing height. The engine note changes as it circles the DZ for the second time. Is something wrong? The pilot and navigator are peering into the darkness, straining for the first sight of the lights of the reception committee below, but there is no dim-but-reassuring-glow from torches lashed to sticks in the landing ground. The pilot has dropped as far as he dares through the cloud, down to 500 feet, and he comes around for the last time before Pearl hears his voice over the intercom: 'Mission aborted.'

With a sigh, she swallows her disappointment as the bomber turns tail and heads for the Channel.

Had Pearl but known it, on that night of 15 September 1943, the Germans were chasing the Resistance through the woods of Les Tailles de Ruines directly beneath them, and 'Hector', the SOE circuit chief whom she was to join in the field, had been forced to scrub her reception: at the last moment, he had cancelled the order to set out the landing lights. The pilot, likewise, had prioritised Pearl's safety.

Five days later, WAAF Assistant Section Officer Cécile Pearl Witherington was told to prepare herself for her second attempt to drop behind enemy lines. Time and luck were running out. It was the evening of 21 September, the last but one night of the September moon, the twelve-day lunar window which allowed the pilots to navigate by its silvery light. 'It's my last chance,' she said to herself, 'my last chance,' for she knew that if she did not make it that night, there would be no further opportunity until the October moon. From the grounds of Hazells Hall, near RAF Tempsford – a camouflaged aerodrome deep in the Bedfordshire countryside – she gazed imploringly at the waning moon, whose light was fading as fast as the falling leaves of autumn.

The weather had also turned. The fat, yellow harvest moon, which for eleven unbroken nights had enabled Squadron Leader Hugh Verity to deliver secret agents behind enemy lines in his Lysander aeroplane, had vanished. 'This has really been a harvest moon to remember,' the pick-up pilot had said in August, as the secret 'Moon' Squadrons – 138 and 161 – whose base Tempsford was, ferried an unprecedented number of agents in and out of Occupied France. So smooth had been the Tempsford 'taxi run' that King George VI and Queen Elizabeth would visit Tempsford to congratulate the pilots, but for Pearl, as she waited impatiently for her own Tempsford taxi, this was of little consequence. 'Taxi', she now realised, was a misnomer for a flight that was proving so unexpectedly difficult.

For the second time she was to spend her 'last' night on British soil at Hazells Hall, a manor house at Sandy, a few miles west of Tempsford. The hall had been taken into military service as sleeping quarters for senior officers and 'Joes', the agents waiting to go into the field, and was more comfortable than anything the aerodrome could offer – Tempsford itself was a rush job, a collection of Nissen huts quickly built in wartime. Boggy and soggy, its runways were often under water, but it had one redeeming feature: its secret location between the railway line and the Great North Road, where it lay well hidden from the enemy by low hills. So far it had proved undetectable to German military intelligence. 'Find this viper's nest and destroy it,' Hitler had ordered his *Abwehr*, the military counter-espionage organisation, but although at least two German spies were caught in the vicinity and executed, the blacked-out airfield would never be discovered.

The acquisition of Tempsford had, in fact, represented a major victory for Britain's youngest and least popular wartime secret service, the Special Operations Executive (SOE). The 'Baker Street Irregulars', as they were known, since their London offices were in the Sherlock Holmes-territory of 64 Baker Street, specialised in the 'ungentlemanly' warfare of sabotage and subversion, and the new, upstart organisation was deeply distrusted by the Secret Intelligence Service, by the chiefs of the armed forces and, in particular, by the head of Bomber Command, Air Marshal Arthur Harris, who had 'fought to the last ditch' SOE's inopportune requests for a squadron of aircraft for its special operations.

When Harris had rejected Tempsford as unfit for purpose in March 1942, SOE had snatched at this crumb from the rich man's table. By that November, Squadron Leader Verity had taken command of 161 Squadron's flight of six Lysanders for pick-up operations, and there were five Halifaxes as well as two Wellingtons and a Hudson for parachute operations. When Pearl arrived in the autumn of 1943, Tempsford was ready for her.

At Hazells Hall, Pearl is once again getting ready for her first mission as a secret agent. Lily, the stout woman from the French

Section of SOE who has come to dress her, has laid out her clothes on the bed.

'Well, Pearl, you should know the ropes by now,' Nancy Fraser-Campbell, her conducting officer, says with a laugh. Nancy is a captain in the First Aid Nursing Yeomanry (FANY), and works closely with the dedicated but gullible Maurice Buckmaster, head of the French Section ('F'), and his intelligence officer, Vera Atkins. As is customary with departing female agents, Nancy – although it is more usually Vera who takes on the job – has come down to Hazells Hall to inspect Pearl's costume and to check that it will pass scrutiny in France. Nancy has become a close friend of Pearl's during the latter's training, and Pearl finds her presence reassuring.

Lily is insisting that her charge wears woollen underclothes, ignoring Pearl's objections to the winter-weight vest. 'You must wear it tonight, duckie,' says Lily. 'They all say it is perishing cold in the aircraft – all the ones that come back.'

Pearl slips on the vest obediently. Nancy inspects the manufacturer's label of the cream blouse for authenticity, and holds it out to Pearl. Next comes a fine lambswool jumper and a tweed suit: Pearl's 'civvies' have to suit her cover story, that she is Geneviève Touzalin, born in Paris on 24 June 1913, a secretary in the *Société Allumettière Française*, a French match company. 'F' ensures that a cover story is not too dissimilar to an agent's real life experience so that it can be more easily memorised, and Pearl's own birthday is 24 June 1914, while her shorthand and typing are impeccable. Pearl must inhabit her cover story, forget that she is British, remember only her former life in France. SOE's Jewish refugee tailor, who knows how to cut cloth the Continental way, has made her two tweed suits – one *marron*, a rich chestnut brown, the other grey – both of which she has been told to wear for a few days so that they do not look suspiciously new.

Tonight Pearl is wearing the brown suit, for a particular reason. At the last moment, before Marie's failed parachute drop on the night of 15 September, a new briefing had arrived for Vera, who is responsible for the French Section's women agents:

> WRESTLER is taking for herself Frs. 150.000 in a packet to put where she thinks fit. She is taking a packet for HECTOR containing Frs. 500.000 . . . In addition, she is taking a microphotographed target briefing for HECTOR which should be handed to him on arrival. This has been sewn by Miss de Baissac [another SOE agent] into the hem of the brown skirt she will be wearing on the operation. Would you kindly arrange with whoever sees her off that she has this skirt on.

Now, Nancy checks that the target briefing for Hector, stitched neatly into the hem of Pearl's skirt, is not visible. She then checks Pearl's pockets for giveaway bus or cinema tickets. . . Fingers run over old laundry tags and rip them out, or search out an embroidered handkerchief or a tiny bottle of lavender water which might betray its English origin. Pearl heard of a recent slip-up when an agent was sent into the field with a pair of gloves that had 'Made in England' stitched inside one of the fingers. She has already sacrificed her favourite pink Yardley lipstick, giving it to her little sister, Mimi, who is also in the WAAFs and will probably wear it to the next dance at RAF Mildenhall.

Nancy is offering Pearl a Lancôme lipstick, which one of the pilots has brought back from France. It is called Le Rouge Baiser and is bright red: luscious, seductive.

'Oh, I can't, Nancy,' says Pearl. 'You know I hardly wear make-up.'

Nancy, an American-born Scot, is a sophisticated girl who is no stranger to the latest cosmetics, turning heads in the French Section's offices when she wears her kilt with her FANY battledress jacket. She smiles. 'Go on, Pearl. Try it.'

Gingerly, Pearl paints her lips and Nancy pats them dry with a handkerchief. 'There.'

Pearl smiles into the looking glass. Even her teeth have been attended to: F Section's thorough preparation has ensured that she has been sent to a French dentist, who extracted the filling she had been given in London and replaced it with gold.

Pearl frowns. 'I don't like it. I look like a *putain*.' Briskly, she wipes off the lipstick. 'You keep it, Nancy. Give me the skirt.'

The tweed skirt slides easily over Pearl's slim, athletic figure. She is tall, long-legged, straight-backed. Her long fair hair no longer cascades down her shoulders but is twisted and pinned up, ready to tuck under her flying helmet. Her brilliant blue eyes are the most arresting feature in a fresh, oval face which, if not classically beautiful, is attractive and vivacious. Men find her *trés jolie, très sympathique*, with her quick smile and sensitivity to other people's feelings – but there are moments when Pearl's large blue eyes can turn as grey and forbidding as the Atlantic in winter. Promoted quickly to personal assistant, the set of her shoulders indicates that she does not suffer fools gladly. For twelve years she has sat behind a manual typewriter, first in Paris, where she was born and grew up, and more recently in the Air Ministry in London. She is tired of pushing paper. Nor is she now in the mood to brook delay. All through the summer she has been waiting to 'do her bit', as the tide of war turned and the Allies invaded Sicily, and she is hungry for action.

'Operation Wrestler,' reads her mission briefing. 'Christian name in the field: MARIE. You are going to France to work as a courier to an organiser, Hector, who is in control of a circuit in the regions of Tarbes, Châteauroux and Bergerac.'

Pearl glances one last time at her reflection in the mirror, straightens the seams of her beige lisle stockings, and ties the laces of her brown walking shoes in a double knot. It is once again time for her 'last meal' in England.

In the wood-panelled dining room of the hall, she sits down at the mahogany table to eat what she is told is 'an early breakfast'. It is 11 p.m. Stuffed birds gaze down at her from glass cases. She is served a fried egg – a special wartime treat, as the ration is only one egg a week. Although she is not hungry, she eats every last morsel of her toast with Oxford marmalade and drains the last drop of tea from a bone china cup before rising to her feet.

'Pearl,' calls Nancy. 'Your driver is waiting.'

It is nearly midnight when an anonymous Chrysler with blacked-out windows, driven by a young FANY ensign, delivers Pearl to the gates to RAF Tempsford. A sentry steps out, the gates swing silently open and the car proceeds towards the Gibraltar Farm barn.

In the back of the car, Pearl draws aside the blackout curtain and peers out. She can barely see the moon; ragged clouds gust across its face. Rain spatters the windscreen. Trees bend in the wind.

'Rotten weather,' comments Nancy doubtfully.

Pearl bites her lip, but allowes no trace of anxiety to betray itself in her expression. She has long ago learnt to keep a poker face, whatever the circumstances.

The ground crew are clustered around the bombers, which sit like dark moths on the tarmac, waiting to take wing. The Chrysler cruises past the runway on which her waiting Halifax is parked, and draws up at Gibraltar Farm barn. The blonde FANY driver opens the door and Pearl steps out into the cold night, then quickly into the warm fug of the barn, thick with cigarette smoke.

The despatcher from the Halifax, Horton, gives her the thumbs up: the jump is on despite the wild blustery night, as the pilots often have to push their luck. Horton stubs out his cigarette and lights one for Pearl. In a minute, he will bandage her ankles and help her into her overalls and parachute harness.

Nancy is handing her two packets, in her role as Pearl's conducting officer. 'This one's for you, and this one's for Hector. Make sure he gets it.'

'Thanks, Nancy.'

'ID card, ration book?'

'I've got it all.'

'Good show, Marie.' Nancy uses Pearl's codename – it is essential that the aircrew remain ignorant of her real identity, in case they are captured and talk under interrogation – as she rummages in her leather briefcase. 'Vera thought you might as well take another forty Gauloises. We've got plenty.'

Pearl snaps open her cheap fibre suitcase and adds the packs of cigarettes, a box of matches and two bars of Chocolat Ménier. The chocolate has been made in England and impregnated with garlic to make it authentically French, with the same care as the forged ID card and other documents.

'Take this picture of your "parents", too. It might come in handy.'

Pearl takes the blurred snapshot of a formally dressed, middle-aged French couple. 'You're a brick, Nancy.'

'Now, your L-pills. Here we are.' The cyanide pills appear in a pill box on the table, and Pearl picks them up.

'Bite hard on them before swallowing,' remarks an RAF officer casually, studying the met forecast.

'Most people take them with them, Marie,' says Nancy. 'It gives you the option.'

Lethal pills are standard issue for all agents going into the field, allowing them to commit suicide on arrest rather than face torture at the hands of the Gestapo. The SOE rule is that agents must remain silent for the first forty-eight hours after capture in order to allow their contacts time to escape. Pearl has heard that some British agents have had gold signet rings made with a secret compartment for the L-pill, while at Tangmere Aerodrome in Sussex, the wife of one of the escorting officers is happy to sew the pills into the shirt cuffs of the agents who stay with them the night before they go into the field.

'You know Vera isn't keen.'

'Don't worry about Vera.' Nancy wishes for a moment that Vera, the 'brains' behind F Section's Buckmaster, had been able to see Pearl off instead of her.

Nancy, one of the 'intelligent gentlewomen' so indispensable to SOE, is particularly concerned for her friend's safety in September 1943. She is close enough to Buckmaster and Vera to know that the French Section is in crisis, is even now facing a catastrophe. All summer, bad news has been coming over the ticker-tape in Room 52, the SOE signals room, where Buckmaster and Vera spend long hours deciphering the agents' messages. Nancy doesn't know the details, but she has heard the rumours that a key agent, Major Francis Suttill, codename 'Prosper', was arrested by the Gestapo in June. Buckmaster has been worried enough to send his deputy, Major Nicholas Bodington, to Paris to investigate in mid-July. Was Prosper *brûlé*, and his wireless operator, Gilbert Norman, codename 'Archambaud', and his courier, Andrée Borrel, too? If all three are blown, and are being held in the cells of the Gestapo HQ in Paris, does this not spell mortal danger for Pearl?

Prosper's empire is spread over twelve *départements* and thirty-three landing grounds, and has recently broken all records for drops of arms and explosives, receiving 190 containers in just nine days. Prosper is, says Buckmaster, his 'lynchpin'. If the Germans have penetrated Prosper's vast, sprawling circuit, the result will be mass arrests.

Nancy knows that the life expectancy of a special agent in 1943 is short – that of a radio operator was only six weeks in the early days of SOE. When Pearl volunteered for SOE, Vera warned her that only 50 per cent of SOE agents came back.

Pearl knows the odds, and accepts them. She shakes her head at Nancy, giving her back the L-pills in their box. 'No, thanks, Nancy. I'd rather not.'

As she lights a cigarette, Pearl reflects that she cannot imagine voluntarily ending her life, whatever the circumstances. Not when she has fought so hard to return to her beloved France.

Pearl had pulled every possible string to be accepted as a courier to work with Hector – in reality her old school friend, Maurice Southgate – with whom she had grown up in Paris. It hadn't been easy. It had taken all her determination to steamroller Buckmaster into agreeing to recall Hector's current courier, Jacqueline Nearne, an exceptional agent who had survived a year in the field, and to send Pearl in her stead. Jacqueline, not without reason, had been furious with Pearl.

'She's been at it a whole year,' Pearl had pressed Buckmaster. 'I think you ought to send her back to England.'

'But Jacqueline's doing a splendid job,' protested Buckmaster.

'A year's too long, she needs some leave . . . And you know I really want to be Maurice's courier.'

Buckmaster had paused. 'I don't know . . . Jacqueline won't be keen.' He had looked at Pearl, who had showed no signs of leaving his office, and sighed. 'Oh, very well, then. I'll recall her.'

'She didn't half take me for it,' Pearl later remarked: 'You've pinched my job,' Jacqueline had hissed, when they eventually met in the field. 'I didn't pinch her job, as far as I could make out,' protested Pearl, to anyone who might be listening. 'I couldn't make out what she did, anyway.'

It was a disingenuous reply. Pearl knew full well why she wanted to take Jacqueline's job, and it was connected to a secret she shared with very few people.

'Very intelligent, straightforward, courageous . . . with leadership qualities.' As her training report said, Pearl was deeply patriotic. She loved two countries and longed to take the fight to the Germans. But there was another, more personal reason for the burning fury Pearl felt when she thought about the foreign invaders, a fury which drove her to overcome every obstacle. The German army had separated her from the man she had loved since she was nineteen: her fiancé, Henri Cornioley, a Parisian parfumier in his family's flourishing beauty business. The war had divided the couple. She knew that Henri, mobilised into the French army in 1939, had been taken prisoner by the Germans when they overran France in June 1940, and Pearl had not seen him for three and a half years.

Pearl shivers with anticipation. Might Henri have escaped? Could her love be waiting for her on the landing ground? Perhaps she will drop into the arms of the tall, dark Frenchman as she has heard another SOE agent, Odette, had dropped into the arms of her lover, Peter Churchill.

'Marie!'

Pearl awakes from her reverie. Nancy is holding out a slim white box. 'Colonel Buckmaster and Vera would like to give you this. A gift from F Section, with their best wishes. Vera was sorry not to be able to escort you tonight, but she had to go to Tangmere.'

Pearl opens the box and slides out the gold powder compact. It is a thing of beauty, shiny and French and the most valuable present anyone has ever given her. She turns it over and reads the inscription on the back: *Fabriqué en France*.

'I can't take this,' she protests.

'You can always pawn it.' Nancy grins and glances at her watch. 'Right, we should be making a move.'

She has been watching Pearl as she smokes. Her hand is steady. There is no 'trembling cigarette', such as Vera had noticed between the shaking fingers of another agent, Noor Inayat Khan, at Tangmere. Or perhaps it was Cicely or Diana? Nancy can't exactly remember.

'All set, then? Got your pistol?'

Pearl's hand goes to her .32 Colt in its holster and nods firmly.

The girl has backbone. Perhaps she will survive. Nancy stifles a sigh, and squeezes Pearl's hand as she shakes it. 'Best of luck, Marie.'

Flight Sergeant Cole of 138 Squadron revved the engines and taxied down the runway. As he accelerated, there was an ominous change in the roar of the engines and the aircraft lurched to one side.

'What's the matter?' exclaimed Pearl.

'Don't worry, love,' shouted Horton, the despatcher.

The bomber's wheel had veered off the runway, which had been laid on one of the farm's meadows and was extremely narrow. The pilot returned to the start of the runway and took off on the second attempt.

Shortly afterwards, a storm blew up and the aircraft was forced to land at Ford, a naval airfield near Tangmere. Pearl arrived at the base at 1 a.m., a pretty young woman in civilian clothes, and her presence attracted curious stares. Passing herself off as a journalist who had come in search of a story, she was making her way towards the canteen when she met a tall officer in RAF uniform, who addressed her in French. It was Squadron Leader Philippe Livry-Level, the legendary French aviator who, after serving in World War I in an artillery regiment, had lied about his age to the RAF in order to achieve his ambition of active service in the air. Nearer fifty than forty, he had nevertheless been accepted by 161 Squadron as a navigator, exchanging the dark blue uniform of the Free French for the lighter blue of the RAF. The airman had at once guessed Pearl's real mission, and lent her his room in which to rest. It was freezing cold – '*Froid de canard*,' said Pearl – but she was glad of the privacy.

The next night, 22 September, the ultimate night of the September moon, they took off again despite almost complete cloud cover and only the barest glimmer of moonlight. Flight Sergeant Cole was determined to drop his 'Joe' and make it third time lucky for her. Once more inside the cavernous fuselage of the plane, Pearl felt like a trussed chicken, so tightly had Horton fastened the straps of her parachute over her camouflage jumpsuit. Once again her feet grew numb in the bitter cold. Horton pushed a sleeping bag in her direction, shouting an explanation that the benches on which the crew of seven normally sat had been removed to make room for the fuel tanks necessary for the long journey. The roar of the engines was as deafening as ever.

Behind her, carrier pigeons slept in cardboard boxes complete with their own mini-parachutes. Like Pearl, the birds had work to do, in their case they were carrying messages for MI6 – the Secret Intelligence Service.

The pilot flew high over the clouds, following a circuitous route in order to outwit the enemy. Their first target was Detective One, thirty kilometres south-east of Tours, where they had to drop propaganda leaflets. Suddenly, the aircraft ran into flak from German anti-aircraft batteries and seemed to Pearl to jump out of the sky.

'What's happening?' she asked. 'Are they shooting at us?'

'Don't worry,' said Horton. 'It's always like this.'

The flak crackled around them and the bomber roared upward, out of range. Horton lined up the cylindrical boxes of pigeons beside the exit hole in the rear fuselage and grinned at Pearl, yelling, 'Reckon they'll get eaten before they make it back to Blighty.'

As he pushed the packages through the hole and the pigeons spiralled downwards, the throb of the engines lulled Pearl to sleep. Cole flew on over France, navigating by the moon's faint reflection on the river Loire, passing Blois, where an island in the middle of the river served as a landmark to the pilots of the Moon squadrons, over the silver ribbon of the Loire's little sister, the Loir, and then the Cher, before dropping through the clouds to his second target, Wrestler/Stationer 12, seventeen kilometres south-south-west of Châteauroux in the *département* of the Indre.

Horton shook Pearl awake once they were over Hector's circuit, 'Stationer', approaching the dropping zone outside the small town of Tendu. It was nearly 2 a.m. Horton clipped Pearl's parachute to the static line attached to a fixed wire on the rear fuselage, and tapped her on the shoulder. At 850 feet he opened the exit panel. Pearl waited. 'Action stations!' Her heart thudded. This time it was for real. The light flashed red. She had heard stories of agents breaking their noses on the opposite lip of the exit hole, or smashing their legs or their backs or dropping into trees, or even onto the roof of a *gendarmerie*.

Below her, pinpricks of light flashed Morse code. Trees and shadowy buildings were coming closer in the moonlight, and she could smell the air of France, a farmyard smell of animals and rich, damp soil. *Le terroir.* The land. She thought of Henri, of stolen kisses, of whispered promises. She was home again in the country of her birth, the only country she had ever known as home.

The light changed to green. The despatcher raised his hand. 'Go!' Pearl jumped into the darkness. The static lines snatched at her parachute, her rigging lines cleared the tail wheel and, as the canopy filled, her light frame was borne away by gusts of wind into the night.

2

Darkest Hour

It was 11 June 1940. Twenty-six-year old Cécile Pearl Witherington, personal assistant to His Majesty's air attaché, Douglas Colyer, at the British Embassy in Paris, stood staring in disbelief at the great gates of the Residence in rue du Faubourg-Saint-Honoré. They were locked. The windows of the magnificent building were shuttered, and the flagpole bare: no Union Jack waved in the breeze.

Pearl pressed a neatly manicured hand against the small gate to the right through which she usually entered the Residence, but there was no answer to the bell.

A passer-by was watching her, gazing at the empty flagpole. '*Les Anglais?*' The man spat. '*Les Anglais ont foutu le camp!* The English have fucked off.'

Another man shrugged. 'As soon as an Englishman hears talk of war, he shits in his pants.'

Turning, Pearl ran across the road into rue d'Aguesseau where the modern office block in which she and the other secretaries who worked for the Defence Section in the Chancery was situated. Air Commodore Colyer's office was locked. The typewriters were silent. Where was everybody? Duggie, her boss; Sir Ronald, the ambassador? Only eleven days earlier, on 31 May, chefs had been preparing the lavish banquet at which Prime Minister Winston Churchill and Foreign Secretary Lord Halifax had entertained the French premier, Paul Reynaud, to dinner. In their offices, the secretaries had discussed whether this last-ditch attempt to persuade the French to stay in the war would work; the very next day, news had come that the staff at the Quai d'Orsay were burning confidential papers in the garden. The Nazis were at the gates of Paris.

Pearl blinked. The unthinkable had happened. The ambassador, Sir Ronald Campbell, and his entourage had vanished on the night of 10 June, following in the wake of the French government as it withdrew to Tours.

Turning on her heel, Pearl left the building and slowly retraced her steps towards the *Eglise de la Madeleine* and rue Vignon, a narrow street just behind the church where she lived at number 34, in a flat over an *antiquaire,* with her widowed mother, Gertrude, and her two younger sisters: Jacqueline, who they called Doudou, and Hélène, known as Mimi. Suzanne, the sister in age closest to Pearl, had married and moved to England in 1939.

A tall, stylishly dressed figure in a costume made by a Parisian dressmaker, Pearl looked what she was – no mere *dactylo,* shorthand-typist, but a senior PA who carried herself with confidence. Now, however, she hesitated in alarm when she came to the rue Royale. A vast sea of people was pouring down the *grands boulevards* towards the Seine bridges, their numbers swelling with every moment that passed: wave after wave, the rich in cars, the poor in carts or on foot, streaming southwards in flight from the approaching German armies.

Breasting the human current with difficulty, Pearl's mind was still numb with shock at the suddenness of defeat, and the speed with which her adopted country had collapsed. People were fleeing the capital, but she and her sisters had no French relatives with whom to stay, no family in the south to offer them refuge, for despite her impeccable French and neat chignon, despite her birth and childhood in Paris, Pearl was British. Her only asset in the calamitous summer of 1940 was her diplomatic *carte d'identité* and her willpower; her only chance of escape from the Germans was to follow the ambassador and, somehow, cross the Channel to England.

Like most Parisians, Pearl had had no inkling of the imminent catastrophe. Not until 16 May had the news reached the capital that the Maginot Line, the barrier designed to shield the French

Republic from Nazi aggression, had been breached. Her first thought had been for Henri, to whom she was secretly engaged.

Henri Cornioley worked, in a somewhat desultory fashion, at the family's fashionable '*Institut de Beauté*' also in the rue du Faubourg-Saint-Honoré, where he and his family lived in great style and opulence. He was the elder son, with expectations of inheriting a thriving business. The *institut* had been founded by his grandmother after she moved from Switzerland to France with her fourteen-year-old son, Henri's father. When her husband had died, Madame Cornioley had built up her beauty business alone, mixing pots of face cream in her apartment. By the time Henri was growing up, her hard work had paid off: the whole family worked in the family firm, apart from Henri's mother – who was Hungarian – offering hairdressing and beauty care. There were cubicles in the salon for shampoos-and-sets and facials, and in the back rooms, or the 'laboratory', as it was known, Henri experimented with perfumes. The apartment hummed with immigrant energy.

Henri had been helping his father create a new fragrance when his call-up papers arrived, in September 1939. He left Paris with resigned cheerfulness to join the *19e Train Hippomobile*, a horsedrawn-transport company of the logistics corps stationed near Sedan on the Meuse. Autumn was spent playing pelote. Then winter came to the Ardennes.

'We spent the time burying the horses, who died like flies . . . but I didn't have to dig graves in the frozen earth,' said Henri. 'I had a privileged position. I was a machine gunner.' As unprepared as most of his countrymen, as well as the British Expeditionary Force, for the might of the *Wehrmacht*, he had assured Pearl on his last leave in February 1940 that the Maginot Line was impregnable.

Henri had been astonished when the first German bombers burst out of the sky. He and his comrades had begun firing at the Stukas overhead. 'You could be sure that it was a German bomber,' he quipped, 'as we certainly didn't have any French ones.'

Lying along the hedgerows, the men let off volley after volley, until the battery lieutenant shouted at Cornioley: 'You there, stop firing like that! Don't you know the cost of ammunition?'

'No, sir.'

'A franc a bullet! That's what it costs.'

Je dis oui, évidemment, ça fait cher des rafales. Okay, a volley is expensive, but we are here to shoot!' Henri laughed bitterly. 'And then people wonder why we lost the war!'

On 10 May, the day of the German offensive, Henri's regiment was pushing northwards towards Belgium when it was stopped in its tracks by the Panzer columns scything through the forests of the Ardennes, and began to retreat along the path of its advance. Five days later, the RAF failed to break the Germans' pontoon bridges on the Meuse, and suffered devastating losses. The German army, the *Wehrmacht*, swept on, scooping up Cornioley just as he was heating up some coffee for his section in an abandoned village.

Pearl, standing at the door of the family's apartment, wondered briefly if her fiancé was still alive: she had no way of knowing that he had just been taken prisoner somewhere south of Verdun. But as quickly as her fears arose, she suppressed them. There was no help to be had from Henri, and her mother and sisters were depending on her to take care of them, just as they always did.

As she took off her coat inside the family's apartment, Pearl wondered what she was to do: stay in the city and risk being rounded up by the Germans; or go, like the 5 million other Parisians fleeing for their lives? All the female staff of the British Embassy had been ordered home as a safety measure when news came of the German *Blitzkrieg* in May, but where was 'home' for the Witheringtons? As a Briton who resided in Paris: 'I was only local staff,' said Pearl. '*Je n'avais pas de point de chute en Angleterre.* I had nowhere to go to in England.' But she trusted Air Commodore Duggie Colyer, her boss, whose indispensable Girl Friday she was.

Those last days at the embassy had been hectic ones. On 15 May, Pearl was still working for Colyer when he wrote of his horror when 'the Germans won through to the sea'. The air attaché's office was besieged by airmen clamouring to have their equipment transported back to England, and as he negotiated with General Picard at the French War Office to borrow 280 American lorries to save the equipment, Pearl dealt with:

> a constant stream of Air Ministry Officials, shot-down aircraft crews, Belgian refugees etc, passing through the office . . . Belgian Air Officers were constantly on the doorstep asking for aircraft with which to continue the war. Cypher messages poured in for decoding on the X-type machine, which constantly broke down. The office became a rallying-point for all and sundry.

On 3 June, the Germans had bombed Paris in force. Colyer had told Pearl that he was impressed by the Parisians, who were 'very calm', which he thought was 'a good sign for their continued resistance to the enemy', and so was greatly surprised when the French government began to make preparations to leave.

Even at the eleventh hour, it had been hard to believe that the city would fall, and Pearl was sure that, whatever happened, Duggie would look after her.

But on Monday, 10 June, just a month after the invasion of Belgium, 'HM Ambassador left Paris at 9 o'clock in the evening,' recorded Colyer, 'the French government having already left.' Travelling all night, the ambassador and his air attaché reached the Château de Champchevrier, near Tours, at six in the morning.

Before he left, Pearl had obtained permission from her boss to make for Commes, in Normandy, where, in the event of bad news, Colyer had promised to send her a diplomatic pass to allow her and her family to board any English army truck and to take ship to England.

Loyal and obedient, Pearl now waited patiently in Paris for her orders. Mrs Witherington, however, was growing hysterical. Gertrude Witherington, or 'Gee', as she preferred to be known, was fifty-nine years old and had already settled into the role of a querulous and dependent invalid. Abandoned by her alcoholic husband, Wallace, and widowed after his death in 1932, Gee had the added disadvantage of being deaf – not profoundly so, but hard of hearing. Speaking little French, she was accustomed to addressing people loudly and commandingly in English. Pearl who, *faute de mieux*, had become the man of the family, also acted as Mother's interpreter.

Just days after she had stood on the pavement outside her country's embassy, Pearl and her mother and sisters boarded one of the last trains leaving Paris, for Normandy. They had planned, in any event, to spend the summer holidays at a cottage owned by their friend, Madame Pellon, sister to the old antique dealer over whose shop they lived, and the northern coast seemed to offer the best refuge from the advancing Germans. The four women: Pearl, Gee, Doudou and Mimi, snatched up their belongings and arrived breathless and anxious at Commes, near Port-en-Bessin.

Boats were still departing from Cherbourg for England but, as chaos unrolled around them, the women hesitated. It was to prove a fateful decision.

In the face of overwhelming evidence to the contrary, Churchill clung stubbornly to the idea that British troops might remain in France west of Dunkirk. In response to fresh pleas from the French premier, Renaud, he had told a horrified British War Cabinet in London on 1 June that more British troops had to be sent across the Channel, this time to Brittany and Normandy. The former prime minister, Neville Chamberlain, and Halifax, had remonstrated fiercely with him: it was against all military logic. But Churchill had remained obdurate: 'The British Expeditionary Force must immediately be constituted, otherwise the French will not continue the war,' he declared.

Churchill envisioned a British enclave in Brittany, a base from which the French might develop 'a gigantic guerrilla'. A spy in the 1890s and a former cavalry officer in the 4th Hussars, the prime minister had seen guerrilla action in South Africa and Cuba and believed from the earliest days of World War II that irregular forces might succeed where the regular army failed. He ordered Lieutenant General Sir Alan Brooke, who had only just stepped ashore in England after Dunkirk, to return to France to create a bridgehead in Brittany – the 'Breton redoubt' – with the help of the 1st Canadian Division. Brooke's troops were still landing in the north-western ports as late as 13 June, the day before Paris fell.

The German advance on Paris was swift and deadly. On 14 June the triumphant German army took possession of the French capital, its camouflaged lorries rolling down the Boulevard Saint-Michel full of tall soldiers 'with eyes like glacier lakes' (in the words of Jean-Paul Sartre), as they tossed packets of cigarettes to silent French onlookers.

At last, Churchill accepted that the war in France was lost, and telephoned Brooke to tell him to pull the Canadians out. Three days later, Marshal Pétain, the octogenarian defender of Verdun, replaced Renaud, who had resigned, and broadcast his first message to the French nation, preparing them for capitulation. As he prepared to sign an armistice with Germany, the very next day, 18 June, Brigadier General de Gaulle, the army minister, made his historic appeal over BBC airwaves to the French to continue the fight: 'Whatever happens,' he said, 'the flame of French resistance must not and shall not die.'

In Normandy, meanwhile, a curious paralysis settled over Pearl. As the 'second Dunkirk' gathered momentum, orders and counter-orders producing unparalleled confusion: new troops were arriving, but two trainloads of undamaged British tanks were abandoned; ships from England were unloaded at one quay, while at another units embarked for England. So sudden had been the shock and trauma of French defeat, the pain of not knowing whether Henri was still alive, and so deep was Pearl's faith in Colyer's ability to work a miracle, that she felt unable to come to a decision or to take action to save herself without his guidance. Trustingly, she watched and waited for her orders from Duggie, as the evacuation of Brooke's troops accelerated.

Between 14 and 25 June nearly 145,000 British troops, along with thousands of Poles and other Allied personnel, were somehow embarked from Cherbourg and the north-western ports. The Witheringtons were not among them.

As the last boats left for England, Pearl and her mother quarrelled,

Gee becoming ever more frantic as she saw their last chance of escape slipping away. 'There was panic in the family,' said Mimi, as the four women dithered hopelessly in their Commes cottage.

'We have to go,' urged Gertrude, seizing Pearl's arm. 'I can see Le Havre burning.'

Black smoke was rising from bombed warehouses and oil refineries, blackening the sky over Commes. The smoke blotted out the summer sun and seemed to symbolise the extinction of hope.

'I can't go before I have permission from Air Commodore Colyer,' Pearl stubbornly repeated. 'We have to wait.'

Finally, word came that Pearl's diplomatic pass was on its way, but it would take five days to arrive. The scales fell from Pearl's eyes: there would be no miracle. At last she hearkened to her mother and sisters' pleas. She decided they would go to Bayeux and stop an army truck going up to Cherbourg. Surely it was not too late to hitch a lift back to Blighty?

But when at last the family went into Commes to hail a taxi to Bayeux, they were too late. 'Everyone laughed at us,' said Mimi.

'There's no petrol,' said the *garagiste*.

Eventually, a kindly French farmer took the women in his horse and cart. Mimi remembered the painful moment: 'We had to leave our black cat behind, but George, our Sealyham terrier, was loaded on and our scant luggage and ourselves, and off we went. The farmer dumped us on the outskirts of Bayeux early in the morning.'

As the Witherington women stood dolefully at the roadside, two dirty and dejected French soldiers hove into view. All was lost, they said. The Germans were on their way.

'Pearl scooted over to the nearest garage to commandeer a vehicle, to no avail,' said Mimi. 'There just wasn't any petrol, and the last English army lorry had passed at 6 a.m. It was 9 a.m. Gosh, there we were, stranded. Then we were overrun by the Germans.'

The Witheringtons hurried back to Commes and awaited the Nazi invaders in trepidation. As the Germans reached Normandy, Mrs Witherington decided to go into hiding, leaving the isolated cottage and asking a neighbouring farmer for shelter. 'We hid in a farm because my mother had heard that the Germans were raping girls,' Mimi recalled. 'It rather frightened us, I must say.'

Days passed as the Witheringtons laid low at the farm. In the end, however, it seemed safe to resume their normal lives. 'We stayed a week,' noted Mimi, 'but nothing happened.'

Emerging from their refuge, Doudou and Mimi discovered that the Germans were, surprisingly, very friendly when they appeared on the cliff path in front of the cottage. They bore gifts of cigarettes and chocolate, and clicked their heels at the sight of the knot of women. One of the soldiers, in his smart grey uniform, was just showing the two pretty, blonde English girls his identity disc, when an officer rode into view on horseback. He too made polite conversation, this time in English.

'It's good to speak English,' he said. 'When we get to England, it'll stand me in good stead.'

'You'll never get to England,' retorted eighteen-year-old Mimi. 'Never!'

As her two young sisters chatted flirtatiously with the soldiers of the *Wehrmacht*, Pearl suffered agonies of remorse. She bitterly regretted her decision to wait for orders and blamed herself for the predicament in which she had put her family. The longed-for letter had arrived at last from Sir Ronald, the British ambassador, ordering all personnel to leave for England. He himself had successfully embarked from Saint-Jean-de-Luz, on the Atlantic coast.

As high-ranking diplomats arrived back in London and clerical support staff were left trapped in France, Pearl felt a keen sense of abandonment. She had not shouldered her responsibilities: she had put her mother and sisters in peril.

But the Witheringtons were not alone in their misfortunes, and Pearl took some comfort from helping two other Britons who were also marooned in France. An Irishman, Private Paddy Moffitt of the 23rd Field Royal Artillery, and his fellow soldier, Bill Davidson, had escaped from a column of prisoners at Saint-Valéry-en-Caux and were trying to walk home – without any boots. Armed only with a compass, the men had retraced their steps through the battlefields until they reached the French coast.

'Only twenty-two miles from the coast of Britain,' wrote Paddy in his diary. 'On the Sunday evening we sat looking across the Ocean, wondering if we would ever get home.'

Hidden by clergymen, milking cows into their water bottles, sleeping in hay barns, they arrived finally at Port-en-Bessin and were wading through the shallow waves looking for a fishing smack to take them across the Channel when they were picked up by a Frenchwoman, who gave the four bedraggled soldiers a lift in her car to the Witheringtons' cottage.

Doudou and Mimi had spent the day on the beach. 'When we came back from swimming we found the shutters closed,' recalled Mimi. 'I thought, "Crikey, they've caught our mother, or Pearl."' Inside, Pearl was talking to the escaped soldiers in whispers. She and her sisters gathered money, food, clothes and maps and sent the men on their way south, on bicycles. 'They couldn't speak a word of French . . . With a heavy heart we waved them off with our blessing.' Little did Paddy or Pearl know that before many months had passed, their paths would cross again.

In July, the trains started running again – they had stopped immediately after the fall of Paris in June. By now the Witheringtons were virtually penniless and their plight was growing desperate. Pearl's sense of guilt was overwhelming as she counted her dwindling francs and contemplated an uncertain future: 'There was no more petrol, the trains had stopped running, and we had no money . . . We suffered so intensely at that time that it makes me ill to talk about it. It chokes me up, even after all these years.'

As talk of internment camps for foreigners and deportation to Germany began to circulate, Pearl's paralysis at last lifted. Jumping on her bicycle, she cycled to Bayeux where she was advised by Colonel de Job, French interpreter to the *Kommandantur* of Bayeux, to return to Paris and apply to the American ambassador, William C. Bullitt, for help. The US was still a neutral country maintaining diplomatic relations with Vichy France, but the ambassador might assist an Englishwoman in distress. Afraid of leaving her mother and sisters alone, Pearl knew that she had no choice.

In Paris, the ambassador received her kindly. But even as she waited anxiously for accreditation from the Air Ministry in London, French *gendarmes* were knocking on the door of the cottage in Commes, demanding that Mrs Witherington and her daughters report daily to the *Kommandatur* of Port-en-Bessin.

The mood of the invaders was changing. A few days later, as Doudou and Mimi pushed their bikes up the steep hill in Commes, two German soldiers accosted them and held their bikes. This time Mimi's fears that she and her sister would be pushed into the bushes and raped seemed about to be realised. 'They just wouldn't let us go,' said Mimi. The two frightened girls called out, but no one heard them: their big sister was away and their hard-of-hearing mother was asleep in the cottage.

Mimi tried to wrestle the handlebars of her bicycle from the grasp of the tall German soldier. '*Nein, nein,*' he said, smiling slowly at her and placing his muscular hand over her small, freckled one. The moments ticked by, it was growing dark and the soldiers still blocked the way.

When one of them took another step forward, Mimi flushed with anger: 'If you don't leave us alone,' she announced, 'my sister and I will report you to your *Oberleutnant*. Do you understand?' It did the trick.

Their reprieve, however, was only temporary. Shortly afterwards, all Englishwomen in the area were ordered to be interned in a camp at Falaise. The Germans had detained foreign men immediately after the occupation of Normandy; now the women's turn had come.

Internment meant being put on a train to Germany. In this crisis, and in Pearl's continued absence in Paris as she put her case to Bullitt, Mrs Witherington suddenly showed her mettle. Calling on the *Kommandantur* of Port-en-Bessin, she pleaded to be allowed to take her daughters home to Paris where, she promised, they would report daily to the authorities.

Behind the *Kommandantur*'s desk was a large poster showing an English army officer with a monocle, Sam Brown belt and swagger stick, his hands on his hips and a smile on his face. A broken-down

French family sat at his feet with the caption: '*Ce sont les anglais qui vous ont fait ça*. It's the English who've done this to you.' It seemed unlikely that he would agree to Gee's request as she stood before him, middle-aged, infirm but dignified, in her old-fashioned summer dress. One of the girls was crying.

'We want to go home,' Gee enunciated carefully. 'Our home is in Paris.'

The *Kommandantur* tilted back his chair and stared at the old Englishwoman. There was a pause, and Gee's lip trembled. To her surprise, the German shrugged: 'You are free to go, *Gnädige Frau*,' he said.

In August, the Witheringtons were finally reunited in Paris, where Pearl had found a temporary solution to their money troubles: she was at last receiving an allowance from the American ambassador.

Arriving in Paris barely a month after the city's fall, just after 14 July, Bastille Day, Pearl had been astonished to find herself surrounded by Germans: 'They were everywhere. I was in the middle of a war.'

All along the rue de Rivoli, as far as the eye could see, were giant swastikas, five or six storeys high, reaching right up to the Place de la Concorde. German music was playing, and people sat listening to it.

'*C'est pas possible!* It wasn't possible! Imagine someone arriving *chez vous*, someone you don't like to start with, who moves in, who gives you orders . . . "We're in charge now, this is our country, do as you're told." For me, this was unacceptable, right from the beginning.'

The Parisians watched sullenly as the Germans paraded daily in the Champs-Elysées, as Goering made a luxurious home for himself in the Luxembourg Gardens, and as cinemas, theatres, nightclubs and cafés were taken over exclusively for German patronage. When the Witheringtons went to the opera to see Serge Lifar singing one evening, they were amazed to see 'a sea of uniforms'.

In the first months after the armistice the Nazis behaved very correctly, but *korrektion*, correct behaviour, swiftly shaded into arrogance.

A shortage of cigarettes was one rapid consequence of defeat and occupation: soon people were smoking leaves, and a cigarette butt became a treasure. 'One of the Germans' favourite pastimes was to seat themselves on the terraces of restaurants in the Champs-Elysées, flicking their cigarette ends into the street,' remembers Philippe de Vomécourt, one of three brothers from Lorraine who would later play a crucial role in the French Resistance. 'The people of Paris knew that as they stooped to pick it up, the Germans would hoot with laughter and point at the French, scavenging their fag-ends, but the need for a smoke often overcame their humiliation.'

Pearl felt intense anger. She had spent her whole life in the French capital. She loved two countries and watched with rage the German violation of her beloved France:

> I was furious at the way they behaved in France. People who have never lived in a country occupied by Germans can have no idea what it was like. They took whatever they wanted . . . There was no liberty. You never knew what restrictions were going to be levied next. And there was always that fear. The knock on the door in the middle of the night, after which people disappeared. It roused in me such fury that we had to get away from Paris and do something about it.

Nor was she the only person to feel this way. On the pillars of the rue de Rivoli were posters with photographs of the first French resisters to be shot, while people caught after the curfew were taken to the Gestapo and summarily executed during the night. 'Yet,' said Pearl, 'even in the trauma of defeat there were French people who from the first were fundamentally opposed to the Occupation: a moral resistance . . . The sort of people who helped me and my mother and sisters as we crossed France . . . in our efforts to reach England.' There was as yet no organised resistance, although Pierre de Vomécourt, one of the three resister brothers, had boarded the last ship from Cherbourg and arrived in London in order to promote the idea of a new fifth column in France, resourced from England.

Already the thought had occurred to Pearl that she could be more useful in France helping to drive the Germans out, rather than staying in England once she had delivered her mother and sisters to safety. That summer in occupied Paris, she heard the voice of Winston Churchill on the crackling wireless in the flat, coming over the airwaves of the BBC through the static. At a late-night meeting on 16 July 1940, the very same day that Hitler signed Fuhrer Directive No. 16 authorising Operation Sealion, the invasion of Britain, Churchill ordered Hugh Dalton, the minister of economic warfare, to set up a new secret organisation, the Special Operations Executive: 'Now set Europe ablaze,' he commanded him.

Pearl heard the prime minister's call to arms: 'Churchill said at the beginning, "*Mettez le feu à l'Europe.*"' In a famous passage in his memoirs on 10 May 1940, the day on which he succeeded Chamberlain as prime minister, Churchill wrote: 'I felt as if I were walking with destiny, and that all my past life had been but a preparation for this hour and this trial.' As she listened to him, Pearl felt that she, too, was walking with destiny. 'I believe profoundly in destiny,' she said.

For five months, the Witheringtons remained in Paris. Pearl's thoughts returned constantly to Henri. Was he alive? Was he suffering in the stalag where he was a prisoner of war? There was one very thin silver lining to the clouds of war, however. As she and her sisters shivered in the flat in rue Vignon, wartime conditions broke down old enmities and even seemed to bring some unexpected benefits: united by their common concern for Henri, Pearl and Henri's parents – who were opposed to Pearl and Henri's relationship on grounds of wealth, or Pearl's lack of it – drew closer together and, for the first time, Monsieur and Madame Cornioley received their son's fiancée at their apartment. In a remarkable change of heart, in fact, Monsieur Cornioley, seeing that Pearl, clearly a competent woman, had lost her job at the embassy, took her on as an assistant at the *Laboratoire Cornioley.* Pearl began to learn the beauty business, showing the same shrewd head for figures that Henri's grandmother had done.

In Paris, however, the situation was worsening. The persecution of the Jews was becoming more overt: on 3 October 1940, a German edict ordered all Jews to declare themselves to their employers, and on 19 October, the Vichy government of Marshal Pétain published its own *Statut des Israelites,* forbidding Jews from holding public office. As noisy anti-Semitic demonstrators threw bottles in the Champs-Elysées, factories fired Jewish workers, and racist oppression spread to all foreigners. One day, at the beginning of December 1940, one of Doudou and Mimi's former classmates came to the door in a panic: 'The Germans are rounding up all the English in the sixteenth arrondissement,' they were told. 'You have to get out before it's too late.'

'We were living in the ninteenth arrondissement,' Pearl remembered. 'Mummy said, "I don't want to be caught by the Germans, we're going . . ."'

The smart 16e arrondissement was not far away. It was only a matter of days, hours even, before the Germans came knocking on their door. Once again the family of women packed their few possessions and went into hiding. George the Sealyham was given to friends. Two French families took them in for a few days, while Gee waited for Pearl to find a way for them to cross the demarcation line into the relative safety of the Free Zone, established on 11 July 1940 when France was divided into the German Occupied Zone in the north and Marshal Pétain's Vichy regime in the south.

Still Pearl hesitated. One day, however, the policeman at the Prefecture where the family had to sign in every day – due to their status as foreigners in the city – gave her a tip-off: 'Don't wait . . .' There would be no second chances. On 9 December 1940, the Witheringtons fled the capital.

For the second time they were on the run: Pearl, her frail mother, and her two pretty sisters, against the might of the German war machine.

3
The Longest Winter

IT WAS bitterly cold in the harsh winter of 1940–41. As Pearl set out with her mother and sisters on the night of 9 December 1940 to catch a train and secretly cross the demarcation line into the Non-Occupied or 'Free' Zone, she had no idea how to achieve this, her first clandestine act of the war. Her British passport was hidden in her underclothes; she had no *Ausweis*, official pass, to show the police when they reached the border; nor any false ID papers to flourish in her bid to smuggle her family across the demarcation line. But the *gendarme* at the Prefecture had let the Witherington family sign in for two days, giving them a headstart in their bid for freedom, while a kind friend had paid for their tickets. The four women, a conspicuous little party, hurried to the station to catch the next train south towards the spa town of Vichy, seat of Pétain's government.

Marshal Pétain had bluffed the French people into thinking that honour could be salvaged from defeat. Saluted by Nazis generals, he had shaken hands with Hitler at Montoire, some eighty miles south-west of Paris, on 24 October 1940, and proclaimed: 'It is in the spirit of honour, and to maintain the unity of France, that I enter today upon the path of collaboration.'

With this action, the word 'collaboration' took on a new, shameful meaning. The photo of the handshake with Hitler went around the world, confirming that the Führer had a new ally, for Vichy was unique in being the only government in Occupied Europe to agree willingly to the occupation and division of its country. France had become a vassal state, although this was not at first evident to many French people, who were confused by Pétain's actions:

Philippe de Vomécourt would write that the majority believed that 'to refuse to collaborate, even more to resist actively, was to commit a crime. [Pétain] succeeded in driving France and Frenchmen into further agonies of conscience and division.'

For refugees like the Witheringtons, it was hard to know whom to trust. Simply by looking at the other passengers on the train, they had no way of knowing who was a collaborator and who was not. Certainly the majority of the population supported Pétain, and blamed the previous government for their country's defeat, believing that the old marshal had had no choice but to sign the armistice in the face of the overwhelming might of Hitler's 'New Order'. Their attitude was *attentisme*, wait and see – they would sit on the fence, for it seemed inevitable that Hitler would invade England and win the war he had begun. For Pearl, therefore, finding someone willing to help her among the rows of closed, wary faces sitting opposite her in the railway carriage seemed well nigh impossible.

Pearl had decided to split the family up in order to look less conspicuous. She and her mother had a turbulent relationship; Mimi, in particular, was Gee's pet, and was best at handling the stubborn matriarch, so it seemed the wisest policy to put the two of them together in one carriage, while Pearl and Doudou sat in another. Doudou could be trusted not to talk or draw attention to herself as Pearl started her dangerous quest: hunting anxiously for a *passeur*, smuggler, who was prepared to take them across the border.

Pearl's greatest fear was that Mrs Witherington, who spoke only the poorest French and looked conspicuously English, would inadvertently give them away. The girls, on the other hand, were bilingual, and spoke French with a delightful Parisian accent. 'We could pass for French,' said Pearl, 'but Mother, with her accent, never could.'

She had impressed on her mother before they left the importance of leaving any talking to Mimi. But Mrs Witherington had brought a picnic with her to eat in the train, and wasted no time in unpacking it.

'Eat up, Mimi,' whispered Gee loudly. 'You need to keep your strength up.'

'*Non, Maman*.'

'You've hardly touched a morsel.'

'*Shh, Maman*.' Mimi shook her head. '*Je n'ai pas faim*. I'm not hungry.' She was feeling too nervous to eat.

'It's a lovely chicken, dear. Very moist.'

To keep the peace, Mimi nibbled on a small piece of breast and chewed on some bread, although she felt it would choke her.

Gertrude Witherington, meanwhile, seemingly blissfully unaware of the danger they were in, tucked into her picnic as the train sped towards the border, never doubting that Pearl would find a way. She always did.

The mining town of Montceau-les-Mines in Saône-et-Loire, south of Dijon, lay on the border between the Occupied and Free Zones. By the following summer, there would be a number of local people in the area operating as underground guides, willing to smuggle refugees over the demarcation line, but in the depths of the freezing winter of 1940 it was an untried, dangerous adventure for four women, one of them nearly sixty and with an ailing heart, to take to the fields and woods in the darkness: had Pearl even known the route. Added to this, German soldiers were patrolling the train, examining travellers' papers, inspecting ID cards, demanding to see official passes.

Pearl was on tenterhooks as she perched on the edge of her train seat, listening to the conversations around her. Her senses quivered as they would during *la clandestinité*, when she would go underground as a secret agent. In the secret world, the best agents developed a highly tuned intuition, which they called their 'antennae', and relied upon to sense danger. Fear drove Pearl now to this heightened sense of alertness, for she knew that in revealing herself she would be risking not only her own life but the lives of her mother and sisters: if she made a wrong judgement, she could be denounced to the Germans.

Leaning forward, she listened intently. A man in the corner of the carriage was talking in a local accent to some friends. One remark in particular caught Pearl's attention: '*Il parlait de faire passer les chevaux*. He was talking about smuggling horses.'

Horses. If he could take horses over the line, Pearl reasoned, he could take people. She decided to follow him if he got up. The man was talking quite openly about fooling the Germans. It was time for a bold stroke. She waited until he rose from his seat, and slipped behind him into the corridor.

'*M'sieur?*'

The *passeur* bent his head towards the young woman who was tapping him on the arm. '*Oui, madame?*'

'*Je suis anglaise*,' whispered Pearl. 'Can you help me?'

'You need to make the crossing?'

Pearl nodded. 'There are four of us,' she said. 'Can you do it?'

'*Avec plaisir, madame*.'

'You're sure? My mother is with us.'

The *passeur* smiled at Pearl's anxious face. He was a dark, stocky man, dressed in well-worn country clothes with a flat cap and boots. He looked like a man who worked with horses and dogs, and had a kindly expression.

'*Ne vous inquiètez-pas*. Don't worry. You must get out at Montceau-les-Mines.'

'But our tickets are for Vichy.'

'I will see to it. Get off the train. Wait for me.'

'Pearl put all our eggs in one basket,' remembered Mimi, who had been watching negotiations through the corridor window of her carriage.

Pearl beckoned to her sister, who joined her in the corridor. '*Ça va!* I've found someone who'll take us across, Mimi. Tell Maman to prepare herself.'

Montceau-les-Mines was, by good fortune, the smuggler's home town. As the girls helped their mother down from the train under cover of darkness, their Good Samaritan, who had already paid for the supplement on their train tickets, bought them a 'coffee'– made from grilled, ground barley – at the station café to warm them up. As the train shunted slowly away from the platform, the four women crept out of the station and followed their guide up a country lane.

Very soon, the lane petered out and they were on a muddy path. It was pitch dark and Pearl and Mimi supported Gee as she stumbled and nearly slipped on the frozen puddles. The little group passed a farmhouse. Dogs barked at the sound of their feet on the gravel. 'Mummy, with her bad heart, could only go slowly,' said Mimi.

As they crouched behind a hedge for a rest, they heard the tramp of marching feet. Heavy boots struck the frozen rutted earth and the sound rang out in the cold night air. Men were singing German marching songs. The crunch of boots came closer.

'You must hide,' hissed their guide. 'Get in the ditch, now!'

He threw Gee's blanket over his bicycle, and told Pearl and her sister to pull their skirts down over their 'pale legs', just as the German patrol marched past them on the other side of the hedge.

'My poor mother got entangled in some bramble bushes,' said Mimi. 'Our hearts were beating fast.' The women held their breath as the patrol passed within inches of them, and then vanished into the night.

They walked for so long that they lost track of time. Footsore and weary, they crept through fields and woods, struggling not to lose sight of the dim figure of the *passeur* ahead of them. Eventually, they came to a field that he said was near the demarcation line. The three girls urged their mother not to talk as they walked along a lane with high hedges, which led onto a road.

They could see the barrier now, guarded by armed sentries in their grey uniforms and coal-scuttle helmets. A swastika banner was suspended above the barrier and a powerful searchlight swept the road. The *Wehrmacht*, and not the French police, manned the demarcation line, which stretched for 1,200 kilometres across thirteen *départements*, and divided the more industrialised north from the less populated south. It was a formidable barrier to cross, and Pearl stared with dismay at a bright beam of light as it swung from side to side.

The *passeur* put his finger to his lips. 'We cross now,' he said. 'Hurry, please.'

For a moment the women hesitated.

'*Dépêchez-vous!* Hurry up!'

'We went off at a fast trot,' said Mimi. All of a sudden, the searchlight began to swing their way. 'I heard my mother gasp, "Oh my God, we are done for!"'

'Run!' cried their Good Samaritan, waving away their thanks. 'Run!'

The smuggler leapt onto his bike and pedalled away into the darkness as the women darted forward across the road, the girls clutching their mother's hands as she stumbled in the beam of light. But luck was on their side. The German sentry guarding the barrier to their left happened to look the other way as they crossed, and the little party made it to the other side.

'Our safety – a café on the unoccupied side – we had made it!'

The women were almost crying with relief.

'Was I all right, Pearl?' asked Mrs Witherington. 'I didn't let you down. I didn't talk, did I?'

Pearl squeezed her mother's arm. 'No, Maman,' she said. '*Tu étais super!* You were an absolute brick.'

Tired but elated, the women travelled on to Vichy, their original destination, where Pearl had planned to apply to the American ambassador for help, but she was told that nothing could be done for her.

'Try your luck in Marseilles,' said the Americans.

Disappointed and hungry, the women stuffed newspapers into their wet shoes and hiked on, crossing frozen rivers, surviving on hunks of black bread and fruit for five days before finally arriving at Marseilles railway station on 15 December.

At Marseilles station entrance barrier, Pearl was shocked to see the Vichy police stopping passengers in the queue ahead. 'Your papers, please.'

They were asking for identification papers, and she had none. Telling her mother to stay out of view, Pearl quickly sent a message to the American Embassy via a kindly passenger, asking for someone to collect them.

'Sure enough they did, bless them,' remembers Mimi.

The Americans did more, offering Pearl a job, which also temporarily solved the family's financial problems. In rue Paradis, in the old quarter, they found a cheap, flea-ridden hotel where the girls slept three to a bed, giving their mother a single bed of her own. There were food shortages, and it was a rough, hard three months.

The old quarter of Marseilles had a reputation for toughness and defiance, the *tabacs* and bars in the narrow streets sheltering many refugees on the run from the Nazis. Escaped airmen and army personnel were interned in the medieval Fort Saint-Jean, the older of the two fortresses which dominated the harbour of the *Vieux-Port.* The internees were, however, allowed out by day if they gave their word of honour that they would not escape, and several young airmen and soldiers dined with Pearl, Doudou and Mimi on a variety of dubious wartime dishes served in the cheap brasserie opposite the Hotel du Paradis. According to Doudou: 'The lights, or lungs, in wine sauce were delicious.'

On Christmas Day 1940, American diplomats from the embassy invited Pearl to come and cheer up the troops at the fort. The prisoners had fattened up a pig called Hitler, which they were preparing to eat when Pearl entered. Paddy Moffitt, the Irish soldier whom Pearl had helped when he escaped to Normandy in the summer, was himself a prisoner in the fort. He noticed 'a girl who came in with some officers', and he and Bill Davidson shouted from the parapet: 'Miss Witherington! Pearl!'

The two men ran downstairs to find Pearl, who was surrounded by a mêlée of troops of all nationalities.

'I asked an officer if it was Miss Witherington,' said Paddy. 'Yes, it was her!' A joyful reunion followed, and Paddy and Bill joined the other servicemen who met up with the Witherington girls in the old port.

Both men were determined to escape and, before long, Davidson had joined the French Foreign Legion, while Paddy had taken the road over the Pyrénées to Spain – it was the most common escape route back to England, for once in Spain there were boats from Gibraltar. For the Witheringtons, however, there was no hope of following in his footsteps. The three girls were young and fit, and could easily have followed a guide on the mountain trails. But for Pearl it was out of the question: she and her sisters could not abandon their mother, who was too unwell to hike over the mountains.

Months dragged by. Pearl realised that her only hope was to begin the laborious process of applying for exit visas.

Snow fell in the *Vieux-Port*. It was icy cold.

Feeling against the British had hardened in Marseilles after the Royal Navy had sunk the French fleet at Mers-el-Kébir, Oran, on 3 July 1940. The wounded sailors had been disembarked at the port. It was hard for many Frenchmen to realise that Pétain now headed a collaborationist government. The Vichy French fleet could not be allowed to fall into the hands of Hitler and when French commanders rejected the Royal Navy's ultimatum to scuttle it or sail to join the British, Churchill had taken the painful step of ordering the bombardment of the French warships. Some 1,250 French lives had been lost.

'I have never been so ashamed and disillusioned by Britain as I was the day I saw the wounded French sailors on the wharf,' remarked Nancy Wake, an Australian journalist who later became an SOE agent ('the White Mouse'), but who at the time was living in Marseilles with her husband. 'We had been allies just a short time ago . . . The German propaganda machine had a field day . . . It made the French people, already suspicious of involvement, think twice before they included themselves in subversive activities.'

Nevertheless, there were exceptions: men and women who realised almost immediately that Pétain was no more than a puppet figurehead. French aristocrat Charles d'Aragon had no illusions about peace with honour, writing in his journal in the autumn of 1940: 'We have been beaten everywhere. It's shameful . . . *le déshonneur submerge tout*.' Visiting Vichy, he almost bumped into the 'saviour' of France in the bar of the Hotel du Parc and was struck by the showy pink carnation in Pétain's buttonhole and his excessively familiar manner, surprising in an old warrior: 'I had the feeling of being at the heart of a ridiculous Olympus, a new and pitiful mythology, a gossipy court.'

For the dismayed aristocrat, it was 'the longest winter', as the cult of Pétain grew and there was no organised resistance. But there were acts of opposition. In March 1941, for instance, the son of General d'Astier de la Vigerie was arrested and imprisoned for distributing oppositional tracts. Shocked by the sight of his old friend Jean-Anet, an early *résistant*, being escorted through Toulouse (for distributing clandestine papers), Charles d'Aragon reached out from the solitude of his estates and began writing for the clandestine press, too.

The green shoots of resistance were piercing the frozen earth.

4

Escape

IN MARSEILLES, scattered Britons were gradually regrouping. For an Englishwoman like Pearl in the city, it was only a matter of time before she bumped into the legendary Captain Ian Garrow, a survivor of the 51st Highland Division, who was one of the first to organise escape lines to Spain in the winter of 1940. She began working with the Scot, who became chief of the British escape organisation in Marseilles later known as the 'Pat' organisation, after the famous Lieutenant Commander 'Pat' O'Leary, RN, the *nom de guerre* of Belgian army doctor, Albert Guérisse. Garrow and 'Pat' helped many agents and shot-down aircrew, while three of SOE's best couriers – Andrée Borrel (Denise), Madeleine Damerment and Nancy Wake (The White Mouse) – served their clandestine apprenticeship in the organisation, and Nancy Wake was herself one of Garrow's couriers.

Pearl's baptism by fire in the escape lines introduced her to clandestine techniques such as cut-outs and letterboxes (houses where messages could be left). She learnt the smell of danger in the narrow streets where informers were quick to betray suspects to the Vichy police. All too often, supposed 'safe-houses' turned out to be traps, as SOE agent Gerry Morel discovered in Marseilles in October 1941.

On his way to a safe-house, he pushed through the dark alleys of the *Vieux-Port*, crowded with seamen and prostitutes. Ignoring the cries of '*Hallo, chéri*!' that greeted him at every doorway, he reached his destination: 12 rue de la Colline Noire.

A woman opened the door to him. '*Bonsoir, monsieur.*'

'I've been sent by Gaston,' said Morel.

The woman looked sharply up at the dark stairs that led to the second floor.

'Send him up,' a voice said.

In the shadows on the top floor was a man. Morel had left his revolver with the lawyer who was his contact: the times when he might have to fight his way out of a situation were outnumbered by those when he might be searched.

The man in the shadows said: '*Tu viens de la part de Gaston?* You come from Gaston?'

'Yes.'

'Come in, please.'

Morel went past the man, through the doorway into the attic. It was in darkness.

'I'll turn on the light,' the man behind him said, clicking a switch.

Three members of the *Milice*, the Vichy collaborationist paramilitaries, faced Morel across the narrow attic with drawn machine pistols.

In the *Vieux-Port*, Pearl watched from the shadows the struggles of the earliest resisters against Pétain's police, and saw the battle lines laid down between collaborators – supported by the acquiescent majority – and the few brave souls determined to resist the Nazi regime. It only deepened her determination to play her part in the 'secret war'.

'I knew very well what I wanted to do,' she said, 'for I had become more or less mixed up with the story of resistance in Marseilles.' She had cut her teeth during the winter of despair.

In the New Year of 1941, an English diplomat at the American Embassy asked Pearl to help him organise a Red Cross boat to transport wounded servicemen and refugee women and children home to England. For two months she negotiated with the Germans, but just when the boat was due to sail they withdrew their authorisation. Most British prisoners subsequently revoked their parole and, like Moffitt, disappeared over the Pyrénées.

By the spring, only a handful of British remained in Marseilles, and the Witheringtons' spirits were at a low ebb until they heard, to their great relief, that their family's exit visas had finally been granted.

With hopes high, the little group of women again set off for the station. This time they were catching a train to the French frontier with Spain at Cerbère–Portbou. At the Spanish customs, officers asked if they had anything to declare. The answer was nothing – they were penniless. A female officer began to search Mrs Witherington, but as she attempted to undress her, Gee raised an indignant hand to her corset.

'What are you looking for?' demanded Pearl.

'Money.'

'I told you we don't have any.'

'I've never seen the English travel without money.'

Pearl glared at the woman. 'Have you never heard of refugees?'

The few pesetas Pearl had been advanced by a representative of the British ambassador to Spain only took them as far as Barcelona. The next day, the family travelled on to Zaragoza and Madrid, where Spanish soldiers took pity on the hungry women and gave them food. On 14 March they finally arrived in Lisbon, and Pearl found rooms in an English guest house. The financial situation was desperate until Pearl applied to the air attaché. As usual, she was immediately employed – in fact, the air attaché was so impressed by his new PA's efficiency that she was afraid to put her name down in advance for a boat to England; it was certain that her boss would veto it.

It was tempting to stay in Portugal, a neutral country far from the privations of war, rather than pursue their goal of reaching England. Lamps burnt brightly in the streets, the city was bursting with Allied troops, nightclubs were open: 'The first time I ventured into a *boîte de nuit* was in Portugal,' Pearl remembered, while Doudou and Mimi persuaded her to stay up all night with them to watch the sun rise on Mount Cintra.

Three months passed. 'We lacked nothing,' said Pearl, in comfortable Portugal, but the handsome officers held no interest for her. Her thoughts turned constantly to her fiancé, Henri. She had not seen him for over a year: 'I was just living and waiting for a boat to Gibraltar', hoping against hope that in time Henri, too, would be able to join her in England.

But a rumour reached Pearl that Henri was imprisoned in Miranda, the notorious Spanish prison camp where hundreds of prisoners of war were held in appalling conditions; Moffitt, who had followed a goat herd over a mountain pass and walked straight into the arms of the police, was incarcerated there. Pearl and Henri had been writing to each other during the Phoney War, which had ended on 10 May 1940, but his letters had ceased, and she had not seen him since his last leave in January that year. Her anguish only grew when she heard that Moffitt had collapsed after days spent filling baskets with stones. Then the rumour was corrected: Henri's name was not, after all, on the prison lists. But if he was not in Spain, where was he? Was he even alive?

In his freezing stalag, Henri vowed that he would not spend another winter in Germany.

'My first winter in Germany: *oh là là*!' The cold was frightful, the food too. 'I said to myself: "*Ah ça, mon vieux*, you won't survive another winter here in a country where they have cold winters." It was one of my reasons for escaping from Germany.' As he and his fellow prisoners laboured first at erecting barbed-wire fences around their camp, and then at cutting down the barbed-wire fences on the Siegfried Line, Henri dreamed of freedom.

He was one of nearly 2 million French prisoners of war sent to different stalags in Germany, and most probably found himself in Stalag VB, near the border with Switzerland. To attempt an escape was extremely risky: all frontiers were heavily guarded, and Alsace and Lorraine, through which he would have to travel if he escaped successfully, had been annexed by the Germans in 1940. But locked up, humiliated, angry, many Frenchmen were determined to escape – 40,000 were to do so. From their stalags, they looked west to France, to *la patrie*. Henri was one of these.

Spring softened the landscape. In the summer of 1941, the men were let out of the camp to help bring in the harvest. As he tied up sheaves of corn, an owl flew out of a nearby wood. Henri, who loved animals, took this as a good omen – he had kept a pet baby black rabbit while in the army, warming it in his jacket as his regiment advanced from Beaumont-en-Argonne, in the Ardennes, until the moment when the Germans overran them and he released it into the fields of Lorraine. In July, the prisoners were split into small groups and set to muck-raking in the villages. One day, a German asked for four or five volunteers to work by the canal. Swimming and sunbathing, Henri recovered his strength.

'I said, "Listen, mates, we've lived like kings for the past fortnight . . . *C'est le moment ou jamais* . . . It's now or never, it's time for us to fuck off out of here."'

Four other prisoners agreed to make a run for it with him. The next morning, they took the canal path as usual, then ran for the fields.

After forty-eight hours of marching in fierce storms, the men reached a mountain pass, the Col du Donon, high up in the Vosges Mountains in Alsace. It was 737 metres high, the gateway to liberty. Drenched and exhausted, they were breasting the pass when they found themselves face to face with a German guard post.

'*Halt!*' The Germans raised their rifles. Henri and his friends turned and ran for their lives. Three men were recaptured, but Henri himself escaped to a woodcutter's cabin where he and a fellow POW sheltered overnight. The next day, they cautiously retraced their steps: they had no alternative but to cross the pass if they were to reach France. A German sentry spotted them and fired warning shots, but the two men separated, hurling themselves down the mountainside by different paths to the plain below.

Vineyards, fields, houses rose out of the early morning mist. A peasant told Henri that he had reached a town called Raon-sur-Plaine. Cycling on to another village on a bicycle lent to him by a friendly mayor, he took charge of three more escapees: two Poles and a North African. On 1 September 1941, he led them triumphantly into Bourg-en-Bresse, west of Geneva, and thence to Mâcon, on the river Saône. Demobilised (due to Vichy France's peace agreement with Germany), free at last, Henri crossed the river into central France and turned his face towards Paris and his waiting family.

But, just as Henri gained his freedom in France, his fiancée quit the Continent.

On 8 June 1941, Pearl's chance had also come. An old banana boat named the *Avoceta* sailed into Lisbon harbour, bound for Gibraltar in a British convoy. It was now or never. Without stopping to ask her boss's permission, Pearl shepherded her mother and sisters onto the heavily overloaded vessel, which was carrying 250 English refugees.

With difficulty, the girls found a cabin for Gee, while Pearl and her sisters slept on deckchairs under the stars as they chugged down the coast. They ate an unrelenting diet of sardines, the only food available, until four days later when the boat docked in Gibraltar. They had been luckier than they knew. On her next mission, the *Avoceta* was sunk by a German U-boat. Only one lifeboat was picked up, with few survivors.

The English refugees were transferred to the *Scythia*, a Cunard liner which had come up from South Africa with RAF personnel bound for the UK. The Witheringtons spent two weeks on board her in Gibraltar, where Pearl took the opportunity to let her hair down. According to Mimi, 'We had a super time as there were no women on the Rock, and parties were given by the Royal Navy.' Some of the best parties were on HMS *Ark Royal*, and Pearl, slim and sun-tanned, her hair bleached by the Mediterranean sunshine, attracted quite as much attention as her two sisters. The three girls danced on deck as the band played 'If You Were the Only Girl in the World,' and 'When Nightingales Sang in Berkeley Square.'

One night, on their return to the *Scythia*, the high-spirited sisters were promptly put on a charge and confined aboard for three days: 'Disciplinary action has had to be taken against three civilian passengers who failed to return by the time stated on their pass,' recorded the Daily Orders of commanding officer Squadron Leader Stansfield. 'Pearl, Doudou and me,' scrawled Mimi proudly on the paper.

The *Scythia* was carrying 2,500 service personnel and refugees, including, by good fortune, Paddy Moffitt, when she and another liner steamed out of Gibraltar in a convoy accompanied by two warships and submarines. The long voyage passed without incident.

On Sunday, 13 July 1941, the *Scythia* sailed into Greenock in Scotland. After fleeing Paris over a year before, the Witheringtons had taken the long way round to a country that only their mother knew. They had only the clothes they stood up in.

5
Pearl

'As for my childhood,' said Pearl. 'I never had one.' Her early years were too painful to talk about.

Born in Paris on 24 June 1914 to a British couple domiciled in the French capital, Wallace, secretary to a Swedish paper manufacturer, and Gertrude Witherington, Cécile Pearl Witherington had seemed destined for a very different upbringing, for there were few indications of the burdens that were to be placed on her small shoulders. On the contrary, she was born into the comforts of a well-to-do expatriate household. Her father, a high-living English gentleman – for such was Wallace's aspiration – had brought his pretty wife to fashionable Paris not only because it was his place of work, but because one could live there with far less expense and more amusement than in London.

After Pearl's birth, Gertrude had taken her baby to be registered.

'What is the infant's name?' asked the registrar.

'Pearl,' answered Gertrude.

'But this name is not French,' protested the official. 'Your daughter must have a French name.'

Gertrude considered the matter for a moment: 'Cecilia,' she replied.

'*Ah, oui, Cécile,*' said the registrar.

'Cécile *Pearl*,' said Gertrude firmly. The Frenchman could say what he liked: her daughter was English, and her name was Pearl.

As the baby grew, Gee sang nursery rhymes to her in English: 'Rock-a-bye-baby' and 'Little Miss Muffet.' She spoke to her in English, told her English fairy stories. She taught Pearl to read and write from English story books, observed English customs, such as the obligatory plum pudding at Christmas, and lived a proud but increasingly lonely life as an outsider in French society. 'We were born in Paris and had never lived in England, but we were brought up to be more English than the English, as is often the case with the English who live abroad,' noted Mimi. England itself, the country their mother called home, was a strange, mythical place. Pearl did not visit it until she was twelve. For her, Paris was always home.

Gee was naturally shy, and found mixing socially difficult. Her isolation was increased by her deafness, which was severe enough to make conversation difficult in a group of people; she preferred one-to-one conversations, when she could more easily lip-read. Learning a foreign language presented an insuperable difficulty; and, as pregnancy followed pregnancy, Gee lost the inclination to try.

'*Je ne comprends pas*,' she would say, as the puzzling conversations swirled about her. People spoke too fast; she couldn't understand them. When she asked them to repeat themselves, they laughed at *Madame l'anglaise* with her blank face, and shrugged their shoulders.

Cosmopolitan Wallace Witherington, on the other hand, was an expert linguist, fluent in five languages; in fact, no two people could have been more different in their attitude to language and travel than he and his wife. But none of this was apparent to either of them when Wallace first brought his new bride to France.

Son of a prosperous architect, Wallace was descended from Northumberland gentry, the owners of Cartington Castle, near Rothbury. They became a distinguished military family: Squire Richard Witherington was immortalised in the fourteenth-century 'Ballad of Chevy Chase', which praised him for fighting to the death after his feet were hewn from under him in battle:

For Witherington my heart was woe
That ever slain he should be:
For when both his legs were hewn in two
Yet he kneel'd and fought on his knee.

The family motto is: 'I will not fail.' The courage of the Witheringtons became legendary, while the story of Richard Witherington inspired the Royal Navy to name one of their 'W' class destroyers after him.

Wallace was to be the last English male descendant of the Witheringtons; by the time of his birth, on 22 April 1879, the heroic Witherington legacy had largely passed the family by. After the deaths of his parents, young Wallace went to London. There, in 1910, he met his bride-to-be: Gertrude Florence Hearn.

Gee was living at 32 Clarendon Road, Putney, a suburb on the south side of the river Thames. She too, was motherless, and was keeping house for her brother, Charles Joseph, a dried-fruit merchant. Born in 1881, in Hounslow, Gee was two years younger than Wallace. The story went that her brother, Charlie, who sang in the same choir as Wallace in a Putney church, brought his friend home after choir practice one evening and introduced him to his slim, brunette sister.

Gee was swept off her feet. Wallace was charming and handsome and his life seemed impossibly glamorous to a sheltered spinster getting on in years. Like his father, Wallace had trained as an architect, but his personality disinclined him to study and he had abandoned architecture for the post of secretary to Baron Victor de Foch, a wealthy Swedish nobleman and supplier of paper for bank notes. Crossing the world's oceans, from Buenos Aires to Canada, the gregarious young secretary revelled in the globe-trotting life, which enabled him to perfect his languages.

Wallace and Gee's marriage was solemnised on New Year's Eve, 1912, at Wandsworth Register Office: Wallace was thirty-three, Gertrude thirty-one. He had rescued her from the life of a superfluous woman, for she had no occupation or profession: her only vocation was marriage. Wallace may also have given her a step up the social ladder: Gee's father, George Frederick Hearn, was a retired condensed-milk merchants' manager, while Wallace Seckham Witherington gave his profession as 'Director of a Public Company.' Both parties lived at Clarendon Road, for a time, but their destination lay across the Channel, where

Wallace's Parisian apartment was ready and waiting to receive his new wife.

Marrying Wallace and moving to the City of Light seemed like an awfully big adventure to Gee. The tall, timid brunette assumed that she was making a good match when she accepted a proposal of marriage from the dashing man-about-town who promised to take her abroad. At first all was well; Wallace moved his bride into his office apartment at 34 rue Vignon, a respectable address on the right bank of the Seine, and she delighted in her new domain: the two elegant, shuttered rooms overlooking the street, the master bedroom with a view of the courtyard, the spiral staircase to the kitchen and two other bedrooms. Marrying late, by the standards of the day, she was in a hurry to start a family and quickly became pregnant.

The arrival of Cécile Pearl, their firstborn, was greeted with joy; her two names representing the two cultures in which her parents – separately – felt at home, and between which their daughter would easily move.

A spate of babies then followed, which Wallace could ill afford. According to Pearl, 'In the space of nine years, he produced eight children (four of whom died young). But he never managed to meet their needs. Besides, he was never there.' Tony Thomson, Pearl's nephew, remarked that, 'Wallace enjoyed the bottle and the betting shop.'

After World War I, Wallace lost his job, segueing effortlessly into a life of leisure. 'He'd lived a luxurious life. And he was certainly lazy,' said Pearl. Wallace's wide circle of friends made a point of looking him up whenever they came to Paris. Rising late, he would stroll out of the apartment at eleven in the morning, not returning until two the next morning. His family barely saw him.

Gee was almost permanently pregnant, but her four male babies died of a 'blood disease' (probably haemophilia). The four girls who survived, however, consumed the family's dwindling resources. More and more, Gee turned to her elder daughter for help.

'Wallace always spoke French to Pearl,' her nephew noted.

'Gertrude was a Brit who said "Non", but Pearl quickly became fluent.' From the age of eight, Pearl was Gee's link to the strange, foreign world outside the 'little England' she had created within her flat. Perhaps as a result of this, Pearl did not go to school until she was thirteen, although she practised her reading on the advertisements on buses and lorries in the rue Royale.

The situation became desperate: Wallace had hardly two sous to rub together and, anyway, alcohol took first claim on his purse. Gee would send Pearl out to find money: she could not return until she had some:

> It was I who went to whichever bar [Father] was in, to collect twenty francs a day. The barman served as an intermediary, and gave me a box of biscuits as a present at the same time.

If Pearl failed to find her father, or the money had already gone down his throat, there was another alternative:

> I had to go to one of his friends who lived on the other side of the Seine . . . I'm simply telling you this to give you an idea of what made me a fighter in my life. First I had to telephone from the hotel opposite us to see if I could go there. This friend lived beside the *Institut de France*, on quai Visconti. From rue Vignon, I had to go right across the Tuileries Gardens to reach him, so that he'd give me the the money I needed in order to go shopping for lunch.

In the morning, Pearl runs down rue Vignon towards the Tuileries Gardens, entering from the Place de la Concorde and walking the dusty length of the gardens until she reaches the footbridge, the Pont des Arts, which leads to the *Institut de France*. Breathless, she rings the bell, and is given a grudging twenty francs; then it is time to hurry back again, to go to the market. Her mother is waiting; her sisters are hungry, and so is she.

Sometimes, though, there is no money. Her father has vanished; his friend doesn't answer the bell. Still Pearl stops by the market;

the stallholders are taking a long lunch before opening again at four o'clock. While their backs are turned, Pearl dodges behind a stall and rummages through a sack of potatoes. Some of them are on the turn, smelly, squelching, half-rotten, but her small fingers root through the spuds, her eyes flicking assessingly over some nearby haricot verts as she drops half-edible vegetables into her pinafore pocket. She keeps a weather eye out for the stallholder, listening for the roar that will tell her she has been spotted. But Pearl is a practised thief, an Artful Dodger determined to survive. She knows the streets, the argot of the traders, their customs and habits.

At home, her sister Suzanne is crying again. Her buttocks are red, the skin weeping from neglect. Overwhelmed by her continual pregnancies and miscarriages, and the bitter disappointment of bearing dead sons, Gee is proving to be an inadequate mother. Unequal to the task of the day-to-day care of her babies, depressed by her isolation and lack of family support in the foreign capital, and increasingly alienated from her drunken, absentee husband, she hands over the care of her squalling infants to Pearl, and a Belgian refugee, Lucie, who comes to live with the family in 1918.

Wallace descends into full-blown alcoholism. Pearl's anger grows as she watches her father's condition deteriorate. She concludes that he lacks the force of character, the mental capacity to face up to life. To *faire face à la vie*, to face up to one's challenges and responsibilities becomes, for Pearl, the most important human quality.

Debts pile up. One afternoon, at the age of eight, she comes home to find all the family furniture piled up on the pavement. She bursts into tears and howls of rage. 'Be quiet!' she is sharply admonished. Later, she learns that her father has failed to pay the rent for their flat for the whole of World War I. In desperation, Gee turns to her brother, Charlie, who comes over to Paris and settles the arrears, so that the family can move back into their home. Watching her bed being carried back into the apartment, Pearl learns a sharp lesson on the insecurity of life.

She blames his friends, who enable him to keep on drinking. Pearl is only eleven or twelve when she challenges one of her father's friends, imploring him not buy Papa another drink. It is brave of her. This particular *copain* helps them out financially – he has come to take her out to lunch – but her father is ill and she knows very well that he is still drinking: 'If you didn't all keep buying him drinks, he wouldn't be in the state he is now,' snaps the fierce little girl. The man avoids her eyes; he never comes back.

Pearl can hear the voices echoing in her head, Wallace's mates: '*Tu veux un verre? Prends donc un verre.* Fancy a drink? Go on, have one. *T'as envie d'un verre? Prends-le donc.* Feel like a drink, old man? Just the one.'

There are angry rows between her parents, and Pearl grows to dread the nightly arguments, raised voices, tears. Her own fury grows at her drunken, spendthrift father and the situation in which he has put his family, and she promises herself that when she grows up, she will never quarrel with her husband in front of her children.

In January 1922, Gee gives birth to her last daughter, Mimi, in the British Hospital in Paris – she is the only one of the four girls to be born in hospital. Her mother tries to breastfeed her, but she has no milk. The baby chews on Gee's nipples until they are red and raw, wailing miserably, until Pearl can bear it no longer and runs out to the pharmacy to beg for some formula. But the chemist has had enough of foreigners who live on tick: 'I can't help you, young lady.'

'The baby's hungry, she's crying,' pleads Pearl.

'*Écoutez!* This has gone on long enough.'

'Please, monsieur.'

The chemist stares at the skinny little girl in her hand-me-down coat and tatty shoes.

'*Je ne peux pas*,' he repeats.

At the boulangerie, the baker's wife refuses her a baguette. There is no more credit for Madame Witherington, not until she pays her bread bill. The shouts and insults of the shopkeepers pursue young Pearl down the street, in full view of the other customers.

As her marriage broke down, and the girls grew older, Gertrude proved herself unexpectedly resourceful. Appearances were to be kept up, at all costs. She dressed all four of her girls alike, in clothes handed down from their English cousin, Patricia, exquisitely sewn by her mother Olive, Wallace's sister. *Les petites anglaises,* Pearl, Suzie, Doudou and Mimi, in their English fashions, became a familiar sight in the neighbourhood. 'Do you know how old I was when I got a dress that I chose for myself?' asked Pearl, later. 'Twenty-seven.'

Pearl wore her aunt's cast-off shoes, too. They were a size too small, as Pearl was tall for her age, so her cramped toes became permanently bent and painful. But to wear one's cousin's cast-offs was not unusual at the time.

'We didn't have any money, but we weren't unhappy,' remembered Pearl. She longed for roller-skates, but her mother couldn't afford them. She loved the countryside and the seaside, and longed to live there; she wanted to learn the piano; there was no money for lessons. There was not even a few *centimes* for the Punch and Judy show in the Champs-Elysées. 'It didn't kill me.' Pearl was tough.

She hugged tight her few, happy memories: playing hide and seek with Lucie, their unpaid nanny; an outing with Pearl's father to the circus when she was six and her first sight of an elephant; another outing with Papa, when she was twelve and he took her to the lido, where she developed a passion for swimming. But her happiest memory was of the day in 1922 when, after eight years confined in the city, she first saw the seaside.

Cornwall was a revelation. Aunt Olive had invited her nieces for a holiday in Portscatho, on the Roseland Peninsula, where she and her husband, George Naylor, had a summer house called Water's Edge. Pearl loved the old house with doorways so low one had to stoop to enter the dark interior; the fishing trips on her uncle's boat; the old harbour where the cottages tumbled down to the sea and where the pilchard fishermen taught her to row. Pink hydrangeas sat in front of blue doorways; Uncle George bought her ice cream; Aunt Olive took her to the beach. But these were rare treats.

On their return to Paris, the owner of an English *salon de thé* took pity on Mrs Witherington, whose poverty was no less acute for being genteel, and offered to pay her to do his washing. Every day Lucie, the mother's help, scrubbed white tablecloths and Gee ironed them. Lucie 'more or less brought us up', recalled Pearl. She herself did no housework, and her position in the household was becoming clear: she was the man of the house. When a letter arrived for Gee from the tax office, she turned to Pearl. Wallace, as usual, was absent: 'God knows where he was.' The twelve-year-old Pearl hurried down to the tax collector and ran through the figures until he was satisfied with the Witherington accounts.

Although she could speak French like a native, Pearl could not write it. The street urchin had never been to school, despite her father's promises that next term, perhaps, she could go. She was thirteen before the priest at the local Protestant church entered Pearl for the *École Britannique* in rue Guersant, a tram-ride away from her home in rue Vignon. The church paid her fees, and her school dinners. The Witherington girls were all charity cases.

It was a shock for Pearl to discover the extent of her illiteracy. Having learnt French phonetically, she had not the least idea of spelling or grammar. Nor had she ever learnt mathematics. Mornings began with a French *dictée*, for the school was bilingual, lessons being taught in French in the morning and English in the afternoon. Every morning, Pearl received a scolding from her teacher as she put two 'p's in *apercevoir* or misspelt *ils appellent* as *ils appelant*.

'Copy out your dictation as many times as you have made mistakes,' ordered Mademoiselle. At first even that was impossible, for the new girl made a mistake in every word: the other pupils laughed at her howlers. 'I had terrible gaps.' For three years Pearl, ashamed that she could not write properly, struggled to catch up. She dedicated evenings and weekends to her homework, which included *la sténo*, shorthand and typing in both languages, for the school prepared its pupils for commercial positions and a bilingual secretary commanded a higher pay grade. Luckily, she had a photographic memory.

Gee now designated Pearl the family breadwinner, and moved her into Wallace's back bedroom overlooking the courtyard. 'It was the best room in the house,' noted Mimi, who felt a certain resentment at her elder sister's privileges: she had to share a room with her two elder sisters. Gee took the other bedroom and Lucie bedded down on a mattress in the kitchen.

Pearl understood her mother's logic: 'Well, I'd taken his place, without even knowing it, without realising it.' As for her father, the father who'd bred children and then abandoned them: '*Je ne pige pas!* I just don't get it,' she exclaimed in disgust. As Wallace continued his rake's progress, his daughter absorbed lessons she would never forget: self-control, duty and restraint. She squared her shoulders: she would make up for Papa's deficiencies.

There was to be no academic qualification for Pearl, no *baccalauréat* (the school-leaving certificate essential for higher education) even though she was an able student who loved reading, immersing herself in the novels of AJ Cronin or spy stories such as *Louise de Bettignies: Sister in Arms*, about a woman agent who ran an escape line from Belgium to France in World War I: 'I said to myself, that's the kind of thing I'd really like to do.'

No sooner had Pearl passed her commercial diplomas than she was removed from school, after just three and a half years. Further education was an unaffordable luxury. Mimi and her sisters, however, continued their education. Mimi entered the Protestant school when she was ten: there were different rules, different responsibilities, for the firstborn.

'My mother was very strict, and much more so with me than my sisters,' says Pearl. Chastisement for her 'elephant' of a daughter was constant: 'You, you great big elephant!' said Gertrude, as her tall elder daughter proved clumsy, dropping a teacup. As their unhappy mother's hand would fall upon Pearl, she in her turn often delivered *une bonne fessée,* a sharp slap, to her little sisters, who, in her opinion, were allowed to do just as they pleased. The three younger girls formed a unit apart from Pearl, who was three and a half years older than Suzie and nearly nine years older than Mimi, to whom she was closest. Enviously Pearl watched as her sisters were given opportunities that had been denied to her, such as outings at a British sporting club, which she would have enjoyed. Pearl had grown into a bold, athletic girl who dreamt of swimming the Channel or becoming a famous aviator like Amy Johnson or Lindbergh. Solo exploits fascinated her, and martial music thrilled her. When she saw soldiers marching to a military band, she longed to fall into line with them and march in step.

More and more, the crowded, claustrophobic flat felt like a prison. Gee still lived *en vase clos*, cut off from the world. 'We knew few people outside,' Pearl recalled. Gee lacked real friends. 'She had none,' said Mimi. 'Mummy hated France.' The family also kept themselves to themselves partly because of their straitened circumstances.

Since there were no tea parties for Pearl, she made her first friends in the public parks. One day in the Tuileries, a little boy approached her: 'Can I borrow your skipping rope?'

It was Charles Delaunay, the son of painters Sonia and Robert Delaunay. Soon he was spending every Thursday with Pearl and her sisters.

In the few short years in which Pearl was at the *École Britannique*, she began to emerge from the shyness that was a legacy of her upbringing. She made friends with a girl named Evelyne Cornioley, who lived nearby: her family's apartment was in front of the *Madeleine*, Pearl's behind it. But although they lived in the same *quartier*, the two girls inhabited vastly different worlds. The Cornioleys were French citizens, although of Swiss origin; like the English Witheringtons, they were Protestants. Unlike them, they were fabulously rich.

One day, coming back from the market with her mother and sisters, Pearl caught a glimpse of Evelyne with a tall, dark-haired teenage boy. It was her friend's brother, sixteen-year-old Henri Cornioley. They were going home together to their apartment on the rue du Faubourg-Saint-Honoré, a road so grand that it housed a string of embassies and fashionable boutiques.

'Hurry up!' Mrs Witherington exhorted her elephant of a daughter, who was staring after Evelyne and her handsome companion. 'Don't dawdle, Pearl.'

Henri vanished almost as swiftly as he had appeared. Later, Pearl learned that he had been sent to Switzerland for his health; he had a weak chest and there were fears that he had tuberculosis, although later he was diagnosed as suffering from the after-effects of diphtheria.

Yet more pressing concerns overwhelmed the family. It was 1931, and Pearl was seventeen. Wallace returned to England and would die the following year of tuberculosis, on 29 August, in a South Kensington consumption hospital, aged only fifty-two. The need for money was urgent. Mrs Witherington was a single mother so poor that she could not afford a ticket home to England; but nor was it easy to find employment for a young English girl, a foreigner in Paris, without a work permit.

There was only one thing to do: fake the paperwork. While in the offices of Thomas Cook, arranging for Pearl to sell paper roses on Queen Alexandra Rose Day, Gee heard an exciting rumour: there was a position open for a 'young person' at the British Embassy, in the office of the air attaché.

She hurried to the owner of *Maison Beresford*, a dress shop near their apartment, and begged a favour. Would *Monsieur* write a letter saying that Pearl was in his employ?

'*Pas de problème*,' replied the kindly shopkeeper. 'Consider it done.'

The next day, the embassy offered Pearl a month's trial. A door had opened into a secret world: the 'oddly scented, half-witted' world of 1930s diplomacy. The contrast to Pearl's previous life would be startling.

6

A Forbidden Romance

To a nervous junior cypher clerk like Pearl, no environment could have presented a greater contrast to her own impoverished home than the Residence of His Britannic Majesty's Ambassador to France at 39 rue du Faubourg-Saint-Honoré. A canny purchase by the Duke of Wellington from Napoleon's sister, Pauline Borghese, in 1814 ('the purchase is a remarkably cheap one' wrote the Duke, pleased to have only paid 863,000 francs on behalf of his master, George III), the building had become the first permanent British Embassy abroad, a symbol of the might of the empire. In a stroke, Pearl had exchanged chaos for order, poverty for sumptuous riches, conflict for calm.

'Here I was, nesting high up in a corner of my safe, new world,' wrote Valentine Lawford, a junior secretary in the Diplomatic Service, when he first arrived at the Paris Embassy in the 1930s. Seventeen-year-old Pearl also felt safe and secure, perhaps for the first time, within the microcosm of England and Englishness which the Residence represented. It was a narrow world, bounded on the north by the Faubourg, on the south by the Avenue Gabriel, on the east by the Hotel Crillon, and on the west by the President's Palace, and it seemed to represent 'the centre of the civilised universe'. How inviting and romantic it appeared to *les jeunes gens de l'Ambassade*, the young people at the Embassy. 'The shops of the Faubourg,' exclaimed Valentine, 'exuded a perfume sweeter, subtler, headier than anything I had known in Piccadilly.'

The scents breathed in by Pearl would have been those of rose, jasmine, lilac and lavender: Roger et Gallet's luxurious shop lay directly under the block of new offices in rue d'Auguesseau where she worked for the air attaché, across the street from the Residence. The soaps and scents whose odours came wafting up the stairs to the freshly painted offices were much favoured by the female clerical staff; the gentlemen wore Guerlain toilet water.

In those 'modern' offices, there was also order and grandeur. The Service attachés worked closely with secretaries like Valentine in the Chancery, who were housed in rather older quarters – the converted embassy stable in the courtyard opposite, a stone building still decorated with the heads and forelegs of two horses over the door.

On the walls of the buildings were rows of photographs of embassy staff (from which the female members had been rigorously excluded). Men in high collars and generous moustaches surveyed the women who, like Pearl, worked as cypher clerks, decoding the messages sent in secret code from London, as well as from the faraway outposts of the British Empire. Little had changed in this period *entre deux guerres*, and little seemed likely to change: the time-honoured rituals of leaving one's *carte de visite* or arranging the placement at dinner occupied the ambassador's wife, Lady Tyrrell, while the measured tread of her husband, Lord William, and his entourage between the antechamber and the throne room, the Salon Pauline and the ballroom, filled the dusty hours.

The spirit of the Iron Duke still hovered over the Residence, but another equally imperious feminine spirit dominated the interior: that of its earlier mistress, the beautiful but troubled Pauline Borghese. Her message that she was Queen of Hearts was conveyed in the glowing white marble sculpture of Princess Pauline posing as 'Venus Victorious' in the entrance hall of the Residence – a statue Pearl would have passed most days, while in Pauline's gold and blue bedroom, Pearl would have noticed another unusual item: a gilded bronze cup modelled on Pauline's breast, in which her servants brought her milk. The intimacy of the room conveyed a sense of being in the presence of the dead woman; and Pearl, with her interest in women heroines, learnt of Pauline's unhappy history, which carried echoes of her own. For Pauline, too, had been an exile. In 1793 she had fled Corsica and, like Pearl, had become a refugee in Marseilles. The princess had '*le sentiment justifié d'avoir été choisie par le destin*' – she felt herself to be, with some justification, 'chosen by destiny', too.

Pearl passed her month's trial at the embassy with flying colours, and would work there for nine years. Her wages were 1,000 francs a month, which she handed straight over to her mother. She was only paid local rates, well below that of the English staff, but it was better than the 500 or 600 francs she would have earned in a shop. And in the evenings, after work, she gave English lessons, the proceeds of which she kept as pocket money.

Pearl's regular income revolutionised the life of the family, and gave Pearl new status within it. The cost of living remained much lower in Paris that it was in London – a major reason why Gertrude remained trapped in the city she detested – and money stretched further than it would have done in England.

As an office worker, Pearl began to grow apart from her dependent family. She considered herself shy, but she was also determined. The timidity, the fear of groups, which she professed to suffer from all her life – hating to go to a party or to enter a bistro alone – affected her in public situations: 'I feel paralysed.' But it was coupled with a need to prove herself. Pearl, a keen swimmer, had followed with admiration the career of nineteen-year-old Gertrude Ederle, who in 1926 had become the first woman to swim the English Channel, and resolved to show similar will-power in conquering her shyness.

Pearl had grown to her full height of 5' 8", the same height as her mother. Her long, corn-coloured hair fell halfway down her back, but in the office she always wore it up, twisted into a chignon or French pleat, with a centre parting and a few curls teased over her forehead. Elegant and striking, she turned heads in the embassy, for Pearl had a secret taste for luxury, preferring to have her dressmaker copy the current fashions in suits made of good-quality material rather than buying cheaper outfits. Lithe, slim, with excellent deportment and wide blue eyes, she began to attract attention; a year or two in the embassy, even in the typing pool, gave her a new polish and confidence. Her efficiency at work, as well as her natural intelligence, was also noticed, and praise brought a greater sense of self-worth and identity. She was proud to be English, but could also say: '*Je suis Parisienne*.'

Pearl had not forgotten her first intriguing glimpse of Henri Cornioley, and asked Evelyne about her brother. Three and a half years older than Pearl, Henri was soon obliged to do National Service in the French army. Just before he left for Tunisia, in 1930, Pearl caught another tantalising glimpse of the young man when she was walking along the Champs-Elysées with Evelyne and her younger brother, Charles, and Henri passed by.

'He didn't even say "Bonjour", or ask how we were.' Pearl was mortified. Evelyne's big brother had ignored the two girls.

Henri returned from his military service fit, muscular and tanned by the North African sun. His ill-health had vanished and he, too, had gained in confidence. 'He joined our group,' remembers Pearl. 'That's how it started: with a very deep friendship, on my side at least.'

It had become a weekly ritual for Pearl to meet her friend Evelyne, who was engaged, and who brought along her fiancé and her brother, Charles, and this was the group her elder brother Henri now joined. It soon became natural for Henri to fall into conversation with Pearl, to walk beside her as Evelyne chatted to her fiancé ahead of them. Young Charles acted as a chaperone of sorts but, as Evelyne listened to her brother's deep voice and Pearl's laughter behind her, she began to suspect that her best friend was falling in love with Henri. According to Pearl:

> One fine day, his sister suddenly turned to me and she said: 'I presume when you come out with us you come out with me, and not my brother?' And I thought, to hell with that. I said, 'If that is the way you are going to look at it, mate, I've had it. I am not going out with you any more.

The following week, Pearl stayed huffily at home instead of joining the group. Evelyne, equally offended, did not contact her. But Henri missed his sister's friend: the outing seemed curiously dull in Pearl's absence.

The following week, Henri came to call on the Witheringtons in rue Vignon. 'Why are you hiding away?' asked Henri.

Pearl made a little *moue*, pouting disdainfully, but said nothing.

'Why are you pulling that face? What is it, Pearl?'

Pearl shrugged. 'I know what your sister thinks.'

'What? What does she think?'

'You know, Henri.' Pearl looked at the ground. 'She thinks I want to be your friend rather than hers.' She paused. 'Evelyne thinks that I prefer you.'

'And do you?'

Pearl blushed. 'I like you both the same.'

'Well, come back, then.' Henri smiled, his brown eyes meeting her blue ones. 'It isn't any fun without you.'

Pearl allowed herself to be persuaded but, all too soon, Evelyne was married and the group disintegrated. So Henri asked Pearl to meet him alone.

By now, alarm bells were ringing in the Cornioley household. There, Pearl had previously been received as Evelyne's school friend; to receive her as their elder son's girlfriend was a very different matter for Madame Cornioley.

Pearl's direct conversation shocked the older members of the family: 'My, you're a tough one,' remarked Henri's aunt reprovingly one day. 'People have always said you're very hard.'

'*Ce n'est pas moi qui suis dure, c'est la vie!* It's not me who's tough, it's life!' Pearl had retorted.

Her spirited attitude, however, attracted Henri, whose own comfortable family background bore such a contrast to hers, while her strength appealed to his gentler character. One day he kissed her.

On 12 August 1933, a day Pearl would never forget, Henri proposed marriage. She was not altogether surprised: their relationship had the intensity of first love. 'So I said, yes – I agreed.'

But Henri's proposal came with a qualification: 'You have got to understand that I cannot marry you at present,' he said. 'It is out of the question because I have to look after my mother and sisters and you will have to wait.'

Pearl understood. 'I can't leave Mummy and my sisters,' she responded.

She was only nineteen, he twenty-two, when they became engaged. 'That was very young, for those days.'

When Pearl confided to her mother that Henri had proposed marriage, Gertrude forbade any talk of an engagement, and a major battle ensued between mother and daughter. Pearl could see the situation from Gee's point of view: 'She was alone with me as sole support of the family . . . my sisters were obviously much younger. She looked on my leaving home with horror.'

Henri's family was equally opposed to the match. One day, when Gee was away at the seaside at Wissant, where she took groups of children for English conversation, Henri's father invited Pearl to go for a walk. He raised the subject of the relationship, not once but many times: 'He took me all through the streets of Paris, telling me that his son wasn't worth it.'

But Pearl refused to be bullied. 'I told him that I had no plans to marry Henri – at present. *On est de très bons amis.* We were just "good friends".'

Monsieur Cornioley was a wealthy businessman who was not used to being contradicted. The young Englishwoman was to give his son up at once. It was his wish.

'Whether or not we might marry one day,' Pearl remembered replying, 'I can't say. But we have a great friendship and you are not going to break it. I am sorry, I am going to go on seeing him.'

Monsieur Cornioley had exploded with rage. 'I will never receive you again,' he declared, turning on his heel.

His reasons for his opposition to the match were easy to understand: the Cornioleys lived in luxury while the Witheringtons were not only foreign, but poor as church mice.

'My family's "*Institut de Beauté*" was based in a huge apartment in the rue du Faubourg-Saint-Honoré,' recalled Henri. 'The balcony was seventeen metres long!' Situated in the same prestigious road as the palace of the President of the Republic, in the heart of fashionable Paris, the Cornioley family business was booming in the 1930s. 'I had an extraordinary childhood,' said Henri. '*Une jeunesse dorée . . . C'était l'opulence, chez nous.* It was a golden childhood, lived in the lap of luxury.'

None of this impressed Mrs Seckham Witherington, however. She considered that Henri was not a 'gentleman': his family was in trade. 'She thought he was a pedlar, going around delivering potions on his bicycle,' commented Pearl's nephew.

According to Mimi: 'Mummy didn't like him at first, because he didn't have a proper job.' And there was another consideration: hard-up as she was, Gee could not afford to entertain. 'Mummy didn't like him to come round . . . So [Pearl] met him outside . . . They did quarrel, Mummy and Pearl; they were distant from each other.'

Pearl made a final effort to bring her mother round: 'I took her out for a Welsh rarebit, because it was something she was very fond of, to this special place in Paris.'

But when Pearl confessed to Gee that Monsieur Cornioley had forbidden her to visit his apartment, her mother was horrified: 'What? Not accept one of my daughters in his home, and kick her out?' she exclaimed. 'Well, we'll see about that. Henri can't come to me, then.'

Outcasts from both family homes, Pearl and Henri could only meet in public, but this parental opposition only strengthened their love, and the forbidden romance blossomed.

'Pearl was very preoccupied with Henri,' recalled Mimi, describing him as 'typically French . . . tall, very thin, with glasses, a chain smoker.' Cultured and amusing, for all his lack of a formal education he was everything Pearl wanted; he offered an ease and sophistication sorely missing in rue Vignon. And Henri was equally obsessed with Pearl. For the first time in her life, she felt valued, not for what she could provide, but for herself.

Whatever the weather, the young lovers used to meet on one of the public benches – 'our bench' – in the Champs-Elysées, where they held hands, kissed and dreamt of a shared future. They had much in common: both their mothers had chosen a foreign first name for their babies, which they were not allowed to use. For Pearl, 'Cecilia' had become 'Cécile', while in Henri's case, his mother's choice of 'Villy', after a *bled* or lake in Switzerland, had been changed to 'Willy' by the registrar at the *mairie* – the infant had emerged as Henri Charles Willy. Both had a cosmopolitan background: Pearl's family hailed from across the Channel; Henri's from Eastern Europe. They had a language in common (Henri never learnt English), and a religion, as both were Protestant.

It was Henri who returned Pearl to the Christian faith. As a child, she and her sisters had attended the Protestant church, but had never been baptised, for which Pearl blamed her father. When she was sixteen, she turned to the pastor for help, but as her mother had already been to see him several times to beg for financial aid, when Pearl arrived, thinking that she was also asking for charity, the pastor had refused to see her. In fact, she had come for advice about her difficult relationship with her mother. Pearl never forgot the rebuff.

'That marked a turning point for me,' she says. 'I never wanted to hear a word about God after that – until the day when I met Henri.'

Henri told her that one could not live without religion. Slowly, Pearl began to change her mind.

For the next three years, Henri tried different jobs. His education had been interrupted by illness and, like Pearl, he had not passed his *baccalauréat*, and had few qualifications. On his return from National Service he worked in a factory manufacturing street lights, in a shop, and then had begun a new enterprise with a friend, cleaning carpets. These ventures failed, and it became apparent that Henri had not inherited the family flair for business. But there was little need to work, since his parents gave him a generous allowance and, indolent and charming, he drifted back to the *Laboratoire Cornioley*, where he was happiest developing his nose for perfumes and running errands for his father.

In Pearl's place of work, however, the British Embassy, she was being heaped with new responsibilities. By 1936 the tension was palpable, the mood alarmist, as volunteers flocked to fight in the Spanish Civil War. The British ambassador, career diplomat Sir George Russell Clark, had argued for the closest possible cooperation with France in order to preserve peace, but by 1937 his successor, Sir Eric Phipps, was warning the Foreign Office that the atmosphere in France was dangerously defeatist in the face of Hitler's territorial ambitions. He resigned, disgusted, in 1939 and as Europe hurtled towards war, yet another British diplomat was handed the poisoned chalice that was the Paris Embassy.

Fortunately, Sir Ronald Campbell, who was appointed in July 1939, was able to turn for help to the rising star of the Defence Section, air attaché Douglas Colyer. Wing Commander – later Air Commodore – Colyer had arrived as an exciting new broom in 1936; born in 1893, he had a distinguished record, having served in the Palestine Brigade of the RAF and had been awarded the Distinguished Flying Cross in 1918. Tall at 5'11", with hazel eyes and thick black hair, Colyer was a handsome and forceful presence as well as an accomplished linguist, having qualified as a Russian interpreter as well as being fluent in French and Spanish.

The air attaché's verve and charisma became the talk of the embassy. Pearl was impressed by what she heard. Colyer in turn was impressed by her expertise, and she soon found herself promoted to become his personal assistant.

In 1938, the new king, George VI, and his wife Queen Elizabeth, paid a state visit to France. Colyer was attached to their suite and afterwards received the *Légion d'Honneur*. Said a press release:

> A man of great organising ability, and with a keen eye for detail, he does not spare himself when there is an urgent job to be done. He expects that those working with him will give everything they've got, too. But he never asks anyone to work longer hours than he works himself.

Pearl never minded working late for 'Duggie', as she called him in her private thoughts. Like his junior officers, the shy secretary was soon put at her ease in the commodore's presence. She became devoted to him. She was twenty-two in 1936, he forty-three. He was, she wrote, so warm, so human, so understanding.

One day she confessed to a colleague: '*J'ai beaucoup aimé Duggie*. I'm very fond of Duggie.'

'Well,' came the reply, 'he is very seductive.'

'That's not what I mean,' Pearl had replied indignantly, feeling herself blushing with embarrassment. There was nothing physical in her feelings, she protested. They were *copain-copain*, mates.

Pearl was a person who developed intellectual rather than physical relationships, considering the brain to be the most erotic organ. But she admitted to a tendency to put someone she liked very much on a pedestal, and Duggie was certainly at the top of hers. It is likely that he filled the vacant role of father-figure for his young PA. Here was a man in command, one she could respect and admire, unlike her real father, for whose memory she felt only contempt. She hero-worshipped 'Duggie', who became her patron and mentor.

But Pearl had lost sight of Colyer in June 1940, although she would later learn that he had taken efficient charge of the evacuation of refugees from Saint-Jean-de-Luz, near Biarritz. His final act had been to embark the FANY drivers and other women and children on HMS *Nariva*. On a wet and stormy night, Colyer had caught a sardine boat from Bordeaux to England, virtually the last man off, in the best tradition of the service. On 25 June he disembarked at Plymouth, writing that his 'Odyssey was over.'

Pearl's, on the other hand, had only just been beginning. Her boss had taken care of the woman refugees at Bordeaux – but not of his devoted PA. In the confusion he may either have sent her Diplomatic Pass too late or the post was delayed. She, too, had been forced to become a refugee, and to undertake a far more dangerous Odyssey across war-torn Europe to England. But Pearl bore no grudge against her boss: on board the *Scythia,* she and Gee, Doudou and Mimi, were excitedly craning their necks for their first sight of Scotland.

7
London At Last

A STEADY drizzle was falling as the *Scythia* steamed up the Firth of Clyde towards Greenock on 13 July 1941, but no rain could dampen Mrs Witherington's spirits. She craned her neck for the first sight of land and burst into tears as she stepped ashore on Scottish soil. The girls shivered. The temperature was several degrees colder than it had been in Gibraltar, and they could barely understand the Glaswegian accents of the porters who directed them to the railway station.

Their first thought was to find their sister, Suzanne, who lived at Stooper's Hill, in Benington, near Stevenage, with her husband and baby. Having had no news of her family since their telegram the June before saying they were leaving Commes for Cherbourg, Suzie had given up hope of ever seeing them again. 'She thought we'd died,' said Mimi, later. Suzie was in her kitchen when she heard her mother's voice calling her name. She ran to the window, looked out 'and nearly fainted'.

The reunion was joyful, but brief. Leaving her mother and sisters with Suzie, Pearl travelled on to London, a city she had never visited before. On Bastille Day, 14 July, she found herself a room in a YWCA hostel in Mornington Crescent, the warm welcome she received inclining her to think more kindly of the Church.

Money problems, as usual, were pressing: 'We only had what we stood up in,' recalled Mimi, so, four days after landing in England, she and Doudou joined the WAAF (Women's Auxiliary Air Force). 'Serve in the WAAF with the men who fly,' said the recruiting posters, an inducement to many pretty and patriotic young women like Mimi, who was to meet her future husband, Squadron Leader Tom Oddie, in the force.

On arriving at Loughborough Flying Training Command, the girls' story was widely reported in the press:

> **Walked a thousand miles to be WAAFs**: Hélène, aged 19, and Jacqueline, aged 21, wanted to join the WAAF. So these two sisters: fled from Nazi-ruled Paris, walked most of the 1,000 miles to Lisbon, hid in ditches from German sentries . . . lived for five sleepless days and nights on . . . small hunks of black bread.

Pearl did not make the headlines. Instead, having settled her sisters, she trod the streets of south London before renting a small flat for her mother on Streatham Hill.

Pearl's first sight of the war-torn capital shocked her. Two months earlier, on 10 May, the House of Commons and Westminster Abbey had received a direct hit from the *Luftwaffe* in one of the heaviest air raids London had endured. It was the night of a full moon. *The Times* had reported the result of this 'intense and indiscriminate attack':

> The debating chamber of the House was wrecked, the roof of the Members' Lobby pierced . . . Big Ben fell silent, its face blackened and scarred. Today the Abbey is open to the sky. The roof over the lantern, the low square tower at the centre of the Abbey, has fallen in . . . The Deanery of Westminster is destroyed, and the dean, Dr. de Labillière, and his wife have nothing but the clothes they were wearing.

'London can take it,' was the message of the capital during the Blitz, but as Pearl walked past bomb craters and ruined houses and read the daily lists of casualties, she mourned for the devastated city. It stood in stark contrast to the Paris she had left, which had been declared an 'open city' before it fell to the Germans and had therefore saved its historic buildings. She was, however, impressed by the Londoners' spirit of defiance:

> England was determined. The English were in it up to their necks, against the whole world . . . When I arrived in July 1941, I saw Londoners go down into the underground stations every night to seek shelter from the bombing . . . People were organised to sleep in sleeping bags three layers deep all along the platforms. The next day they started again, and that went on for months.

The war news, however, was uniformly depressing. In Libya, Rommel was winning the desert war, Crete had fallen to the Germans and, despite rolling out the red carpet for Harry Hopkins, President Roosevelt's personal envoy, the Americans had still not come into the conflict. Despite Hopkins's robust expressions of sympathy for Great Britain as she stood alone in January 1941 – 'We're only interested in seeing that that sonofabitch, Hitler, gets licked' – Churchill was no nearer his goal: the United States remained aloof from the faraway European conflict.

Physically present in London, but equally aloof, was the tall and prickly figure of Brigadier General Charles de Gaulle, leader of the Free French, who had been airlifted to Britain on 17 June 1940, carrying with him, said Churchill, 'the honour of France.' From his first meeting with the junior general in France, the prime minister had admired his resolution. On Bastille Day 1941, as Pearl arrived in London, de Gaulle sent a defiant message to the independent French newspaper in London, *France*: 'Today, as a year ago, we recognise only one foe . . . We shall fight him with every weapon. True to ourselves, we are sure of remaining true to France.'

Anthony Eden, the new foreign secretary, put on an equally brave face to *The Times*, announcing that the Government 'looked forward to the day when the Champs-Elysées will once more echo with the measured tread of the gallant fighting forces of a France restored to independence and greatness . . . *Vive la France!*'

In fact, most people in France looked upon de Gaulle as a crackpot; bitter and depressed, they had made their choice for Pétain but, for a few, the maverick general served as a symbol of hope. The three de Vomécourt brothers had responded to his appeal on the BBC to French officers and soldiers on British soil to keep the flame of French resistance alive. 'We could not admit the idea that France had lost a war against the Germans,' said Philippe. 'We had lost a battle but not a war. The war was still going on, and we must help to win it.'

Ordinary men and women in London were also inspired by de Gaulle's stand and his majestic insistence that 'We are France.' A South London shop assistant, eighteen-year-old Violette Bushell, went to watch the Free French troops marching down Whitehall on Bastille Day 1940, only three weeks after de Gaulle's escape. Violette, who was half-French and worked at the Bon Marché store in Brixton, was excited to see the general in his blue and gold képi lay a large laurel wreath at the foot of the Cenotaph. It was bound with a tricolour ribbon and bore the inscription, *Les Français Morts*. Coming sharply to the salute, the general roared: '*Salut aux Morts!*' His troops saluted in turn, and cried: '*Vive la France! Vive Général de Gaulle!*' The crowds had burst through the police cordon and mingled with the troops. Later that afternoon, Violette had met a French soldier in Hyde Park, and asked him home for tea. Etienne Szabo would become her husband, and Violette a secret agent like Pearl.

Pearl, too, may have left her office at the Air Ministry in Charles Street, W1, to watch the Free French on their parades. She adored martial music and might even have been tempted to fall into step with the marching soldiers, sailors and airmen, and the French Foreign Legion, smartest of all in their steel helmets and white knitted scarves. Like Violette, she felt deeply for Occupied France *sous la botte*, under the jackboot.

On her arrival in London, Pearl had contacted the air attaché's administration in London. She was at once employed as PA to the director of Allied Air Forces and Foreign Liaisons. It was a responsible job, with better pay; but her heart was not in it. Staring out of the office window, her thoughts returned constantly to France. She became determined to go back, to find Henri; together they might fight the secret war against the Germans. But she knew that first she would have to train as a secret agent – an arduous, potentially dangerous undertaking.

As this desire crystallised within her, it began to fill her every waking moment. Pearl knew she had special gifts to offer: she spoke French like a native, she knew the country. But they were going to waste: 'My idea in volunteering for the clandestine war was that I would be more useful in France, trying to help throw the Germans out, than staying in England, pushing paper around.'

La paperasserie, paperwork. Pearl was tired of filing after twelve years in the civil service, tired of living in digs in Willesden with two other secretaries. She wanted action:

> I burned with intense anger. It's true. Anger against all these unfair things . . . and remember, I'm a child of the 1914 war. I hated the Huns . . . It was something I really felt deep down inside me . . . I can't explain it. I suppose it's a love of France, a love of England. A hatred of what was going on. It was just a drive within me. Occupation is completely different from receiving bombs. Neither is funny. But with an occupation you are with it all day and night. If you are caught during curfew, which is between eleven at night and six in the morning, you are taken to a police station and if anything happens to a German soldier during the night, then you are taken out and shot.

Pearl had another motive too: 'I wanted to prove myself . . . because I am very shy. So I wanted to prove something to myself.' Once Henri's love had given her confidence. Alone in London, she missed him intensely: 'There was the sadness of wondering what was happening to him, and where he was.'

Months had gone by without news of her fiancé. She had not seen him since his last leave in February 1940, and her initial relief at delivering her family to safety in England had long ago given way to a mood of grey despair. In her dingy, chilly Willesden bedroom in north-west London, just as when they were teenagers and exchanged diaries, Pearl faithfully wrote in her journal in the hope that one day she would be able to show it to Henri. But at night, alone in her narrow bed, misery engulfed her. She lay awake, weeping, afraid that he was dead – dead of an illness caught in the stalag, or shot trying to escape.

The weeks passed. But, at last, when she had almost given up hope, a letter arrived from Henri's grandmother in Lausanne in late September. In neutral Switzerland, out of reach of the German censor, she was able to give Pearl the news that Henri had escaped that month and was in France. He was alive; there was even an address near Mâcon to which Pearl could write.

Overjoyed, Pearl dashed off a letter. To evade the censor, she asked a friend in the Lisbon Embassy to help by allowing her to use the diplomatic bag. In this way, the couple were able to correspond freely.

'My dear love,' wrote Henri, 'this is the 931st day of our separation . . . News from you is the only joy in my solitude' while, 'the only thing that helps me endure this separation is faith,' he wrote on another occasion. 'Have faith, my love.'

Pearl needed to find a secret, underground way of returning to France. It was her only hope of finding Henri again and of fighting with him in the Resistance. He might, of course, escape to England and train with her as an agent, but first she knew she must contact the shadowy, secret service that she had heard sent women as well as men behind enemy lines.

People called it 'the Org' or 'the racket'. Only Churchill and the Cabinet, the Whitehall mandarins and the top brass knew its real name: the Special Operations Executive (SOE).

Fresh from France, in a country which was new to her, and in which she had few contacts, Pearl decided to approach her boss in the Air Ministry, Air Commodore Beaumont, and ask for an introduction. 'And [Beaumont], knowing my ex-boss in Paris [Colyer], said, "Oh, Pearl wants to go into France." And he put his foot down. So that was a closed door.'

Getting back into France 'wasn't easy', she would recall later. 'The career officers of the regular forces didn't like SOE at all. To them, we were only amateurs. My old boss said to me: "You're not going to work with those people." He made me shut the door of SOE.'

Pearl tackled Colyer face to face, but to no avail. 'I don't want you mixed up with that crowd,' he repeated.

In fact, Colyer had Pearl's best interests at heart. In the autumn of 1941, the RAF was deeply suspicious of SOE, which was in competition with it for the use of its bombers. New ideas of irregular warfare put forward after World War I by Liddell Hart, who argued that irregular forces could win victory without the sacrifice of trench warfare, had influenced the creation of SOE. But such dangerous, new-fangled theories cut little ice with Sir Charles Portal, chief of the air staff. All Portal knew was that the 'Baker Street Irregulars' were new and untried. SOE was only one of nine wartime secret services, including MI5, MI6, the escape service (DF), the decipher service, 'black' propaganda (propagada to enemy countries, organised by the Political Warfare Executive) and the deception service, all clamouring for scarce resources. Portal told SOE's Harry Sporborg, controller of Northern Europe:

> Your work is a gamble which may give us a valuable dividend or may produce nothing. It is anybody's guess. My bombing offensive is not a gamble. Its dividend is certain; it is a gilt-edged investment. I cannot divert aircraft from a certainty to a gamble which may be a gold-mine or may be completely worthless.

Worst of all, in Portal's view, was the ungentlemanly idea that an agent, in civilian clothes, was licensed to kill:

> I think that the dropping of men in civilian clothes for the purposes of attempting to kill members of the opposing forces is not an operation with which the Royal Air Force should be associated . . . there is a vast difference, in ethics, between the time- honoured operation of the dropping of a spy from the air and this entirely new scheme of dropping what one can only call assassins.

In the face of such disapproval, Pearl's wish to join 'the Org' and become a female 'assassin' looked doomed to failure.

8

The Baker Street Irregulars

When Winston Churchill gave the minister for economic warfare, Hugh Dalton, the command, 'Set Europe ablaze,' on 16 July 1940 – thereby marking the creation of the SOE – he may not have foreseen the bitter rivalries that would ensue; nor would he have cared.

Churchill was utterly determined to push through the creation of a new instrument of war. In South Africa, the Boers had put a price on his head: '£25 – dead or alive.' His personal experience as a spy, his knowledge of guerrilla fighting, had convinced him of the value of irregular forces. On that fateful day, 16 July, when Hitler ordered Operation Sealion, the invasion of Britain, and the British Expeditionary Force was still licking its wounds after Dunkirk, Churchill resolved to set up a new secret service. It would be his baby, and he would protect it throughout its short life.

The rapid collapse of France in the summer of 1940 had forced a revolution in British strategic thinking. Britain stood alone, and in that 'detonator' summer, Whitehall departments normally at each other's throats suddenly found themselves in rapid agreement. If victory was to be plucked from the jaws of defeat, the War Cabinet agreed on 25 May, it must bring economic pressure to bear on the enemy 'by a combination of air attack on economic objectives in Germany and on German morale and the creation of widespread revolt in her conquered territories'. To stimulate this revolt 'was of the very highest importance. A special organisation will be required.'

Three days after Churchill appointed Hugh Dalton as controller of the new organisation, a secret paper was signed by the former prime minister, Neville Chamberlain, on 19 July. This was the founding charter of SOE, set up, on Churchill's authority, 'to coordinate all action by way of subversion and sabotage against the enemy overseas. This organisation will be known as the Special Operations Executive.'

SOE was to be defined by secrecy. Wrapped in mystery, it would go on to operate under various aliases – the Inter-Services Research Bureau, Room 055A, War Office, HQ Special Training Schools, the Joint Technical Board among others – and the identity of Sir Frank Nelson, Sir Charles Hambro, Brigadier Gubbins and other senior staff, their names hidden by a plethora of acronyms, would also be a military secret of a high category.

It was to be, the charter stressed, 'a secret or underground organisation'. As to its scope, 'sabotage' was a simple idea: it meant smashing things up. 'Subversion' was a more complex concept. It meant the weakening of, by whatever 'covert' means, the enemy's will and power to make war, and the strengthening of the will and power of his opponents including, in particular, guerrilla and resistance movements.

In a famous letter written to Lord Halifax the foreign secretary, Dalton declared: 'We must organise movements in enemy occupied territories comparable to the Sinn Fein movements in Ireland, to the Chinese guerrillas now operating against Japan, to the Spanish Irregulars who played a notable part in Wellington's campaigns . . .' Britain was to have her very own fifth column behind enemy lines, influenced by the romantic legends of Michael Collins in Ireland and Lawrence of Arabia, both personal friends of Churchill.

Behind the official language lay a personal grouse of Churchill's. He was exasperated with MI6, otherwise known as the Secret Intelligence Service (SIS), which was run by Sir Stewart Menzies, always known as 'C'. As long ago as April 1938, after Chamberlain had returned from Munich promising 'peace in our time', C had been tasked with setting up a new department for special ops, Section D ('Destruction'). It had been headed by the flamboyant figure of Major Laurence Grand, a professional if somewhat eccentric soldier. Tall and thin, with a black moustache, he never wore uniform, always had a long cigarette holder in his mouth, and was never without a red carnation in his buttonhole.

Grand bubbled with ideas for dirty tricks to destroy Germany's economy, such as blowing up the Iron Gates on the Danube to disrupt the flow of Romanian oil into Germany. The swashbuckling atmosphere prevalent within 'D' intrigued a young intelligence officer, Captain Bickham Sweet-Escott, when he was called for a mysterious interview at the War Office in March 1940. As would happen with many SOE recruits, he had come to the interview by way of the old-boy network, his tutor at Balliol College, Oxford having tipped off another old Balliol man at Section D who was looking for a German speaker.

In a bare little room on the ground floor were two chairs, a table, a very dirty inkwell, and an ashtray made out of the lid of a cigarette tin. Opposite Sweet-Escott sat an officer in civilian clothes who closely resembled Sherlock Holmes. He gave his codename as 'Goodwill'.

'For security reasons, I can't tell you what sort of job it will be,' said the officer. 'All I can say is that if you join us, you mustn't be afraid of forgery and you mustn't be afraid of murder.'

Sweet-Escott was undeterred. At a second meeting a week later at Saint Ermin's Hotel, near Queen Anne's Gate, Escott was taken upstairs to the fourth floor. A burly ex-petty officer, who went by the name of Cornelius, barred his way.

'This is Escott,' said Goodwill. 'Take a good look at him because he is going to be one of us.' Cornelius stared, and admitted him.

His head full of forgery and murder, Escott entered the offices of 'D'. There was no purpose or plan he could discover, no documents or files to study. He learnt that he had joined a unit known simply as 'Section D', but that that was a phrase he must never use outside the building.

Soon Escott found himself helping Cornelius pack bags of detonators, explosives and limpet mines in the Balkan Section. In May and June 1940, Section D embarked on a series of Bond-style missions, salvaging Continental gold, diamonds and platinum from the advancing German army but, on the whole, 'D' was a spectacular failure. In July 1940, it did not have a single agent in Western Europe between the Balkans and the English Channel.

Churchill was fast losing patience. The last straw was a bungled attempt to sabotage the Swedish iron-ore fields, despite the prime minister having personally ordered Grand to 'press the button' on several hundred pounds of explosives.

The situation was critical. The Blitz began on 21 October 1940 – rather than setting Europe ablaze, it was the British capital that was on fire. The sky over the London docks was red from burning factories as the *Luftwaffe* pounded the capital. As Marshal Pétain prepared to meet Hitler, Churchill drove to Broadcasting House. He wanted to appeal directly to the French to keep faith with the British. Speaking French with a strong English accent, he broadcast that night over the BBC:

> Here in London, which Herr Hitler says he will reduce to ashes, and which his aeroplanes are now bombarding, our people are bearing up unflinchingly. Our air force has more than held its own. We are waiting for the long-promised invasion. So are the fishes.

It was stirring rhetoric. But time was running out, and Churchill had known that he had to move from rhetoric to reality. Less than two months into his premiership, which had begun on 9 May, he had brutally snatched back Section D from Stewart Menzies. The Secret Intelligence Service had failed to deliver, despite the fact that it was one of its largest units.

Churchill plucked it away to form the foundation of his own creation, SOE.

The rupture was like a bad divorce, wrote one historian: Menzies' 'subsequent behaviour only too often resembled that of an embittered ex-spouse'. He brooded in the shadows, and his implacable hostility to SOE would create major problems.

The 'jealous rivalry' of C scuppered SOE's first attempts to get its agents into France. A Captain F.H. Slocum RN had set up a private navy on the Helford River in Cornwall in order to land agents on the Breton coast, but C, supported by the Admiralty, vetoed the use of Slocum's boats by SIS's rival 'firm'. This had forced SOE to resort to other means to infiltrate France by sea, and it would not be until as late as 1942 that an SOE agent would reach France: Captain Peter Churchill, codename 'Michel', arrived by submarine and canoed to the beach near Antibes.

The dislike between the two 'firms' was as virulent as it was mutual. As late as 1943, SOE officers wrote of their surprise at discovering that 'contrary to what they had been educated to believe – the principal enemy was Hitler and not their sister organisation.'

Significantly, Menzies had been in charge of Section D's communications. 'C's people controlled Section D's communications, its codes and cyphers,' said Escott. This control continued after Section D was incorporated into SOE, and meant SIS could read SOE's messages. It could keep the new secret service on a tight rein.

From the start, there was a fundamental conflict between the professional agents of SIS, intent on the quiet collection of intelligence, and the 'amateurs' of SOE, whose job it was to create loud bangs.

'The battle we were forced to fight against those who should have been our friends,' noted Escott with surprise, 'was at times no less bitter than the battle against our enemy.'

Churchill's first act was to sweep away 'D's ramshackle apparatus and create a new organisation with country sections for each territory in which it operated. In November 1940, SOE moved to 64 Baker Street, soon expanding into neighbouring office blocks: Norgeby House at number 83; St Michael's House at number 82; and nearby flats at Montagu Mansions and Berkeley Court. A neat black plaque outside 64 Baker Street announcing that these were the offices of the 'Inter-Services Research Bureau' misled chance callers, while those who were admitted rarely used their own names: the new boss of 'the firm' – at its inception, Sir Frank Nelson – was always referred to as 'CD'.

In November, another key figure in SOE strode into the

corridors of Baker Street for the first time. Forty-four-year-old Brigadier Colin Gubbins was a professional soldier with first-hand experience of guerrilla warfare, having been shot at from behind hedges by men in trilbys and mackintoshes in Ireland. He was also the author of a handbook on guerrilla fighting, the *Partisan Leaders' Handbook*. Spotted by Dalton at a dinner party, Gubbins became SOE's director of training. His background in the War Office, where he had worked in a unit developing irregular warfare, now also incorporated into SOE, qualified him perfectly to bring an element of professionalism to the motley crew of civilians who were attempting, not altogether successfully, to get SOE off the ground.

Gubbins, a born leader of men, summed up the situation at a glance:

> At the best SOE was looked upon as an organisation of harmless backroom lunatics which, it was hoped, would not develop into an active nuisance. At the worst, it was regarded as another confusing excrescence . . . As a whole it was left severely alone as a somewhat disreputable child.

At the heart of the Special Operations Executive lay its French Section, known universally as 'F'. It was first started in Paris by Section D's Leslie Humphreys, who had set up escape lines for British servicemen but was less successful in his attempts to recruit agents. Nevertheless, F Section demonstrated the way in which, despite the ostensible separation of interests between SOE ('special operations') and SIS ('intelligence gathering') laid down in SOE's charter of 19 July 1940, the new 'firm' began developing a structure in the field which almost exactly paralleled that of SIS.

It explained, to some extent, C's fury; he and his ruthless deputy, professional spymaster par excellence, Claude Dansey, continued to pursue their own agenda: to take back special ops from Churchill's noisy baby.

In November 1940, the same month that Gubbins strode into Baker Street, Major Henry Marriott, formerly a Courtauld representative in Paris, took over from Leslie Humphreys as head of 'F'. The following spring, he was joined by another British officer, thirty-eight-year-old Major Maurice Buckmaster, who was to become one of SOE's most controversial figures.

Born in 1902, Buckmaster had been unable to take up a scholarship to Oxford when his father went bankrupt, and instead had become a private tutor to a wealthy family. Subsequently a Ford manager in France, he knew the country and its language well, but had no experience of special operations. Despite this, Buckmaster had received a mysterious posting to join 'a secret organisation in the War Office'.

Like Pearl, Buckmaster loved two countries and, like her, a deeply felt experience lay behind his motivation to join the cause of French resistance. On the morning of 2 June 1940, he and the remnants of 50 Division had stepped ashore from their Dunkirk troopship onto Dover beach. The young officer had been surprised by the holiday mood, by the happy groups of women running down to the harbour with sausage rolls, Bovril and cocoa to welcome 'the scruffy warriors of Dunkirk'. He wrote:

> The thought went through my mind that the Dover reception committee must think we were returning from Norway or some victorious campaign about which . . . we had not heard. We were, after all, part of a beaten army . . . We just knew that the British Expeditionary Force had ceased to exist.

He realised that 'the only way to win the war was to land again, at some far distant date, on the continent of Europe, equipped with weapons superior to the enemy's and in even greater numbers.' He promised himself that he would be part of resistance by 'the real France', for whom he was convinced that the collaborationist Pétain did not speak. 'The real France', for Buckmaster, meant General de Gaulle, and the Free French troops whom in September 1940, he had escorted down the west coast of Ireland in the flagship HMS *Devonshire* to Dakar, west Africa.

Arriving for the first time at the grey, five-storey building at 64

Baker Street on 17 March 1941, Buckmaster took the wobbly lift up to his office on the fifth floor. It had a bare and deserted air. Knocking on Marriott's door, he opened it. There, on the other side of the only other desk in the room was Marriott, known in SOE as 'HM'. He appeared dispirited and, in fact, was soon to retire because of illness.

Buckmaster was told that he was to be the French Section's information officer. But, as he discovered to his dismay, 'F' had made a slow start. Buckmaster's duty, as he understood it, was, in Churchill's words, to 'stir the torpid Frenchman'. His personal assistant, Vera Atkins, a Jewish Romanian 'enemy alien' whose naturalisation he would facilitate, had been one of Humphreys' spooks in SIS.

Buckmaster remembered asking his commanding officer what his new duties would be.

'The general idea,' explained HM, 'is to see what we can do about getting information about Occupied France. We need to find out what sort of targets we should concentrate on attacking.'

'What sort of information is available?' Maurice asked.

HM had shrugged. 'Very little.'

'What about Secret Service reports?' Maurice inquired.

'Oh, no, we don't get those. Can't get hold of them,' replied HM.

Buckmaster's elation, by this time, was fast disappearing. Settled at his new desk, he picked up the receiver on the 'scrambler' and telephoned a colonel in the Intelligence Department. What exactly was he to do in 'F'?

'Subversive activities,' the colonel explained.

'I've gathered that, sir, but what kind of subversive activities?'

'I'm not too clear myself, but I think the idea is to sabotage industrial installations in France,' the colonel said.

'This isn't a Secret Service affair then?'

'Heavens, no, old boy. Special Operations . . .!'

Staring at his empty out-tray, Maurice had had an idea. He remembered the Bottin, a reference directory listing all the industrial and commercial enterprises of France and, since there was no Bottin in Baker Street, went to the War Office to borrow one.

Over several days, he laboriously listed the names of refineries that might become the targets of sabotage. On a Monday morning, Maurice presented the list to Marriott: 'Oil refineries, sir. I think they should be our priority targets.'

Marriott studied the list. 'Good God, Buckmaster! Are you off your head? These are sugar refineries!'

This story, related by M.R.D. Foot, official historian of SOE, is damning confirmation of the black hole in F Section's intelligence in the spring of 1941. With no access to SIS intelligence, SOE remained severely handicapped by its inferior position in relation to its parent service.

F Section's existence was 'Top Secret'; so secret, in fact, that pretence was kept up that it did not exist at all. Most importantly, it was to be kept a secret from General de Gaulle and his head of military intelligence and operations, André Dewavrin – codename Colonel 'Passy' after a metro station in Paris.

Passy, formerly an agent of the French Intelligence Service, the *Deuxième Bureau*, had been one of the first Frenchmen to come to London to join de Gaulle at the end of June 1940. His meeting with the general had been a 'glacial' encounter: 'The only contact I felt with the general,' wrote Passy, 'was his grey, piercing gaze.'

But de Gaulle was leader of the Free French and a potent symbol of resistance. Having established his HQ at 4 Carlton Gardens, in the spring of 1941 it was decided to give him a French section of his own.

The new Gaullist section was to be named 'RF', *Republique Francaise*, to distinguish it from 'F'. The matter required delicate handling. Harry Sporborg, SOE's regional controller of Northern Europe (a former solicitor in Slaughter & May), hosted a splendid lunch at the Ecu de France, a restaurant in Jermyn Street. Over a fine claret, he introduced Colonel Passy, the guest of honour, to Eric Piquet-Wicks of the Royal Inniskilling Fusiliers – Sporborg's choice as head of the new section. After coffee, Piquet-Weeks was shown his new office at 1 Dorset Square, in a house recently vacated by Bertram Mills Circus.

At an even more impressive luncheon at Claridges in June, Sir Frank Nelson – CD – then broke the news officially to Passy that SOE already had a French section that was trying to work in France, quite independently of de Gaulle.

The Frenchman had smiled impassively. 'Passy had somewhat naturally known about it all for some time,' commented Bickham Sweet-Escott.

The rivalry between the two French sections in SOE – the British-run 'F', soon to be known as 'Buckmaster's Boys'; and the Gaullist 'RF' Section – was intense from the start.

'We had practically no means, while the English had everything available,' complained Passy. As French exiles in London, de Gaulle and Passy had no resources: they were dependent on their hosts for accommodation, financial support, aircraft and weapons. Resentful suppliants, who seemed to Churchill to delight in biting the British hands that fed them, de Gaulle and Passy nevertheless had some advantages over 'F': de Gaulle took first pick of the Frenchmen who arrived in England eager to continue the war and who were sent to the Royal Patriotic School at Wandsworth for screening. The majority of French refugees naturally chose to join de Gaulle, which left 'F' with the difficult problem of finding potential secret agents who were fluent in the language.

To have two French sections in SOE seemed unnecessary duplication, but there were solid reasons for doing so. First, French security was considered to be risky. Memories were fresh of the humiliating failure of the Gaullist attack on Dakar in September 1940, known as Operation Menace; but what mattered more to the Foreign Office was that the secret of the enterprise seemed to have been exceptionally badly kept. Dozens of stories of indiscretions in shops and bars went around London as soon as the operation was over, meaning that information may well have reached Vichy and forewarned the Germans. British staff had become reluctant to pass secrets to the Free French; The Foreign Office, therefore, had put pressure on SOE to form its own French section.

A second, powerful argument for the need for an independent,

British-led French Section was de Gaulle's rigid veto on direct action against the Nazis in France.

When Pierre de Vomécourt arrived in London in June 1940, he went first of all to see the Free French, but found no interest from de Gaulle in the idea of a fifth column: 'de Gaulle feared that active resistance and sabotage would provoke reprisals,' said de Vomécourt. Many Frenchmen chose for this reason to serve in 'F' rather than 'RF'.

Pierre wanted arms and training without delay. He went next to the War Office, where he was given an introduction to Gubbins, and became 'Lucas', the first SOE French Section organiser of a network or 'circuit' of resisters.

In October 1941, Buckmaster was promoted to head of F Section. Pearl had by then probably met him socially. She was precisely what 'F' was looking for: bilingual, street-smart, keen, intelligent and resourceful. Desperately short of recruits – Passy was still creaming off the Frenchmen arriving at the Wandsworth Patriotic School – it was likely that Buckmaster spotted her as potential agent material. He may have entertained her at his flat at Pelham Court, in Chelsea, or lunched with her at Caletta's in the King's Road, to which he was accustomed to take agents, many of whom he knew personally.

However it happened, Buckmaster's private diary showed that he met Pearl on 11 November 1941, just a month after taking over from Marriott. 'Pearl's ring inscribed,' reads the entry. 'It shows that they were in contact and clicked,' says Michael Buckmaster, his son.

In the continuing turf war between Stewart Menzies of the SIS, and Sir Frank Nelson of SOE, however, SOE was on the losing side: C had the upper hand over CD.

Most importantly, it was C who had personal access to the prime minister. Personalities mattered to Churchill, who detested the abrasive Socialist 'Dr Dynamo' – Hugh Dalton's nickname. Churchill had given Dalton the job of SOE minister as a sop to the Labour leader, Clement Attlee, but that didn't mean he had to like him. To Churchill, Dalton, an Old Etonian, was a class traitor.

Dalton had indeed been situated in the heart of the Establishment.

His father had tutored George V; Queen Victoria once described the young Hugh as 'Canon Dalton's horrid little boy.' Churchill felt the same way: 'Keep that man away from me,' he said. 'I can't stand his booming voice and shifty eyes.'

Disappointed by his lack of access to the prime minister, Dalton was also frustrated by the tight rein with which the Foreign Office held SOE, which he believed prevented SOE becoming a 'Fourth Arm' of warfare, after the three regular services, as he envisioned: 'You should never be consulted, because you will never consent to anything,' snapped the Socialist at the urbane foreign secretary, Viscount Halifax. 'You will never make a gangster.'

Menzies, however, was riding high with the prime minister. He had gained Churchill's ear when the code-breakers at Bletchley Park cracked the Enigma code on 22 May 1940, and 'Ultra' – the program set up to monitor and discipher the Enigma signals – became the single most important source of secret intelligence about the enemy. Churchill described the Ultra transcripts as his 'golden eggs', and ordered Desmond Morton, his personal intelligence advisor and a former SIS agent, to arrange for C to deliver them daily to Downing Street: 'These are to be sent in a locked box,' he wrote, 'with a clear notice stuck to it, THIS BOX IS ONLY TO BE OPENED BY THE PRIME MINISTER IN PERSON.'

Every day, Menzies delivered the Enigma messages in person to 10 Downing Street. He carried them in a buff-coloured box to which only Churchill had the key, which he kept on his watch chain: opening the box was an exciting ceremony for the ex-spook prime minister. C had wormed his way into the inner circle at Number 10. Dalton, by contrast, remained in the doghouse, growling with frustration.

Sir Frank Nelson, the first CD of SOE, retired the next year (in the spring of 1942), burnt out perhaps by his continual sparring with C. It was looking as though SOE would fall into the same trap as Section D – the failure of their *coups de main*, isolated acts of sabotage against the enemy, creating a vicious circle. Because it had no achievements to show, SOE could not advance against enemies at home; and because there was no progress against its enemies at home, it could achieve nothing in the field. A solid wall of enemies seemed to confront the young 'firm'.

But the invasion of Russia by the Germans, Operation Barbarossa, on 21 June 1941, changed the British situation overnight. On Bastille Day 1941, as Pearl's train drew into Paddington station after leaving her family in Stevenage, *The Times* was announcing a vital piece of news: the Anglo-Russian agreement of mutual assistance 'against Hitlerite Germany' had been signed by the British ambassador in Moscow, Sir Stafford Cripps, and Stalin.

On the same day, German news agencies announced that Panzers were outside Kiev, and 'the route to Moscow is opened'. Outraged by the news, the French Communist Party vowed to begin the fightback against its occupiers. On 20 October 1941, a young Communist, Gilbert Brustlein, assassinated Lieutenant Colonel Karl Hotz, the military commander of Nantes, probably the most important Nazi in the west of France.

It was the darkness before the dawn. The fuse of resistance had been lit.

9

First Flames

JUST TWO months after Buckmaster's arrival at Baker Street, on 6 May 1941, a parachute drifted over the *département* of the Indre in central France. The Whitley bomber that had dropped the parachutist waggled its wings and disappeared into the night sky.

Georges Bégué, alias 'George Noble', radio operator, landed softly in a freshly mown field, picked up his heavy suitcase in which his primitive 'biscuit tin' radio was hidden, and began walking towards Vatan. The peasants in the neighbouring farms slept as he passed. At a *petit bistrot* he ordered, '*Un café bien chaud*,' before tramping the twenty-three kilometres to Valençay.

The blind drop of 'George I' – after him, all radio operators were for a time known as 'George' – marks the *département* of the Indre as 'the true point of departure for active resistance in France,' wrote Georges Bégué, the first F Section secret agent to be parachuted behind enemy lines in France.

Georges had come, not by chance, but at the invitation of Max Hymans, former Socialist deputy of the Indre, who had written to the War Office in London in early 1941 offering to receive a British officer on his estate. Hymans's brave, isolated initiative allowed SOE to start recruitment in an area which was strategically and technically important: France would prove the most important theatre of operations for SOE in Europe, while Georges himself had been dropped just south of the demarcation line in the Free Zone.

Reads Hymans's citation for the OBE:

> Monsieur Hymans immediately put all his resources at the disposal of the first British-led resistance group in France and in

> so doing exposed himself and his family to the gravest dangers . . . Resistance to the policy of the Vichy Government in 1941 required the greatest courage and faith in the allied cause. Monsieur Hymans shirked no danger and no responsibility . . .

Three days after meeting Hymans, on 9 May, Georges made his first radio transmission to London from a safe-house in Châteauroux. Baker Street was overwhelmed with joy to receive the coded signal that Georges was at 28 de la rue de Pavillons, and that the first 'letterboxes' were being set up: one at Renan's the pharmacist in the rue des Mandarins and the other at the *garagiste*, Marcel Fleuret.

Bicycling through le Berry, as the region was known after its ancient dukedom, Georges also searched for suitable dropping zones that summer: 'The environs of Châteauroux are rich in areas which are suitable for landing grounds and parachute drops on the edge of the woods,' he reported.

The very next day after that communication was received, Pierre de Vomécourt (Lucas) and Roger Cottin – 'Roger *les cheveux blancs*' because of his white hair – were also dropped 'blind', that is, without a reception committee to meet them. Pierre at once contacted his brother, Philippe, at his château, Bas Soleil, at Brignac, ten miles east of Limoges, where the three brothers, encouraged by Pierre's news that they would have influential backing from London, divided up France into three areas of influence. Pierre was to take Paris and the north, where he became organiser of the first circuit – 'Autogiro' – and played an essential role in making the argument for active resistance to the Nazis. Jean focused on eastern France, and Philippe on the Non-Occupied Zone south of the Loire.

As proof of its good faith, Baker Street arranged through Georges's wireless for the very first supply drop of arms to be at Bas Soleil on 13 June; Philippe, codename 'Gauthier', and his gardener's son, hurried to hide the heavy containers in the shrubbery. When he opened the first one, the surprised baron discovered it was full of limpet mines for blowing up ships – of little use, since they were over a hundred miles from the sea. But there were also tommy guns, daggers and plastic explosive.

F Sections's first agents – George I, Pierre and Roger – were Frenchmen. Their arrival was due to the decision of Marriott's deputy, Thomas Cadett, a former journalist at *The Times*, to break the rule that only British and Commonwealth citizens could be deployed by F Section. When the RAF unexpectedly offered two of their Whitley bombers from which to parachute SOE agents into France, Georges, already trained as a wireless operator, had been the first man ready; none of the ten British agents in training were ready to go in May.

On the night of 6 September 1941, however, six more parachutes floated over a field belonging to wealthy farmer Auguste Chantraine ('Octave'), mayor of Tendu: Ben Cowburn, ('Benoit') a Lancashire oil engineer; Michael Trotobas ('Sylvestre'); Victor Gerson ('Vic'); George Langelaan; the French count, Maurice du Puy; and André Bloch, their 'radio'. All landed safely and fanned out through the countryside.

A '*résistant* from the first hour', Chantraine volunteered his farm, his family and himself to the cause of a resistance that was, said Georges, 'particularly designated under the name of "action" from that moment, in order to distinguish it from "intelligence". And action,' he boldly proclaimed, meant 'the uprising of the French and their participation in combat.'

'*G. Bégué fut le premier*, Georges Bégué was the first,' wrote an unknown witness. '*Cette petite voix dans la nuit, c'était celle de l'Espérance.* This small voice in the darkness was the voice of hope.' And this voice of hope quickly swelled to a chorus.

10

Enter 'Hector'

ONE DAY, on the steps of the Air Ministry in London, Pearl bumped into a childhood friend, Maurice Southgate. They had been schoolmates at the *École Britannique* in Paris, but had not seen each other for two years.

Southgate, like Pearl, had been born in 1914 to English parents in Paris, where he had spent his childhood and schooldays. Over six feet tall, slim, artistic and highly intelligent, he was a gifted draughtsman who excelled at art school. After graduating, he became a furniture designer and later a successful interior designer. Pearl and Henri had kept in touch with Maurice as he studied design at the *École Boulle* in Paris, and watched his career flourish; and Pearl had been at the British Embassy when in 1939, at the outbreak of war, Maurice had reported to the ambassador as one of the first to volunteer for service. She knew that he had joined the RAF and served as a sergeant interpreter with the British Expeditionary Force at Reims, before being evacuated to England. Now, fate seemed to have brought them together again, as they stood face to face on the steps of the ministry.

They stare at each other, and burst out laughing.

'Good God, Maurice. Is it really you?'

'Pearl!' Maurice beams at her. 'This is extraordinary. What are you doing here?'

'I'm working for old Beaumont at the ministry. But how are you, Maurice? I heard you nearly died on the *Lancastria*.'

'Yes, that was a close shave.' They embrace, kissing on both cheeks in the French fashion.

'I nearly bought it. Had to swim for hours, and the sea was on fire from the burning oil.'

'But you're all right, thank God.' Pearl hugs him on the steps, ignoring the curious glances of passers-by. 'What happened? Tell me all about it.'

They walk down the road together to the nearest Lyons Corner House where, over a cup of tea and a bun, Maurice pours out his adventures. On 17 June 1940, he had been among the last troops to be evacuated from Saint-Nazaire aboard the *Lancastria*, bound for England, but during the crossing the ship was dive-bombed by German aircraft and set on fire. Of the 5,000 men aboard, more than 3,000 perished. As the ship sank, Southgate had managed to swim away and survive for several hours before being picked up by another boat.

His miraculous escape, he now tells Pearl, had made him more determined than ever to make his contribution to the war effort. He, too, feels that in some strange way he has been saved by destiny for a special purpose.

Pearl takes a deep breath. She knows she can confide in Maurice.

'You know, Maurice, I really want to return to France, to help the Resistance,' she says.

Maurice grimaced. 'You want to go back? You've only just got out.'

Pearl nods. 'I know . . . but I want to help the war effort, too. It's a waste of time, staying here in London.'

'But how would you manage it? How would you go underground?'

Pearl lowers her voice. 'There are ways. I asked my old boss, *mon ancien*, Duggie Colyer.'

'And what did he say?'

'No. Out of the question.' She mimicked the air commodore: "*Vous n'allez pas travailler avec ces gens-là*. I'm not having you working with that gang."'

'*Hein*.' They have both slipped into French, unintelligible to listening ears. Both of them are familiar with the posters like the one on the wall behind them which warns: 'Careless talk costs lives.' It is safer to talk in French, which comes as naturally to them as English.

'*Je me suis dit, "C'est un sacré culot!"*' exclaims Pearl, her cheeks flushing with remembered anger. 'I said to myself, "He's got a bloody nerve!"'

Maurice's face is serious. 'Perhaps he was thinking of you, Pearl. You'd be taking a hell of a risk.'

'I've made up my mind.' She leans forward: '*Je suis anglaise et un Anglais est encore plus têtu qu'un Breton, ça c'est vrai!* I'm English and an Englishwoman is even more stubborn that a Breton, you know that!'

'You mean you're as stubborn as a mule,' agrees Maurice with a laugh. 'And what about Henri? Is he over here, too?'

'No, he's still in France. I haven't seen him for a long time. You heard he escaped?'

'*Oui*. That's wonderful.' He pauses. 'I imagine he's part of your plan?'

'I want us to work together in the Resistance . . .' Pearl stares at Maurice. 'What about you, Maurice? Is your wife still in France?

'She's in hiding. She's safe, I think.'

'You must miss her.'

Maurice nodded. 'I'm back in the RAF . . . stuck in England, like you. We're in the same boat.' His expression is disconsolate.

'Is it something you'd ever think of doing?'

'Going back, you mean?'

'*Oui*.'

'I wouldn't know how to go about it.'

'I can give you a contact,' whispers Pearl. 'There's a man I know . . .'

Maurice's eyes brighten. 'What about you? Have you volunteered?'

'Not yet. I'm waiting for a letter from Henri. I want him to come to England so that we can do our training together and then we can drop into France in the same team. I still haven't heard from him . . .'

'I see.' Maurice looks thoughtful.

'But you could go in first . . . We could join you.'

'Give me twenty-four hours to think about it.'

The next day Maurice gives Pearl his answer: '*Oui.*'

Pearl put Southgate in touch with Major Buckmaster, and he joined SOE in May 1942. Southgate's perfect French and knowledge of France qualified him ideally for the French Section; he began his training as a secret agent and was quickly promoted to squadron leader, as Pearl continued to wait patiently for an answer from Henri.

'I didn't want to miss the boat with Henri,' she had explained to Southgate, anxious not to go into France just as Henri arrived in England. It was a foreign country to him and, speaking no English, he would be lost without her.

Pearl had thought hard about how to phrase her letter to Henri, before writing in her rounded, confident hand to him that she recommended him to '*faire une cure d'oranges*'. 'Taking the orange cure' was code for travelling to neutral Spain – that way, he could join her in England.

She would dream that she and Henri were at Wanborough Manor, the paramilitary training school outside Guildford, where Southgate was about to start his training. Only French was spoken at Wanborough, where its commanding officer, Major Roger Vaughan de Wesselow, an urbane and astute former officer in the Coldstream Guards, crucially spoke the language himself – although not to a high standard – and kept a close watch on the recruits' fluency.

January 1943. In her Mayfair office, Pearl inserted a new carbon into her Corona manual typewriter and hit the keys with unusual force. Christmas had come and gone. She had attended one or two dances, at 1s 6d a time, and danced with a few officers. Another WAAF secretary, twenty-seven-year-old Joan Arkwright, recorded how, after watching *The Gang Show* in the WAAF NAAFI together, 'the sergeant said "Surely I'd found a boyfriend", in the same tone as she would say, "I suppose you've had tea". In the forces,' wrote Joan, 'a boyfriend seems to be one of the necessities of life.'

But Pearl had no eyes for other men. It was the New Year, and her patience was wearing thin: she had received no message from Henri.

'He hadn't understood,' Pearl concluded. But it was also possible that having already once been being taken prisoner and escaped from the Germans, Henri had no desire to risk his neck again. He would have had to contact an escape line, cross the Pyrénées into Spain, and probably find himself arrested by the *carabiñeros* and in jail or a concentration camp such as Miranda: he was not RAF personnel, who could apply to the British Consul. It would have required both motivation and money to take the boat for England, as Pearl had done. Henri preferred to wait, to his fiancée's chagrin – but the enforced delay may have saved Pearl's life.

Pearl is still waiting for a letter when, in mid-January, Maurice Southgate, who now goes by the codename 'Hector', arrives in London from his final training and meets her in a Marylebone hotel. Pearl notices that he is wearing a black leather jacket, a blouson that he is wearing in before his parachute drop into France.

'Drink, Pearl?'

'Lemonade, please.'

'How about a Dubonnet and bitter lemon?'

Pearl shakes her head. 'Just lemonade.'

'Still on the wagon, old girl?'

'You know I'm always on the wagon, Maurice.' Watching her father's descent into alchoholism has affected Pearl.

Maurice grins at the barman. 'Double Scotch for me,' he says.

Hector was waiting impatiently for the date of his parachute drop. He had received his mission orders: to take command of a wide-ranging SOE circuit codenamed 'Stationer' in the Auvergne. An SOE circuit, or *réseau*, consisted of a network of French resisters or 'subagents' organised by a British-led team of circuit chief, radio operator and courier, who could supply them with arms and explosives from England so that together they could build the Resistance.

Southgate's orders were to build on the foundations laid by two earlier agents, Baron Philippe de Vomécourt and Ben Cowburn, in the region around the town of Châteauroux in the *département* of the Indre. The small town, which nevertheless boasted a railway station, lay 269 kilometres east of Paris, nearly 100 kilometres south of Blois in the southern Loire, a remote region in the green heart of France, *la France profonde*, where life had changed little over the centuries.

But for all its remoteness, the people of Châteauroux did not lack courage. It was there that the wealthy farmer Auguste Chantraine – Octave – had developed his contacts with the French Communists, *the Francs-Tireurs et Partisans* (FTP), as the partisans were named who were striking the first blows against the occupiers.

Hector parachuted into the Auvergne on 25 January 1943. Accompanying him was a female courier – pretty, dark-haired Jacqueline Nearne, who had been brought up in Boulogne and returned to England to fight. The rest of his team: radio operator, George Donovan Jones, codename 'Isidore'; and Irishman Brian Rafferty, were waiting for him. The great 'Stationer' circuit was about to burst into life.

As he left the dropping zone in the cold dawn light, Hector alarmed Jacqueline by stopping a peasant who was up early and asking him in English, 'When's the next bus coming?'

Jacqueline scolded her boss. Rafferty's last boss, Charles Hudson, had just been caught. One could never be too careful: peasants sold their produce to the Germans; women slept with the enemy; walls had ears; informers were all around you, as former agents had learnt to their cost.

11

Heroes and Traitors

SEPTEMBER 1941. In the streets of Châteauroux, Nazi radio-direction finding vans were closing in on Georges Bégué – George I – whose radio the Gestapo found they could easily jam. In the early, heroic days of SOE, Georges's short-wave Morse transmitter and receiver weighed thirty pounds in its small fibre suitcase and trailed at least seventy feet of aerial; it was far too bulky to be easily hidden. There were also the fragile crystals, which Georges kept wrapped up in his pyjamas. Patiently tapping out his encrypted messages to London, Georges used the dangerous poem-code system often broken by the Germans: Tennyson's poem, 'In Memoriam', was requested by more than one agent as his code before going into the field. It expressed the weight of fear that lay upon every agent, and seemed like a personal appeal to the Home Station:

> Be near me when my light is low,
> When the blood creeps, and the nerves prick
> And tingle and the heart is sick,
> And all the wheels of being low . . .

One day, Georges was interrupted by a Vichy police inspector searching his room between two transmissions. 'I was very lucky not to be caught that day,' he wrote. 'It was evident that the noose would tighten sooner or later round our necks, and that we should make other arrangements. However, I had to continue . . .'

Alone and indispensable, George I was the only wireless operator available to arrange SOE's first Lysander aeroplane pick-up on 4

September 1941, piloted by Wing Commander W.J. Farley, commander of the newly formed 138 Squadron. It was an historic landing as the first Allied plane touched down on the soil of enemy-occupied Europe, scooped up Pierre de Vomécourt, a.k.a Lucas, who carried the first report on the situation in the field, and set down agent Major Gerard Morel in his place.

The detection vans were becoming swifter and more deadly during the three months Georges transmitted his messages in Châteauroux: a long transmission would bring them to the door within thirty minutes. Waiting in an upstairs room for his scheduled transmission time – known in SOE slang as his 'sked' – it occurred to Georges that in order to reduce the risk to radio operators such as himself, the BBC evening broadcasts to France might be used instead to send a personal message to agents on the day when a plane was coming. The reception committee for the parachute drop could even listen in their own homes to the coded messages. For example: 'Pierre is well,' over the early evening broadcast would mean the operation was on. But if at 9.15 pm they heard: 'Pierre sends greetings,' it would mean the operation had been scrubbed. Georges's brainwave was the beginning of SOE's unique system of *messages personnels*, 'personal messages' – but it would take time to develop.

In the narrow streets, the Vichy police from the *Brigade de Surveillance* at Limoges were multiplying their identity checks and searches of individual houses, and the live letterboxes used by agents were exposed to greater and greater danger. 'This system by which agents left messages for each other at the houses of French resisters, revealed itself from the start to be very impractical and often dangerous,' wrote Georges.

At the end of September, Max Hymans, the deputy who had invited the first SOE agent into France, asked Georges to stop using Fleuret's garage as a letterbox, as his wife was becoming nervous. It was, however, too late: the Germans had already set a 'mousetrap' or *souricière,* watching the house closely for the agents' comings-and-goings. On 5 October, the garage-owner was arrested, and deported; his wife was caught two days later. The letterbox's address had been found in Morel's papers when he had been arrested two days earlier, after a tip-off.

The police were hot on Georges's heels. They kept the Café du Faisan, one of his favourite haunts, under close surveillance, and their patience was shortly rewarded. Although Georges himself slipped the trap, '*le Capitaine anglais Langelaan*' and his 'accomplice', Liewer, were arrested; '*le Capitaine britannique Trotobas*' was the next to be taken – men who had first parachuted into Auguste Chantraine's field earlier that month. Finally, on 9 October, the police arrested Bouguennec, another agent who also stepped into the Fleuret mousetrap. In his trouser pocket was a scrap of paper with an address in Marseilles: the Villa des Bois.

Max Hymans, who had slipped out of Châteauroux just two days before the police came to arrest him, at once warned Georges, who fled to Perigueux. He, too, had been given the same address: the sinister Villa des Bois on the Corniche at Marseilles. This was said to be a safe-house used by another agent, Christophe, code-name 'Turck', a French architect, who had been dropped during the August moon with Jacques de Guélis, F Section's briefing officer.

De Guélis had returned to London with Lucas, but in September and October eight more agents had arrived. All had instructions to contact Christophe at the Villa des Bois.

The Limoges *Brigade de Surveillance* set a second mousetrap at the villa from 11 October. They did not have long to wait. The trap was manned by someone who closely resembled Christophe in voice and appearance, and who invited any telephone callers to come to the safe-house. The Gestapo caught Jacques de Guélis's lover, Georgette Dunais, as well as two other Englishmen, Hayes and Le Harivel.

On 26 October, George I himself walked into the trap. The Germans congratulated themselves: they had caught the wiliest mouse of all: '*Le pseudo Georges (en réalité Bégué) . . . est un des principaux chefs de cette organisation*. The so-called George, really Bégué, is one of the principal chiefs of this organisation.'

Max, however, was too smart for his enemies. He had returned to Marseilles armed with new false papers and had telephoned

Christophe at the Villa des Bois: '*J'étais sur mes gardes*,' he said. '*Le téléphone répondit, mais je ne pus avoir Christophe au bout du fil.*' The man on the end of the line didn't sound like Christophe, and when he insisted that Max call at the villa, even supplying the address when he feigned ignorance of it, Max's antennae twitched. He stayed away and subsequently escaped to England.

The Germans and the Vichy police were laughing. They had effectively rolled up 'Autogiro', F Section's first circuit, or so it seemed, within six months of its inception.

George I was 'blown' and so was Max, even if he had managed to escape. Georges was imprisoned in the Vichy concentration camp of Mauzac in the Dordogne, while another radio operator, André Bloch – 'George IX' – was caught ten weeks later. Tortured by the Gestapo, he kept silent and was shot. Now the radio link was broken. All SOE agents in the field were cut off from Baker Street. It was the beginning of the 'dark age' for F Section.

In central France, the two de Vomécourt brothers, Pierre and Philippe, toiled in a lonely vineyard. Although farmer Auguste Chantraine was labouring to rebuild the old circuit around Châteauroux under the direction of Philippe de Vomécourt, Pierre ('Lucas') was desperate to find a new 'radio', which Baker Street was having difficulty in providing. Lucas was also short of money, for the early agents were supplied with few funds: perhaps £100 to last indefinitely. For months, the three brothers had financed themselves, and Lucas urgently needed to wire Baker Street for more money.

It seemed a stroke of luck when Lucas ran into a charming young female agent in Paris. Her name was Mathilde Carré, codename 'Lily', and she worked for *Interallié*, a Polish espionage network.

'My organisation has been blown, my chief arrested, but my "pianist" and I can help you,' explained Lily ('pianist' was agent-speak for their radio operators). '*La Chatte*,' the Little Cat, as Lily was known, purred that she longed to work with Lucas and become active again.

Pierre de Vomécourt took care only to give Lily his codename of Lucas, and to keep his real identity secret. Lily promised to send Baker Street a message asking for money. A few days later, a contact handed Lucas the sum required.

In Baker Street, Buckmaster was elated to receive the signal that Lucas and another agent, Roger Cottin of the white hair, were still alive. Neither Buckmaster nor Lucas suspected that the delightful Lily was a 'ghost', a double agent.

The Little Cat was in fact the mistress of German *Abwehr* Sergeant Hugo Bleicher. The signals Baker Street had received had been transmitted from a German-controlled radio post and were composed by officers of the *Abwehr* (counter-espionage). Bleicher, the fabled 'Ace of the *Abwehr*', who, although only a sergeant, soon revealed himself to be one of the most skilled German intelligence agents, had planted his mistress on the unsuspecting Lucas.

In early January of 1942, Lucas asked fellow agent Major Ben Cowburn (Benoit) to lunch to meet the beautiful Cat:

> It was a cheerful lunch in a deluxe black-market restaurant. The lady was slim and pleasant . . . She told us what a catastrophe it was that 'Armand', her Polish chief, and most of his network had been taken, and how lucky she and a few others had been to escape. She was very happy to meet us, and very talkative. She rejoiced in the codename of 'Victoire' and the nickname of 'La Chatte'. She obviously liked the company of men and loathed other women. She appreciated blue funny stories. I had a collection of these . . . the lunch was a great success.

'Lily' operated out of *La Chatterie*, the cattery, with four captured radio transmitters tuned to the London wavelengths. She knew all the codes, the 'skeds' for transmissions and the prearranged security checks, and signed her German-dictated signals under her codename of 'Victoire' – victory.

But when Lucas asked the Cat to provide some forged identity documents, and the very next day she produced a bundle of over-perfect false papers bearing genuine German stamps, as well as a photo of Michael Trotobas and asked Lucas if he knew him, the agent at last smelt a rat.

He confronted the Cat: 'Where did you get all those genuine passes? Are you working for the Germans?'

The Cat confessed 'the wretched truth'. Cowburn noted that, 'Lucas could, of course, have killed her on the spot, but decided not to.'

Instead he challenged her. 'Why not become the greatest of all "treble agents" by working for us?' She jumped at it: Lucas's force of personality had turned the Cat a second time. She agreed to help the Allies while maintaining her contacts with the *Abwehr*, earning herself the title of the 'Mata Hari of World War II.'

She and Lucas soon persuaded the Germans that they should go back to England together, holding out the bait that they would bring back a British general.

At midnight on 12 February 1942, Buckmaster sent a naval motor torpedo boat (MTB) to pick up Lucas, Cowburn and the Cat from the Breton coast at Locquirec. Madame 'the Cat' Carré wore a red hat so that the Germans patrols would know not to challenge her or her companions. A rough sea blew up as the dinghy from the MTB came ashore to pick up the Cat and, as she threw her suitcase into the rocking craft, it capsized and she toppled under the waves. It was a bedraggled Cat, in her dripping fur coat, who was rescued by a naval commander on whom she vented her fury on the Breton beach, watched by the Germans huddled behind the sand dunes.

Lucas and the Cat were finally picked up by an MTB on the night of 26 February. Buckmaster sent Major Nicholas Bodington, former Paris correspondent of the *Daily Express*, with a party of armed Royal Marines, to supervise 'Mata Hari's' embarkation.

She spent the rest of the war in Holloway prison.

After warning Buckmaster that Bleicher had been using the captured transmitters, Lucas returned to France. In April 1942, he and Roger were arrested by Bleicher and sent to Colditz. The 'Ace of the *Abwehr*' had, finally, snuffed out 'Autogiro', although the irrepressible Cowburn would ultimately escape over the Pyrénées to England.

It was a melancholy tally of failure; of intrigue, ineptitude, treachery and betrayal. In the south of France, another circuit also promised more than it could deliver in 1942: SOE was duped by an artist named André Girard, who tricked F Section into believing that he could raise a 'secret army'. The top brass in London pricked up their ears at the sound of 'Carte', as both Girard and his circuit were known, but it was rolled up by the Gestapo after one of its agents fell asleep in a railway carriage and was captured with a briefcase containing a list of all the members of the circuit. Carelessness once again had cost many lives.

Grimly, Cowburn reckoned up the balance sheet:

> The casualty rate had been enormous. Almost all the men sent to France in 1941 had been wiped out. I myself had escaped only through the most extraordinary combination of circumstances. I had been unable to blow up any of my targets. [The oil refineries that Cowburn had been ordered to sabotage had been too closely guarded for him to plant his explosives.] The enemy had penetrated us. Our equipment and means of communication had proved inadequate.

On the credit side, Lucas had captured the Cat from the Germans, and had provided Baker Street with a means of counter-penetration. He and Cowburn had also laid the foundations for a future network: 'We had also obtained a great deal of experience,' wrote the engineer, 'which is said to be cheap at any price.'

12

Churchill and SOE

At his desk in 10 Downing Street, Winston Churchill brooded over the war news. On Sunday, 7 December 1941 he had been dining with the American ambassador, John G. Winant, and Averell Harriman, Roosevelt's special envoy, when at nine o'clock he had switched on the wireless and learnt of the Japanese attack on Pearl Harbor.

Within minutes, the transatlantic phone had rung. It was Franklin D. Roosevelt. He told Churchill that he intended to ask Congress to declare war on Japan. The prime minister concluded that Hitler's fate was sealed: 'I went to bed,' he recalled, 'and slept the sleep of the saved and thankful.'

His new-found optimism was reflected in SOE, where by 1942 the cloak-and-dagger exploits of the 'gentlemen amateurs' were meeting with fewer sneers than formerly. This was in part due to the departure in February of 'Dr Dynamo', who had been sacked for using the SOE telephone-tapping facility to listen in on the conversations of his fellow Labour ministers. He was replaced by a Conservative peer and Churchill loyalist, the tough but tactful Lord Selborne, with whom the prime minister had an easy relationship. 'Top', as Churchill affectionately nicknamed him, fought a shrewd battle for SOE in the 'Whitehall war', the upshot of which was that in June 1942, Stewart Menzies of the Secret Intelligence Service finally, and with deep reluctance, allowed SOE its own independent signals directorate with its own cyphers and radio organisation.

Churchill told his aide, Desmond Morton, that it was time his two secret services stopped squabbling. He pored over the new quarterly reports compiled by Selborne of his agents' achievements across the globe. The reports were necessary, Top had explained, as he slipped them onto Winston's desk:

> As my department works more in the twilight than in the limelight, [and] I should like to keep you informed regularly of the progress of the brave men who serve in it.

Within the files were acts of piracy as bold as Drake's, guaranteed to please a former naval minister: in January 1942, seventeen SOE men took part in an operation to capture the 7,000-ton Italian liner *Duchessa d'Aosta* lying at harbour in the Spanish island of Fernando Po. Subsequently, the corvette HMS *Violet* seized the whole flotilla, worth nearly £1 million, on the high seas. This success story was 'manna in the desert to SOE in its early lean years'.

'SOE continues to stoke the flames,' boasted Selborne to the prime minister, who was entranced by the exploits of his brave 'irregulars'. At his desk, Churchill scribbled his comments in the margins of the reports, enquiring anxiously about the fate of individual agents. What had happened to them after they were captured? Had they been rewarded for their efforts?

The story of SOE weapons-instructor Lieutenant Fernand Bonnier de la Chapelle, who on Christmas Eve assassinated the pro-Nazi Admiral Darlan, was particularly impressive. Before he was shot at dawn on Boxing Day, the twenty-year-old agent had refused to give away his co-conspirators.

In Czechoslovakia, two SOE assassins liquidated the hated *SS Obergruppenführer* Reinhard Heydrich in Prague on 27 May 1942. As Heydrich's chauffeur-driven Mercedes slowed to negotiate a corner, two Czech paratroopers, Jan Kubis and Josef Gabčik, stepped into the road and attacked the open-topped limousine. Gabčik's Sten gun jammed at the vital moment, but Kubis threw a Mills bomb, which killed their target. Like many SOE 'successes', however, it came with a heavy price in appalling Nazi reprisals against the civilian population.

When, in February 1942, the Germans changed their U-boat cipher 'Shark', it became unreadable to Bletchley Park, and C's 'golden eggs' lost their value. Now it was Selborne, not C, who had privileged access to the prime minister: during the bitter months of 1942, when U-boats were sinking rising number of Allied convoys and Britain seemed to be losing the Atlantic war, Churchill found consolation in SOE stories of derring-do.

Yet Churchill's depression deepened. In March 1942, in the grip of his 'Black Dog', he confessed to Roosevelt: 'When I reflect how I have longed and prayed for the entry of the United States into the war, I find it difficult to realise how greatly our British affairs have deteriorated since December 7.'

It would take a year before the Bletchley Park codebreakers cracked the changed 'Shark'.

Nor was there much to console Churchill in France where, following the Allied invasion of North Africa, the Nazis had marched into the Non-occupied Zone in November 1942 and now occupied the whole country.

But SOE in France had a gift for regeneration after every false start. Stubbornly, it would spin 'a sort of Penelope's web, continually unpicked by the Gestapo, of which the bloody threads were obstinately re-knotted night by night'.

A new and gifted SOE organiser parachuted into northern France on 1 October 1942. The legendary Major Francis Suttill, codename 'Prosper', a barrister by profession, was sent in to build a new circuit on the ruins of 'Autogiro' and 'Carte'. He rapidly created a powerful network, 'Physician', based in Paris, with the help of his two resourceful women couriers, Andrée Borrel (Denise), and Yvonne Rudellat (Jacqueline), and his 'pianist', Gilbert Norman (Archambaud). So fast did the circuit expand – with the help of contacts provided by the failed 'Carte' organisation – that Baker Street sent Prosper a second operator, Jack Agazarian (Marcel), at the end of the year.

As Prosper's web extended all over northern France, it began to look as if 1943 would be a make-or-break year. Could a secret army rise against the occupiers? Baker Street asked the indomitable Ben 'Benoit' Cowburn, to return on a third mission in April 1943, to set up a circuit in Troyes.

Before doing so, Benoit was given the task of delivering a new set of crystals to Major Suttill in Paris. But Benoit had been shaken by his experiences with the Cat: treachery had made him ultra-cautious, even to the point of insisting on jumping 'blind' on his second mission for fear of being received by a 'contaminated' committee. 'Contamination' had become something to be greatly feared:

> We had begun to use certain words which were to enter the vocabulary of secret agents. These were 'contaminated' and 'sick'. A person who was under surveillance by the enemy was 'contaminated'. He was at liberty and normal in appearance and might not be aware of having been spotted. Yet he was not only in great danger himself but, like the carrier of a dreaded microbe, could contaminate others.

The Cat had been a 'lady-virus' who had tricked them, and now every door seemed to bear a question mark: was it a mousetrap? Cowburn's senses were on the alert at all times, and he took extraordinary precautions to avoid unnecessary risk. Nevertheless, Captain John Barrett, his last 'pianist', had been arrested. It was with reluctance that Cowburn made his way to Paris to an address in the Avenue de Suffren.

The apartment was occupied by a delightful old lady who at once summoned 'Denise', Prosper's courier, Andrée Borrel, a twenty-two-year-old French nurse who was SOE's first woman agent to be parachuted into enemy-occupied territory. That afternoon, Denise took Cowburn to meet Prosper at the Gare Saint-Lazare.

As Prosper – born in Lille, only half-French and possessing a Belgian accent – could not pass as a Frenchman, he relied on Denise to explain the details of daily life and to travel with him almost everywhere. He was waiting at the station when she and Cowburn arrived.

'Thanks,' said Prosper, taking the crystals. 'Is there anything I can do for you?'

'I don't think so. I have my own radio operator and I'll soon be on my way to Troyes.'

'I'm glad to meet someone who believes in the self-contained unit! Nevertheless, I'd like to put you in touch with someone . . . I'll see you in the Avenue de Suffren tomorrow.'

Cowburn was impressed by Prosper's personality, which acted as a magnet to others less forceful and quick-witted; he was said to have recruited the writer, Armel Guerne, as his lieutenant when, in December 1942, Prosper and Denise had demonstrated Sten guns to an interested audience in a Montmartre nightclub.

Cowburn was anxious to leave for Troyes. The next day, Prosper came to see him in the flat. There were several other visitors: Cowburn remarked that there seemed to be 'too many of us in one flat'. Prosper agreed, but what could he do? He was overloaded. London kept sending him people, who told their friends about him, and so there was a 'Special Agents' Club'. It was: 'The same old story. The small world of resistance rallied to a strong personality, to one who would never refuse help and assistance.'

The smallness of the 'resistance world' was underlined when the friend Prosper introduced to Cowburn turned out to be 'Cinema', an agent recruited long ago by Philippe de Vomécourt whom he had already met, and who ran the 'Cinema-Phono' circuit. Cinema's real name was Emile Garry, which reminded everybody of filmstar Gary Cooper, hence 'Cinema'.

After a quick beer with Prosper and Cinema, Cowburn left Paris. 'It was the last time I would see that fine man, Major Suttill.'

By April the following spring, the German mood had hardened in Paris. Snap checks were frequent: lines of French police were drawn across the street, while behind them would be a number of German plain-clothes men from Heinrich Himmler's *SS Sicherheitsdienst* or SD, the Nazi party's security service, which was at daggers drawn with the military's security service, the *Abwehr*. The growing rivalry between the older *Abwehr* and the newer SD, Himmler's baby, to some extent paralleled that between SIS and SOE in England. Equally virulent and counter-productive, the struggle between the two German security services followed a trajectory by which the *Abwehr* lost ground to the SD, just as SIS did to SOE.

Both the *Abwehr* and the SD were known as the Gestapo, but the SD was the more to be feared. If you were carrying a parcel and hesitated for a moment, they would pounce on you. In the metro stations, police waited in the underground passages to demand papers, frisk people and open parcels. Going down the steps from a sunlit boulevard and being suddenly challenged in the narrow passage below felt like entering a rat trap.

In the same month, in London, Pearl was about to get a great boost to her morale.

It was a personal friend of Pearl who finally opened the door of SOE to her. Madeleine Currall had worked with Pearl before the war in the British Embassy in Paris, and in 1943 was PA to the permanent under-secretary of state at the Foreign Office. One day, in April, they met for lunch and Pearl poured out the story of her difficulties with Colyer.

'*Ne t'inquiète pas*,' replied Madeleine. 'Don't worry. Leave it to me.' The PA put in a discreet word on behalf of her old friend. 'The next thing I knew, an ecstatic Pearl was ringing me up, saying, "I'm in!"'

Pearl knew only that Madeleine 'did business with the service which interested me, whose name I did not know. It was called the Inter-Services Research Bureau then . . .' It was widely believed that the agents worked for the 'War Office'. 'It was all very secret and hush-hush,' commented Nancy Fraser-Campbell, who had joined SOE in 1942.

Shortly after Madeleine's intervention, a mysterious telephone call was made to Pearl on her home number at 117 Pullman Court, Streatham Hill, SW2, where she was living with her mother.

'Tulse Hill 3192.'

'Miss Pearl Witherington?'

'Speaking.'

'An appointment has been for you with Colonel Buckmaster. Please go to the following address . . .'

Buckmaster was waiting for her at the flat in Orchard Court in which he briefed the agents. By the beginning of 1943, Baker Street was reserved for planning operations and intelligence.

At Orchard Court, it was the irrepressible Park the janitor, formerly a bank messenger in the Westminster Bank in Paris, who presided over the agents' movements, who said, 'Strip, lad,' to the new recruits and, when an agent was down to his birthday suit, presented him with his imitation French clothing made by SOE tailors. He would then fold and press the discarded uniform, careful to put paper around the buttonholes. He had a prodigious memory and knew every agent by his fieldname.

Since agents were not meant to meet each other in England more than could be helped, it was Park's job to 'spirit people from room to room in the nick to time,' wrote Buckmaster, 'his tact and popularity enabling him to move people from the briefing room . . . with the agility of the characters in a French farce.' When the flat was crowded, Park would even move one of his charges into the famous black bathroom, in which an agent often cooled his heels in the dry, black-tiled bath, doing *The Times* crossword, until Buckmaster was free.

In Pearl's case, it seemed as if her interview was a virtual formality: 'Pearl interviewed me,' admitted Buckmaster, later. Pearl asked if she could replace Jacqueline Nearne as Southgate's courier, arguing that it was high time to recall her. Buckmaster agreed. 'I know PW well,' Buckmaster wrote in a final reference for her dated 14 September 1943. 'She is capable and brave.'

Pearl explained the misunderstanding with Henri, who had apparently failed to understand her request that he should 'take the orange cure' and come to England. Buckmaster listened sympathetically. After she had gone, he scribbled a brusque comment: '[PW] has a French fiancé in France who is stated by some to be a simpleton.'

Captain Selwyn Jepson of the Buffs, the thriller writer who was recruitment officer for F Section, interviewed Pearl in May 1943; later that same month, Pearl formally applied to be enrolled in the

First Aid Nursing Yeomanry, the FANY. The role she selected was 'Clerk', to which Pearl added, 'Secretary'. She gave her age as twenty-eight, her religion as Church of England, and added that she had a St John First Aid certificate, shorthand, typing and fluent French. Her boss, Air Commodore Beaumont, provided a service reference.

By 15 June, Jepson was writing to the FANY adjutant stating that he had no hesitation in recommending Pearl for 'confidential work . . . This lady has qualifications which render her valuable for special operation duties.'

Lieutenant Macfie of the FANY Corps, a friend of Pearl's, also wrote to Mrs Phyllis Bingham, former confidential secretary to the FANY commandant, Marion Gamwell, saying that she considered Pearl 'eminently suitable' for confidential work. Mrs Bingham headed the so-called 'Bingham's Unit', which provided potential female secret agents with the cover they needed to disguise the real nature of their training. Filed as F17 ('F' for F Section), Pearl was now a FANY.

Pearl left London for the leafy lanes of Surrey, reporting to Wanborough Manor, an Elizabethan manor house at Puttenham, on the Hog's Back outside Guildford, for preliminary paramilitary training. Wanborough was one of over seventy country houses that had been requisitioned by 'the Org' for training purposes (and one that gave SOE a new nickname: the 'Stately 'Omes of England'). Pearl was one of three women and fourteen men in Party 27AA. She was also, without doubt, one of its keenest recruits.

13

Offering Death

ON 8 June 1943, Pearl entered Wanborough smartly dressed in the uniform of a FANY subaltern. As Ensign Witherington – with a 'raspberry pip' insignia on her shoulder – she was, as she put it later, 'disguised as a FANY': her real identity as an SOE trainee was hidden under the convenient cover that she had joined the First Aid Nursing Yeomanry.

The FANY, a volunteer corps formed in 1907, had served gallantly in World War I and had a reputation for recruiting pretty, well-bred girls. The youngest SOE agent, twenty-year-old Tony Brooks, recalled waiting outside 6 Orchard Court and seeing 'one of those terribly secret cars that SOE used, an enormous great American gas-guzzling station wagon, painted in sand and spinach but with civilian number plates . . . driven by an extremely glamorous girl in a very smart FANY uniform.' They drove up Baker Street 'and she took her hat off and her long blonde hair rolled down right onto her shoulders . . . I thought it would be a good thing to remember when I was facing the firing squad.'

The link between the SOE's French Section and the FANY had arisen through a chance encounter in early 1942 between Highlander Colin Gubbins, head of training at SOE, and his Scottish neighbour, FANY commandant Marian Gamwell. It had become clear that the shortage of men made it essential to recruit women for France: 'SOE recognised that to do what it wanted to do it had to have women,' wrote Pearl. 'Heated discussions followed when the idea of using women for underground work was first put forward,' noted Vera Atkins. 'Wireless operators and couriers were wanted, and women were suited to the job as they could move about more freely in occupied territory. Men were more suspect.'

Selwyn Jepson, SOE's senior recruiting officer, was responsible for female recruitment. He faced opposition from the powers-that-be, who said that a woman, under the Geneva Convention, was not allowed to take part in combatant duties, which they regarded resistance work in France as being. The charter of the Auxiliary Territorial Service (ATS), the women's branch of the army, prohibited their carrying arms, but the FANY, a civilian corps, was allowed to do so. Jepson persevered:

> In my view, women were very much better than men for the work. Women, as you must know, have a far greater capacity for cool and lonely courage than men. Men usually want a mate with them . . . There was opposition from most quarters, until it went up to Churchill.

The prime minister, whose articles Jepson, formerly a literary agent, used to place in the *London Magazine* when Churchill was an impecunious Conservative MP, once again broke the deadlock.

> Churchill growled at me, 'What are you doing?' I told him what I was doing. He said, 'You're using women in this?' I said, 'Yes, don't you think it is a very sensible thing to do?' and he said, 'Yes, good luck to you.' That was my authority!
>
> The one woman who was not against it was the woman known as the 'Queen Bee' [Commandant Marian Gamwell], who was the chief of the FANYs. With her connivance, I dressed my recruits in FANY uniforms, which were very pretty and very nice and gave them complete cover.'

In April 1942, the War Cabinet had taken the decision to recruit women for the field, although this remained secret until after the war for fear of a public outcry if it were known that women were being sent on dangerous missions, especially those women who, like Violette Szabo and Odette Sansom, were mothers. 'Yet all the time,' writes Dame Irene Ward MP, 'secure from public comment, women were volunteering for, and serving in, the most hazardous of operations, where physical as well as moral courage was a paramount necessity.'

Their motives varied. There is a suspicion that some agents desired self-immolation: that they welcomed death. Agent George Millar, organiser of the 'Chancellor' circuit, was deeply unhappy when he volunteered for SOE: when Major Lewis Gielgud (brother of the actor), interviewed him, he 'believed that he was offering death. And I wanted a useful death and then peace.'

Death might also be embraced as the price of revenge, and revenge against the hated enemy was certainly a motive for women agents like Szabo, who vowed to shoot a German after her husband was killed at El Alamein. Yvonne Cormeau, a radio operator, had also lost her husband in the war. No longer wanting to live without the man they loved was a good enough reason for such women to volunteer.

The war was a time of moral clarity when, for SOE agents, the cause for which they fought was manifestly just: good against evil. There was no ambiguity. Pearl herself had a driven quality, a 'fury at the Germans who had snatched her sweetheart from under her nose', says Maurice Buckmaster's son, Michael.

All the female agents were united in thinking that they had the qualities to do a man's job. 'The sort of person who volunteered,' noted Vera, 'was someone prepared to operate on their own with a considerable amount of courage and prepared to take the very considerable risks of which they were made fully aware . . . We assessed their chances of coming through at no more than fifty per cent.' Like the men, she said, they were told of the risks they ran and given the opportunity to pull out during training. 'None did so.'

Faced with Vera across the desk, briskly enumerating the risks of betrayal, imprisonment, torture and death, it might have been hard for a woman to back out at the last moment. As Vera knew, many unsuitable candidates were weeded out in training; but some were not. Of SOE's women agents, the vast majority were sent to France, often with tragic results. Of the fifty-two who went, seventeen were arrested and twelve died in concentration camps.

Impelled by a desire to escape into action, women volunteered, sometimes quite impetuously. They knew they had a special skill, fluent French, but they generally had no inkling of the shadowy organisation for which they would work, its chain of command, or its overall strategy, to which they would be subject. In fact, the majority of women going into Occupied France, unlike Pearl or Andrée Borrel, had little idea of conditions in the field, or the magnitude of the sacrifice which might be required of them. Like Millar, they offered themselves, trustingly, to the SOE web.

At Baker Street, the office staff knew that the agents might 'come to a sticky end', as SOE agent Tony Brooks puts it. FANY Captain Nancy Fraser-Campbell, who was working for Colonel Bourne-Paterson in the Ops Room, remembers an agent asking her on the eve of his departure if he could bring her back anything from Normandy.

'The chance of his coming back seemed pretty remote,' said Nancy, but she replied, '"A Camembert cheese."'

Four months later, she was astonished, on opening the office door, to be met by a strange odour. There on the windowsill was an enormous Camembert, brought back by Lysander aeroplane. To Nancy's annoyance, as she had hoped to take the cheese back to her family, 'Bourne-Paterson sent out for some bread and they all tucked in.'

Recruiting women agents disturbed some senior SOE figures. Brigadier Dodds-Parker told Pearl: 'I always felt terrible about sending young women over, but of course they were jolly useful as wireless operators. You see, the excuse of staying at home was much more logical for a woman than a man.' It was true – a woman could stay at home all day and not look suspicious. But the (male) radio-operator Georges who stayed at home did seem strange: why was he not out working?

Women could pass as housewives or office workers. They needed to look ordinary, said Buckmaster:

> They were in no way conspicuous. The last thing we wanted in them was eccentricity. We denied them glamour, in their own

interests; we made them look as homely and unremarkable as we could.

Pearl was parachuted into France wearing a 'woolly' under her tweed suit, a pair of cotton stockings and brown walking shoes: no silk stockings or red cloche hats of the kind sported by 'Mata Hari' Mathilde Carré were provided by the SOE tailor. One agent told Buckmaster, not altogether accurately, 'We were just ordinary people, not particularly brave.' Odette Sansom was nearly turned down by Jepson on initial interview, because of her 'huge' personality.

Entry into SOE was by invitation. It operated like a privileged club, staffed by the officer class, mostly from the public schools and Oxbridge. Dalton, Hambro, Brook and Buckmaster were all Old Etonians; Selborne, grandson of the great Lord Salisbury, Winchester and Oxford; Sporborg, Rugby and Cambridge. Bourne-Paterson attended the Scottish Eton, Fettes, and Caius College, Cambridge. City solicitors Slaughter & May, and Courtaulds, supplied sharp brains and entrepreneurship.

Vera Atkins, by contrast, had a more exotic background: her real name was Vera Rosenberg and she was born in Romania to a German Jewish father and South African Jewish mother, whose maiden name, Etkins, she anglicised. Buckmaster was helping her with her naturalisation. Her position in 'F', however, would give ammunition to its enemies, who asked: 'How can we trust "F" when its intelligence officer is an enemy alien?'

Nor did the rumours end there. There were mutterings that Vera had been in Budapest with Leslie Humphreys before the war, when he was still spying for SIS, and it was even whispered that Buckmaster's deputy, Major Nick Bodington, was a 'mole', planted in F Section by professional spymaster, Claude Dansey, deputy to Stewart Menzies of SIS. Bodington had twice failed entry into SIS. Had Dansey found another, more useful role for him, relaying the contents of coded messages back to SIS during the first two years when it controlled SOE communications? No wonder SOE was obsessive about leakage and worried about its porous walls. Within the labyrinthine and incestuous secret world, it paid to watch your back.

Unlike the senior staff's backgrounds, the agents were a mixed bag: 'We were thought of as a group of renegades,' said Pearl. The women ranged from working-class baker's assistant, Andrée Borrel, to the Mauritian aristocrat she served in the Parisian *boulangerie* in the Avenue Kleber, Lise de Baissac. There were acrobats (the Newton twins); actors (Dennis Rake); architects (Roger Landes); journalists (Nancy Wake); schoolmasters (Harry Rée and conscientious objector Francis Cammaerts). Michael Trotobas was a chef at Stoke Poges Golf Club; Noel Burdeyron was second head waiter at the Dorchester; Brian Stonehouse a fashion artist for *Vogue*; John Goldsmith was a racing trainer; James Amps a jockey at Chantilly; and William Charles Grover-Williams, a racing driver.

'Buck's Boys,' remembers Noreen Riols, who worked as a decoy girl – one of the women whose job it was to flirt with trainee agents to see if they would spill their secrets – at Beaulieu, 'were usually between twenty and thirty-five, courageous, highly motivated, idealistic – and always devastatingly handsome'.

It took just seven weeks to turn civilians into secret agents. On 11 January 1943, the first female student, milliner Vera Leigh, entered Wanborough. She flew to France by Lysander aeroplane in May, and was arrested by the 'Ace of the *Abwehr*', Bleicher, five months later. Four more women arrived at the manor on 16 February, of whom the only one to survive would be Yvonne Cormeau, who parachuted into France in August 1943 to work for George Starr, codename 'Hilaire', in Gascony. Also in Party 27X were Yolande Beekman, a London shop assistant who became a radio operator and was dropped into France in September 1943; Noor Inayat Khan, codename 'Madeleine', an Indian princess who had become a corporal wireless operator in the WAAF and was the first female 'pianist' to be sent to France; and Cicely Lefort, a doctor's receptionist and courier to Cammaerts. The fourth doomed woman was Diana Rowden, who came from an army family and was convent educated.

Reservations were expressed about some of the students: Noor was 'not quick (or) clever', reported her trainer. Cicely was 'very ladylike and English': the Lysander pilot, Bunny Rymills, who flew them from Tangmere, remarked that Cicely 'looked like a vicar's wife. Her French did not seem all that hot.' Noor was wearing a green oilskin coat, which showed off her glossy brown hair and gentle brown eyes. Only a trembling cigarette betrayed the girls' nerves.

All four were landed by Lysander on the night of 16 June in a pick-up operation arranged by F Section's efficient new air movements officer, Henri Déricourt, a former French Air Force pilot who had escaped from Marseilles to England. After training on Lysanders, Déricourt was parachuted back into France in January 1943; since March, the tempo of pick-ups had increased under his management, while on the night of 15 June, two Canadian agents, Frank Pickersgill and John Macalister, were also dropped into France to start a new circuit, 'Archdeacon'.

Buckmaster was impressed with the way in which Déricourt, who also conveniently acted as postman for the agents' mail on the 'Lizzy' (Lysander) flights, seemed able to avoid German scrutiny. Vera, on the other hand, distrusted the flashy, handsome, fast-talking pilot when she was sent to report on him in 1942:

> When I saw him, my heart sank. Possibly it was his slightly mocking attitude, perhaps it was that he didn't seem to look one straight in the face; but I came back and said that I didn't like him, and that I wouldn't trust him.

Her doubts were ignored, however, as was MI5's negative report, when Nick Bodington vouched for the Frenchman personally. It was to prove a fatal error.

In Surrey, Pearl threw herself enthusiastically into the Wanborough routine. The women, formerly excused physical exercises, now joined the men's classes. In the mornings they learnt to handle and fire revolvers, pistols and light automatic weapons and practised tapping out the alphabet on the Morse buzzer; in the afternoons, they hurled hand grenades in a chalk quarry on the Hog's Back and blew up trees – Pearl was taken outside by a sergeant-instructor and shown how to put a detonator into a primer and how to put the primer into a 'six-inch brick' of explosive; she was then required to apply the brick to a tree of her choice, and to bring it down herself. A swim in the private pool set among pine trees rounded off the afternoon. No one stayed up late after dinner, for reveille was at 0600 hours, followed by physical exercises and all-in wrestling.

Early on in her training, Pearl found the same sergeant-instructor surrounded by a great array of light weapons. Under the shade of the copper beeches, he broke down and put together a tommy gun, a light-machine gun, a Colt automatic and the .45, a Browning, a French light-machine gun, a Schmeisser and two different sizes of Lugers, as well as a small Belgian pistol. The class followed suit. 'We shall be firing with every one of these this afternoon and every day,' he barked at them. 'You'll soon get used to them, even if they appear confusing to begin with.'

A few yards away, a corporal was teaching a second class the art of signalling with an Aldis lamp. A third class was a lecture on bridge demolition, which included the formulae necessary to give the precise amount of explosive required to blow up a bridge of any given size. After lunch, the students moved on to time-pencils (delayed fuses) and instantaneous fuses, followed by shooting practice.

Pearl took to guns like a duck to water: 'Outstanding. Probably the best shot (male or female) we have had yet,' enthused her report. She also scored highly in physical training: 'Good. Very determined. Strong, though not naturally agile.' As for explosives and demolition: 'She is extremely keen on this,' said her trainer, 'and would like to specialise.'

Her aptitude for Morse code was, however, nil, although as a former Girl Guide who had mastered semaphore, she had expected to find it easy: 'I was desperate because I couldn't do it. I said to myself, "If I can't understand it, they won't take me."' There was daily practice. 'Little by little, the speed on the Morse buzzer increased,' recorded Peter Churchill – but not for Pearl. Finally, she went in despair to the commandant, Major Ward, who had taken over from de Wesselow: '*Ecoutez, c'est épouvantable, ce sacre Morse.* Look, it's hopeless, this dreadful Morse. *Je peux pas, j'y arrive pas*, I just can't do it.'

The commandant saw that she was on the verge of tears. 'There's no need to worry,' he said. 'Why are you getting in such a state? If you can't do it, you can't do it! *Ouf!*'

Pearl could have hugged him when he explained that the purpose of Morse training was simply to select those students suitable for training as wireless operators.

On 8 June, like the other recruits, Pearl signed the Official Secrets Act. 'I cannot sufficiently stress the importance of security,' announced Ward in his opening address. 'Nobody outside this school knows what goes on here, and nobody must know.' All letters were censored, telephone calls forbidden. Local people were simply told that commando training was going on at the manor, although the students were allowed to visit local pubs, which led to talk in the Windmill Inn at Ewhurst of 'funny business' going on over the hill.

Buckmaster made a point of visiting Wanborough to assess the recruits. 'They were offered strong drink and their reactions under its influence was studied. Did they talk in their sleep? If so, in what language?' Woken by a sudden bright light in the middle of the night, did they exclaim, 'God Almighty!' or '*Nom de Dieu!*'?

Pearl impressed Ward with her 'excellent security', dispelling any lingering prejudices he held against the female sex: 'This student, though a woman,' he wrote, 'has definitely got leaders' qualities . . . Cool and resourceful and extremely determined. Knows what she is in for and is anxious to get on with it . . . She possesses a strong and rather dominating personality. Very capable, completely brave.'

Colyer, in the meantime, had been annoyed to see Pearl 'strutting about' dressed as a FANY. As head of personnel in the RAF, he decided to do something about it.

Air Commodore Beaumont, Pearl's most recent boss, summoned her and asked, 'Why are you in FANY uniform?'

'I don't know.'

Beaumont grunted. 'You belong to the RAF.'

'And that is how I became a WAAF instead of a FANY,' noted Pearl. She was given an honorary commission as WAAF Assistant Section Officer Witherington, but she remained 'double-hatted' as a FANY ensign, to the bewilderment of her sister, Mimi, who was perplexed to see Pearl going in and out of the Streatham flat when she was on leave, wearing first a light blue and then a khaki uniform. Possibly she was copying Maurice Southgate, who also had a penchant for wearing alternate army and RAF uniforms while on leave in London after transferring to F Section (according to SOE folklore, his mother's neighbour had remarked to her: 'I never see your two sons go out together').

'No one must know what you do here: not your mother, your sister, your brother,' the trainees were told. Pearl told her mother that she had joined the FANYs, and Gee, as well as Pearl's three sisters, no doubt believed that she was still in a secretarial role. Mimi was more persistent; but Pearl had no trouble in parrying her family's questions as secretly she travelled up to Arisaig, on the west coast of Scotland, for further commando training.

This training would include twenty-five-mile treks over the mountains; it rained almost every day; and there were no crossroads, or even roads, churches, post offices or rivers to assist recruits in their map-reading. Navigation was done by means of the compass, and several F Section trainees would find themselves lost in the mountains. The recruits also practised firing tommy guns and revolvers; and exploding high-powered charges; canoeing; and swimming with 'clams', limpet mines.

One wet day, two of the group were passing a famous salmon stream. As one of them watched the fish leap up a wall of descending water and fall back into the pool below, he fingered the small slab of plastic explosive in his pocket. 'Are you, by any chance, thinking what I am thinking?' asked John, the first officer.

It was the work of a moment for his companion, Alfred, to insert a detonator into one end of the plastic mould, hold the electric wire that ran into the detonator, and to swing the charge gently round his head, like a lasso, letting it drop into the middle of the pool.

Both men lay down close to the bank as Alfred touched off the charge. 'Here goes!' he said, and several tons of water rose fifty feet into the air, revealing the stunned salmon on the bed below. As the water crashed back into the pool, John dived in and wrapped his arms around the largest fish. After an exhausting struggle, he landed the salmon and wrapped it in his trench coat.

That night, instead of the usual bully-beef, mashed potato and neeps for dinner, a twenty-four-pound salmon was served.

Living off the land, trapping, stalking and shooting game came naturally to Pearl but, as the weeding-out process continued, she became preoccupied with the thought of saying goodbye to her mother. Some of the women trainees seemed to have little idea of the task that lay ahead, thinking that they had been recruited as bilingual secretaries (Noor's trainer wrote that she 'came here without the foggiest idea what she was being trained for'). Pearl, however, after her experiences in Marseilles, knew that she might be killed at the hands of the Gestapo.

She asked for an interview with Buckmaster: 'I held myself responsible for Mummy, and I thought if something happens to me and I don't come back, what is going to happen to Mummy? . . . Vera said, "Let's see the colonel", and so she made the appointment.'

However, when Pearl put the question to him, Buckmaster's answer was: 'Supposing a bomb hits you in London, what is going to happen to your mother?'

'I was absolutely furious.' As usual in times of trouble, Pearl turned to her old boss, Colyer. 'I said I must have some kind of reassurance of what is going to happen to Mummy, because honestly this won't do.'

Colyer heard her out sympathetically, and said he would see if the Air Ministry could help.

Pearl remained upset and critical of Buckmaster, who worked long hours in the office and displayed 'tireless zeal', as his masters noted, but had a tendency to lack 'fixity of purpose' and to become 'enmeshed in detail'.

'Not one agent liked Buckmaster, not one,' confessed Pearl.

During her training, Pearl did, however, grow close to Nancy Fraser-Campbell. Who no doubt conveyed to Pearl the prevalent mood of excitement in June within F Section, which had been building ever since the 'MOST SECRET Invasion Directive' of 12 May 1942 from the chiefs of staff to SOE setting out its 'collaboration in Operations on the Continent'. Now, in 1943, 'the Org' was waiting on tenterhooks for clarification of its role in 'Overlord', the invasion of France.

In the 'Invasion Directive', the War Cabinet had finally approved plans for Anglo-US operations in Western Europe, culminating in 'a large scale descent on Western Europe in the Spring of 1943.' SOE was to have a vital role, building up and equipping paramilitary forces in the occupied countries, although 'particular care is to be taken,' stated the chiefs, 'to avoid premature large scale risings . . .'

For months, SOE had waited for official recognition of its role. A wave of euphoria swept through Baker Street on 20 March 1943 when, after two years' 'civil war' with SIS, the chiefs of staff finally issued their official directive to the SOE. The parameters between SIS and SOE were at last clearly defined.

'We'd become the first organisation in the history of British warfare with a licence to commit sabotage,' crowed Leo Marks, SOE's brilliant young cryptographer. Henceforth SOE would be responsible for conducting clandestine warfare and building up secret armies. Most controversially, its quota of aircraft was to be increased at the expense of Bomber Command.

Churchill asked the Air Ministry for a force of ninety-three aircraft. At the meeting of the Defence Committee on 2 August he emphasised:

> The immense value to the war effort of stimulating resistance amongst the people of Europe. He recognised that acts of rebellion against the Germans frequently resulted in bloody reprisals, but "the blood of the martyrs was the seed of the church", and the result of these incidents had been to make the Germans hated as no other race had ever been hated . . .

The debate over aircraft allocation raised SOE to a higher status. Its requirements were now 'high priority'.

The mood in Baker Street was upbeat as Buckmaster was promoted (to colonel). 'We drank champagne out of paper cups,' recalled Noreen Riols, 'when Buck got his pips.' Nancy and Pearl would have known of Buckmaster's promotion: the tall, cherubic-faced former major, with blue, slightly pop eyes, who fervently believed 'that all his geese were swans,' had been duly rewarded for his devotion to duty.

In the signals room at Norgeby House, Room 52, the clack of the teleprinter was non-stop as the machines relayed 'Top Secret' messages from Grendon and Poundon home stations, where up to 2,000 FANYs decoded the agents' traffic. The messages brought Buckmaster, 'anxious mother' to his 'boys', closer to the agents in the field.Vera developed a particular talent for deciphering the coded messages, often mutilated so that they were all but impossible to read.

In April 1943, the news out of France was encouraging. Francis Cammaerts, a former conscientious objector, was successfully dropped into south-east France to run the 'Jockey' circuit. There were good reports from RF Section, too. On 16 April, General de Gaulle recalled Colonel Passy; Pierre Brossolette, a founder-member of the *Conseil Nationale de la Résistance* (CNR); and Tommy Yeo-Thomas, a.k.a the 'White Rabbit', the first British officer to take part in a Free French mission, 'Operation Arquebus', intended to weld together the different resistance groups. Picked up by Lysander, by midnight all were safe in London.

It looked, said Tommy, as if 'both sides had finally noticed that they were fighting the same war'.

But then a gloomy message is received in Room 52. It is from

Adolphe Rabinovitch, a young Russo-Egyptian Jew who is agent Peter Churchill's radio operator. Rabinovitch reports that Churchill and his lover, Odette Sansom, have been arrested after being found in bed together in the Hotel de la Poste in Saint-Jérioz, Haute-Savoie (proof, if proof was needed, of the danger of sexual relations between agents). Buckmaster urges Rabinovitch to come home, but he insists on staying to warn Cammaerts.

Two days later, the teleprinter spews out a new message, one to which Vera at once alerts Buckmaster. It is from Prosper, as agent Francis Suttill is always known. He has suffered a devastating loss. The Gestapo have caught two sisters, Germaine Tambour, formerly secretary to 'Carte' and her sister, Madeleine, whose apartment was an important 'letterbox', the meeting-place for Prosper's team: his 'pianist', Gilbert Norman, courier Andree Borrel, even Peter Churchill. Ten agents have used the Tambour letter-box. Prosper has realised to his horror that he had a 'contaminated' contact from the start, in the person of Germaine Tambour. He offers the Germans a ransom for the sisters' release, but when he hands over the money, the laughing soldiers release two old prostitutes instead.

On 16 June 1943 – as Pearl started her training – a flight picks up Jack Agazarian, who has fallen out with his chief, and delivers Noor Inayat Khan as the new 'radio' for Garry's Phono circuit. So acute is the shortage of 'pianists' that Buckmaster overrides her poor training reports, and sends the naïve writer of stories for children out to work. Pearl will be much needed when her training is finished.

In France, the invasion was expected daily. In every *bistrot,* bar and apartment where the agents gathered, the longed-for landings, the *débarquements,* were on the tip of every tongue. But in faraway Casablanca, planning was going in quite a different direction. Roosevelt and Churchill had agreed on 18 January that the principal operation in the European theatre that summer should be the invasion of Sicily. As a sop to Stalin, who was not present at the conference but who was pressing for a second front, and under pressure from Churchill, the combined chiefs of staff also agreed to launch limited offensive operations from England, the most important of which was to be an attack on the Cotentin Peninsula, France, on 1 August 1943.

As Churchill took the salute in his tropical suit and topi, and posed for his end-of-conference photograph, dressed in his usual double-breasted navy woollen pin-stripe suit and Homburg hat, his mouth clamped on his cigar, headlines in the press screamed: 'An invasion of Europe within nine months.' But by April of that year, it was obvious that the opening of a front in the western Mediterranean ruled out any attack on France: the Allies had only enough landing craft for Sicily, so cross-Channel operations were out of the question.

Painfully Churchill mulled over the facts. How was he to tell Stalin that he was reneging on his promises? Bitter telegrams flew between London and Moscow. Russian blood had been spent at Stalingrad, and the Allies seemed strangely reluctant to match Russian suffering with their own. Churchill feared that without a second front, Stalin might even capitulate and sue for peace.

It only took the prime minister a week to come up with an ingenious solution. On 10 April 1943, he instructed the chiefs not to divulge the decision to cancel the invasion of France: 'These facts should not become known'. Instead, it was time for a new strategic deception scheme, one that appealed to Churchill – with his passion for the unorthodox – almost as much as special ops. He ordered General Morgan, Chief of Staff to the Supreme Allied Commander (COSSAC) to prepare:

> Camouflage and pretence on a most elaborate scale . . . Very large preparations should be made at the embarkation ports, and the assembly of the greatest amount of barges and invasion craft should be made, culminating in July and August.

Churchill's wishes were formalised in a directive instructing Morgan to plan for a full-scale attack on the Continent as early as possible in 1944, and to prepare 'an elaborate camouflage and deception scheme to pin down the enemy in the west and keep alive his expectations of attack in 1943.'

The deception scheme was named Operation Cockade. Lieutenant Colonel J. H. Bevan, the controlling officer of the London Controlling Section for Deception (LCS), received his brief: 'To prepare deception plans on a world-wide basis with the object of causing the enemy to waste his military resources'. Lieutenant Colonel J.V.B. Jervis Read, head of 'Ops B' at the LCS, drew up the details of a tripartite operation, of which the first part, 'Starkey', was the notional attack by fourteen British and Canadian divisions to establish a bridgehead on either side of Boulogne between 8 and 14 September. Three weeks later, an American corps would notionally sail from the UK to capture Brest, while a further 'attack' would take place on Stavanger in Norway.

On 30 April, the chiefs of staff ordered service commanders to cooperate in the preparation of the phantom invasion, Operation Cockade, '. . . a vast scheme of cover and deception'. The Double Cross Committee (under orders to provide 'channels of deception according to the plans of the controlling officer') was to leak the news by 'special means', via the 'controlled' German agents run by the committee; through the BBC; by planting false stories in the press; and even by forging letters to POWs packed with false information to fool the German censors.

Cockade was a secret of the highest classification, and one that was not shared with SOE. One of the Double Cross Committee recalled:

> They were regarded as horribly insecure. They weren't brought in on any of the really secret stuff. They were simply regarded as terribly amateurish.

The country sections, including F, were considered to be as leaky as a sieve – but even sieves have their uses. At this vital juncture, Bevan decided that SOE had a role to play in strategic deception: it was 'a legitimate organisation for exploitation as the disposal of the London Controlling Officer.' What this meant was that F Section would be duped, for the sake of the war effort. It would also inevitably increase the risk factor for agents already in the field, as well as those, like Pearl, about to go in.

The men in the know, or 'Cockaded' about the deception scheme, were limited to the charmed circle close to Churchill. They included Harry Sporborg, deputy head of SOE, and Brigadier Gubbins. Buckmaster was to remain 'not Cockaded', i.e. in the dark. As Sporborg said: 'Clearly, if deception is involved, Buckmaster is the last man you want to know about it.'

Cockade, however, was disastrously flawed from the start. '[The operation] had originally been devised to shroud a real invasion of France,' wrote Sir Michael Howard, official historian of strategic deception in World War II. 'Once the decision not to invade had been taken, the LCS had to throw Cockade together at very short notice, but now not based on any real event, just a few spoof advances.' Set in these terms, Cockade was about to become a cock-up.

Buckmaster was given orders to bring back his key agent, Prosper, from France for an urgent briefing. On the night of 14 May 1943, Squadron Leader Verity landed his 'Lizzy' on a bumpy field in France, and Prosper scrambled in.

The next morning, the agent stood at the door of 6 Orchard Court. Buckmaster was waiting for him.

14

The Prosper Disaster

COLONEL BUCKMASTER'S private diary reflected his agitated state of mind in the days before Prosper's arrival, as his entry on Sunday, 9 May revealed: 'Hideous muddles, in the office.'

Buckmaster's maddeningly obscure diary did not go into details, concentrating in the main only on social events, but several cryptic entries indicated his sense of crisis. As usual, he was working flat out. Through the long hours, Buckmaster's thoughts were in turmoil: not only had Brigadier Gubbins suddenly ordered him to bring back his key agent, Prosper, to London, but CD had given 'F' some startling, secret news, of the utmost significance. Buckmaster recalled:

> In the middle of 1943 we had a top-secret message telling us D-Day might be closer than we thought. This message had been tied up with international politics on a level far above our knowledge and we, of course, acted upon it without question.

The date of the invasion of France, 9 September, was the momentous news he was about to share with Prosper: the greatest secret of the war.

On Saturday 15 May, 'Prosper arrived,' recorded Buckmaster in his diary. 'And Antelme and Suttill out,' he added, indicating that he was taking Francis Suttill, Agent Prosper, and another agent, Mauritian major France Antelme, codename 'Renaud', out to dinner.

Over dinner, the conversation was serious, lively, and acrimonious. A heavy burden would be placed on Prosper's shoulders if he was to prepare for a general rising of the Resistance in support of Allied landings in early September.

Prosper was concerned about security issues, about carelessness and ineptitude at Baker Street which was endangering agents' lives, as well as the logistics of the coming invasion. He and Antelme had many issues to raise with their chief.

As the men discussed the incipient invasion – which they had been led to believe was just around the corner, the landings scheduled a mere four months away – they remained painfully unaware of the net of deception that separated them from the men above them. Churchill's orders had gone out from Downing Street to his deception controller, Bevan; to the Double Cross Committee; the chiefs of staff, all the way down to Gubbins and Sporborg of SOE: but Buckmaster and F Section's agents were not among their number.

Many years later, Buckmaster seems to have realised that he and Prosper were pawns in the deception game. He gave the BBC a fuller account of those fatal May days:

> In May 1943, a message came from Churchill through Gubbins, that he wanted Prosper brought back immediately, because Churchill wanted to meet him. He was closeted with Churchill and the Cabinet Office for a long time. Churchill said that Stalin was bullying him into making more trouble in France.
>
> Churchill said: 'Are you prepared to risk your life in these circumstances? I want you to make as much disruption as possible. Ignore the security rules, stir things up.'
>
> Prosper said: 'Yes, sir.'

In fact from 4 May–4 June 1943, Churchill was in New York for a meeting with Roosevelt. He could not have met Prosper, as Buckmaster alleges. It was probably Gubbins and his deputy Sporborg who asked Prosper, on the prime minister's orders, to 'make a fuss', and intimated that the invasion could be expected imminently. 'Stirring things up' in France would also have been a strong nod to Stalin, who was still expecting a second front there; the need to placate the Russian thorn in his flesh would have been at the forefront of Churchill's mind as he boarded the *Queen Mary* to cross the Atlantic.

* * *

By Sunday 16 June, Prosper, Antelme and Buckmaster were hard at work discussing preparations for the expected landings. 'Office 9.30 a.m.,' scribbled Maurice in his diary. 'Prosper had lunch at Caletta's,' he added, after entertaining the agent at his favourite King's Road restaurant.

On Monday, it was the turn of France Antelme (Renaud) a middle-aged businessman with important links to French bankers, who had first been sent into France in January 1943: 'Antelme 11.30 a.m. . . . Antelme to dine.'

Antelme received his instructions to organise food supplies and finances for a landing force, but the next day's 'F Section meeting' descended into chaos. Operation Cockade Starkey had been 'mounted in too much of a hurry in summer 1943 to mis-persuade the Germans that an invasion of France was imminent and would take place in early September.' Time was short to raise money, organise field kitchens and food supplies, stockpile enough weapons and train raw recruits to shoot and use explosives. Loyal and dedicated, Prosper and Renaud still had many questions.

'Bloody awful afternoon,' wrote the harassed Buckmaster. 'Many rows.' On 20 May: '12.30 Prosper left,' recorded Buckmaster with evident relief. 'And Renaud.'

Internal dissension continued, however. 'Many messages,' recorded Maurice three days after Suttill's departure. 'Had rows.'

When Prosper and Antelme returned to France, 'both men assumed that there would be a major Allied landing in 1943,' wrote Prosper's son, Francis J. Suttill. Prosper had been warned to expect more sorties by the June moon than had reached him in the previous six months. Not only do records show a 'massive' increase in June *parachutages*, drops, to his circuit, which received 190 containers in nine days, but the amount of *matériel de guerre,* weaponry, dropped to all the French networks also rocketed: for example, kilos of high explosive jumped from 88 kg in January to 10,252 kg in June; Sten guns from a mere 87 to 2,353.

'F Section was doing exactly what everyone would do if you expected an imminent invasion,' commented Francis J. Suttill.

However, Prosper was seething with rage at the inefficiency of SOE desk officers. On 19 June, he criticised London for sharing the addresses of Prosper's cancelled letterboxes with other intelligence sections, even agents of DF, the escape section:

> Your conception of a letterbox appears to be a place where an agent, usually covered in mud, carrying an obvious suitcase, can turn up at an unreasonable hour to be lodged and fed and watered for up to three weeks.

He was especially concerned for the safety of the recently arrived Noor, codename Madeleine:

> Madeleine was apparently given the Monet letterbox in spite of the fact that it is cancelled since February (cancellation confirmed personally by me in May visit). Please take disciplinary action. Had Madeleine gone there yesterday she would have coincided with one of the Gestapo's periodical visits to that flat!

While Prosper called for disciplinary action to be taken against the agent who passed on the address of the Monet letterbox to his number two, it was the slackness at Baker Street, staffed largely by enthusiastic volunteers, that most irritated him:

> The whole system of giving to any agent a letterbox of another agent *is an obvious invitation to disaster for that circuit*. (I hope I make myself clear. I state, in parenthesis, that it is now 0100 hours 19th June and that I have slept 7 hours since 0500 hours 15th June). The answer is quite obvious. If you give a letterbox to an agent it *must* be given on the understanding that is it to be divulged to *NO ONE, whatever the circumstances, without the consent of the organiser of the circuit to which the letterbox belongs* . . . *All* my letterboxes and passwords *now in force* will be cancelled from midday 19th June and will remain cancelled till I receive your W/T message, 'The village postman has recovered . . .'

Prosper sensed that the bubble was about to burst. Instinct told him that his circuit was in mortal danger: the virus of contamination, or 'plague', as Albert Camus calls it in his novel, *La Peste*, was jumping circuits, while in the rush to get everything ready for 'D-Day', F Section was breaking its own security rules and precipitating disaster. Mournfully, Prosper predicted that if F did not accept his suggestion to cancel all letterboxes, they might as well file his report for production 'on the inevitable eventual post mortem of the "feu" [the late] Prosper organisation.'

The greatly increased number of Allied planes going over to drop arms began to attract enemy attention: Operation Cockade 'Starkey' was putting the Germans on the alert. On 20 June, there were four *parachutages* round Blois, and the enemy set up road blocks.

It was to be a good move on the part of the Germans. The two Canadian agents, Pickersgill and Macalister, who were to start up the 'Archdeacon' circuit, were received on 15 June in the Cher valley by a lieutenant of Prosper's named Pierre Culioli, with whom they stayed while he tried to improve their false papers. On 21 June, he was driving them to the station to take the train to Paris when, in the small town of Dhuizon, they ran into a German control point. Hearing the Canadians' strong accent, the Germans arrested the agents.

Culioli managed to drive off with one of Prosper's couriers, Yvonne Rudellat, but crashed the vehicle into a wall, later claiming that he intended to kill them both (it is equally probable that he was simply trying to escape). Both he and Yvonne were badly injured.

German soldiers searched the wreck of the vehicle. In the boot they found Culioli's briefcase, containing vital papers. There was also an envelope with two crystals, addressed to 'Archambaud', the codename of Prosper's radio operator, Gilbert Norman, at 102 Avenue Henri-Martin, Paris 16e.

Shortly after midnight on 24 June, the Gestapo called on Norman, who was living with an old friend, Laurent, and his wife.

The Germans rapped on the door of the flat, shouting, '*Ouvrez, police allemande!*' Norman was sitting at the kitchen table. Spread out in front of him was a mass of ID cards, on which he was painstakingly resetting the photographs of the principal agents of the circuit, as demanded by new regulations. On Prosper's card was his address. That night Norman, the Laurents and Andrée Borrel were all arrested.

The same morning, Suttill returned to his digs, a small hotel in rue Mazagran. He had taken room 15 under the name 'François Desprée'. He climbed the stairs to his room, taking care not to disturb the *patronne*. As he turned the key in his lock, on the other side of the door three SD men drew their Lugers. Prosper pushed the door open and stood, framed in the doorway; a violent scuffle ensued before Prosper was overpowered and led bleeding away.

15

Radio Games

DESPITE THE unfolding drama in room 52, the SOE signals room, Buckmaster remained stubbornly optimistic. There was another section meeting on 10 August: 'Fairly good results,' he reported two days later.

On Monday, 23 August, Buckmaster met 'Witherington' to talk about her training, and agent George Hiller, who was waiting to go to the Lot in south-west France. Extraordinarily, there was no mention in Buckmaster's diary of the arrests of Prosper and Gilbert Norman in late June; probably because he could not allow himself to believe that the urgent 'flash' messages coming over the teleprinter were true.

The first report of Prosper's arrest had come over Norman's radio on 25 June. Buckmaster's response to the operator's message of 27 June, which was transmitted under duress – Norman purposely used his 'bluff' security check and omitted his 'true' check – was a severe reprimand: Buckmaster accused Norman of 'a serious breach of security which must not, repeat must not, happen again.'

It seems incredible that the head of F Section was not prepared for this eventuality. To omit the true check was code for: 'I am in German hands.' Norman, tapping out a message in Morse dictated by the German standing over him in his cell was warning Buckmaster, in the only way that he knew how, that he was under arrest. As he slowly tapped the keys, he prayed that Buckmaster would understand. Instead, he was ticked off like a naughty schoolboy.

The first hint of any action taken by Buckmaster was his diary entry of 22 July: 'To Tangmere [airfield] with Nick and Aggie [Jack

Agazarian].' He was bidding farewell to his deputy, Major Nick Bodington, who had volunteered to go to Paris with Agazarian to discover the truth about Prosper. Among all the sketchy entries in Maurice's diary, noteworthy for what it omitted as much as for what it revealed, is one telling entry on 1st August: 'Bad news re Nick.'

Shaken by Bodington's confirmation that Prosper and Norman were 'gonners', Buckmaster was forced to confront the truth that Norman's radio was being 'played back' by the Germans. There was a further tragedy, too: Bodington had returned alone after sending twenty-four-year-old Aggie to a letterbox where he, too, was arrested by the SD, the Nazi party security service. All five men – Prosper, Norman, Aggie and the two Canadians – were now in the hands of the Gestapo at 84 Avenue Foch. It was later reported that Prosper was tortured for seventy-two hours, chained to the concrete floor, his arm broken.

'The entire Prosper organisation is destroyed,' reported Bodington. 'Prosper should be considered dead.'

Buckmaster ordered some of his agents home, but decided to leave Noor in Paris. She was the only wireless operator working in the capital and was too valuable to bring back.

In the face of the evidence, it seemed that Buckmaster remained strangely in denial. Plaintively he asked Marks, the SOE codemaster, if he thought Norman had been caught, and continued sending Norman messages in the hope of prolonging his life: since every radio operator had a distinct 'fist' (his own particular touch, or style, on the keyboard) on his wireless transmitter – not easily copied by a German radio operator – Buckmaster thought that this would persuade the Gestapo to spare Norman, as they would need to keep him alive to send back 'their' messages in the right 'fist'.

Buckmaster did the same for John Macalister, the Canadian 'piano' to Frank Pickersgill. Pickersgill had a girlfriend in London, Kay Moore, who took the same bus to Baker Street as Maurice Buckmaster. One day, near Christmas 1943, he asked Kay if she would like him to send a message to her boyfriend. 'Yes,' replied Kay. 'Tell him the samovar at number 43 is still bubbling.'

Kay met Buckmaster again on the bus in the new year and asked him if he had an answer to her message.

'Yes. The reply was: "Received."'

Kay gasped. 'What's wrong?' she demanded.

'Nothing,' replied Buckmaster. He continued to deny that there was a problem, but Kay knew her boyfriend was in enemy hands and that a German was operating his radio: Frank would never have sent her such a formal reply.

On 29 June 1943, Dr Josef Goetz, the German radio-mastermind at Avenue Foch, returned from paternity leave to find his cells full of SOE agents. He had not planned their capture, but the gratifying Gestapo haul now had him rubbing his hands. It was time for the *funkspiel*, the German radio game with Baker Street, to commence.

Goetz had an inestimable advantage. When Bodington returned from Paris in late July, he brought crushing news. The bombshell he dropped was that Henri Déricourt, the SOE air movements officer, was a German spy, a double agent who had been working for the Germans for months.

Déricourt had told Bodington that he was in great danger, but would not be arrested while they were together or in lodgings he found for him. It could only mean that Déricourt was a Gestapo agent. It was not necessary to say any more. Bodington could work it out.

The man who Buckmaster had implicitly trusted to organise the infiltration of his 'Boys' into France was, in fact, an agent of *Obersturmbannführer* Karl Boemelburg, head of the SD at 84 Avenue Foch. As agent BOE (Boemelburg) 48, the pilot lived around the corner from Avenue Foch at 58 rue Pergolèse, and was on cordial terms with his controller, Karl, who frequently entertained him at the Gestapo chateau at Neuilly. While arranging Lysander and Hudson aeroplane receptions for Buckmaster at fields all over northern France, Déricourt had shared his flight plans with Boemelburg and his deputy, Kieffer. He had also copied the agents' mail, which was ferried back and forth to Britain by the pilots. 'I hate treason but I love traitors,' was one of Boemelburg's favourite sayings, and in Henri Déricourt, he had found a traitor *par excellence*.

It was a further catastrophe for Buckmaster, coming on top of Prosper's arrest. With Déricourt's help, Dr Goetz had built up an extensive picture of F Section, its staff, its structure and its agents, information he had put to good use as he began his skilful interrogation of Prosper and Norman.

Prosper held out for the first forty-eight hours according to the SOE rule, but Norman cracked. It was hard to believe that he would do so. Antelme, who had returned safely to London, told Penelope Torr, F Section's records officer, that Norman 'would have shot himself rather than talk or transmit under duress.' Against this remark, Buckmaster pencilled: 'Agree.' But, by 7 August, Antelme's study of the texts coming from Norman's radio convinced him that they had betrayed enemy control, and 'F' ceased to believe them. As a result, Goetz gained only a limited advantage from Norman's set, although Macalister's set, captured with all its codes at Dhuizon, proved a different matter: Goetz's wireless game through this set was so successful that for ten more months, 'F' continued to drop arms to the bogus circuit, 'Archdeacon', where an SS squad leader, Joseph Placke, was successfully impersonating Pickersgill.

Gilbert Norman would become an easy target for 'turning' after exploding with anger on reading Buckmaster's ticking-off to his signal that omitted the proper checks. London had broken its own security rules, to which Norman had always adhered; he was also undermined by the inexplicably wide knowledge of SOE that his interrogators appeared to have. But he had a third, more compelling reason to cooperate: the Gestapo were holding his 'untameable' lover, Andrée Borrel, and they threatened to harm her if he did not talk.

Norman became the key to Prosper's secrets. Present during Prosper's interrogation by Goetz's chief interrogator, *Sturmbannführer* Hans Josef Kieffer, Norman prompted the German's questions, filled in the gaps. It was an incredibly demoralising experience for Prosper to be betrayed by his trusted 'radio' and, weakened by torture, he may have been tempted to succumb to the Gestapo's offer of a deal by which his life and Norman's, and the lives of their French subagents, would be spared, in exchange for their names and addresses and the whereabouts of the circuit's arms dumps. There was, however, no reliable evidence that Prosper ever agreed to such a pact.

Placke testified in 1946 – when he was trying to save his own skin – that after forty-eight hours of interrogation, Prosper gave the address of George Darling, with whom arms were stored at Trie-Château, near Gisors. According to the SS leader, who was one of the party who arrested Darling:

> [Prosper] wrote Darling a letter, telling him to 'give the arms to the bearer'. [Darling, on seeing] Prosper's handwriting, led the way on his motorcycle, to the cache in the woods, and helped load them onto a lorry. Then he was told to put his hands up . . .

Darling died in a hail of bullets, and the legend of Prosper's perfidy began.

Déricourt's biographer, Jean Overton Fuller, who was also his lover, claimed that Prosper 'concluded the pact with Kieffer' only about twenty-four hours after his arrest: an unlikely event given that this would have broken the most fundamental rule of SOE to remain silent for forty-eight hours, and that Goetz, Kieffer's superior, was away until 29 June. The writer, Armel Guerne, one of Prosper's lieutenants, claimed that Prosper signed the pact in fury because he believed himself betrayed by the faceless men above him, specifically Claude Dansey, deputy head of the SIS, for whom Déricourt allegedly also worked. It was 'Uncle Claude' who gave Prosper to the enemy, said the writer. It had been a triple cross: 'The betrayal came "from London, from the top office".'

Guerne's story was that Prosper threatened London that he would bring the whole of the Resistance out, at the risk of their massacre, unless the High Command ordered an immediate invasion. 'To stop him, London gave him away to the Germans.' After Prosper's threat, said Guerne, 'the British guaranteed him the invasion would be mounted before 1 July.' It was a promise made 'in perfect bad faith', because it was known that before 1 July he would be arrested. How did London tell the Germans? asked Déricourt's biographer, Fuller. 'By Déricourt,' came the reply.

Perhaps a sixth sense told Prosper that he was being duped in the service of Operation Cockade, the game played for high stakes in which he – and, indeed, Buckmaster – were both victims. But it would not have been enough to make Prosper, 'one of the most trustworthy, brave and resilient officers' in SOE, in the words of his boss, forget all his training and trust the word of the Gestapo. It was more likely Gilbert Norman who agreed to lead his interrogators to the arms dumps.

Perhaps the most convincing proof of the radio operator's guilt was the deposition of Maurice Braun, number two in the 'Publican' circuit, who met two other agents in Fresnes prison, Worms and Fox.

'Worms sidled up to me. "We're being watched," and Fox said in a low voice: '*Gilbert nous a vendus*. Gilbert has betrayed us.'

'There's no point in hiding anything,' added Worms. '*Gilbert a tout dit et même donné le code*. Gilbert has told everything and given the code.'

It was a shame, remarked Ernst Vogt, one of the interrogators, that Gilbert Norman had such a good memory.

The legend that Dansey deliberately planted Déricourt in SOE and used him to sell the rival 'firm' down the river in the summer of 1943 has persisted; it was the subject of a BBC *Timewatch* programme in 1986, although M.R.D. Foot repudiated the allegations in the *Observer*.

Whatever the truth, it was enough for Déricourt to be a double agent for him to do incalculable harm, as his infiltration of F Section enabled him to pass priceless information to his German masters. But the ghost lived on tenterhooks, always afraid that his cover would be blown. When Nick Bodington had returned to France with Agazarian on the morning of 23 July, a bare four weeks after the first wave of Prosper arrests, Déricourt had met him. The double agent had thought Buckmaster's deputy had come to kill him.

Alone with Bodington, the ghost's eyes were pleading. '*Tu es venu pour moi, n'est-ce pas, Nic?*' he said. 'You've come to kill me, haven't you, Nick?'

'*Non*,' an as-then unsuspecting Bodington had replied, '*je ne suis pas venu pour toi*.'

The next morning, Bodington tossed a coin with Aggie, who called 'Tails' and lost. The young man kept the fatal appointment at the contaminated letterbox, and was arrested. Déricourt knew that Norman had been taken, and had tipped off Bodington, which was why he sent young Agazarian to keep the appointment in his stead. But why need anyone have kept it? Because otherwise Boemelburg would have known that Déricourt had warned Bodington, and both of them would have been arrested. There had to be one sacrificial lamb, and Déricourt had chosen Agazarian, whom he disliked.

Prosper's son, however, did not blame Déricourt for his father's arrest: 'My father was threatened by gross incompetence, not betrayal,' he says.

Prosper arrived at Sachsenhausen concentration camp on 3 September 1943. On 23 March 1945 he and another agent, Charles Grover-Williams ('Sebastian'), the ex-racing driver, were told they were to have a medical. In the white tiled room they stood in turn against a wall. The men thought their height was to be measured; instead, a slot in the wall opened, and they were shot in the back of the neck.

Even now, seventy years later, a swirling mist of doubt and uncertainty surrounds Prosper's role in 1943.

In Paris, the August of 1943 shaded into September. Noor was still at large: Déricourt the 'postman' sent her final report back to London by Lysander aeroplane. Written *en clair*, not in code, in loopy, childlike writing, it conveyed a spirit of innocent optimism. She thanked Vera Atkins for her gift of a brooch in the shape of a bird that she had given her on her departure:

> Your brooch has brought me luck . . . The news [of the invasion of Sicily] is marvellous and I hope we shall soon be celebrating . . .

> Someday, if possible, please send white mac, FANY style. It's grand working with you. Lots of love, Nora.

The Germans, however, were demanding something more from Déricourt. It was time to send another lamb to the slaughter.

16

Agent Marie

THE BEAULIEU 'Finishing School for Agents' was buried in the heart of the New Forest, on the estate of Lord Montagu around Beaulieu, Brockenhurst. Lessons were held at the 'house in the woods' where Edward VIII had met Mrs Simpson. 'Most officers dressed every night for dinner,' recalls decoy girl Noreen Riols. 'It was all terribly pukka.' At these 'Group B' schools (Group A were paramilitary training schools), any pretence that the agents were there for commando training was dropped and they were, for the first time, told the true nature of their mission.

Behind the cloak was the dagger: under the watchful eye of Colonel Frank Spooner, a former Indian Army officer, assisted by Scotland Yard detectives, trainees were taught silent killing by two former Shanghai policemen, Sykes and Fairbarn, who told their pupils that 'a knife should be used as delicately as an artist uses his paint brush.' SOE had many varieties of knives: there was the dagger issued to British parachutists, which the French called a *cran d'arret*, a knife with a blade that fixed with a catch when it was opened. 'The blade was two-sided at the point, and it was altogether a beautiful and practical knife,' said George Millar, organiser of the 'Chancellor' circuit, who became very attached to his: 'I could not bear to part with it.' Then there were daggers that fitted into pipe stems, or behind a lapel, and tiny, lethal knives that fitted into fountain pens or inside a shoe.

Added to these were pistols that fitted snugly into shoulder holsters, and powerful revolvers, as well as PIATs (projector infantry anti-tank weapons) and bazookas, and lessons in railway sabotage and the wrecking of factories. Students were roused in the middle of the night by staff dressed in mock SS uniforms, who shook them awake, shone bright lights in their faces, shouted '*Raus, du schweinhund!*' and subjected them to mock interrogations. Some students, like Pearl, took this training seriously and later testified that it saved their lives; others told the pseudo-Gestapo to go away, and paid the price.

It was time to prepare the trainees for clandestine life. Pearl was sent on the 'standard Organiser's 96-hour scheme' with an alias, 'Pearl Wimsey', and a cover story that she was on sick leave from the Air Ministry and was spending a holiday in Birmingham. Nervously, she caught the train on Monday morning, 8 August 1943, and found lodgings at 10 Wheeleys Road, Edgbaston, before telephoning her contact, a man named George Bluck. She then made the first of several 'mysterious' calls to Bluck's printing works.

Pearl's time in espionage did not have an auspicious start: 'Wimsey's approach to Bluck was extraordinary to a degree, and she could hardly have excited more suspicion by her methods,' read the disapproving report on her efforts. 'The telephone operator said Bluck's co-director was all agog to know who his girlfriend was.' Wimsey was 'completely put off by being asked on the telephone whether she was Miss Wimsey,' apparently stuttering out a cock-and-bull story that she needed a book printed, and was too 'nervous' to meet Bluck at his works unless he came down the steps to find her.

Despite Pearl's strong personality, she was shy and often had to force herself to enter a crowded restaurant or meet a group of strangers. Unsophisticated, bound to Henri since her teenage years, she was unused to meeting strange men. Her next task was therefore even more of an ordeal: she was to be tested by an agent provocateur to see if she could keep a secret.

The most famous temptress at Beaulieu was a woman named Fifi, whose task it often was to go to bed with trainee agents to see if their pillow talk gave them away. That evening, she and a Major Dykes were to meet Pearl at the Grand Hotel in Brighton at 6.30 p.m.

Noreen Riols, another Beaulieu decoy girl, who shared a room with Fifi (although not her bedroom duties), recalled her role in testing a trainee's discretion. On the night of the rendezvous, the conducting officer would say to the agent: 'This is our last night. We'll celebrate. Let's go out to dinner!' Once at the hotel, Noreen would greet the agent and ply him with drinks. A telephone call would come for the conducting officer, who would excuse himself, and leave the decoy alone with her prey.

> On the balcony of the Royal Bath Hotel in Bournemouth, on a warm night with the sea and the moonlight, he [the agent] would soon suggest that we spend the night together. That was my lead-up. Finally he talked . . . The Brits were pretty stiff, but foreigners sometimes talked. I understood – they were far from home.

Days later, as the trainee agent was being interviewed by Colonel Woolrych, the officer in charge at Beaulieu, Noreen would walk into the room.

'Do you know this woman?' the colonel would enquire coldly.

Noreen remembered one agent rising in astonishment, then fury, before shouting: 'You bitch!'

For Pearl, the bait was not to be the handsome major, but Fifi, posing as a journalist. The trap was carefully set: 'I intended to ask [Wimsey] for a drink at the American Bar,' explained Major Dykes. Fifi, loitering nearby, would be invited to join them. 'Having indicated that Fifi was a person who could be of use, but having given no reason to the student that she was anything to do with the organisation, I intended leaving . . . when the student could not very well depart without appearing rude, or hurried, i.e. when she had a full glass.'

The plan, however, went awry, partly because of Pearl's habitual punctuality. She arrived promptly at 6.30 p.m at the Grand and, seeing no one of the major's description in the hotel lounge, bolted into the Ladies' retiring room. Perhaps a woman more worldly-wise might have bought herself a Dubonnet and bitter lemon and lingered at the bar, but Pearl had too many painful memories of her father's alcoholism, and did not drink. After ten minutes, she fled into the unfamiliar streets. Lost, she took refuge in a cinema, before trudging back to her digs.

'Wimsey should have been briefed to remain for one hour at the RV,' read the report on the fiasco. 'Major Dykes did not turn up with Fifi until 6.40 and consequently no meeting took place.'

The major had earlier parked his car outside Bluck's works to check on Pearl. He watched as she arrived for her four o'clock meeting with her contact; she arrived early, checked her watch, doubled back, and 'hung about in a rather forlorn manner' until Bluck drove up. Neither Bluck nor Dykes was impressed.

The next day went a little better. Pearl managed to code a letter in the Playfair cipher she had been taught, based on a square containing twenty-five letters and numbers. She also gave a reasonable account of herself to the police, who were also used in this sort of training, when they called at her digs on the pretext of an ID check. Pearl managed to avoid a few 'elementary traps': refusing to sign her name on a piece of paper she was given, and keeping up her cover that she was a shorthand-typist by taking down dictation. But the final report on her performance was damning: 'Miss Witherington does not appear to have tackled the scheme with sufficient imagination or drive. She . . . approached the work with the attitude that everything was rather too hard.' She had failed to find any letterboxes (one of the tasks she had been given), and was altogether 'too cautious'.

'End of a perfect day, I don't think!' wrote Pearl miserably in her journal as she left Birmingham.

She was given another chance. On 19 August, Pearl was sent to Portsmouth as an assistant to George Hiller, the organiser in the area. Hiller, a cool-headed future diplomat, who would be sent to the Lot to run the 'Footman' circuit, may have inspired Pearl with confidence. Certainly, she was less nervous as she set about recruiting new contacts. Despite 'mumbling' the password, Pearl made contact successfully with a Mr Glover in the lounge of an hotel: she pretended to wait for a friend but, said her report: 'Mr Glover thinks it would have been less conspicuous had she bought herself a drink at the bar . . . Miss Witherington seemed concerned about restrictions in the prohibited areas.'

The next day, however, Pearl finally plucked up enough courage to approach the bar:

> On the pretext of purchasing a bottle of Dubonnet, Miss Witherington again entered into conversation with her contact. She proceeded to recruit him as an agent capable of giving information about local troop movements . . . Evidently she has benefited by the lessons she learned.

But, even so, at the end of the fifth week's finishing training, Pearl's final report was lukewarm: 'She is of average intelligence and fairly practical, but rather slow in picking up new ideas,' writes the Group B commandant on 26 August. 'She is inclined to imagine difficulties which do not exist and to see the gloomy side of things . . . Lacks initiative and drive . . . Loyal and reliable but has not the personality to act as a leader, nor is she temperamentally suited to work alone.'

Buckmaster ignored this lack of enthusiasm for his protégée, which contradicted other reports of her leadership skills. His instincts were sometimes surer than those of the instructors (Francis Cammaerts was another great agent whose poor reports were also overruled), and Pearl was finally given her cover story. She was to be 'Geneviève Touzalin, secretary in a French match company, born 24 June 1913, address 34 rue Vignon, Paris, privately educated, place of work – Cours Vendôme until May 1940, when she moved to Cannes and then Marseilles. 27 March 1943 moved back to Paris and now resides at 1 Avenue du Parc Monceau.'

Pearl repeated her story until she was word perfect. One of the most touching pieces of evidence in her personal file is the sheet of paper on which she has practised her new signature, 'Geneviève Touzalin,' fifteen or sixteen times. An early attempt is crossed out, but as she continues, her firm, upright hand – an emphatic 'T' and vigorous, curling 'z' – grows bolder and more confident. It is the hand of a woman with more potential than her instructors realise.

Three days later, Pearl moved to Ringway, Manchester, for parachute training with Miss Watson, her conducting officer, who shared her training. 'Both these students were reasonably fit on arrival and did as well as could be expected in the PT,' wrote the commandant, Major Edwards. They were 'in good spirits and seemed very happy. [Miss Watson] was the less frightened of the two.'

Pearl was not the only student to be terrified of jumping. The balloon drop, whereby the student dropped from a balloon tethered by a hawser to the ground, gave a sensation of height that paralysed Captain Oliver Brown, a trainee who went up with a friend: 'I just sat there on the edge and I said, "Well, for Christ's sake kick me up the arse, Charles, or you'll never get me out.'

Pearl and Miss Watson made three jumps. They trained with the men, and were made to jump first in order to shame the men into not showing their own terror: 'What was really rather clever of [the instructors] was that there were several girls on the course who were going to be parachuted into France, and they always made a girl go out first,' recalls another trainee. Despite her fear, 'Miss Witherington profited by being able to talk quite frankly about her feelings, and took the shock extremely well,' noted the commandant. 'She is much stronger than she looks.'

But Pearl, despite the success of her final, night jump on 2 September, was not impressed. The men were allowed four practice jumps and, after their drop into France, which counted as their fifth, qualified for their parachute wings. The women did not qualify; it was a case of blatant sexism she never forgot.

The September moon was drawing closer. Buckmaster's diary recorded a visit from Pearl on 9 September: 'Pearl and Antelme came in.' As usual, Buckmaster took Pearl and France Antelme to dinner in a King's Road restaurant. Her final days were passing in a blur.

On 10 September, however, the day after her meeting with Buckmaster, the postal censorship service intercepted a letter that it passed to 'F' with a warning note about 'Miss Pearl Witherington who has recently been taken on by the Organisation.' According to the intercept, Pearl had returned to Paris after leaving Marseilles and had a contact, a Miss Lynham, who was working for the enemy in the German GHQ at Maison Lafites.

Agent Marie could not be allowed to return to France without thorough investigation.

It is almost more than Pearl can bear. After weeks of training she is prepared for France; physically fit, word perfect on her cover story, raring to go. She has dared to allow her thoughts to turn to Henri waiting for her somewhere in France, to imagine their reunion. She hopes fervently that Maurice Southgate (Hector) now running the 'Stationer' circuit in the Auvergne, has got in touch with her fiancé as she has begged him to do: but there has, of course, been no word from the field to let her know if he has been able to do so. Radio operators have more important messages to send than news of ill-starred lovers chasing each other across war-torn Europe. The diplomatic bag is no longer bringing her Henri's letters, but she knows he has not, could not, forget her.

Called in for questioning about the intercepted letter, Pearl gives a robust defence: the statements about her are untrue; she did not return to Paris after leaving Marseilles, and last saw her acquaintance, Miss Lynham, in December 1940. Impressed by her appearance and demeanour, her interrogators consider her answers and decide to brush aside the censor's concerns.

At the bottom of the page, Buckmaster adds his own handwritten comment. 'I know PW well . . . [she] is capable and brave. I agree there is little risk and she can go.'

As his major circuit in France disintegrates, Buckmaster needs to replace his lost 'boys', the ones taken by the Gestapo. He must infiltrate urgent replacements. Among the first agents to go will be the woman he knows well: Pearl, a.k.a Agent Marie.

She has no idea of the danger of being run by the colonel.

Pearl's next action indicates her anxious frame of mind in these final days. In her lunch hour, she catches a bus to Oxford Street with a friend from the Air Ministry who has been trying for some time to persuade her to visit a clairvoyant. Pearl is curious: in Paris, her friend the writer (and secret agent), Armel Guerne, had often talked to her about seeing into the future. Walking along the busy street, she sees the sign and enters the dark booth at the back of the shop.

'How much?'

'Two shillings and sixpence.'

Pearl sits down. The woman is staring into a crystal ball. She regards Pearl carefully and tells her that she will give her *la boule vierge*, the virgin's ball. The clairvoyant has divined correctly, for, despite her long engagement to Henri, Pearl lives at a time when 'nice girls don't', and she has met no one during her two years in England to make her change her mind.

The clairvoyant asks Pearl to hold the ball for several minutes; then, without touching it, wraps it in a mauve handkerchief. She turns the ball inside the cloth, and tells Pearl her past life. To Pearl's surprise, her reading is accurate, to the tiniest detail.

Suddenly the clairvoyant says: 'You want to change your work, so what is it you want? What are you going to do?'

'I want a great change, that's all I can tell you.'

'Give me your hand.'

Laughing, Pearl proffers her palm, and the woman says: 'You'll come out of this very well.'

'What about Henri?' asks Pearl. 'Can you tell me about my fiancé?'

'Henri . . .' The woman doesn't answer. 'After the war,' she announces, 'you'll go to the United States.'

On 13 September, Pearl at last receives her mission briefing for Operation Wrestler. She is to work as a courier for an organiser. The message is signed 'Hector'. Buckmaster has kept his word: Pearl's orders are to work with Maurice Southgate, her old friend.

Two days later, on 15 August, the day on which Agent Marie is told she will parachute into France, an addendum is added to her briefing. Her role in the field is to be 'Organiser', her territory, Clermont-Ferrand. From the beginning, Marie is to be given responsibilities far beyond those of an ordinary courier.

Happily, Pearl is able to make arrangements for her mother: in a letter dated 16 September, perhaps written at Hazells Hall, Pearl wrote to Vera Atkins confirming their arrangement that Mrs G. F. Witherington would receive £9 a month, deducted from Pearl's annual wage of £350 per annum. 'Dear Miss Atkins,' wrote the dutiful daughter, listing her mother's and sisters' birthdays, 'I also ask you to kindly send my mother extra sums for birthdays and Xmas . . . I hope I am not causing you too much trouble and would like to say how grateful I am to you for your kind help.'

At Orchard Court, Buckmaster bids Pearl luck. Neither he nor Vera is free to act as her conducting officer for the night of her jump, so Nancy will go instead.

Agent Marie dislikes protracted farewells. Jumping into the American station wagon standing at the kerbside, she tells her FANY driver to hurry. The girl opens the throttle and together they roar up the Great North Road towards Tempsford.

17

Henri

THE WIND was stronger than she had expected, and Pearl snatched a quick upward glance at the dark, receding shape of the aircraft that had abruptly decanted her into the night sky. 'I sighed with relief that I'd got out without breaking my nose on the other side of the exit hole – as sometimes happened to parachutists.' The cream canopy of her parachute swung violently from side to side, carrying her far away from the lights of the torches below. Within seconds, the ground rushed up to meet her and she landed with a thump in a clump of bushes.

Pearl's parachute wrapped itself around her, a billowing balloon of silk with a mind of its own. Turning away from the wind, she punched hard at the release button of the harness until finally the chute lay in limp folds at her feet, and she was able to tear off her overalls. 'I was dying to spend a penny,' she told Nancy Fraser-Campbell, later. 'It was all I could think about. I wasn't frightened at all; I just wanted to go behind a bush.'

Rising to look about her, Pearl took a few uncertain steps forwards, and then stopped. Water: only the sheen on the surface had alerted her. There was a lake ahead and several electricity pylons, whose humming wires she had missed by a hair's breadth. A thin ground-mist swirled about her. The silence was broken only by the lowing and the heavy shifting of limbs of the white Charolais cattle on the other side of a hedge, telling her that she was not alone.

Then, out of the mist came a high-pitched whistle. Pearl listened. The whistle came again, on two descending notes.

'Henri?' she called softly. 'Henri! Is that you?' He had come to meet her, as she had hoped! She ran towards the tall figure of her fiancé looming out of the dark.

'Pearl?' came the loud whisper. '*C'est toi?*'

Pearl stopped in her tracks. She would know that voice anywhere: it was not Henri after all, but Maurice Southgate – Hector – her new *chef de réseau*. Her first pang of disappointment at not finding Henri running towards her was swept away in an overwhelming wave of relief: oblivious to danger, she felt like shouting for joy. She was alive; she was standing on the soil of France, and her long fight to return was over. How extraordinary to see her old friend emerging from the mist like a friendly phantom. It would never do to throw herself weeping into the arms of Hector, an officer unlikely to appreciate feminine displays of emotion but, as he hurried towards her and kissed her warmly on both cheeks, she hugged him, feeling, for the first time in a long time, a man's two-day old beard against her skin.

Before she could open her mouth to ask where Henri was, the burly figure of Auguste Chantraine – Octave – the farmer who had earlier received Ben Cowburn, appeared beside her. He seized Pearl's hand and pumped it warmly.

'*Tout va bien, Mademoiselle? Tu n'es pas blessé?* You're not hurt?'

Pearl shook her head. She had been luckier than other agents who had wrenched their ankles on landing, broken limbs or backs. Luckier by far than those agents who, even as Marie rolled onto the soil of the Indre in the Southern Loire, and sprang smartly to her feet, were being dropped straight into the arms of the Germans.

Octave took her by the arm. '*Tu viendras chez moi à la ferme.* You're coming to stay with me on the farm.'

They were hurrying her away from the dropping zone. Maurice Southgate, organiser of the vast 'Stationer' circuit ranging from Tarbes to Châteauroux to Bergerac, had a reputation as one of F Section's luckiest agents – as well as one of its most careful. He had been an army officer before joining the RAF, and disapproved of the poor security that led some reception committees to indulge in noisy congratulations when new agents fell from the sky. '*Ça ne risque rien!* There's no risk!' was the invariable response of the excited Frenchmen who greeted the agents struggling out of their parachutes. '*Ça ne risque rien*,' they repeated when Hector remonstrated with them as they seized the silken bounty that the agent was attempting to bury according to his instructions, to bear it away to their wives and girlfriends to make blouses, petticoats and even wedding dresses.

Pearl hesitated, looking around in vain. Of Henri Cornioley there was no sign. It was 2.16 a.m., and she was tired and thirsty after long hours in the bowels of the bomber. She reached for the thermos that she had been given before take-off, and unscrewed the cap. Perhaps the tea would still be warm. But as the liquid touched her lips, she spluttered and spat onto the grass. '*Quelle horreur!*' The flask was full to the brim with rum.

'Marie!' called Southgate, careful to use her codename in front of Octave. 'Where's your luggage? How many suitcases did you have?'

'Two.'

'Did you see where they went?'

Pearl shook her head.

'Probably in the drink,' said Southgate. 'Let's go.'

'*Allons-y!*' Octave was nudging her down the lane. Reluctantly, she followed the farmer, leaving the reception committee deftly loading the contents of the containers that had been sent down with her onto carts, for the field had to be clear before dawn.

When they arrived at Octave's farm, the yard was still shrouded in darkness. Pearl could barely make out the outline of the farmhouse, the courtyard with its dung heaps and rusting machinery, and the plough horses in their stables.

'This way.' Southgate led her to a barn and pushed open the door. Inside was an enormous haystack. '*Bon!* You can sleep up there.'

Pearl stared at her chief in his dark leather jacket and cap pulled low over his head. He had smeared mud over his face, and looked very different from the last time she had seen him in the uniform of an RAF squadron leader in Whitehall.

'Where's Henri, Maurice?' she asked, breaking into English. 'Did you give him my message? Does he know I'm here? Is he all right?'

'*Sois tranquille*. Calm down.' Southgate smiled. 'We knew you were coming when we heard your *message personnel* over the BBC – "*Mimi vous dit merci pour son joli cadeau*." Mimi says thank you for the nice present. It was confirmed at 9 p.m. Now get your head down before you wake up the whole farm.'

'But what did you tell Henri?'

'I said that I had news of the fiancé who bore the name of a precious stone. Now, go to sleep.'

While Pearl tossed and turned on the haystack, Southgate spent what remained of the night methodically checking her false papers. He was concerned that her papers looked less than authentic. Next he counted the 500,000 francs she had brought for him, and the 150,000 that were for her.

Later that morning, he woke her. As Pearl climbed down the ladder of the haystack, brushing off her crumpled skirt, and slipped on the brown brogues she had been given in London, Southgate regarded her with amusement.

'Sleep well?'

'Yes, thank you.'

'You were on top of a whole stash of arms.' He laughed at her surprised face. 'There's twenty tons of explosives under that hay.'

It was a long speech for the normally taciturn organiser. 'Let's go,' he said.

'Where are we?' asked Pearl.

'Luant,' came the reply. Later, Pearl would discover that they were in fact outside Tendu, where Octave was mayor, but the hyper-vigilant Hector had decided that the fact had to be hidden from Pearl, in case she was arrested and tortured, and implicated the farmer.

Together, Pearl and Hector catch the train to Châteauroux, capital of the *département* of the Indre, eighteen kilometres away to the north-east. Pearl assumes their destination will be the Café du Cygne in rue Diderot, the letterbox she has been given in her briefing should she miss her reception committee and need to contact Hector but, instead, he leads her across the road from the station to the Hotel du Faisan, the best hotel in the town.

'Wait here.' Hector holds open the door. '*Prends un café.*'

'Aren't you coming in?'

But her leader has vanished as mysteriously as he had arrived.

Pearl enters the Hotel du Faisan cautiously. The vestibule is empty. In the salon, a young woman is polishing a table. '*Numéro dix*,' she says, without pausing in her dusting. When Pearl reaches the bedroom, she takes a deep breath before knocking. The door opens immediately and a hand pulls her sharply inside.

'Henri!'

Henri is shaking with emotion as he pulls her towards him with one hand and shuts the door with the other. 'Pearl! Oh, Pearl, is it you, is it really you?'

As he embraces her, Pearl feels his whole body tremble as if it had been he, not Pearl, who jumped the night before.

'Pearl.' Henri can barely speak as he holds her tightly to him. 'I never thought I'd see you so soon. Is it really you?' he repeats.

'Didn't Maurice tell you I was coming?'

'He said you'd started training . . . That you wanted to know I was in France before you began your training.'

'Yes, I did. You'd joined his group, he said.'

'After I'd escaped, I ran into him in Tarbes. He told me that he was working for the Resistance. That's when I decided to join him.'

Pearl buries her face in his jacket. '*Tu me manquais, Henri*. I missed you, Henri.'

'And I you. God, how I missed you, Pearl.'

And, as he kisses her, his trembling ceases. They stand for a long time with their arms around each other, not speaking.

But as he holds Pearl in his arms, in her neat tweed suit, Henri catches sight of her English brogues: '*Mon Dieu!* What have you got on your feet?' He stares at her leather walking shoes. 'You'll have to change those shoes, Pearl.'

'I know. It was all they had in London.'

'They're a dead giveaway.'

'What shall I do?'

'My sister can lend you something.'

There is barely time for breakfast together before Hector reappears. 'I've got a room at Limoges where you can spend the night, if you don't mind a few fleas,' he tells Pearl. 'Can you drive her there now, Henri?'

There was no time for Pearl and Henri to linger in Maurice's rented room to consummate their relationship after their long separation, however much they might have longed to do so. After dropping Pearl off at Limoges, Henri continued on to Paris, under orders from Hector to speak to his father urgently about Pearl's false *carte d'identité*, a poor fake. Fortunately for Pearl, Monsieur Cornioley agreed to pretend to employ her as a beauty representative; he had accepted Pearl after she worked for him in the autumn of 1940, and was prepared to take the risk. Her new papers would provide vital security but, until then, it was imperative to lie low, out of sight of the Gestapo and the feared *Miliciens*, the Vichy military police who, as Frenchmen, were far more likely to see through her disguise than the Germans.

In Limoges, Pearl fell into an exhausted sleep in Maurice's rented room. She had no nightdress, as all her clothes had been lost with her suitcases, and slept in her combinations for more than eleven hours. When she awoke, her body was covered in bites. She inspected the mattress, but there seemed no sign of an infestation until she turned the bolster over, and an army of fleas jumped out. Pink and itching, longing for a change of clothes, Pearl was taken that morning by Hector to the little town of Riom, north of Clermont-Ferrand in the Auvergne.

She sheltered in Riom in a safe-house in rue de l'Amiral Goubeyre, the home of Monsieur Dezandes, former principal of the local college of fine arts, who had been dismissed for refusing to follow Pétain. For three weeks Pearl washed out her underclothes every night and hung them by the fire to dry, a habit guaranteed to arouse suspicion when she temporarily went into hiding, as she awaited her new false papers, with Southgate's radio operator, Amédée Maingard ('Samuel'), who had rented a room from a milliner. When Southgate had eventually recovered Pearl's suitcases from the water, he had delivered them to Maingard and asked him to dry her clothes. But his landlady did not allow *des petites filles*, lady visitors, and Maingard, a Mauritian aristocrat with exquisite manners, had watched nervously as the new girl hung her bra over the clothes-horse in his bedroom: 'He was terrified the landlady would walk in and see my knickers hanging up to dry.'

The safe-house with the Dezandes became 'a haven of peace' for Pearl and Francis Cammaerts ('Roger'), the former conscientious objector who ran the neighbouring 'Jockey' circuit and was also taken in by the Dezandes. 'Monsieur and Madame Dezandes took a terrible risk sheltering agents,' Pearl said. Occasionally, Madame Dezandes rustled up a cold duck, but generally Pearl and Francis ate in black-market restaurants in order not to endanger the family, only taking breakfast with their hosts. The first meal of the day was a brief affair, since there was no tea, coffee or chocolate, and even less milk. Instead, their hostess would grill barley and grind it down to make ersatz coffee.

One day, Hector decided to introduce Pearl to the *agent de liaison* responsible for the Auvergne, telling the young man that he wanted him to meet a recently arrived agent. When 'Marie' kept the rendezvous in the park at Clermont-Ferrand, the agent looked shocked as she emerged from behind a tree: '*Il attendait un bonhomme, pas une bonne femme!* He was expecting a chap, not a woman.' Pearl was sure Maurice had done it on purpose.

Pearl had arrived in the deeply rural, rugged Auvergne in the autumn, and was at once seduced by the beauty of the vineyards surrounding Clermont-Ferrand, a town she had never visited before. The vine leaves were turning yellow and red in the October sunshine; in the park, scarlet canna lilies stood in rows. West of the town lay the Puy-de-Dôme, oldest and tallest of the towering volcanic mountains that dominated a region where the Gaullist leader Vercingetorix once made his last stand against Julius Caesar. Proud and independent, the people of the Auvergne spoke their own dialect of the Southern French '*langue d'oc*', lit bonfires on the dômes to celebrate the summer solstice, and were rumoured to still worship the Celtic god, Lug. Their women wore clogs and embroidered aprons, made Cantal cheeses and cooked with locally grown puy lentils. Traditions were carefully preserved, while the Virgin Mary was particularly venerated, just as the mother goddess of the old religion once had been.

Beauty was deceptive, however: it hid sharp German eyes. Cammaerts's courier, forty-two-year-old Irish yachtswoman, Cicely Lefort, had been arrested in September at Montélimar, his HQ, when she was staying in a house he had warned her not to visit. Unable to answer a German question, she was sent to Ravensbrück. She had only lasted three months.

Both Cammaerts and Southgate made security a priority, asking their agents to work out a good reason for their actions, in case of snap controls or surprise arrests. During her training, Pearl had been shown how to roll up a secret message and insert it inside a cigarette: some agents amused themselves smoking their counterfeit cigarettes in front of the Germans, although Pearl was not so rash. Southgate did his utmost to prepare her for *la clandestinité*. She was told to write nothing down – 'Never, never, did I carry a written message' – to memorise every message: 'I was just one of the very, very, very lucky ones, but then I was also very careful what I did.'

'When I arrived in France, I got a hat with a fairly big brim so that if I didn't want anybody to see who I was, I could put my head down and they wouldn't see me.'

Confirmatory news came that Monsieur Cornioley had put Pearl on the books of one of his subsidiary cosmetics firms, Isabelle Lancray. Monsieur Cornioley showed his faith in Pearl by giving her a letter on his headed business writing paper, as well as other documents confirming that she was one of his beauty reps. She knew that they would get her through the Gestapo's 'first questioning', although if this didn't satisfy them, 'then you had to go through the mill.'

Jacques Hirsch, son of a Jewish *résistant* family who owned a confectioners in Paris, but who were in hiding near Brive, escorted Pearl to the *mairie* of Montaut-les-Créneaux in the Gers, and helped her obtain an authentic identity card in the name of Marie Jeanne Marthe Vergès, travelling rep. With her case of beauty samples, and in her best chestnut brown suit, Pearl was ready to start work as Hector's second courier, in addition to his existing courier, feisty Jacqueline Nearne, who was refusing to go home to England.

Pearl's briefing of 13 August 1943 ordered her to get in touch with an important French Resistance leader:

> Through Hector you are to make contact with a French Colonel, who acted under Isidore and who has been described to us having under his command a considerable number of men in the '*maquis*' [resistance groups, named after the Corsican scrub which provided cover for the partisans]. You are to explain our requirements to him and if satisfied with his reaction to these requirements, to arrange for the receipt by him of the materials and finances of which he stands in need.

'Isidore' was the codename of another radio operator, George Donovan Jones, who had been parachuted into the Auvergne the previous year. On 24 September 1942, a three-man team – organiser Charles Hudson, Irishman Brian Rafferty, and 'pianist' Jones – had come to start 'Headmaster', a new circuit based at Clermont-Ferrand. Hudson was caught, and Rafferty had taken over direction of the circuit. Then Jones had been badly injured in a bicycle accident, losing the sight of one eye, but he nevertheless had continued to transmit from his hospital bed, with the connivance of the doctors and nurses. By 25 January 1943, he had been well enough to receive Southgate and twenty-four-year-old Jacqueline.

Southgate's original tasks had been to take over from Ben Cowburn the Châteauroux circuit, which was based on Chantraine's contacts with the French Communists. He was also to build on possibilities offered by an old friend of Cowburn's, Charles Rechemann, near Tarbes and Pau in the foothills of the Pyrénées. Hector was in touch with Rafferty's network in the Auvergne, and Jacqueline spent many hours on trains bearing messages from

'Stationer' to the neighbouring circuit in the elongated area bounded by Paris, Clermont-Ferrand and Toulouse.

In the early summer of 1943, however, the loquacious Rafferty had given the game away: he was heard saying, as he left a Clermont-Ferrand café: 'Yes, it's a fine moonlight night, we shall have great fun.' He had been followed and caught on his way to a parachute drop.

Jones was also arrested, and tortured by the SS at the notorious prison at the Château de la Malcoiffée after a *Milicien* reported his arrest to the Vichy Gestapo chief, SS *Sturmbannführer* Geissler. Handcuffed every night to a chair, one night the fiery Welshman had smashed the chair, jumped from a third-floor window onto a flat roof below and dropped to the street. A village blacksmith had cut off his handcuffs, and put him in touch with Hector. After crossing the Pyrénées, Jones had finally reached London.

Rafferty had not been so lucky. He gave nothing and nobody away under interrogation; he was shot at Flossenbürg late in March 1945.

Eight months after his escape, Captain George Donovan Jones, MC, would be parachuted back into France. Renamed Agent 'Claude', he was ready to start a new circuit in the Sologne.

After Rafferty's arrest, Buckmaster had asked Southgate to take over the Auvergne circuit. 'Stationer' was now expanding in an area strategically significant for the Allied invasion: vital south–north rail and road communications lay through central France, essential for German troop movement.

Unlike Suttill's Paris-based network, 'Physician', which had recruited metropolitan intellectuals, 'Stationer' was a country circuit, and therein lay its strength. Prosper's circuit and its sub-circuits had never managed to rid themselves of the Parisian flavour that turned out to be their undoing, but Maurice Southgate's 'Stationer', like agent George Starr's 'Wheelwright', was different. Both networks were catholic in their choice of assistants: Southgate's varied from exceedingly tough near-gangsters to the wealthy Maingard.

Pearl's task was to take over the work of the imprisoned G. D.

Jones. If her report was positive, a new agent would be sent from London to take over the circuit. Her orders were also to recruit.

> You must make it clear to the Colonel that our need is for resolute men who will take their orders from us and nobody else, and who will attack those targets given them by us. We should contemplate financing such a group on the basis of something under 1000 francs a head per month, and that we envisage an expenditure in the neighbourhood of 750,000 a month.

She was also given her password, used to identify other agents in the field: '*Eh bien! Vous êtes allé vous promener dernièrement?* Have you been out walking recently?'

The correct reply was, '*Un peu, mais on use les semelles par le temps qui court.* A little, but the soles get worn out nowadays.'

Amédée Maingard, nicknamed Dédé, was to act as Pearl's 'radio' to communicate with the group, and they would work closely together. He was one of a number of F Section's best agents, including Claude de Baissac and his sister, Lise, to come from Mauritius. British subjects, they were bilingual in French and English, at a time when 'F' was in hot competition with the Gaullists for potential agents and most Frenchmen joined de Gaulle. 'F' was grateful to the Mauritians and Canadians who swelled their numbers. Maingard, received with Harry Rée near Tarbes in April 1943, had set up his radio post at Montauban.

Henri reappeared just as Pearl was setting out to meet the colonel she had been instructed to contact. He had brought her a pair of his sister Evelyne's boots from Paris, *des bottilons en tissu*, cloth ankle boots, in place of her conspicuous English shoes. Cork-soled, with a slight heel, they were unmistakeably French. Pearl was mightily relieved. 'They were better too,' she wrote, 'because my feet got so cold in the winter, when I was travelling by train.'

It is difficult to overstate the danger Pearl faced at this point. The tide of war was turning in the Mediterranean, but in France the Germans were increasingly ruthless now that they controlled the whole country. Heinrich Himmler, head of the SS, was crowing with delight at the arrest of Prosper. Himmler himself personally controlled the *Sicherheitsdienst*'s (SD) radio game with F Section from his headquarters in Berlin, the *Reichssicherheitshauptamt* (RSHA). He was convinced that winning the *funkspiel* against Baker Street was the key to victory in the secret war: and there was no doubt that he was winning. Himmler and his colleague, Admiral Canaris, who ran the military's security service, the *Abwehr*, were deadly rivals. Both services were popularly described as 'the Gestapo', but in fact they were distinct. During Pearl's first months in France, Himmler was discrediting Canaris, and the hated SD gained the upper hand. In the Avenue Foch, SD HQ, the screams of tortured agents fell on deaf ears.

In the field, Pearl was cut off from news, although Hector told her of the fall of Prosper. But politics contributed to her difficulties on the ground: from the start, she was thrown into the maelstrom of rivalries and personal grudges, which tore the Resistance apart.

The repercussions of the Prosper disaster had fallen most painfully on the area of France known as the Sologne. Between the Loire and the river Cher, in a triangle bounded by Orléans, Tours and Vierzon, were sited most of Prosper's dropping zones – thirteen out of thirty-seven in his 'Physician' circuit – and there the weight of German reprisals fell on his French subagents.

Encouraged by the success of the Allied landings in North Africa in late 1942, new recruits had flocked to join Prosper's lieutenant, Pierre Culioli, at his headquarters at Meung-sur-Loire, an outpost of 'Stationer'. His group of local resisters had grown in size to hundreds of young men eager to rise against the hated invader, but they were short of weapons or training. But on 21 June the Gestapo had caught Prosper's lieutenant and he was arrested in a *rafle* or round-up, after the vastly increased numbers of aircraft flying over the area because of Cockade and the rain of *parachutages* attracted German attention.

Nor had the Gestapo, of course, kept the terms of the 'pact' not to kill the agents once they had their names, and the locations of the arms dumps. The local *Feldkommandant* sent in 2,000 soldiers, who rolled up the circuit with clinical efficiency. At least 400 resisters were killed, according to Pearl, who first estimated the deaths from the collapse of 'Organisation X', as she described the Prosper network, at that number. Other estimates put the figures much higher, at 1,500.

A local priest, the Abbé Pasty, curé of Baule, had felt 'an explosion of joy' when he had first met Culioli. Now the Sologne lay bleeding. The priest tormented himself with questions:

> Why had the Germans surrounded this area of the Sologne? Who informed them?
>
> How, in one fell swoop, was nearly the whole 'Prosper' network betrayed so precisely to the Germans? Who gave them the address of 'Prosper', arrested two days after Gilbert (Norman), and so many others?

The abbé blamed the 'War Office', a term used by many Frenchmen to distinguish F Section agents, commanded directly by the British, from the Free French agents run by Colonel Passy's BCRA (*Bureau Central de Renseignements et d'Action*). The abbé was nearer the mark than he realised in blaming faceless men in Whitehall.

British strategy had run into profound difficulties in France by the autumn of 1943. When it became clear that the expected invasion would not, after all, take place in September, the secret armies SOE had been carefully building up had to be pacified. It was a difficult task. Resistance morale was at an all-time low. Operation Cockade Starkey had been badly bungled. Although no deliberate sacrifice of agents had been intended, the outcome was nonetheless tragic. Returning from London in May 1943 under orders, so he believed, to put his circuit on the alert, Prosper had – against all his instincts – compromised security in his bid to prepare for the 'imminent invasion'. The deception scheme resulted in a deliberate increase in RAF sorties to his dropping zones and put the wind up the Germans, as intended. They had swooped on the Resistance, who became Cockade's sacrificial lamb.

Lieutenant Colonel Bevan, the deception controller at the

London Controlling Section for Deception, later confessed that he was 'deeply unhappy' at the unintended consequences for the Resistance: Prosper and the other penetrated circuits had been delivered to the Germans, who had been allowed to make spectacular gains. Buckmaster would later conclude that, 'Prosper did as he was told – and got captured and killed. He gave his life, as ordered.'

And from the French point of view, Perfidious Albion was once again in the dock.

SOE, in the person of Sir Charles Hambro – CD before Gubbins – argued that the only way to counter the deterioration in Resistance morale was to provide 'a steady flow of greatly increased deliveries of arms'. But chief of the air staff, Sir Charles Portal of Bomber Command, refused to offer more than twenty-two bombers to do this.

The Free French had also been dealt a mortal blow. In June 1943, a telegram had arrived for General de Gaulle and Colonel Passy in Algiers, announcing that Jean Moulin, codename 'Rex', former *préfet* of the Eure-et-Loir *département* and first president of the *Conseil National de la Résistance* (CNR) – the only man able to unite the warring factions of the Free French – had been arrested at Caluire, a suburb of Lyons, on 21 June, three days before Prosper had been taken.

De Gaulle had ordered his aide-de-camp in France, Captain Serreules, to help 'Rex' escape, without success, and only Moulin's heroism in the face of torture prevented a total collapse of the French underground.

Early in July, an inmate of Montluc prison, Christian Pineau, was summoned to shave a dying man.

> *Il avait reconnu Rex bien qu'il fût couvert de plaies et de traces de coups reçus . . .*
>
> He recognised Rex even though he was covered in wounds and bore traces of recent blows. [Rex] recognised him, but he was too weak to speak to him.

Almost unidentifiable after his treatment at the hands of Gestapo chief, Klaus Barbie, Rex died alone, somewhere in France or Germany on an unknown date.

Days later, de Gaulle's aide-de-camp Serreules was caught with a list of 400 members of the French underground. It was proof to Winston Churchill of the danger of Gaullist over-centralisation, and led to the destruction of the organisation.

BCRA had to start all over again.

Churchill's irritation with de Gaulle had risen to fever pitch in 1943: he even proposed that the War Cabinet consider a break with the French leader. They refused, telling the prime minister that the withdrawal of the Free or 'Fighting' French would mean the loss of 50,000 men from the Resistance. Churchill remained obdurate, however, telling the controller of SOE, Lord Selborne: 'We must be careful that the direction of the French resistance movement does not fall into the control of de Gaulle and his satellites here.'

The Resistance had gained ground as the Germans imposed forced labour in German factories on young Frenchmen, and thousands of *refractaires*, fugitives from labour conscription, had taken to the woods and the hills. British subsidies to the Resistance had increased in June 1943 to the sum of 80 million francs to take into account these swelling numbers.

Churchill, persuaded by his aide, Desmond Morton, that de Gaulle was simply advancing his own political interests, finally ordered Selborne to withdraw subsidies from the general:

> Let me have your proposals for carrying on the underground work without admitting de Gaulle or his agents to any effective share in it, and without letting any sums of money get into their hands.

Foreign Secretary Anthony Eden and Selborne were horrified. De Gaulle's leadership was 'solid', said Selborne, and the fledgling *Armée Secrète*, Secret Army (all parties of resistance in France would eventually come under the banner of the FFI), would disintegrate if he were removed. Nor could Britain abandon the young French *refractaires*, who were supported with ration cards through the French Committee in London. 'They have gone hunting a very big tiger with us,' Selborne told Winston in colonial language designed to appeal to him, 'and we cannot leave them in the lurch.'

Eventually, the prime minister agreed to continue the subsidies: news of the June arrests of Prosper and Jean Moulin had touched him personally. On reading in the monthly SOE report that the Germans 'succeeded in capturing some important men and a very few British officers', he had circled the words 'British officers,' with a thick pencil, and scribbled in the margin: 'What happened to them?'

In September 1943, Buckmaster's orders to Pearl followed the official line: damp down guerrilla activity in France. 'Don't touch Gaullist networks, or meddle with SIS.' But Agent Marie was soon to discover that 'there was an abyss between London and what we had to do here, and they couldn't possibly imagine what was going on . . . They had a general overview, but all the details . . . It's sometimes the details that count.'

The Germans had watched the 'bandits', as they termed the *maquisards*, degrade the German war machine over the last year: 1943 had been 'a serious turning point in the interior situation in France'. Not only were murders of members of the *Wehrmacht*, and acts of sabotage against *Wehrmacht* installations, railways, and supply lines on the increase, but in certain districts 'organised raids of gangs in uniform and civilian clothes on transports and military units multiplied.' By December, it had become 'impossible to dispatch single members of the *Wehrmacht*, ambulances, couriers or supply columns without armed protection to the 1st or 19th Army in the South of France.'

When she met Colonel Villiers, chief of the Gaullist 'Gaspard' *maquis*, Pearl was to realise quite what a misunderstanding had arisen between Baker Street, Rafferty and Jones. 'Well, this is very funny,' Pearl had said to herself, as she listened to Villiers talk politics. 'It was a Buckmaster circuit, because Rafferty had been in contact with these people before he had been caught.'

She had leant forward and asked: 'But you're a Gaullist organisation?'

Villiers had laughed proudly. 'Yes. I have 22,000 men . . . our *maquis* covers four or five *departéments*.'

'*Oui, c'est bien gentil, mais vous voulez quoi?* That's all very well, but what do you want from me?' asked Pearl.

'*Eh bien, des armes*.'

Pearl had to refuse the colonel his arms: her orders were not to meddle in politics. She was only there to help the resisters, and she had been ordered not to work with the Gaullists for security reasons. All the same, Pearl managed to lay the foundations for future cooperation.

Baker Street recognised that her mission had not been an easy one: 'The colonel was a touchy, difficult and elusive man, but by her tact and perseverance Witherington succeeded in effecting a very satisfactory liaison with him.'

Pearl had another reason for refusing to supply the Gaullists. She distrusted the circuit because of its size, just as her instincts told her that Hector's own network, 'Stationer', was dangerously large: 'In my opinion, it was much too big.' The smaller and more concentrated a network was, the better.

As Pearl struggled to bridge the abyss between London's view and the situation in the field, she learnt to rely on her wits, just as she had done as a child; particularly when, within three weeks of her arrival, Hector was recalled to London. He would stay away for three months.

So far Pearl had no permanent accommodation; she had failed to find a lodging in Châteauroux, the largest town in the area, as staying with the Dezandes permanently would not have been secure – 'safe-houses' were for short-term stays, and difficult to find. Suspicious landladies slammed the door on her; the woman who served her in the *boulangerie* might be sleeping with the enemy, tempted by Gestapo money to inform on her for the majority of people still supported Pétain and believed that the German 'New Order' was there to stay. Pearl was running out of options. The only solution for her as a courier seemed to be to sleep on the railway trains as she carried messages between the far-flung outposts of Southgate's empire.

Just before he left, her chief gave her a tip: to travel at night when there were fewer people around, and to buy a first-class, annual season ticket, as it would allow her to avoid long queues and dangerous questions from the *Milice* at the ticket office. It was expensive, but a price worth paying to avoid the German controls.

Pearl took Southgate's advice. She prepared for life on the trains with the utmost care, plaiting her long blonde hair 'in the Teutonic fashion', and winding her plaits around her head. She surrounded herself with pro-German magazines such as *Signal* and *Carrefour*. 'I didn't look French.' With her new ID and ration cards, a photo of Pétain in her pocket, her face scrubbed clean, her blue eyes wide and innocent, Agent Marie endeavoured to look as pro-German as possible.

18

Explosions Arranged

A TELEGRAM had arrived for Pearl at Clermont-Ferrand. Amédée Maingard passed her an ultimatum from Baker Street: 'Blow up the Michelin factory, or we'll bomb it.'

Pearl was horrified: the Michelin factory in Clermont was in the north of the town, surrounded by houses. It had been manufacturing tyres ever since the niece of Scottish chemist Charles Macintosh, who had discovered that rubber dissolves in petroleum, had married Edouard Daubrée, owner of a farm machinery business, and begun making a few rubber balls for her children. The Michelin brothers, who had taken over the business, were collaborators supplying the *Wehrmacht*: in June 1943, Rafferty had blown up 300 tons of tyres before his arrest.

SOE had been ordered to step up sabotage in 1943, after the postponement of the 'invasion' and the lifting of the SIS ban on sabotage in the Unoccupied Zone, which had followed the German occupation of the whole of France. Now, 'F' was keen to show what its saboteurs could do.

Former chef Michael Trotobas – whose *nom de guerre* was le Capitaine 'Michel' – ran the 'Farmer' circuit in Lille in north-east France, a cradle of the Resistance, where Communist *routiers*, lorry drivers, carried hidden SOE containers as armed SS guards sat beside them in the cabs of their lorries, and had already undertaken many successful derailments of trains.

In the spring of 1943, the chiefs of staff had decided that the important SNCF (the French national railway) locomotive works at Fives, an eastern suburb of Lille, should be destroyed: RAF air raids had failed to do so because of the heavy anti-aircraft defences in northern France. The chiefs had asked Brigadier Mockler-Ferryman, the director of the London group of SOE, whether his agents could blow up the loco sheds, and he had jumped at the opportunity to demonstrate that SOE action could be more accurate than bombing. Trotobas had offered to undertake a sabotage attack; Bomber Command had received the news with derision, but had reluctantly agreed to Gubbins's request for a pause in the bombing.

On 27 June, Trotobas and twenty *cheminots*, railway workers, had planted their explosives. At 2 a.m. a series of loud explosions had shaken the city, and the loco works had burst into flames. Trotobas radioed London: 'OPERATION COMPLETED.' However, when the signal was passed on to the chiefs and the Air Ministry, their response had been sceptical: 'Tell your man to send photographs of the operation area.'

Trotobas had returned to the smouldering ruins, wearing his best suit and carrying a forged pass describing him as a manager of the SNCF industrial insurance company. The SD officers had allowed him to take photos, even holding the flashlights to illuminate the twisted steel and collapsed buildings. The pictures were sent to a Normandy letterbox. On opening the package, the RAF had found a small card: 'With the compliments of the Resistance.'

Tragically, in the following November, the SD raided the safe-house where *le capitaine Michel* was hiding: his deputy, Lieutenant Reeves, codename 'Olivier', had been arrested and tortured and allegedly pointed out his organiser's hideout to the Gestapo. On entering, they had found Trotobas in bed. A shoot-out had followed in which Trotobas killed the Gestapo leader before being himself killed.

By 1943, the first American agents were joining the secret war. Chicago-born Ernest Floege, codename 'Alfred', took part in Operation Scullion to blow up the shale oil refinery near Le Creusot. Alfred had been dropped near Tours on the night of 13 June to start the 'Sacristan' circuit, a year after the Americans had first come riding into town under the leadership of Colonel William J. 'Wild Bill' Donovan, a much-decorated hero of World War I, who had visited London in the spring of 1942 and persuaded Frank

Pearl's mother, Gertrude, at the time of her marriage to Wallace Seckham Witherington in 1912

Pearl (standing) and her sisters: Suzanne, Jacqueline ('Doudou') and Hélène ('Mimi')

Pearl with her sisters and Uncle Charlie (Charles Joseph Hearn), who had come to Paris to pay her father's debts

Air Commodore Douglas Colyer, CB DFC, Pearl's employer as air attaché at the British Embassy, Paris, until June 1940

Flight Officer Pearl Witherington in WAAF uniform

Vera Atkins as WAAF squadron officer 1946

Colonel Maurice Buckmaster, head of F Section, Special Operations Executive

Sir Stewart Menzies or 'C', head of the Secret Intelligence Service and Churchill's wartime spymaster

Major General Colin Gubbins or 'CD', head of the Special Operations Executive from September 1943–June 1946

Andrée Borrel, alias 'Denise', Prosper's courier

Major Francis Suttill, alias 'Prosper'

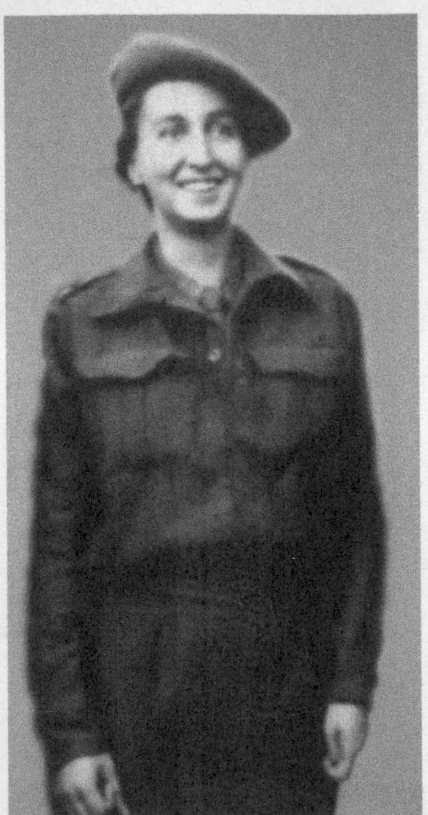

Pearl as *le lieutenant 'Pauline'*,
SOE circuit chief, the
'Wrestler' *maquis*, June 1944

1re Classe
CARTE
payable à TOULOUSE
VERGES Marie
Chautaiseau
06.7.9.10.11.15

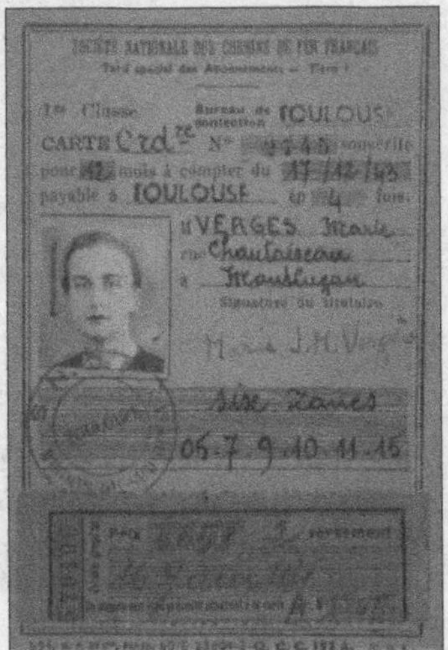

Pearl's false identity card in the name of Marie Vergès

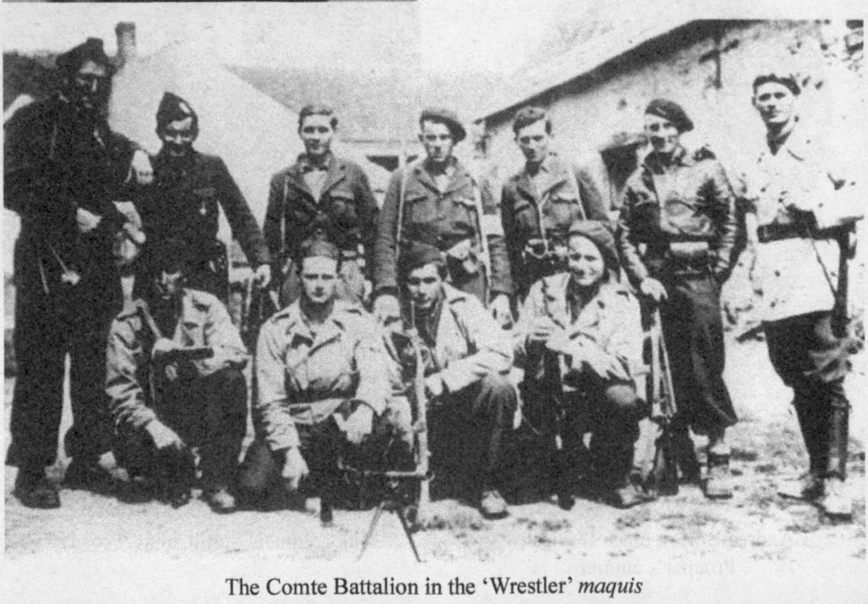

The Comte Battalion in the 'Wrestler' *maquis*

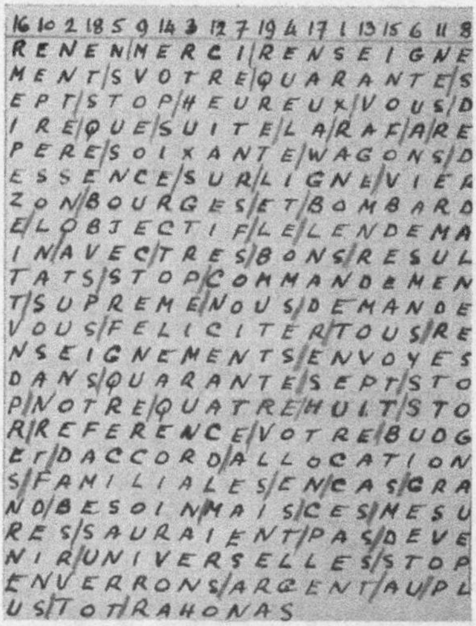

16 10 2 18 5 9 14 3 12 7 19 4 17 1 13 15 6 11 8
RENEN/MERCI/RENSEIGNE
MENT/SVOTRE/QUARANTE/S
EPT/STOP/HEUREUX/VOUS/D
IRE/QUE/SUITE/LA/RAF/A/RE
PERE/SOIXANTE/WAGONS/D
ESSENCE/SUR/LIGNE/VIER
ZON/BOURGES/ET/BOMBARD
E/LOBJECTIF/LE/LENDEMA
IN/AVEC/TRES/BONS/RESUL
TATS/STOP/COMMANDEMEN
T/SUPREME/NOUS/DEMANDE
VOUS/FELICITER/TOUS/RE
NSEIGNEMENTS/ENVOYES
DANS/QUARANTE/SEPT/STO
P/NOTRE/QUATRE/HUIT/STO
R/REFERENCE/VOTRE/BUDG
ET/DACCORD/ALLOCATION
S/FAMILIALES/EN/CAS/GRA
ND/BESOIN/MAIS/CES/MESU
RES/SAURAIENT/PAS/DEVE
NIR/UNIVERSELLES/STOP
ENVERRONS/ARGENT/AU/PL
US/TOT/RAHONAS

Code message from London to Pearl thanking her for her telegram informing Special Forces HQ of German petrol train, which the RAF bombed 'with very good results'. The petrol was intended for the 'Das Reich' division, who were attacked by Pearl's units on 16 August 1944. The message reads: 'The Supreme Commander asks us to congratulate you on all the information given in 47.'

General Heinz Lammerding with one of the 'Das Reich' Division's panzers in the background

The Trochet family farm, Loir-et-Cher, France

Jedburgh 'Julian', left to right: Lieutenant Brouillard; Major Arthur Clutton, alias 'Stafford'; and Sergeant James Menzies

Major General Botho Elster smiles as he surrenders his 19,000 troops to the Americans in September 1944

The 'Wrestler' *maquis*, Captain 'Comte', Pearl, Perdriset (in breeches), Henri (background), and Kneper

Pearl and Henri:
married at last,
October 1944

Pearl and her daughter, Claire

Henri (left) and Pearl (right), with Maurice Southgate,
his parents and his French wife in Paris, soon after the war

HM The Queen presents Pearl with her CBE, Elysée Palace, Paris 2004

Pearl with her parachute wings

F Section Memorial at Valençay on the twentieth anniversary of its inauguration, 6 May 2011

Nelson to send a large mission from Baker Street to Washington. Appointed director of the Office of Strategic Services (OSS), Donovan, a man of 'Irish charm and tireless energy', worked closely with his friends in SOE, and by September the Special Ops (SO) branch of the OSS was virtually fused, in north-western Europe, with London's SOE.

The Americans brought their own energy to a very British organisation (when SOE's Sweet-Escott stopped off at Gander Bay, the US base in Iceland, en route to Washington in July that year, he noticed that each pat of butter he was given for breakfast was stamped with the legend, 'Remember Pearl Harbor'). But energy and courage were not enough. In December 1943, Floege's thriving *réseau* outside Angers came to an abrupt end when his son and courier was arrested in a routine raid and broke under interrogation: forty-five members of the network were arrested, although Alfred himself escaped.

There were by now many more resources at SOE's fingertips than when it had first started. The Americans were with them, and even the RAF had been forced to come around to their methods. But, once again, it was to be their 'brain' rather than 'brawn' approach that brought dividends. By the summer of 1943, agent Harry Rée, who ran his own circuit, 'Stockbroker,' had discovered a new, less risky method of carrying out sabotage: blackmail.

The Peugeot motor works at Sochaux were making tank turrets for the Germans, as well as Focke-Wulf engine parts. The RAF had made several attempts at bombing it, but the factory was a small target in a populous area of town requiring precision bombing: on 14 July, a night raid had missed the factory by a kilometre and killed hundreds of townspeople. Harry called on the director, Robert Peugeot: 'We want to blow up your factory.'

'Blow up . . . are you mad?'

'I am a British officer, Monsieur Peugeot. I am not mad.'

'A British officer? Really? How can you prove this? Why should I believe such a fantastic story?'

Rée saw that Peugeot was afraid that he might be an agent provocateur trying to lure the industrialist into saying something incriminating. He offered to arrange for the BBC to repeat any message Peugeot gave him before the seven o'clock news the evening after next.

'You can arrange this?' Peugeot asked. 'Well, prove it. Have them say, "*La guerre de Troie n'aura pas lieu*. The Trojan War will not take place."'

Harry's wireless operator sent the message on his next 'sked' and Buckmaster agreed to the plan. F Section was by now using *messages personnel* extensively in order to confirm the identity of their agents to French people with whom they were in contact, and in particular to those from whom they borrowed cash on the promise of reimbursement after the war (no written receipt could be given). Instead, the contact chose a random phrase for repetition by the BBC's French service, and once he heard it repeated, 'the Frenchman was convinced, as if by magic,' said Buckmaster. 'The money was handed over without a qualm.'

Harry convinced Peugeot that, one way or another, his factory would be blown up: if the saboteurs did it, they could place their explosive where it would do the greatest harm to production and the least to the fabric of the factory; if the RAF bombed it, the damage would be incalculable. The industrialist was convinced, put Harry in touch with two of his foreman, and on 14 May 1943, explosives in the factory were detonated.

Weeks later, the Germans sent a replacement tank press by barge through the Canal du Doubs – Harry and his saboteurs attacked and blew up the barge, blocking the canal to the fury of the Germans, who used it to pass midget submarines from the Loire to the Mediterranean.

Buckmaster, encouraged by the success of Rée's blackmail of Peugeot, had decided to pass on the idea to other circuits where it might also be effective and so when, in October, a call had come through to SOE from the ministry of economic warfare suggesting the Michelin factory as a target, Vera Atkins had duly sent a message to Amédée Maingard.

Pearl at once set up a meeting with her new friend, Colonel Villiers (in reality, a Monsieur Ingrand, the commissioner for tourism in the Auvergne), and told him that she had received an ultimatum. 'What do you want to do about it?' she asked.

Pearl doubted whether his men had the experience to mount a successful sabotage attack, for when she had enquired at their first meeting how exactly the *maquisards*, his fighters, had learnt to use the arms and explosives sent from London, his reply had been: 'By trial and error.'

'*Quoi? Mais c'est pas possible!*' gasped Pearl.

She had at once offered to train the sabotage team herself. Pearl had excelled at demolition during her training, and specialised in calculating the right formulae to blow up a train, a railway bridge, or a factory without causing collateral damage. She had the knowledge; but she also knew how traditional the men of the Auvergne were. If the *maquisards* didn't want a woman, she tactfully suggested, she could send someone else, such as Amédée.

The reply came from the *maquis*: '*Ils ne veulent pas de femme.* They don't want a woman.'

Pearl soon realised that 'Gaspard', codename for Emile Coulaudon, the renowned leader of the sabotage team of the Auvergne *maquis*, was a misogynist. He would not take orders, let alone instruction, from her. '*C'était incroyable!* It's unbelievable,' muttered Pearl to herself in frustration, as her offers of training in demolition were repeatedly rebuffed – Maingard was too busy with his own work to have time to train the recalcitrant and inept would-be saboteurs. It was Pearl to whom he had given the responsibility, knowing that Baker Street trusted her and that she was a trained organiser.

Gaspard's men continued to plant their SOE supplied explosives, but although a further 40,000 tyres were destroyed, production at the factory continued unabated. Pearl reported:

> This was solely due to the lack of sabotage instruction at that time in the region. The sabotage parties were exceedingly keen . . . if they had been trained, they would certainly have done much better.

Pearl did manage to train Jacques Dufour, codename 'Anastasie' of the Limousin *maquis*. Dufour, who later worked with Violette Szabo, became a daring saboteur whose exploits elicited a Gestapo reward for his capture. But her patience was wearing thin with Gaspard, as the Michelin factory continued to churn out tyres for the Germans.

When illness prevented Pearl from keeping a rendezvous with Gaspard, she sent Henri in her stead. He stood all night on the train from Paris, where he was still working with his father, but when he alighted at the little Auvergne stop, the *maquisards* failed to recognise him – or pretended not to: the locals were so distrustful of strangers that when the tall Parisian with his metropolitan accent walked into the hamlet, the peasants muttered to themselves in their local patois, Auvergnat, and refused to serve him. They eyed him up and down, this well-dressed stranger in fashionably framed glasses, his dark hair styled the Parisian way, standing at the bar, drumming his fingers and calling for service. Henri, a chain smoker, lit up. Cigarettes were luxury indeed. Was he a collabo, perhaps? It was best to keep silent. Trust nobody. The men turned their backs and affected deafness.

'I had a devil of a job even getting a *casse-croûte*, a snack,' complained Henri.

Henri, whom Buckmaster had marked down as a 'simpleton', could sometimes behave stupidly. He had none of Pearl's chameleon-like ability to fit in with all sorts of people, to empathise and listen and ultimately win acceptance. The 'meeting' with Gaspard had to be chalked up as yet another failure: Henri gave up without exchanging a word with him, and took the train back to Paris.

Furious at this muddle and confusion, Pearl cut all contact with Gaspard, whose blundering team had by the spring of 1944 made three failed attempts at sabotaging the factory, including one that flooded it but again did no lasting damage. She was angry, too, with the Michelin brothers, who had promised to allow a targeted sabotage attack but had gone back on their word. It was time to take a tough decision.

On 11 March 1944, Pearl wrote a report to Buckmaster, which was flown back to London by Lysander:

From Marie: Michelin

1) I regret to inform you that the proposed sabotage of Michelin has completely fallen thro' in spite of repeated attacks. The management, after agreeing to the proposed destruction, refused to collaborate and still do so. Villiers's sabotage leader has been arrested: he tried to set fire to the M factory by putting thirty incendiaries in one work shop, he did not take into consideration the working of the '*dispositif de sécurité d'incendies*', (fire safety system).

2) I wish to put on record the management's attitude vis à vis the sabotage plans. They refused to believe the R.A.F. will have time to bomb Clermont-Ferrand before an Allied landing: in the meantime they are working, turning out material and making money whereas if the sabotage had taken place when proposed they would be doing none of these today. They are playing for time.

After six months in the field, Agent Marie's attitude had hardened towards French collaborators. It had been a bleak, miserable winter, trying to survive on the trains. For three months she had searched in vain for a room to rent and had barely slept on the long overnight journeys to distant parts of Hector's sprawling empire. One of her regular routes, from Toulouse to Riom, meant leaving at 7 p.m. and arriving at 11 the next morning. Cold, shivering, only allowing herself cat-naps in case she dreamt of her family and muttered a word or two of English, she became increasingly exhausted: 'I travelled mostly at night . . . in unheated trains. That wasn't funny.' If she were arrested: 'We did know that we would be tortured. That we did know.'

Added to this knowledge was the fact that other agents were still successfully being picked off. In November, a woman informer, jealous of the beautiful Noor Inayat Khan, betrayed her for 500 francs. Noor had been arrested with her wireless and codes, allowing Goetz, the Gestapo mastermind at Avenue Foch, to prolong his radio games with Baker Street. Meanwhile, Pearl's next-door circuit, Claude de Baissac's 'Scientist', west of 'Stationer', had also been infiltrated that summer when a retired French army officer, Colonel André Grandclément, was 'turned' by the Gestapo after his wife was arrested. He had led the Germans to the arms dumps. As with Prosper, mass arrests had followed.

That time, there was a reckoning. In 1944, Roger Landes, codename 'Aristide', and de Baissac's former radio operator, was sent to rebuild the ruined circuit, and tricked the traitor into believing that London was sending a plane for him and his wife.

Landes and the *maquis* led the couple into a forest. 'This way,' said the *maquisards*, pointing to a woodland path. Grandclément realised his situation, and kissed his wife goodbye. As he walked ahead, a *maquisard* shot him. Landes then put the muzzle of his .45 automatic to the back of Madame Grandclément's head and fired once. The blood spurted from her forehead and she fell to the forest floor. Landes said:

> We were discussing with the other men from the *Maquis* who is going to kill the woman, me being in charge of the group, well, it is my duty to do it. We couldn't let her go, you see, because if I had been arrested all my group would have been arrested. I was responsible for the lives of my men, I'd got to protect my men . . . I didn't sleep for a week after that because it was the first time I'd used my pistol and I had never shot anybody before.

It was a difficult choice, but the only one Landes could have made. Captured Resistance fighters were not treated like regular soldiers by the Germans and sent to prisoner of war camps. Instead, Hitler's secret 'Commando Order' of 7 October 1942 had decreed:

> In future, all terror and sabotage troops of the British and their accomplices, who do not act like soldiers but like bandits, will be treated as such by the German troops and will be ruthlessly eliminated in battle.

All sabotage parties, in uniform or out of it, armed or unarmed, 'are to be slaughtered to the last man'. Those arrested by the French police were to be handed over to the Gestapo. Landes knew what that meant: *Nacht und Nebel*, night and mist – extermination in the death camps.

The stress and fear took its toll on Pearl. There were narrow escapes. One day she was sent on a dangerous mission to transport a Eureka beacon – one half of a new radar device to help pilots locate landing grounds (the other half of the device would be fitted into the navigator's cabin and could pick up the beacon's signal from seventy miles away, overcoming the difficulty of landing agents in cloud or ground mist). The transmitter was fitted into two large, heavy suitcases, weighing nearly a hundredweight, which she could not carry alone, so she took with her Jacques Hirsch, whose brother Pierre was now Hector's second radio operator. Both knew that the contents of the suitcases were immediately incriminating.

Pearl and Jacques were to take the Eureka by train to be hidden in the chimneybreast of a farm, where it was to guide Allied pilots on their way to bomb the south of Italy.

'Jacques was in a blue funk', she wrote. 'I always admired his courage, because his fear never stopped him working.' Rejected by the army as a Jew, Jacques had become a lawyer whose phenomenal memory allowed him to memorise the entire railway timetable – to be a Jewish agent, like the Hirsches, and radio operators, Eric Rabinovitch and Gaston Cohen, required a special kind of courage.

Pearl's own heart was in her mouth as the pair lugged their suitcases past the *gendarmes*, the *Miliciens*, the knots of German soldiers at the train station. The two couriers had to look as casual and confident as possible, and not betray the weight of the suitcases by their bearing. At any moment the shout could come: 'You there, stop!'

'We always risked that,' said Pearl. '[That] someone would see us and ask us to open the case.'

On 28 January 1944, Maurice Southgate, a.k.a Hector, was dropped back into France in a non-moon period, landing on one of George Starr's grounds. Baker Street promptly began overloading him with work, just as it had done Prosper.

'Plenty to do, and how!' noted Hector. Buckmaster ordered him to organise a reception for about twenty agents during the February moon, but sent him down first to Tarbes, at the foot of the Pyrénées, to receive three new agents: 'Frank, Martial and Gaëtan'. Southgate introduced Gaëtan to his contact, Monsieur Untal, the *econome*, bursar, of the Poitiers *Lycée de Garçons*, and told him to get a new set of identity papers. For some reason, Gaëtan failed to do so; nor did he succeed in finding new landing grounds around Montluçon.

'Sent him back to Poitiers with a raspberry,' wrote the exasperated organiser. A 'very mysterious letter' subsequently arrived from Gaëtan asking Hector or Marie to meet him at Poitiers railway station with a new *mot de passe*. 'This letter arrived too late for either Marie or me to keep the appointment,' wrote Hector. 'The whole letter and story seemed phoney.' He began to suspect that Gaëtan was a double agent.

Like all the best SOE agents, Southgate lived by the motto, *Dubito, ergo sum* – I doubt, therefore I survive. But despite his suspicions, he knew he could trust Agent Marie to handle the situation: her instincts were almost as good as his. He despatched her to Poitiers.

Pearl took the train from Montluçon. Hector had told her to go directly to the bursar's office: 'Don't talk to a soul. Go past the office and straight up to the first floor.'

When Pearl reached the address and drew level with the office, the concierge leapt out from behind his desk: '*Où allez-vous, madame?*'

'*Je vais à l'économat.* I'm going to see the bursar.'

'*Foutez le camp ici, la Gestapo est là!* Fuck off, quick, the Gestapo are here!'

'But I've got to find out about Untel . . .'

'*Foutez le camp, je vous dis!*' the concierge hissed. 'Bugger off!'

Pearl turned on her heel and ran round the corner. The place was swarming with Gestapo: she had been about to walk into a mousetrap. Panting with fear, her heart thumping in her chest, she took a long, deep breath, slowed her pace to a walk and looked around. No one was watching. Putting a scarf over her head, she slipped into the nearest church and lingered an hour, before darting into another church. There was no train back to Montluçon till late that evening and so, for the only time in her life as a clandestine, Pearl acted the tourist, whiling away the afternoon in the churches of Poitiers.

'Marie returned very excited, saying that the Econome and his wife had been arrested,' recorded Hector matter-of-factly the next day.

He wasted no time before sending her on another risky mission, however. Two new agents had arrived by parachute with funds for him and he needed her to collect the cash urgently: 'Go to La Châtre. There's no password. We don't know anybody there, and they don't know us; if you're stuck, say you've come to see Robert . . . You'll just have to cope on your own, Marie.'

La Châtre is a small and charming town about forty kilometres south-east of Châteauroux. As usual, Pearl follows orders and makes her way to the grocer's shop-cum-bistrot whose address she has been given. She enquires for a Monsieur Langlois.

His wife stares suspiciously at Pearl: 'My husband's out.'

'I really need to see him. Umm . . . it's about some money that's arrived. I've come to collect it, for my *chef de réseau*.'

The woman knows nothing so Pearl asks when she can come back.

Madame Langlois shrugs: 'Tomorrow, if you like.'

But there are only three trains a week between Montluçon and La Châtre: Pearl has to wait until the day after the next. It is an anxious time for her.

When she returns, she sees the head of Madame Langlois through the bistro window and has an intuition that there is going to be trouble: her 'antennae' are quivering.

A man enters, whom she has never seen before. His expression is guarded, surly. 'Bonjour, madame.'

'Good day,' says Pearl, smiling.

'Well, I'm Robert. But I don't know you!'

'I don't know you, either, as a matter of fact.'

Robert stares at her, unsmilingly. Without a word, he jerks his head towards a winding staircase, and Pearl follows him up to an empty room. He tells her to sit down and fires questions at her but, since he and Pearl work for completely different circuits, none of the names Pearl give are familiar to him.

Pearl begins to panic, sensing his growing distrust: 'Do you know Amédée Maingard, our pianist?'

'*Non*.'

'What about Jacques Hirsch, and his brother, Pierre?'

'Never heard of them.'

'You must know "Gaspard" at Clermont, and the Auvergne *maquis*,' says Pearl pleadingly.

Robert turns and spits on the floor. '*Non, madame. Connais pas*.'

Pearl is filled with an increasing sense of foreboding. She is not a practising Christian, but she utters a silent prayer . . . 'Dear God, please God, tell me what to say.' She casts frantically in her mind for a name to give that this man might recognise, and suddenly it comes to her: Octave, the farmer at Tendu, where she was dropped. Tendu is not far as the crow flies, west from La Châtre.

She is loath to play this last card, for she knows she is breaking Hector's strict security rules, but it is her last chance.

'Do you know Octave?' Pearl asks.

'*Non*.'

'But you must know him. Octave is Monsieur Chantraine, the mayor!'

'*Ah, oui, oui . . . Oui!*'

'I was parachuted onto his field at the end of September!'

Four or five men suddenly burst through the door.

'They were about to kill me,' said Pearl later, of the *maquisards* who had stormed in: Robert had made up his mind that she was a *Milicienne*. She had met the wrong man, for Hector had meant her to meet a resister named Robert Chabenat, not the bistrot owner. Luckily the Langlois family were in fact ardent *résistants*, so it was just an unfortunate case of mistaken identity.

'He was all set to bump me off,' Pearl would tell Henri later. '*Il avait eu l'inténtion de m'étrangler.* He was planning to strangle me.'

That Christmas, Pearl went to Paris to spend the time with Henri and his parents. After their early difficulties, the family had taken her to their heart, and she was touched that Monsieur and Madame

Cornioley risked inviting her to stay in their apartment in the Faubourg-Saint-Honoré to share their Christmas dinner. As they sat around the table, she felt truly accepted as Henri's fiancée, their engagement acknowledged by the whole family, including Evelyne.

By inviting her to stay, Pearl knew the Cornioleys were sharing her risk, and she loved them for it. She tried her best to minimise the danger to her hosts: with a big hat that she had bought specially to disguise herself pulled down over her face, she ran in and out of the apartment without being noticed. 'I don't think anyone realised I was there,' she says. 'I was English and I had gone to England.'

Perhaps the brief taste of comfort and warmth in the Cornioley apartment, where business continued as usual and wealthy women, whose husbands profited from the German occupation – women who knew nothing of rationing and queues and suffering – continued to shop on the black market and have facials at the *Institut de Beauté*, upset Pearl, for she collapsed after Christmas.

Pearl was suffering from acute neuralgia and rheumatism. The lack of heating on the trains, the lack of sleep, the need to stay constantly vigilant, had worn her down. She was ill for three weeks. She lost six or seven kilos, came out in a skin rash, and was homesick for her family, of whom she had no news. But, most of all, Pearl missed Henri. Before her parachute drop, she had dreamt of working side by side with him, but this was not how events had turned out. Instead they were still apart, after the briefest of reunions; he remained in Paris, and her love for him felt almost as thwarted as it was in London.

Isolated and lonely, she retired to the little room in Montluçon, where she had finally found a landlady who believed her story that she was a beauty rep and, sick and weary, she rested and slept. She still hadn't slept with Henri and, looking in the mirror, she wondered whether he would even want her now. His kisses had become a distant memory.

And then came the news that she had been secretly dreading: the Gestapo had caught Octave. She heard that he was arrested and deported in December – had her conversation with Robert Langlois harmed Octave?

Knowing that in all likelihood he would never return, Pearl mourned the fate of the French resisters who not only sacrificed their own lives, but saw their families suffer, their wives and children taken, their farms burnt. Perhaps at that moment something died in Pearl: a certain innocence, a belief in justice.

At that point, a lesser woman than Pearl might have given up: she seemed to have reached the limit of her endurance. But while she had been changed, she refused to be broken. She would show that Octave had not died in vain.

With steely determination, Pearl typed her final report on Michelin and sent it to Baker Street by Lysander aeroplane. There would be no more fudge or compromise with collabos. *Either you are with us, or you are against us.*

Agent Marie's orders had been to stop Michelin tyre production, if not by sabotage, then by other means. She wrote grimly:

> Our boys are very good at precision bombing. If it is decided to destroy Michelin by bombing the factory, the RAF could also bomb Bergougnan where they are turning out material exclusively for the Huns.
>
> There is very little defence around Clermont-Ferrand and what there is, is mobile. I hate to suggest this bombing of Michelin, but Villiers and I think it would give the management a lesson . . .

On 5 April 1944, Marie added a further report: 'Michelin was well pin-pointed and destruction complete in main factory. People in Clermont say many of the incendiaries were duds. Casualties: about 16 killed and 20 injured. Sanatorium damaged by blast, no casualties or damaged material. Re my para 3 above,' continued Marie ominously, 'Hector will deal.'

19

Churchill to the Rescue

As PEARL criss-crossed France on the lonely night trains, she was mercifully unaware that on the other side of the Channel, SOE was fighting for its life. In the winter of 1943–44, 'the Org' faced the greatest crisis of its history.

At his desk in Norgeby House, cryptographer Leo Marks stared with growing horror at the message from Holland that one of his brightest radio signal masters had just put under his nose: 'I think you should take a look at this, sir.'

The message confirmed the head of codes' fears that there was something very wrong with SOE's Dutch traffic. As both cryptographers knew, every SOE radio operator had a different 'fist', his own particular touch on the keyboard, but this pianist's had changed. The signal master had decided to find out why. He had ended his own transmission 'HH', meaning 'Heil Hitler', the signature of every German agent. Back had shot the reply: 'HH'. It was the damning proof for which Marks had been waiting: the Dutch section ('N') was enemy-controlled, its agents blown.

When Marks showed the message to Brigadier Nicholls, head of signals, he, too, was convinced. But convincing the 'Mighty Atom' (as Marks nicknamed Gubbins) was a different matter altogether, until two Grendon FANYs, Mrs Denman and Mrs Brewis, spotted a telltale mistake. 'Cucumber' and 'Kale' – all Dutch agents were named after vegetables – had made a strange spelling error. In their transmissions, they spelt 'price' not the Dutch way, '*prijs*', but the German, '*preis*'.

By September, the cat was fully out of the bag. A top-secret message came from C's Berne Station: 'Sister service totally infiltrated by Germans. We therefore urge you to break off all contacts with their agents and keep clear of them.' Two Dutch agents, 'Sprout' and 'Chive', had broken out of Haaren prison and escaped to Switzerland, where they had informed the British consul that, when they landed in Holland, the Germans had been waiting for them on the dropping zone. Haaren prison was full of SOE agents.

The Germans were chuckling over the success of 'Nordpol', their deception of N Section. They knew SOE's codes and passwords and, posing as the (captured) agents, were regularly exchanging traffic with London over dozens of captured sets.

Menzies – C – was triumphant at this evidence of SOE incompetence, which promised victory in his turf war with CD; while Portal, the chief of the air staff, threatened to ground all SOE flights. Forty SOE agents had been caught on landing in Holland, in the largest single SOE disaster in the field throughout the war.

On 1 December 1943, 'Bomber' Harris, who feared for the lives of his aircrew, announced that all SOE air operations were cancelled. The day after the RAF's bombshell announcement, Clement Attlee, deputy prime minister, summoned Selborne to a special meeting to set up a full enquiry into the Dutch disaster. Selborne immediately recalled Gubbins, who was in Cairo with Churchill, to London.

In the absence of Churchill, SOE's creator and protector, the crisis was escalating, but the prime minister was too ill to return from Egypt. After celebrating his sixty-ninth birthday with Stalin and Roosevelt at the 'Big Three' Teheran conference, Churchill had collapsed with pneumonia and was unable to fly home. He had spent Christmas convalescing at Eisenhower's villa near Carthage, and was still in Marrakesh in January when Desmond Morton, his aide, handed his master the report on the German penetration of SOE marked 'Most Secret and Personal'.

The hand that held the knife was C's, but it was Morton who twisted it, saying:

> I have always held the view that on technical as opposed to political grounds at least part of the work for which SOE is now responsible should always have been carried out by C.

The chiefs of staff criticised SOE for not halting operations to Holland in August 1943 and ridiculed its 'small-scale sabotage in France'. They demanded 'coordination with SIS . . . unification of intelligence and subversive activities and the institution of a single system of clandestine communications.'

The proposal amounted to the abolition of SOE.

As Churchill lingered in the Moroccan sunshine, Selborne sprang passionately to SOE's defence. He drew up a thirty-page list of all SOE's successful special operations, including the liberation of Corsica in October 1943 ('primarily an SOE operation'.) Admitting the Dutch tragedy, he argued that elsewhere SOE had triumphed, despite the nature of its work, which always exposed it to contamination. On 14 January 1944, he pleaded eloquently before Attlee for SOE also to be given its chance at Operation Overlord, as the real D-Day was codenamed.

'The Org' was doing something new, and its agents had to start from scratch:

> . . . To learn and devise the techniques of subversion, sabotage without any nucleus of experienced professionals to guide them, as in other Services and Government Departments. This Service is accordingly continually growing in efficiency, and daily developing the art of warfare in a new sphere. Notable special operations already stand to its credit, and all that it asks is that it should be given the confidence which it deserves and be freed from the feeling that any setback which the fortunes of war bring is going to be made the occasion by other Departments for immediately demanding its dismemberment.

As Buckmaster admitted: 'We have been called "amateurs".' They were civilians drafted in as a brand-new instrument of war. No blueprint for special ops existed.

> In June 1940, there were no British troops under arms on the Continent of Europe . . . Invasion of our homeland seemed imminent. Victory, in which we all so passionately believed,

> seemed a far-off mirage . . . Naturally enough, mistakes were made.

These words fell on deaf ears. The Defence Committee decided that 'SOE should now be placed under the control of the Secretary of State for Foreign Affairs.' Only Anthony Eden, Secretary of State for War, opposed the amalgamation of SIS and SOE: he knew that ever since August 1943, the Overlord planners had been incorporating SOE into their strategy for D-Day's Normandy landings – Operation Neptune – a combined seaborne and airborne landing on the Channel coast.

On 17 January, Churchill returned, weak but resolute, to 10 Downing Street. His direct intervention again saved SOE, and flights to Holland were resumed.

It was the last time he would have to defend his accident-prone offspring against its enemies. 'Brave and desperate men could cause the most acute embarrassment to the enemy,' wrote the prime minister, 'and it was right that we should do all in our power to foster and stimulate so valuable an aid to Allied strategy.'

The Free French also realised that 'without Churchill there was nothing to be done'. Baron Emmanuel d'Astier de la Vigerie, head of the early Resistance movement 'Libération', a lean, mercurial left-wing poet and a key figure in General de Gaulle's retinue, called on Churchill in London:

> The English secret services wanted to treat the French uprising as if it did not exist . . . Like de Gaulle, Churchill was a hero out of the Iliad; the lone and jealous governor of the British war effort. To go and see the polite and self-effacing Attlee, or Lord Selborne, the affable Minister of Economic Warfare, or . . . General Gubbins, the mysterious manipulator of the initials S.O.E . . . to go and see them was useless.

Only Churchill, fired by imagination or anger, could make any real impact on British strategy. Equally, he needed encounters with charismatic figures like d'Astier, whom he immediately summed up as 'a man of the Scarlet Pimpernel type', or 'Tommy' Yeo-Thomas, another of the 'brave and desperate men', who had just lived up to his nickname of the White Rabbit by escaping the Germans in a coffin in a French motor hearse, to stir him to action. Inspired by heroic tales of agents who jumped to their deaths from the windows of Avenue Foch in order to escape the Gestapo, Churchill would ensure SOE 'had its chance' at D-Day.

But, in the bleak winter of 1943–44, the White Rabbit was in despair. The death of Jean Moulin, president of the *Conseil National de la Résistance* (CNR), had virtually destroyed the Gaullist resistance movement and so Tommy Yeo-Thomas and his close friend, the dark, brilliant Socialist, Pierre Brossolette, also a creator of the CNR, had been sent on an 'RF' mission, 'Marie-Claire', on 18 September 1943 to rebuild the shattered movement. They had found morale at rock-bottom: the promised landings had not materialised and arms were so scarce that patriot groups had feared annihilation.

The bands of *maquis* were growing, but when Yeo-Thomas toured the Lot he had found a camp of thirty men with only one Sten gun and three French rifles between them. The tricolour, with the revolutionary *Croix de Lorraine* – de Gaulle's chosen symbol – superimposed upon the now collaborationist flag, hung limply in the cold morning air. Orders were rapped out with military precision, but there was not even enough ammunition for target practice.

The French leaders had refused to accept London's orders to decentralise the movement, and there had been stormy meetings between the leaders of different factions, while security was so careless that an *agent de liaison* had presented Yeo-Thomas with an envelope addressed to 'M. Shelley', his *nom de guerre*, containing a typewritten list of names and appointments.

With some 32,000 Gestapo hunting Shelley in Paris, he was picked up by Lysander aeroplane on 15 November, intending to return to relieve Brossolette once he had reported to London.

In London, Yeo-Thomas had found the doors of Whitehall shut in his face as he pleaded for arms for the *maquis* and aircraft to deliver them. At last, he had called on an old friend, Major-General Swinton. 'There is only one man who can decide on such an important point, and that is the prime minister,' the general had said, reaching for pen and paper.

On 1 February 1944, the White Rabbit was shown into the Cabinet Room at 10 Downing Street. The prime minister had been sitting at a long table, his back to the windows, smoking a cigar. He had tilted his chair back as Squadron Leader Yeo-Thomas saluted, and looked critically at the stocky, maverick forty-three-year-old standing before him.

'I can give you five minutes.'

Stumbling over his words in his anxiety, Yeo-Thomas had poured out his fears that the *Armée Secrète* (AS) would be wiped out if they didn't receive the arms and equipment he'd promised them. He had painted a picture of dozens of men and women arrested daily in the streets of Paris, or waiting for *parachutages* 'in the darkness in the windy wilderness of central France'.

'Sit down,' said the prime minister. 'What is the organisation of the *maquis* like?'

For forty-five minutes he had listened as Yeo-Thomas asked for 100 aircraft to make at least 250 sorties in every moon period.

Within forty-eight hours his wishes had been granted. Churchill ordered Portal to supply SOE with 100 aircraft, while 12 Liberators, 2 Halifaxes and 16 Stirlings were put at RF Section's disposal, together with large quantities of weapons, equipment and clothing.

SOE had seen off its enemies. After coming within a stone's throw of being abolished, it had reached its turning point – Sir Charles Hambro was replaced as CD by Colin Gubbins, a tough professional soldier able to work with the military as the Chief of Staff to the Supreme Allied Commander (COSSAC) assumed operational control of SOE activities. SOE was no longer a romantic, madcap idea of the prime minister's: following the decision at Quebec to aim for an Anglo-American landing in May 1944, it was becoming a vital adjunct of the chiefs of staff and the area commanders-in-chief. 'At last,' wrote Gubbins, 'we had moved into calmer waters.'

And then in February came news that sent SOE's reputation

sky-high. In Norway, a team of six Norwegian agents, codenamed 'Gunnerside', had blown up the Norsk Hydro, the heavy-water plant at Vemork, the previous year. In February 1944, Knut Haukelid, who had remained on the Barren Mountain, then destroyed the heavy water being moved by ferry back to Germany. SOE, in its greatest coup of the war, had deprived Germany of the atom bomb. This alone justified its existence.

In France, however, the Gestapo arrested Brossolette.

A blanket of fog, which grounded all SOE flights to France, had descended over France and England: '*Nous mangeons toujours de la purée de pois, mais nous aurons du dessert*. We're eating mushy peas but we will have dessert,' Yeo-Thomas assured his friend in a coded message over the BBC. But the pea-souper persisted: the first Lysander sent to pick up Brossolette had been forced to turn back because of poor weather, the second was shot down in flames over the French coast.

Just twenty-four hours after meeting Churchill, the White Rabbit vowed to return to France to rescue his friend. It would prove a vain attempt. Brossolette, too, would be caught by the Gestapo. In Paris, the landslide of arrests continued. The Gaullist élite – soldiers and politicians – were ripe for the picking. General Delestraint, head of the Gaullist *Armée Secrète*, reached his safe-house in Paris, forgot his password, checked into a hotel under his real name, and walked into the arms of the Gestapo. His death was a further blow to the Resistance.

At Avenue Foch, Goetz was running no less than four wireless games with captured wireless sets. For a full ten months after Prosper's arrest, the Germans continued to fool Buckmaster and penetrate his circuits.

Jubilant at the mortal blow they had dealt Prosper, the Nazi command discussed the best moment to reveal their hand. At first, after Noor's arrest, Goetz thought that London had 'twigged'. But in Baker Street, agent France Antelme believed that she was still free, so Buckmaster began a new series of drops in early 1944 to her circuit, 'Cinema-Phono'.

'We [the SD] continued to work the set and to ask for massive receptions,' said Goetz.

'Buckmaster has developed an attitude problem,' confided Marks to his diary, for his warnings that Noor was frantically signalling that she was caught and her set enemy-controlled – she was sending a special eighteen-letter cypher previously agreed with Marks in case of such an eventuality – had gone unheeded.

In the game of cat and mouse, the ingenuity of the Gestapo officers from Avenue Foch was boundless. They waited in 'blown' flats for contacts of a captured agent. They watched as someone approached, even walking a little white dog that had belonged to Yeo-Thomas's *agent de liaison* up and down her street the day after she was arrested. If it wagged its tail at a passer-by, or jumped up, they would be arrested, too.

The Gestapo were wily as well as brutal, but Pearl could be wilier still.

Like the very best agents – Cowburn, Southgate and Philippe de Vomécourt – her 'antennae' grew more sensitive with every month that passed. She knew that Philippe de Vomécourt was the same: on one occasion he was in a hotel with a fellow agent when he woke suddenly in the small hours.

'Get up!' said de Vomécourt to his companion.

'But it's the middle of the night,' protested the other. '*Non, je reste là, je ne veux pas du tout*— I'm staying here, I don't want—'

'*Je te donne l'ordre de sortir d'ici!* Get up, that's an order!' Philippe had snapped.

A few hours later the police raided the hotel.

It also helped that Pearl knew every inch of the Paris streets; while her time at Beaulieu had taught her how to shake off a follower: she would take the métro, get out at a station, walk along the platform, and suddenly jump back into the train at the last minute. Or she might dart into a department store, take the lift down to the basement whilst her 'tail' was held up by a crowd of shoppers and, having gained a lead, take a service passage reserved for employees. Her resourcefulness was evident when she set out to help Jacques Bureau, a victim of Prosper's downfall, in March 1944:

> There existed, at the beginning of resistance in France, one of our organisations whose head was a certain François. [His] radio operator was at Orléans and was known as Archambaud. The courier was 'DENISE' . . . The whole of this organisation was arrested by the end of September last – I understand 600.

Jacques Bureau was said to have repaired the organisation's radio sets and to have contributed to the R/T communications with the UK.

Pearl learnt of Bureau's fate through his wife. Bureau himself was an old friend of Henri's, and Pearl had known him before the war. Sent to Fresnes prison after his arrest, Bureau was subsequently moved to Compiègne, where his uncle managed to save him from being sent to a concentration camp in Germany with the connivance of a *gros bonnet*, a corrupt Gestapo officer. A bribe meant Bureau was sent instead to Brunswick on parole, where he was 'waiting to work for the Huns in an aircraft factory'.

Undaunted by his experience, Bureau had told his wife that he was going to Germany, and was prepared to spy for SOE. His release on parole would cost his wife 50,000 francs.

'Are you prepared to help her pay this sum?' demanded Pearl, of London. 'Madame Bureau is due to leave for Germany but is at present held up, probably due to our bombing of Brunswick . . . I gave her a PLAYFAIR [code] and told her that if you had special instructions I would let her know by this means. JB,' she adds, 'has a very special knowledge of radio research.'

'Yes,' is scribbled in the margin of Agent Marie's report, which was flown home by Lysander in April. 'Please reply by wire authorising payment of 50,000.' Acting on her suggestion, 'special instructions' were sent so that Bureau could spy for Baker Street from Germany.

In April 1944, Pearl used SOE finances to help nine American pilots who had been shot down six or seven months before and who were trying to escape to England. In the build-up to D-Day, more and more sorties over France were flown by Allied aircraft, many of which were shot down by German anti-aircraft defences. Aircrew who survived depended on SOE agents to help them escape:

> The Americans are in trouble up to their necks and in hiding, their chief having been arrested and his wife blackmailing the rest of the party in her desperation to save her husband's skin.

On 26 April, Pearl went to Paris to see a contact about the airmen. 'It is essential that something should be done quickly to help those responsible for the welfare of the nine airmen,' she told Baker Street. 'Their finances were nil last Friday, so I left Frs 50,000 while they are waiting for contact from you. We cannot, for reasons of prestige, cut all contact until we know definitely that the question is in proper hands.' When her instructions came, she promised: 'We shall drop everything to put the men on the escape route home.'

Although by the spring of 1944 Pearl at last had a base in rue Chantoiseau, Montluçon, she was finding her role in the underground more and more stressful. It was, she says, '*stressant*, *fatiguant* . . . I would never have made a spy, I don't have the temperament for it.' Gestapo controls were tighter than ever at the railway stations all over her vast territory of Paris, Vierzon, Châteauroux, Montluçon, Clermont-Ferrand, Limoges, Toulouse, Tarbes and Poitiers.

The longer an agent stayed in the field, the shorter grew the odds against their survival: Buckmaster asked Jacqueline Nearne to return to London for her own safety, but she was reluctant to miss D-Day. Finally, Buckmaster had sent a Lysander for her. Chalked on the fuselage was his message: 'JACQUELINE MUST COME.' Reluctantly Jacqueline had climbed in.

Now, as the circuit's only remaining courier, Pearl's workload was heavier than ever, and her doubts and fears seemed to grow in those final weeks. How much longer could her luck hold? So far she had dodged the virus of contamination, to which so many of her fellow agents had fallen victim. But, as Buckmaster wrote,

Pearl was 'capable and brave', better than she believed herself to be:

> Long journeys by train and by road through continual Gestapo controls were her regular lot. Witherington never hesitated, and for twelve months succeeded in baffling the enemy despite the fact that she was searched for.

Some women agents made themselves up carefully in the knowledge that sex appeal saved lives. Even though Pearl rarely wore make-up, she had other tricks at her command: her slim figure and quick wits could still charm the Germans. It was her practice to ask a German soldier to carry her case and flash him a smile of thanks. In a bus or tram, she learnt to place the radio transmitter she was carrying – the more expendable couriers often transported radio sets for the 'pianists' – onto the lap of the German soldier sitting beside her. When the police entered to search the passengers she would stand up, put her foot on the seat, and slowly raise her skirt to adjust her suspenders.

Pearl's growing premonition that her luck was about to run out perhaps held an element of truth. On her very last mission before D-Day, she took the train from Montluçon to Paris. It was a nightmare journey. Saboteurs had blown up the lines: 'I spent all night changing trains.' As the train clattered into Paris in the late morning, Pearl perched on a washbasin in the toilet: there was nowhere else to sit. She sat on the basin, swaying with tiredness. The train was full to bursting. As she ran a hand through her hair, she noticed a man staring at her.

Suddenly he shoots a question at her: '*Qu'est-ce que vous faites comme metier?*'

'I'm a beauty rep.'

'Really? You don't look much like one.' The passenger gives her a closer look. 'You aren't even wearing make-up, madame!'

'Huh!' Pearl shrugs. 'Do you think I feel like putting on make-up after a night like the one we've just had?'

The man inspects her even more closely. Her nose is shiny, her cheeks flushed. Her fine, fair hair is in need of a wash and her lips are bare of lipstick. Never has Pearl felt more vulnerable. She's sure that he's about to say that she looks a mess.

The man is hesitating, deciding whether to tip off a soldier, when the train pulls into Gare d'Austerlitz. Without a backward glance Pearl jumps down, case of beauty products in hand. Within seconds, she is lost in the crowd.

In London, Mrs Witherington had no idea of Pearl's whereabouts or the nature of her job, although she received regular letters from Vera Atkins. 'We miss her terribly,' she told Vera on 3 January 1944, while a Captain Bissett from the War Office replied soothingly to another letter of hers that Pearl was 'well and busy', and sent £1 for her sisters' birthdays. 'It is very sweet and kind of her to be so generous to such a crowd of us,' replied Gee. Unaware of the danger Pearl was in, she pressed Captain Bissett to allow her 'other two WAAFs', Doudou and Mimi, to join their sister in a posting in which they could use their French.

Captain Bissett was not encouraging. 'I have made all possible enquiries on behalf of your daughters,' he replied on 24 March, 'but very much regret to say that I find there are no vacancies at all.'

It was an SOE rule that only one member of a family should work for 'the Org', because of the risk, although an exception was made in the case of Jacqueline and Eileen Nearne, as well as the brother and sister team of Claude and Lise de Baissac.

Mrs Witherington was not deterred. Doudou and Mimi were going to London, and 'my other two S/O WAAFs are desirous of calling on you one day next week, if you will be kind enough to receive them.'

An appointment was duly made for 11 a.m. on Friday at Room 238, Bissett's office in the Victoria Hotel, Northumberland Avenue, SW1. He sent an urgent memo to Vera Atkins alerting her to the arrival of the sisters.

'If they turn up at 11 on Friday,' ordered Vera, 'cancel the appointment (as Bissett has made other appointments or some such excuse) and cancel with Room 238.'

For their own safety, the door was shut on Doudou and Mimi.

Pearl had asked for Air Vice Marshall Colyer and Air Commodore Beaumont to be kept in touch with her progress. Beaumont was impressed by what he heard: 'I understand that Miss Pearl Witheringon is putting up a good show.'

But, in the spring of 1944, as the clock ticked towards D-Day, Pearl's greatest test was yet to come.

20

The Fall of Hector

MONDAY, 1 May 1944 dawned fine and sunny. In the morning Maurice Southgate, a.k.a Hector, called at 44 rue de Rimard, a safe-house in Montluçon, to see 'Aimée', his new radio operator. Amédée Maingard, now promoted to Hector's deputy, remained in their shared flat checking two dozen recent telegrams from London.

After lunching with two agents who had just arrived with more messages from London, Hector was dropped off by car in a little backstreet near rue de Rimard. It was 4 p.m. The town was swarming with Gestapo, but Hector was uncharacteristically careless: 'There was a jeep, a vehicle principally used by the Gestapo, hidden a little further down the street,' wrote Pearl, later. 'If he'd seen it, he would never have knocked at the door.' Nor did Hector notice the telltale signal in the window of the safe-house – it was usual to place a vase of flowers or a similar object as a warning sign. Perhaps he already had the look of a man who is 'about to be taken', the look that Benoit (Cowburn) said he could recognise in any agent too long in the field.

Looking back, Southgate could have kicked himself:

> I must admit I was pretty tired as the result of all my movements during the past fortnight, and I can honestly say that for the first time I did not take any elementary precautions in knocking on Aimée's door of the house in the Rue de Rimard. When . . . the door eventually opened, I found half a dozen guns pushed into my tummy, and at the same time saw in my mind four obvious Gestapo civilians walking up and down the Rue de Rimard with

> hands in their pockets . . . I was dragged into the house immediately by those men with my hands above my head.

Like Prosper before him, Hector had met his Nemesis.

Back in the first week in February 1944, soon after his return from London, the 'Stationer' chief had gone to Châteauroux for an important meeting. The snow, which had been falling since Christmas, lay thick on the pavement; people were short of food, clothes and heating, and squabbled over the firewood piled up on the side of the road, cut from the plane trees in the Place Lafayette. Hector could hear the stamp of boots on cobbles as German patrols marched out of their barracks, and women in uniform too, chatting in German: the 'grey mice', ignored by passers-by. At night, air-raid sirens wailed: only the month before the RAF had bombed the *Martinerie*. On the walls were blackout notices, curfew orders, and roughly chalked 'V' signs, with the cross of Lorraine.

Hector melts into the shadows in the Avenue de Verdun. He sees them coming now: Robert Monestier, politician, local leader of the *Mouvements Unis de la Résistance* (MUR), who has requested this meeting with *le capitaine Philippe*, Southgate's field name, and 'Alex', the taciturn Communist big chief from Dun-le-Poëlier, a village in the Cher valley. The Frenchmen fall into step silently with Southgate, and the three men walk up the avenue, past the hospital.

'How was Chantraine arrested?' asks Southgate, without preamble.

The first thing he has learnt since his return to France on 28 January is that the Gestapo have caught Octave. The Tendu fields are a trap now, and he urgently needs to find replacement landing grounds before the next moon. The situation is both more urgent and more difficult than it was when he left, three months ago. Twenty more agents are about to be infiltrated, and he has been given a message over the S-phone – used for ground to air communication – by the pilot who dropped the last batch of agents at Tarbes 'to indicate a landing ground for Major Antelme and party'. All this is weighing on his mind as he turns to Monestier.

'*Par hasard*. By chance.' Monestier shrugs his shoulders.

'Chantraine won't talk,' says Southgate calmly.

Monestier hopes he's right. 'Ah! Philippe and his British phlegm!' The resistance leader steals a glance at the Briton. Tall and thin, with an unmistakeably military bearing, *le capitaine Philippe* is calm, imperturbable, secretive. Under his beret his jutting, aquiline nose reminds Monestier of an eagle's and his gaze is equally watchful. Constantly on the move between the furthest points of his empire, he impresses Monestier as the archetypal secret agent: solitary, intent on his mission, cut off from friends and family.

Hector knows he needs the help of Théogène Briant – Alex – the legendary leader of the Communist FTP, whose underground fighters are the most effective in the area. But negotiations will be delicate. Treading carefully, he raises the question of how the Communists of Dun-le-Poëlier will supply their comrades not only in the Indre but also further afield, in the Creuse and the Dordogne.

'If Alex needs some money to maintain his soldiers, I can let him have some,' Hector murmurs to Monestier.

Alex stiffens. He will only accept funds from the Party and the *Front National*. 'It would be different if you were French,' he says. 'If you were a French officer, I would accept willingly.'

Hector laughs good-naturedly. After a brief discussion, it is agreed that Alex will accept arms and munitions, and his men will participate in attacks designed to 'annoy the enemy 100 per cent through all forms of sabotage, physical, material and moral, especially to undermine his morale.' But the Communist will not take money from *la mission britannique*.

Southgate had never discriminated in the distribution of the arms he controlled – the days were long gone when F Section advised Pearl not to arm Gaullist *maquis*; since then, she had supplied Gaspard (Emile Coulaudon) with explosives to bomb Michelin on the SOE principle that 'the Org' was strictly apolitical, its circuits 'purely paramilitary organisations'. Duff Cooper, British ambassador to France in 1946, would say that in his opinion, F's circuits 'owed a great deal of their military success to their non-political character'.

> British organisers supplied arms to any elements who gave sufficient guarantees of their readiness to execute Allied military objectives . . . Even the Communists benefited, although they were normally reluctant to accept orders from any outside authority.

At 10 Duke Street, London, Colonel Passy, head of the BCRA, took a very different attitude. With only half an eye on the immediate objective and the remainder of his gaze fixed on the post-war political scene, he was resolutely opposed to providing help to the Communists in any shape or form. The British, however, with but one objective – 'the ousting of the Hun from France' – were willing to, and did, supply the Communists under certain, well-defined conditions.

Arming the Communists led to 'frequent clashes' between the British and Free French organisations in London, but these were of no consequence to Southgate and Pearl in the field: in July and October 1943, supply drops of grenades, explosives and machine guns had been made to many resistance groups of differing political allegiances.

Alex proved as good as his word. The scattered hamlets and *demi-bocage* around Dun-le-Poëlier, with the help of Socialist mayor Amand Mardon, replaced the farms lost at Tendu as arms dumps. Frequent contact with Monestier, his adjutant Robert Chabenat – whom Pearl had failed to find in La Châtre – and Commandant Antoine, chief of the *Armée Secrète* in the Indre, consolidated Southgate's network of support.

On 1 April 1944, the moon was favourable and Lysander ops could be restarted. But the 'Stationer' chief was overwhelmed by the number of receptions he was expected to organise in one month, now that Churchill's orders to increase sorties to France had been confirmed by Supreme Headquarters Allied Expeditionary Force (SHAEF). Other circuits in the north and north-west were blown, or under RAF restrictions, and Buckmaster's instructions were to strengthen the northern zone at any cost. 'This operational decision,' he wrote, 'bad as it was for Southgate's circuit, was fully justified by subsequent events.'

'We've got to receive three *parachutages*, each with three people, on the same night,' Philippe told Monestier. 'I've only got forty-eight hours in which to find three landing grounds, three reception committees, and hide nine agents and their stuff until they can reach their destination.'

Monestier and Chabenat hurried to help him, finding thirty men from the Secret Army at Saint-Gaultier to receive one aircraft, thirty more at La Châtre to receive the second; the third would be met near Issoudon.

Hector worked feverishly to unite the Resistance, travelling to the furthest ends of his circuit to visit the *maquis* camps, now stretched over six *départements* – they covered the Massif Central, the deep green heart of the country. In his headquarters of Montluçon, he met Gaspard of the Auvergne *maquis*, and set up a conference of rival chiefs at a farm near Paulhauget in order to coordinate action: a 'Grand Council' was the outcome, with delegates from Combat, *Libération*, and the Communist and Socialist parties. Plans were made for 15,000–20,000 men, armed with British-supplied weapons, to converge on three redoubts between the Loire and Allier rivers in April or May, depending on the date of the Allied landings.

Widely respected by his French comrades, efficient and dedicated, Hector and his team of Samuel and Marie were welding the partisans together as a fighting force ready for the invasion. 'That April,' wrote Southgate later, 'Samuel [Maingard] and I decided to organise all fields for D-Day.'

But little went according to plan. The *maquisards* didn't take kindly to discipline – nor did some of the agents. The *maquis* at Terrasson, instructed by Jacques Dufour ('Anastasie') and 'Martial', disappointed Hector when he visited them:

> Their discipline . . . was nil . . . Two *maquis* boys of Terrasson were killed by the French *Milice* . . . the Terrasson *maquis* wanted to

> avenge these two men and raided the *milice* HQ . . . Returning from this operation they met a German staff car with a General and two colonels . . . and shot them to bits. This obviously did not please the German HQ (Limoges), who sent a reprisal squad to the town of Terrasson, where they burnt many houses to the ground.

Martial, a new agent, had meanwhile gone AWOL, and was ordered by London to return to the UK – 'orders which he also refused to obey'.

Southgate, Maingard and Pearl were anxiously expecting two new radio operators: René Mathieu (Aimée) and Sophie. Southgate dashed north to meet Sophie, who was parachuted to a landing ground near Dun-le-Poëlier, and whisked her over to Châteauroux by car, then by train to Montluçon, where he introduced her to Samuel. It was a relief to have a new pianist, but, 'On the very first night of her arrival . . . we put her on a test, and she proved to be useless as a W/T.'

It was devastating news. Southgate asked Pearl to take care of Sophie and deliver her to Henri, who could put her in a safe-house at Le Blanc, and hurried off to fetch Aimée to take over as pianist. 'Because of the contretemps regarding Sophie's inefficiency and Martial's disobedience, I was behind in my tour and rather tired.'

Harrassed and short of sleep, Southgate was also concerned about the fate of France Antelme, codename 'Bricklayer', a wealthy middle-aged Mauritian. He was one of F Section's most valuable field officers, charged with raising substantial sums from French bankers and businessmen to fund the Resistance.

Returning from his second mission in March 1943, after meeting Monsieur Rambault of the *Banque de France*, Antelme had reported 'to Mr Eden and Selborne on . . . two plans which might have had a profound effect on the course of an invasion of France by the Allies'.

The first was that within a 100-kilometre coastal belt, the branch managers of the *Comptoir National d'Escompte* were to 'secrete and deliver' to the Allied armies a large stock of notes kept for that purpose. Secondly, Antelme was planning 'the feeding of the invading troops' in thirty *départements* with meat, bread, potatoes, vegetables, preserved food and chocolate, for up to 500,000 men. Arms alone would not be enough to defeat the enemy, and the logistics of providing food for the invading force had to be thought through and funded, and it was to Antelme that this vital task was entrusted.

Impatient to return to the field to expedite his plans, Antelme had daily pressed Buckmaster to send him on a third mission. But the head of 'F' had been jittery; on 8 February, after talking to Hugh Verity, who knew Henri Déricourt well, he had finally recalled the air operations chief to England following allegations made that Déricourt was opening courier mail and passing information to the enemy. For many months Buckmaster had refused to believe that the Frenchmant could be a traitor: he had run fifty successful flights in and out of France, while suspicions had also been delayed because Déricourt's codename was 'Gilbert', which was often confused with Gilbert Norman, Prosper's radio operator who betrayed his circuit to the Gestapo.

Repeatedly interrogated in London, Déricourt had proved a match for 'F': 'Gilbert could not be shaken,' reported Colonel R. A. Bourne-Paterson, Buckmaster's deputy. Nevertheless, the decision was taken not to allow the pilot to return to France. Operationally, this had been disastrous, as from the beginning of February 1944, F Section had had no regular Lysander service to the old Occupied Zone. The need was dire: the Gestapo had won 'a major success' with the destruction of Prosper, their 'objective Number One', and in the aftermath of his fall were still 'cleaning up' other circuits to which he was close. It was, wrote Bourne-Paterson drily, 'a rather trying period'.

Against his better judgement, Buckmaster had reluctantly acceded to Antelme's request to be dropped with his radio operator, Lionel Lee, codename 'Daks', and a French woman courier, Madeleine Damerment, to a Phono landing ground on 29 February (1944 was a leap year).

The penny had finally dropped in Baker Street about Garry's

'Cinema-Phono' circuit, originally set up in Le Mans by Antelme himself. It was considered 'highly suspect', wrote Marks:

> Although Buckmaster and George I [Bégué] tried to convince [Antelme] that Noor was caught, and showed him the two-way traffic they'd exchanged with her in an effort to prolong her life, he refused to believe them. Nor would he accept that Phono was blown.

He also refused to drop 'blind'.

'But Phono is blown,' protested Buckmaster. 'We're pretty sure of it. It's too much of a risk.'

Antelme shook his head obstinately. 'I'll be all right. It's my old circuit, I know Garry. It'll be fine.'

'I don't like it, old man.'

'I'm not dropping blind, Maurice. Now that's what I call a risk.'

In what seems an extraordinary error of judgement, Buckmaster, who consistently underestimated the Germans, finally instructed Phono to receive Bricklayer. Signals arranging the drop were sent from Baker Street to Noor's radio – long run by the Gestapo.

Buckmaster took the precaution (as he saw it) of sending in four young agents on 8 February to prepare for Antelme's arrival. One was a Canadian, Robert Byerley; on 10 February, he sent a message, coded on his one-time pad (a more secure coding method than poem codes), confirming his safe arrival, but his security checks were wrong. Bégué at once asked him a test question, to which he should have answered: 'Merry Xmas.' With sinking hearts, Bégué and Marks read the agent's reply: 'Happy New Year.'

There was no doubt that Byerley and his companions had been caught, but still Antelme insisted on proceeding with his plans.

'You are to cut contact with the Phono circuit as soon as you land,' ordered Buckmaster.

In Paris, SS *Sturmbannführer* Hans Josef Kieffer, SD chief interrogator at Avenue Foch, rubs his hands with glee when he receives the message that Antelme will be dropped to a Phono landing ground. The German selects a convenient ground over Rambouillet, just south-west of Paris, for he has important guests whom he wishes to witness the agent's arrival: SS General Oberg, the chief of security in France, and SS *Standarter-Führer* Dr Helmut Knochen, chief of the *Sicherheitsdienst*. Invited to witness the reception of a 'high-ranking British military intelligence officer', the expectant audience is in place by 9.15 p.m.

SS troops encircle the landing ground. The Halifax roars into view. Kieffer's interpreter, Vogt, and his V-men act as the reception committee as the first 'body' descends in the moonlight at 22.45 precisely.

It is Antelme, who rises to his feet and asks: 'Where is Phono?'

The answer he receives is the muzzle of a Luger automatic gleaming in the moonlight.

Antelme is driven to Avenue Foch and interrogated all night. As he enters Kieffer's office, he shouts angrily 'I have been betrayed!' He is taken to the Gestapo torture cellars at rue des Saussaies, but throughout his interrogation and torture, Antelme remains silent. The Gestapo will get nothing from him.

Ominous signals arrive at Baker Street over Noor's transmitter: Antelme has had a nasty accident on landing; he is in hospital with a head injury. London asks Daks, Antelme's pianist, why he has not reported the accident himself; on 24 March, Daks sends a message on his one-time pad confirming: 'Bricklayer is in a coma.' On 8 April he sends two more messages. Marks tells Buckmaster that there can no doubt that Daks and Madeleine Damerment have been caught.

There is a moment's silence. Buckmaster stares out of the window. 'Ah well,' he says, 'it's only agents' lives which are at stake.'

On 20 April, Daks regrets to inform London that Bricklayer has died in hospital.

Among his many other tasks, Southgate had to organise the escape of eminent Frenchmen and women to safety in England. He now found himself, for the second time, in Châteauroux collecting Madame *la Générale* Cochet, whom he was to take to a safe-house at Argenton-sur-Creuse, before she could be flown to London.

Pearl had already attempted to exfiltrate the wife of the major general of the French air force, who was in London with de Gaulle. Southgate had instructed her: '*Tu vas chercher Mme Cochet à Chamalières*. Go and find Mme Cochet at Chamalières. She's got to catch a Lysander . . . This is the address.'

Pearl memorised the address, and duly arrived at Clermont-Ferrand. She waited till the curfew was over, and left the station. The buses were on strike, so she walked all the way to the village of Chamalières and knocked on the door of the house whose number she had been given.

'*Je voudrais voir Madame Cochet, si'il vous plait*.'

The man of the house had just woken up. '*Connais pas!*' he snapped, looking at her blearily.

'She's expecting me.'

'*Non, non, non, c'est pas ici*. She's not here.' He peered at her suspiciously. 'What makes you think I've got anything to do with the Resistance?'

Pearl tried again: 'Geneviève sent me.'

'*Non, non, non, c'est pas ici*.'

Sent away with a flea in her ear, Pearl sat down on a bench. Her mission was a failure. What was she to do?

At that moment, Madame Cochet emerged from the hairdresser's opposite. Relieved, Pearl scooped her up, vowing never to make the same mistake again. She had learnt her lesson – to get every message by heart.

Pearl became more and more necessary to Southgate. Like Maingard, his deputy, she was reliable, dependable, and never spared herself. He knew he could trust her to organise reception committees for the parachute drops. The Indre had become the principal platform for the reception of SOE agents and the arms and materials that were dispatched to neighbouring regions.

The actual date of D-Day remained the greatest secret of the war, but another hint that the landings were imminent came with the return of an experienced team to the Auvergne – Nancy Wake and John Farmer – who were to rejoin the *maquis*. It was yet another responsibility for Hector, who received them. He was dog-tired after the night-time reception, the long briefing, and the counting and checking of money and documents.

Having dealt with Madame Cochet at Argenton, he hurried back to Châteauroux on 29 April to spend the night there, deciding to introduce Jacques Hirsch to the regional military representative of the Indre the following morning, a Sunday. But, once again, treachery was in the air and 'Stationer' at the limit of its security:

> At about 8 a.m. Samuel came to my room, collapsed on the floor after a thirty-mile cycle ride, to warn me not to see this representative, as he had just been arrested in Châteauroux.

It was time to get out of town. The Gestapo were on their tracks. The next day, the two men left for Montluçon. Their train arrived at 11.15 p.m. on 30 April 1944.

On that same Sunday, 30 April, Henri Cornioley arrived late in Montluçon to spend the night with the L'Hospitalier family at 44 rue de Rimard, the safe-house where 'pianist' Aimée was based. Things were 'getting rough,' said Pearl later, and Henri wanted to be part of the action. He, too, smelt trouble: '*Il trouvait que ça sentait le roussi*. Something was up.' There was even talk that the D-Day landings had taken place. Cautious Marie remained at her lodgings in rue Chantoiseau.

On 1 May, Hector was arrested as he stumbled into the safe-house. It had been traced by German direction-finding vans: Aimée was also caught red-handed, surrounded by three transmitting sets.

Too tired to notice the warning vase of flowers in the window . . . such small mistakes made the difference between life and death.

The Gestapo had a rich haul: their greatest prize was Hector himself, but they also found all the documents he had left with Aimée, including telegrams from London, and 1 million francs. He was driven at once to Gestapo HQ in Montluçon, handcuffed, and told to face a wall in a small room with other prisoners. His French guards, young men around eighteen or twenty years old:

> . . . took great pleasure in annoying us by getting hold of our hair, pulling it and bashing our faces against the wall, just for the fun of it. I received a severe knock on my forehead and passed out.

'Ordinary' police methods were used. The prisoners' names were asked, and if they gave it, they were hit on the head and told to shut up; if they did not speak, they were still hit, and asked why they didn't reply. In the meantime, several other prisoners were beaten up in the next room in which a radio set blared forth music to cover their yells of pain. Aimée eventually received this 'entertainment'.

At 9 p.m., the head inspector of the Gestapo walked into the little room in which Southgate was held, pointed a stubby finger, and said: 'Ah, that one.' Behind him was dragged Aimée 'in a shocking condition'. Both men were taken to Montluçon barracks and put in the same cell – '. . . a very foolish thing to do,' commented Southgate, later. All through the night he and Aimée planned their story, deciding not to recognise each other. Finally, 'for the first time in many, many weeks, I had a sound sleep on the concrete floor.'

Four days later, Southgate's interrogation began. 'To my credit, I think I acted pretty well,' he said. At first, he pretended to be a stranger who had just called on the off-chance on Monsieur L'Hospitalier, '. . . but this did not quite satisfy them. The Gestapo chief got hold of a stick and gave me the beating of my life across my back and legs.'

The interpreter spoke much better French. He turned on Southgate, his eyes red with fury, and shouted: '*Schweinhund*. Son of a bitch!'

Southgate smiled innocently.

'*Salaud! Schweinhund!*'

'He then got quite upset with me, and I realised that it would be impossible for me to carry on on these lines, for they had too many documents against me.' Remembering his Beaulieu schooling – "Stick to the truth as nearly as you possibly can" – the captured agent announced that he was going to tell all: 'I thought the best thing was to put them on a false trail, thus gaining as much time as possible to enable the May moon operations to take place.' There were, he estimated, sixty-eight operations to come.

Incredibly, the Gestapo fell for his story that he was working for a Jean Mercier from Paris, who had a beautiful platinum blonde on his arm and gave him sealed envelopes to deliver.

'Do you know what type of job you are doing?' asked the two Gestapo inspectors. 'Do you know what these envelopes contain?'

'*Non, messieurs.*'

'Do you know that you are doing espionage and working against us?'

'I had no idea,' swore Southgate. 'I am so very sorry, gentlemen.'

Ten days later, Southgate and his 'radio', Aimée, were taken under armed guard to the infamous prison at Moulins, Tour de la Mal-Coiffée – in the courtyard, he was sorry to see Madame L'Hospitalier of the rue de Rimard, a grandmother.

Soon afterwards, they were taken to the Gestapo HQ in Avenue Foch.

The Gestapo had been sifting through the papers from the rue de Rimard safe-house, and had found two identity cards: one was Southgate's, under the name of Robert Moulin; 'Unfortunately, the second ID card was in the name of Madame Cornioley, bearing the photograph of Marie.'

Hector did his best to protect Pearl. Despite naming her and Jacqueline Nearne as couriers in the mythical Jean Mercier 'gang' in Paris, he had taken care to give his own room in Limoges as Marie's address, knowing that there were no compromising documents there. As for Jacques Hirsch's address in Toulouse, which he gave for Jacqueline, Hirsch had told him that he would not return to it 'until the Germans have been thrown out of France'. Moreover, Jacqueline Nearne was now safely at home in England. But Marie was not.

In his prison cell, Hector worried not only that he had implicated

Marie, but that also among his papers snatched by the Gestapo was an SOE code to be used in the countdown to D-Day. Based on the fables of La Fontaine, including '*Les animaux malades de la Peste*. The animals ill of the plague', he had been about to distribute the fable code to a dozen people in France – London holding the counterpart of the fable – the addresses being used by Allied HQ as safe and reliable people who could eventually help them during their advance.

> Unfortunately they found three fables which I had just written out and which I was going to ask Marie to take with her to Monsieur Mardon and Monsieur Briant at Dun-le-Poëlier . . .

The Gestapo knew Marie was Hector's courier: they had her identity card and photo, in the name of Cornioley; they had the addresses of the FTP leaders, Mardon and Briant; and they had the D-Day code with which Marie was charged.

Hector put his head in his hands: Pearl was in mortal danger.

21

Countdown to D-Day

PEARL ESCAPED the Gestapo raid by a hair's breadth. When she had woken on the fine, bright Monday morning of 1 May, she had decided on the spur of the moment to go on a picnic with Henri, and had also persuaded Amédée Maingard to accompany them to the river Cher.

At 6 p.m., the little group were sitting on the river bank in the evening sunshine when they caught sight of a cyclist pedalling furiously towards them. It was Monsieur Bidet, father-in-law of the son of the house, Robert L'Hospitalier – 'Marc' – an evader from forced labour in Germany. Henri was the first to jump to his feet.

The cyclist was as white as a sheet: '*La Gestapo est à Rimard*,' he gasped. Monsieur Bidet had just heard that the Gestapo were at Rimard from the local doctor, who had gone there to treat Robert's ill grandmother.

'The Gestapo have come to arrest Robert,' the old lady had whispered to the doctor. 'They're in the house now.'

The doctor had bent closer: 'What do you want me to do?'

Madame L'Hospitalier had gripped his arm fiercely. 'Warn *la mission britannique*.' Moments later, she was arrested by the Gestapo.

The doctor, however, was allowed to leave and was able to convey her warning to Monsieur Bidet, and thence to Pearl, Henri and Maingard before they returned to rue de Rimard.

Pearl was not sure if her intuition of events could be called truly clairovoyant, but she felt strongly that she possessed a sixth sense that warned her of dangerous situations: on 30 April, the night before Hector's arrest, she had felt that danger was near, and had

had a vivid dream that the Gestapo were coming for her. It was one of two premonitions she would have in 1944 that she was sure saved her life: 'It happened to me twice,' she said, later. 'The night before Maurice's arrest, and the night before the 11th of June . . .' It seemed to her, not for the first time, that God or fate was guiding her. It was not her destiny to die that day.

On the night of 1 May, after Hector's arrest, Henri and Jacques Hirsch spent the night in a bistrot, attempting to sleep on a billiard table. Pearl returned to her lodgings. The next morning, 2 May, to their horror they awoke to find German lorries full of soldiers in the town: the Gestapo had sealed off Montluçon after finding the list of the 'Stationer' circuit's landing grounds and were hunting Maingard and Pearl, who had slipped their net the previous day.

The town was completely encircled by troops, German and French. Pearl, Henri, Maingard and Jacques Hirsch managed to borrow a car and somehow outwit the Gestapo. Slipping out of town by the back roads, they only made one stop the next day, at the village of Saint-Gaultier, and sent a message to London: '*Hector est très malade*. Hector is very ill,' signifying that Hector had been taken.

It was the end of 'Stationer'; the group was scattered to the four winds. Amédée Maingard and Robert L'Hospitalier went into hiding. Hirsch fled to Châteauroux. The arrest of Hector was a crisis comparable to the arrest of Prosper the previous summer. Once again, the Gestapo had decapitated F Section's most powerful and effective circuit, but in May 1944 it was even more serious: the invasion of France was only weeks away.

On 3 May, as Pearl and Henri fled the Gestapo, Buckmaster was at his wits' end. Thanks to his bungling, which had allowed the enemy to penetrate and contaminate other circuits, he had come to depend increasingly on Hector to provide the vital Dropping Zones for the munition drops. Now the Gestapo had the list of the DZs: they had seized Prosper's munitions, and were about to seize Hector's. It was a cruel blow: as one resister said, 'Without arms we can only startle the Germans. We cannot fight.' Men without arms could only be helpless spectators to the battles around them.

At this terrible moment, it might have been expected that Pearl and Henri's first thoughts would be for their own lives. Instead they embarked on a dangerous cross-country mission to La Châtre, north-west of Montluçon. They had to find Sophie, the new and incompetent radio operator, who was in hiding there – in a safe-house provided by Gaston Langlois – and tell her that Hector had been caught.

Having warned Sophie, it was time to find shelter.

'Where can we go?' Pearl asks Henri. She has run out of options. Should they stay in La Châtre, or try Châteauroux, like Jacques Hirsch? Montluçon is out of the question. Wearily, Pearl leans on Henri's shoulder. 'What can we do?'

'We should avoid Châteauroux,' says Henri thoughtfully. 'Too many Boches.'

'The Huns are everywhere,' Pearl replies. 'How can we possibly avoid them?'

'I have an idea . . . Some friends who might help.'

'Who, Henri?'

'He's a solid chap. Solid for the Resistance. Name of René.'

'Whereabouts?'

'I'll take you there.'

'But where is it?'

Henri laughs. 'Follow me, *chérie*!'

The couple by-pass Châteauroux, travelling north in the same direction as the river Cher towards the little hamlet of Dun-le-Poëlier, which lies on the edge of the forest of Les Tailles de Ruines. From the crossroads at Dun, Henri leads Pearl to the entrance of a local château, Château Les Souches, deep in the countryside.

'We're here,' says Henri.

'Where?' replies Pearl. 'You can't mean this château?'

'*Non, non*, not the château. This way.'

He leads her up an unsurfaced lane, which stretches from the road towards the tall, iron gates of the château. Behind the imposing gates, to the left, is a square, grey-stone lodge, a two-storey building surrounded by gloomy pine trees through which runs the long, winding drive that leads up to the chateau.

'Come and meet my friend René. He's the *gardien* here.' Henri knocks softly at the back door, which opens at once to reveal the figure of a plump woman in an apron.

'*Bonjour, madame.*' Henri smiles. 'May we come in?'

Within moments, Pearl and Henri are sitting at the kitchen table with the lodge-keeper, René Sabassier, and his wife, and their daughter, Yvonne. René is an ardent resister, and the Sabassier family receive the couple with open arms. He is a friend of the Socialist mayor of Dun-le-Poëlier, Amand Mardon; the hamlet is a hotbed of resistance, and local *résistants* are eager to help.

The mayor finds Pearl and Henri a couple of bicycles; Madame Sabassier cooks for Pearl and Henri, and they are able to rest in safety; even though, by a quirk of fate, the owners of the Château Les Souches, Monsieur Hay des Nétumières and his wife, are firm Pétainists, who cannot be allowed to suspect the presence of an English secret agent and her fiancé at the end of their drive. Under the noses of their employers, with aplomb and courage, the Sabassiers shelter Pearl and Henri.

The Gestapo put up photos of Pearl on 'Wanted' posters all over Montluçon and the surrounding neighbourhood, offering a reward of 1 million francs for information leading to her arrest – a fortune to a poor peasant farmer. The Gestapo are determined to catch Pearl Witherington a.k.a Agent Marie a.k.a Madame Cornioley. They have her ID card and know what she looks like. It can surely be only a matter of time before they have her in custody.

Yet with almost reckless disregard for her own safety, Pearl returns to Montluçon. Within days of her arrival at Les Souches, Baker Street sends a message via Maingard, ordering Pearl to receive an American parachutist, a Major Dussac, and escort him to Montluçon. She is walking into a deathtrap, say the resisters, who marvel at her courage when they hear she is taking the American into town, still full of Gestapo.

The walls of the town are plastered with posters of 'Marie': her image looks down at her from every side. But Pearl sees it is vital to help 'our Allies, important for our prestige,' and she never hesitates.

She returns safely to the lodge at Les Souches, where Henri is waiting impatiently for her: 'Thank God you're back.'

Pearl grins ruefully. 'I made it.'

'I don't know how . . .'

'I'm always very, very careful Henri. I pulled my hat over my face, delivered the airman and came straight back.'

'Thank God,' repeats Henri. '*Le bon Dieu nous protège*. The good Lord is protecting us.'

'I was scared, you know.'

'Come here.'

He embraces her and Pearl reflects, not for the first time, on the difference it makes to have Henri with her at last. Her solitary nine months as a courier are over: she has exchanged the strain of being alone on the trains, the object of suspicious, prying eyes, for an attic room in the lodge, which she now shares with Henri. It is a strange sensation to be together in this room in the forest, on her own with him, but it gives her enormous comfort.

As Pearl sleeps next to Henri on a mattress stuffed with fresh, sweet-smelling straw given to her by Madame Sabassier, the pricking of her nerves is assuaged by his presence. She hears his breathing beside her. When she wakes he kisses her: it is becoming harder and harder to preserve her virginity, as she has promised herself she will do until they are married. She has seen him pretending not to watch her as she washes and dresses in the morning. But they have a war to fight, as she sternly reminds him.

'*Je t'aime*,' says Henri, caressing her as he lies beside her. '*Je t'aime, ma cherie bien-aimée*.' But Pearl is too nervous to relax. At any moment there may be a Gestapo *rafle*, a raid. Soldiers will come knocking at the door in the middle of the night, pushing their way in, their Lugers gleaming in the moonlight.

'Non, Henri,' says Pearl, pushing him away. 'I can't, not now.'

'Then when?'

'Later, I promise.'

He sleeps. She lies awake, knowing that he, too, has a gun. She has lent him her pistol, which is under the bolster. She breathes more easily, knowing that he has the gun and is ready to use it to protect her.

At Gestapo HQ in Paris, the German mood was once again triumphant. When Maurice Southgate was pushed into a corridor on the sixth floor, he was astonished to find himself face to face with another British officer: Captain John Starr, known as 'Bob', who was arrested in June 1943, and who was sitting in a comfortable easy chair, smoking a cigarette in a leisurely fashion. He winked at Southgate. Moments later, the new prisoner was feasting on a meal of soup, German sausage, bread, butter, cheese or jam, with real hot coffee – a welcome change from the ersatz coffee to which he was accustomed – with two lumps of sugar. Behind him, Starr whistled 'It's a Long Way to Tipperary' and 'Rule Britannia'. Southgate was cheered by Starr's behaviour.

He was taken down for interrogation by Dr Goetz and Ernest, a German who spoke fluent French.

Ernest came up close to Southgate with a smile on his face: 'How about it, Mr Hector?'

Southgate 'would not play', and Ernest said: 'Well, Mr Southgate, the game is up.'

'Believe me, you could have knocked me down with a feather,' said Southgate. 'Once more, I could not help thinking of Capt. Starr.' Had the Nazis 'turned' him?

According to Ernest, one of Hector's own agents had recognised his photograph on his identity card and said quite openly: 'Oh, this is Southgate, alias Hector.'

Starr then walked in, went up to Southgate and shook his hand.

Over the next four days of interrogation, Southgate was shocked to see charts of the whole SOE organisation pinned up on the walls of Goetz's office, with photographs of Buckmaster and Major Morel, and the 'Prosper' circuit with photos of Antelme and Bodington.

When the Gestapo questioned him, however, Southgate simply replied that they seemed to know more about it than he did: 'The colonel was very proud and excited: "We know much more," he boasted. "Documents that are sent to your country are read by our people before yours. Do you know Déricourt?"'

'Yes, we did meet in London.'

'He is a very good man of ours.'

Southgate had already suspected that Déricourt was a Gestapo agent, and was shocked to have it confirmed by the Nazi. He was also disturbed by the sight of Starr openly drawing up fresh charts for the Gestapo from SOE documents.

'Why are you doing that?'

'If I don't do it,' replied Starr, 'somebody else will . . . I am gathering very valuable information which may come in useful sometime.'

Knowing that Starr had tried twice to escape, Southgate refused to think ill of him. The two men examined records of past wireless transmissions: 'Both of us were amazed at the ridiculous and foolish things done by London HQ,' said Southgate, later. 'I would even go so far as to call them criminal.' On several occasions, he had had proof of SOE agents being dropped onto grounds held by the Germans, who then used the wireless sets and codes of the new arrivals. However, 'for a long time' the Germans had not realised that F Section's radio operators included not one but two checks on their outgoing telegrams from France to Baker Street: one was the 'true check' and the other the 'bluff check'. Since the German radio operators sent their telegrams with one check only, their messages 'most obviously should have been phoney to London HQ.' But, protested Southgate angrily:

> Time after time, for different men, London sent back messages saying: 'My dear fellow, you only left us a week ago. On your first messages you go and forget to put your true check.' (S/Ldr Southgate would very much like to know what the hell the check was meant for if not for that special occasion). You may now realise what happened to our agents who did not give the true check to the Germans, thus making them send out a message that was obviously phoney and, after being put through the worst degrees of torture, these Germans managed, sometimes a week later, to get hold of the true check, and

then sent a further message to London with the proper check in the telegram, and London saying: 'Now you are a good boy, now you have remembered to give both of them.'

Southgate was furious with Buckmaster for his extraordinary gullibility, demanding that 'the officer responsible for the deaths and capture of many of SOE's best agents, including Major Antelme, should be severely court-martialled.'

'This was clearly the report of an extremely tired man,' commented Buckmaster later, in 1945, for whom it must have made uncomfortable reading.

Southgate was even more upset when, on 2 May, the BBC French service broadcast a message *en clair* warning agents in the field of his arrest: 'Beware of Hector's whereabouts. At Montluçon a big police operation has taken place.' As Buckmaster anticipated, Hector's captors in Paris were furious that the other circuits had been warned, especially when their prisoner taunted them with the news that he still had four radios in operation. At this point, the Gestapo were tempted to kill him.

Buckmaster knew the risk his broadcast would have for Southgate, but it was, he argued, 'an operational necessity':

> 'If necessary, Hector will have to make the ultimate sacrifice. The effect on the prisoner was of course realised, but it was decided to sacrifice the prisoner's life, if necessary, for the sake of preserving the remaining numbers.'

Agents were expendable. The war effort, a month before D-Day, was wholly focused on Overlord, of which the core was Operation Neptune, the Normandy landings.

In August 1944, Hector was deported to Buchenwald.

As they watched their fellow agents fall into the hands of the Germans, a saying became common currency among the more cynical of F Section's agents in France: '*On mange l'orange, on jette l'écorce*. The orange is eaten, the peel is thrown away.'

Was 'F' as cavalier with agents' lives as it appeared to be? In fact, Buckmaster cared deeply for individual agents but he was also, said his son, 'an escapist', a man who 'lived in his own world'. He had 'a second-rate mind,' noted one expert. Increasingly, Buckmaster was unaware of the 'chasm', as Pearl herself put it, between the experience of agents in the field and that of the bureaucrats in Baker Street.

'It was certainly never any part of F Section's intention to send [agents] straight to their death,' wrote the official historian, but 'grievous mistakes' were made in 1943–1944. Drops were made to nine circuits under enemy control in northern France: 'Archdeacon', 'Bargee', 'Butler', 'Delegate', 'Liontamer', 'Phono', 'Priest' and 'Surveyor', including large sums of money. Bricklayer received 1,280,000 francs in February 1944, while 1,757,000 francs were delivered to 'Archdeacon' between June 1943 and June 1944. 'Against stupidity even the gods are silent. *Mit der Dummheit kämpfen Götter selbst vergebens.*'

Buckmaster, however, subject to the demands of his superior officers, could not be held responsible for every error made. There was no signals NCO, as in the regular army, to reinforce Marks's fears that some radio operators were transmitting under duress, and 'He had to delegate so much,' said his son, Michael.

After the war, M.R.D. Foot had asked General Gubbins why he hadn't replaced Buckmaster.

'Replace him with whom?' had come the reply.

The confidence of the German intelligence services had rocketed. Convinced that SOE was in its death throes, the Germans running the successful radio game against the Dutch section sent a gloating message to Baker Street on April Fool's Day:

> IN THE LAST TIME YOU ARE TRYING TO MAKE BUSINESS IN THE NETHERLANDS WITHOUT OUR ASSISTANCE STOP NEVER MIND WHENEVER YOU WILL COME TO PAY A VISIT TO THE CONTINENT YOU MAY BE ASSURED THAT YOU WILL BE RECEIVED WITH THE SAME CARE AND RESULT AS ALL THOSE YOU SENT BEFORE STOP SO LONG.

Hitler and Goering met frequently with Himmler at the SS HQ in Prinz Albert Strasse, Berlin, to study the lists of captured SOE agents: Suttill, Norman, Borrel, Antelme, Lee, Rabinovitch, Southgate, Brossolette and Yeo-Thomas. Brossolette would commit suicide, while Tommy and Eileen Nearne suffered the excruciating torture of the *baignoire* (water-boarding).

At Avenue Foch, Southgate was astonished at the piles of booty, stored there to demoralise captured agents. There were 'quantities of British food, guns, ammunition, explosives . . . dropped mostly to grounds in Normandy where up to ten organisations were all in German hands and had been receiving British material for months and months . . .'

But, in the end, hubris overcame the Germans: 'F' was not quite as stupid as it looked. In the spring of 1944, Baker Street had finally tumbled to the fact that 'something fishy' was going on, and Buckmaster began a double cross of his own. In order to beat the Germans at their own game, he continued with his arms drops to blown circuits in order to bluff the enemy into thinking he believed they were still uncontaminated. He laid his bait for the Gestapo, who snatched at it greedily. Drops were concentrated on the area, which both sides knew were crucial in relation to the battle to come:

> [The Gestapo] were encouraged to believe that we were unaware of the extent of their penetration, and deliveries of stores were continued to circuits known to be Gestapo-operated, in order to give time for new circuits to establish themselves. And new organisers were sent to the field . . .

Odd as it may seem to have delivered tons of expensive arms and explosives, in still more expensive aircraft, with almost irreplaceable aircrew, straight into the enemy's hands, it had an important result. It meant that the Germans, deep in their own deception scheme, did not endanger the new circuits by attacking Allied aircraft. The double-edged sword of the *funkspiel* was turned against the enemy.

By stealth, F Section filled in the interstices between the

contaminated circuits. Softly, softly, Claude de Baissac was sent to Normandy; Major Bodington to Epernay; two Americans, Lieutenant Henquet and Lieutenant Bassett, to Blois; while Cowburn's successor continued his good work in Troyes. Thirteen new networks were established in northern France and, as a result: 'The battle area was by D-Day fairly completely surrounded by F Section circuits.' In all, forty new SOE circuits were in place in France by D-Day.

Unlike Prosper, Hector had trained two deputies and, even more fortunately, both had evaded capture. Pearl Witherington and Amédée Maingard had a crucial meeting on 3 May 1944. Neither was prepared to let their circuit die; in fact, they could not let it die. They and Hector had been waiting to be told their targets for D-Day at the time of his arrest. For the command organisation of SOE, it was an urgent necessity to 'rebuild, and rebuild quickly' in order that the Resistance could meet their targets, which were generally against German army communications.

At this council of war, Samuel and Marie decided how to go forward. Both considered that 'Stationer' was too large in its present form for a single organiser to run. They decided to divide it: Pearl would take command of the northern half of the *département* of the Indre, concentrating on the Valençay-Issoudon-Châteauroux triangle, the historic heartland of central France where F Section's first agent, Georges Bégué, had been dropped three years earlier. Her new circuit was named 'Wrestler'. From 3 May, the home of the Sabassier family, the lodge at Château Les Souches, became her HQ.

Samuel took the south-west of the *département*, now named 'Shipwright'. Jacques and Pierre Hirsch remained with him as his deputies.

Within just a few days in May, 'Stationer', apparently destroyed, was reborn. 'Their agents, orphaned on 1 May 1944, regain the initiative and fly on their own wings,' writes historian Maurice Nicault. 'Swarming' into central and southern France, they liaised with civil resistance movements like the MUR and the *Front National*, but also with the military such as the FTP and the *Armée*

Secrète. The far south of 'Stationer', the Pyrénées and Aquitaine, became 'Fireman', a new circuit run by two Mauritians, the Mayer brothers.

At this juncture, there was probably not another woman in France who could have done what Pearl did. Most of the female agents sent into France in 1943 or 1944 had been captured: their tragic roll-call included Noor Inayat Kkhan, Violette Szabo, Andrée Borrel, Yvonne Baseden, Yolande Beekman, Denise Bloch, Madeleine Damerment, Cicely Lefort, Vera Leigh, Eileen Nearne, Eliane Plewman, Lilian Rolfe, Diana Rowden, Yvonne Rudellat and Odette Sansom; Muriel Byck had died of meningitis, and many others would die in the camps. A few remained in the field: Lise de Baissac, Yvonne Cormeau, Christine Granville, Virginia Hall, Nancy Wake. But none became, as Pearl did, *chef de réseau*, a circuit chief: she rose magnificently to the challenge.

On 15 May, Buckmaster promoted Pearl to WAAF section officer, with immediate effect. She was now officially the circuit commander of 'Wrestler/Marie' in the Indre with Tutur (Berge) as her radio. A woman, a foreigner. The only woman to run an SOE network in occupied France. The *maquisards* shook their heads in wonder at the strange turn of events:

> *Un étranger, et une femme qui était tombée du ciel . . . cela dépassait l'imagination. On ne concevait pas qu'une femme ait pu faire ça, surtout à l'époque et puis, elle était jolie!* A foreigner and a woman, who'd fallen from the sky . . . It was beyond belief. You'd never have thought a woman would have been able to do that, especially in those days, and she was pretty, too! She made the *parachutages* happen, she was our idol, we fought because of her . . .

People found her *sympathique*, warm, likeable, friendly. 'Ah, Pearl,' recalled Henri Diacono, a former W/T operator: 'She was a very pretty girl, she was *très sympathique*. The ambience in general was *très sympathique*. Everybody wanted it that way. We were all young and doing a very interesting training, it was a good laugh.' For Diacono, who'd been bored stiff in the army, fighting in Pearl's *maquis* was much more exciting. 'We were so excited by what we were doing that we didn't think about the dangers waiting for us outside, and we preferred not to think about them anyway . . .'

From 25 May, 'Wrestler' was operational. Pearl took the *nom de guerre* of 'Pauline', and to her troops would be known as *le lieutenant Pauline*. When asked why she chose the name, she later replied that she once had a doll named Pauline; but her choice may also have owed its origin to her long years in the British Embassy, the former residence of Princess Pauline Borghese. Certainly Pauline would become venerated and adored by her troops with the same passion as that felt by her courtiers for Princess Pauline and, as a woman soldier, she would rule the men around her with an authority equal to that of any imperial princess. Indeed, the warrior queen jokingly referred to herself as 'She Who Must Be Obeyed.'

But even with her unique gifts, Pearl knew she could not command alone. She needed Henri, who was rapidly turning from a privileged, dilettante young Parisian into a soldier, too. She loved him and wanted to keep him near. Most importantly, in a world of suspicion, she could trust him. Strong, keen, devoted to Pearl, who would make a better second-in-command? It was an easy choice: she appointed Henri as her second, and he took the *nom de guerre* 'Jean,' becoming known as *le lieutenant Jean*.

Maingard immediately put Pearl in touch with the heads of resistance in the region and they, just as quickly, recognised Pearl's abilities. She had organised parachute drops for Hector before, and would insist on the same security precautions as he had done although, with the excited young volunteers who formed the reception committees, they were often difficult to enforce.

Pearl's reputation spread rapidly. She was 'tall and beautiful, her silhouette instantly recognisable,' wrote one smitten volunteer, Michel Mockers, who recorded that she spoke perfect French, with a slight Normandy accent. Her simplicity and warm smile imprinted themselves on his memory:

> *Le lieutenant Pauline* was an admirable woman who knew how to make herself loved wherever she went . . . She was the *grande*

creatrice, the creator of the Northern Indre sector. It was she who provided the drive, the push . . .

Le lieutenant Pauline could magic from the sky Sten guns, explosives, rocket launchers; even English cigarettes and chocolate came in SOE containers. And, by mid-May, everyone was waiting impatiently for the invasion. The date was secret; but it could not be far off . . .

From Hector's list of contacts found in Châteauroux, the Gestapo were hot on the trail of two particular Frenchmen whose names were on the list: Mayor Mardon of Dun-le-Poëlier, local chief of the Secret Army, and Théogène Briant – Alex – the Communist FTP leader whom Southgate had met in February. The Germans were still under strict orders to mop up the 'terrorists' before the invasion. Did they hear news of the latest *parachutage*, the one that dropped the American, Major Dussac, to the field next to Château Les Souches? Was it that that brought them to the village, Dun-le-Poëlier?

On 1 June 1944, at 6.30 p.m., two Citroen jeeps from the Châteauroux Gestapo drove into the village of Dun and stopped outside the home of Amand Mardon. The mayor, who lived alone with his mother, went out to greet the Germans. They seized him and pushed him into the house. Minutes later, Mardon emerged, his face dripping with blood, his hands tied behind his back, and was driven off in the direction of nearby Villebaslin.

The other jeep stopped outside the home of Briant, who had returned at dawn from a sabotage mission, and was fast asleep. He was also alone, having sent his wife away for her safety to stay with his brother, a gendarme in Châteauroux.

The Gestapo hammered on the door. Receiving no answer, they asked a neighbour: 'Where is Monsieur Briant?'

'Oh, I've just seen him,' replied the woman with apparent innocence. '*Il est parti vers son jardin, une pioche sur l'épaule*. He's gone into his garden with a pick-axe.'

Alex was in fact crouching behind an upstairs window, ready to open fire with his machine gun, but instead of searching his house, the Gestapo drove off towards Villebaslin, where his brother Siméon lived. But, thankfully, the local butcher, also a resister, had seen the

Germans and sent his niece on her bicycle – a pot of milk balanced across the handlebars as her excuse in case she met a German control – to Villebaslin, where she was just in time to warn the rest of the Briant family. Alex slipped away to the forest of Les Tailles de Ruines, where his men were encamped and already planning to ambush the Gestapo and rescue Mardon.

From Les Souches, Henri and Robert Kneper, an escaped prisoner of war who was a member of Alex's *maquis*, cycled furiously after the jeep containing the mayor. It was all in vain. When they arrived out of breath in Châteauroux, the mayor's captors had already taken him to the Gestapo HQ in the rue des Mousseaux.

Within hours, Marguerite Briant, Alex's wife, was also brought in to rue des Mousseaux. She caught a glimpse of Mardon. '*Il était dans un état pitoyable, et n'avait plus figure humaine.* He was in a pitiful state, his face no longer that of a human being.'

For many months, the Führer had been deliberating over exactly when to reveal to the British the Gestapo's penetration of their circuits. Convinced that to do so would cause consternation among the Allies and destabilise their operations, Adolf Hitler waited till D-Day itself. On 6 June, a message came over the ticker-tape in Room 52, transmitted *en clair* over the 'Butler' circuit's radio. Addressed to Colonel Buckmaster, it was laden with a gloating sarcasm reminiscent of the earlier April Fool's Day's telegram:

> WE THANK YOU FOR THE LARGE DELIVERIES OF ARMS AND AMMUNITIONS WHICH YOU HAVE BEEN KIND ENOUGH TO SEND US. WE ALSO APPRECIATE THE MANY TIPS YOU HAVE GIVEN US REGARDING YOUR PLANS AND INTENTIONS WHICH WE HAVE CAREFULLY NOTED. IN CASE YOU ARE CONCERNED ABOUT THE HEALTH OF SOME OF THE VISITORS YOU HAVE SENT US YOU MAY REST ASSURED THAT THEY WILL BE TREATED WITH THE CONSIDERATION THEY DESERVE.

Leo Marks, looking at Buckmaster alone at his desk, would 'wonder what his true feelings were'. He suspected that Buckmaster had never completely shared his conviction that the 'Butler' circuit was blown, and had therefore continued to drop stores – ostensibly to deceive the Gestapo – for he had dropped agents as well.

Shortly before midnight on D-Day, Buckmaster instructed the signals office to transmit his reply *en clair*:

SORRY TO SEE YOUR PATIENCE IS EXHAUSTED AND YOUR NERVES NOT AS GOOD AS OURS BUT IF IT IS ANY CONSOLATION YOU WILL BE PUT OUT OF YOUR MISERY IN THE NEAR FUTURE. PLEASE GIVE US DROPPING GROUNDS NEAR BERLIN . . .

22
Neptune's Trident

D-DAY MINUS five: 1 June 1944. The BBC broadcast its first warning messages to the Resistance: '*Le combat viendra*. The moment of battle is approaching.'

On 3 June, the first 'stand-by' *messages personnes*, coded messages, were read, and lasted for eight hours. It was hard to absorb their portent. The resisters shook their heads in disbelief, pumped each other's hands. At last, the holy grail, the Allied landing so long wished for, envisioned, expected in the autumn of 1943, was within sight. They bent closer to their wireless sets.

In Dun-le-Poëlier, the Gaullist Secret Army was, however, in disarray. The arrest of its leader, Monsieur Mardon, also on 1 June, had caused consternation among his followers, and the political rivalries that had torn the Resistance apart came to the fore: Mardon's men refused pointblank to join Alex's Communists in his camp in the woods at Les Tailles de Ruines.

It was Pauline's first challenge as circuit commander, and she acted without hesitation: 'In the face of the refusal of members of the AS to accept the command of Monsieur Briant (FTP), *la mission* Buckmaster is taking over the direction of all the resisters,' she reported crisply. Breaking into English, she was more frank: the Resistance situation was:

> . . . nothing short of chaotic . . . Monsieur Mardon had not nominated anyone to take over from him and apart from a few odd arms, there was no equipment to speak of. I discovered that in spite of the fact that Monsieur Mardon had had a certain amount of parachute operations, 80 per cent of the arms had

> been given over to the Communists. His various contacts in villages and farms were not organised for guerrilla warfare and it was only after much trouble that we managed to tie things together.

It was no easy matter for Pearl to wrest control from the bombastic Briant, who had seized most of the arms parachuted to the area, but she did so with tact and finesse: 'When M. Mardon was arrested, Commandant Alex called himself the "Chef Militaire Nord Indre," and bombarded me with requests for material and long epistles every day,' she noted. 'He maintained that he had large bodies of troops, but always refused to give me any definite figure.' She remained firm.

> I could see no reason for his receiving arms as I knew perfectly well that he had everything he needed, and I had to use every possible ruse to stave him off. In spite of this, our personal contacts were never stormy; he was not an exceedingly intelligent man and he probably could not see through me.

She had outmanoeuvred the Communist, while remaining on cordial terms with him: quite a feat for a rookie circuit organiser.

Pearl's ability to unite the Resistance and bind them to a common cause was a talent that she had, to some extent, learnt from Southgate. But it was also in her nature, and her charisma led to rapid defections from the FTP: those partisans who weren't really Communists joined her. 'We served as a rallying point for the boys who didn't want to be part of a Communist organisation,' she explained later. 'We were absolutely submerged by all those chaps who turned up and didn't want to follow him.'

But Henri was concerned for the safety of the Communists. 'Those *francs-tireurs* [FTP] are too politicised,' he told Pearl. 'Have you seen that they're walking about with the red star on their uniform? They're very conspicuous, and the Gestapo are out to get them.'

'I know,' said Pearl.

'Well, what are we going to do about it?'

'I'll think of something.'

Sitting morosely in his tent in the woods, Alex complained bitterly that his men were deserting him for Pearl, which meant he had to start a new *maquis* from scratch. Even his best man, Robert Kneper, a former officer in the French army, had gone over to *le lieutenant Pauline*, who continued to fend off Alex's demands with polite letters of her own, which she posted daily in a hollow tree.

By the eve of Operation Neptune, Pearl was in command of fifty men; Alex about seventy. For all his faults, Alex's group was still 'the only one properly organised' apart from Pearl's, and he would soon prove more useful than she could ever have guessed.

D-Day minus one: 5 June 1944. Pearl, Henri and Robert L'Hospitalier are in the kitchen of the lodge at Château Les Souches. The battered radio is the most important item on the kitchen table. It is 9.15 p.m. and the news is over, the supper plates cleared away by Madame Sabassier and Yvonne. They wait for Agent Marie's *messages personnels* to come over the BBC French service.

Out in the English Channel, the van of the invasion fleet is creeping within sight of the Normandy shore.

The radio crackles into life: '*Ici Londres, ici Londres*. London calling!'

Pearl bends closer to the radio. In the kitchen you can hear a pin drop: 'Pour Marie: "*Quasimodo est une fête*. Quasimodo is a festival",' says the announcer, speaking slowly and distinctly. '*Ne folâtrez pas le matin*. Don't fool about in the morning.. *Le Xerxès est un vin d'Espagne*. Xerxes is a Spanish wine. *Une femme fagotée*. An oddly dressed woman.'

The messages are nonsense, but that night they have a special meaning: 'Intensify the guerrilla; sabotage the telephone cables; obstruct the roads; sabotage the railway lines.' The Resistance is to act as Neptune's trident by attacking enemy troops, disrupting communications and blocking reinforcements.

That evening, Lieutenant Pauline issues her call to arms to the men of the Indre. Under cover of darkness, she and Henri steal away from Les Souches with Robert L'Hospitalier – Marc – to the woods of Les Tailles de Ruines, where they find Robert Kneper and knots of partisans camped around a fire. It is a chilly, foggy night in early summer, and the wind is gusting through the trees. The *maquisards* are poking the fire and singing a ragged chorus of '*Le Chant des Partisans*', their marching song.

'*Écoutez, mes amis.*' Slowly the men fall silent, watching Pearl's tall figure standing at the entrance to the camp. She has borrowed a black beret, which sits at a jaunty angle on her fair hair. 'I have something to tell you . . . Something you have been waiting to hear.' She pauses for effect. 'It is good news. Great news . . . the Allies are coming. They are coming tonight.'

There are murmurs of incredulity. Some men rise to their feet, open-mouthed. Others shrug. They've heard that one before.

'Listen to me.' Pearl is standing very straight, eyes shining. '*Je vous donne ma parole,* I give you my word. We have just heard over the BBC . . .'

'*Ah, la radio britannique.*' They are listening now. The BBC has a certain authenticity: it brings the voices of General de Gaulle and Winston Churchill all the way from London.

Pearl continues, speaking with passion the words she has turned over in her mind on her way up to the camp: 'Tonight is the eve of the landings, *la veille du débarquement*, the long-awaited moment. Even as I speak to you, ships are crossing *la Manche* towards the shores of France. They are streaming across the Channel. Thousands of men are coming, with their guns and their tanks, fleets of aircraft. British, Americans, Australians, Canadians, they are all coming to liberate France from the yoke of the oppressor. Freedom is within reach: four years of occupation are about to end. Together we will drive out *les Boches*. Together we will make history. Tonight I call you and all the men of the Indre to arms. *Je vous donne l'ordre de ralliement*. Raise high our standard! Let us fight under the cross of Lorraine. *Vive la France!*'

A bugle sounds and the men in their mud-stained jackets and trousers stand to attention and salute their flag, the tricolour emblazoned with the Cross of Lorraine. It is Kneper, the regular army officer, who tells them to stand easy and raps out their orders: a party is to attack the *gendarmerie* at the nearby village of Saint-Christophe-en-Bazelle and seize any weapons they can; another party is to spend the night cutting down trees and blocking the roads. Yet another party is to cut the railway line by putting explosive charges on the points to derail German trains coming up from the south. And, everywhere they go, the men are to call for volunteers to follow *le lieutenant Pauline* and join them in the liberation struggle.

At Saint-Christophe, the attack is successful and six *Gardes Mobiles* (gendarmes), who have already been resisters in the Dordogne, join the 'Wrestler' *maquis* with their weapons. It is the beginning of an unstoppable movement. Word of Pearl's call to arms spreads like wildfire though the scattered farms and villages and beyond, to the furthest corners of the *département*. Her appeal brings in hundreds of young men who are thirsting for action against the Germans.

'It is the beginning of open resistance to the enemy,' writes Pearl with evident relief. 5 June marks a new phase in her battle to expel the occupier: the dark shadow war, in which she had long been mouse to the Gestapo cat, will give way to a new phase of guerrilla warfare in support of the invading forces.

At last she can make war like a Witherington: her blood is up, the blood of her fighting Northumbrian ancestors. Pearl organises the Nord Indre circuit for battle, confirming that Henri – *Jean* – will be her second-in-command, Marc her radio technician and arms instructor, and Kneper her *agent de liaison*, charged with contacting the heads of resistance movements within the circuit. She still lacks a 'pianist', for Tutur will not return until 17 June.

Henri and Kneper take their wire-cutters and spend the night of 5 June outside, up telephone poles, cutting wires. In her HQ, Pearl listens to the sounds of saws and axes and the crash of falling trees.

On the north side of the river Cher, at Salbris, Philippe de Vomécourt, who went by the field name of 'St Paul', was receiving his own personal messages for his circuit, 'Ventriloquist'. On 1 June:

'*Les sanglots longs des violins de l'automne.* The long sobs of the violins of autumn.' It was the first line of a poem by Verlaine, the sign that the invasion was imminent. De Vomécourt waited anxiously for the second half of the message, telling him that the landings were due within forty-eight hours.

Nothing came.

On 5 June, however, the imperturbable voice of the BBC announcer, unaware of the momentous importance of his words, intoned: '*Blessent mon coeur d'une langueur monotone.* Pierce my heart with languorous monotony.' It was the second line of the couplet: de Vomécourt's own call to action. The baron's heart leapt at the thought that, within two days, Allied forces would be fighting once again on French soil.

Increasingly desperate to rid themselves of 'the terror behind the lines' before the invasion, Germans reprisals had become ever more vicious. In the months before D-Day, 79,000 members of the Resistance were arrested, of whom 50,000 were deported. Philippe de Vomécourt recalled: 'Young men screamed in torture chambers; others fell before the shots of firing squads crying "*Vive la France! Vive de Gaulle!*"'

Patriotism was no longer an abstract ideal: it had become a 'passionate reality'. And the harder the Germans tried to repress the Resistance, the stronger it grew, like a great steel spring which, released on D-Day, uncoiled with all the more force for having been suppressed.

The Germans were listening to the 300 'action' messages broadcast on the eve of the invasion, too. The coded messages were going on for much longer than usual, their sheer number indicating that something was up. When, at 9.30 p.m., the Gestapo wireless section at Avenue Foch picked up Ventriloquist's '*Blessent mon coeur*' action message – which had originally been allocated to the German-penetrated 'Butler' circuit – they realised that it was the signal for the invasion, and at once alerted the German high command.

Their call was ignored. 'Just another false alarm,' was the reaction from Field Marshal Gerd von Rundstedt, commander-in-chief west.

Nor was Field Marshal Erwin Rommel, commander-in-chief of Army Group B, who was responsible for the Channel defences, ready to respond. It was his wife's birthday and the Panzer chief was away on leave in Herrlingen, near Ulm. Normally, he would have been visiting the Atlantic Wall, the defence system that ran from Norway to the Spanish frontier, in which Hitler placed as much faith as the French had once done in the Maginot line.

Rommel, who suspected that the Allies would land in Normandy and was sure that the outcome of the battle would be decided in the first two days, had been devoting his considerable energies to building up the coastal fortifications there, ordering his men to plant 'hedgehogs', tetraheda and Belgian gates – all formidable iron and steel obstacles – as well as spikes, known as 'Rommel asparagus', in the water and on the beach.

A master of mobile warfare who first caught the eye of the Führer when he was his personal escort at the 1936 Olympic Games in Berlin, Rommel 'the Fox' had proposed massing all available Panzer divisions on the coast in order to be ready for the Allies. Like his old foe, General Montgomery, who had employed this strategy against him in 1942 at the battle of Alam Halfa in Egypt, he knew the value of strengthening his defensive front with entrenched Panzers.

But, to his infinite frustration, Rommel did not have a free hand: he was subordinate to Rundstedt and the *Wehrmacht* high command, *Oberkommando des Wehrmacht* (OKW).

Tensions between the German generals had risen to breaking point. Rundstedt, a Prussian aristocrat of the old school, ignored the 'boy marshal, Marschall Bubi', as he nicknamed the Panzer hero sixteen years his junior. He thought Hitler's favourite had been promoted beyond his abilities. The 'last Prussian', as Rundstedt was known, was still clinging to classic German doctrine in Panzer warfare, massing his tanks north of Paris, out of reach of the Allies' naval artillery. In his determination to frustrate Rommel, he had even set up his own command under his favourite, General Leo Geyr von Schweppenburg, commander of Panzer group west.

On 5 June, Hitler, too, was away partying. Holed up at his Alpine residence at Berchtesgaden, he had been hosting the wedding of Eva Braun's sister: his weather forecasters had told him that there was no chance of a break in the weather before 10 June, and the depression over the English Channel was his signal to relax. Circulating with the champagne, Hitler's spirits were high, and he impatiently waved Rommel away when the *Feldmarschall* called at the Berghof to beg for two more Panzer divisions.

Rommel was ready to go down on his knees to plead for more Panzers: his instincts told him that the Allies were coming and coming soon, but Hitler would have none of it. That night, the tipsy Führer swallowed a sleeping draught. Secure in the knowledge that he was right, he ordered his staff not to wake him in the morning.

The Führer was convinced that the main invasion would come at the Pas-de-Calais in July: his spies in Britain – unbeknowest to him 'turned' by the British – had told him so, while the *Luftwaffe*'s spotter planes had also seen tanks, aircraft and landing ships, reporting that eleven divisions were ready and waiting in south-east England to launch an amphibious assault on France. But there was no need to worry, for the invasion was still weeks away . . .

In reality, the tanks were made of cardboard, the aircraft all dummies – they represented the mythical '1st US Army Group', supposedly led by General George S. Patton Jr. The trick was the creation of the London Controlling Section in London as part of Plan Fortitude, the most ambitious deception scheme in the history of warfare.

Unlike Operation Cockade, Fortitude had proved a success – so far. As Churchill had said, when he approved it: 'In wartime, truth is so precious that she should always be attended by a bodyguard of lies.' That protective bodyguard had to be preserved at all costs if Neptune was to succeed.

In the tense first days of June, the secret was holding. Hitler did not suspect that Patton's 'army' was a hoax and that his German spies were all ghosts. Convinced that any landing in Normandy would only be a diversion, he refused to let Rommel have the two Panzer divisions that were positioned north of the Seine, ready to repel the notional 'main' invasion at the Pas-de-Calais. The guns of the Atlantic Wall were trained towards the sea on the coast between Boulogne and the Somme estuary; they were waiting to mow down the Americans as they stormed the beaches there.

Supremely confident, Hitler had been waiting for months for the enemy to come. His frustration was shared by others: 'They are supposed to be coming. Why don't they come?' demanded Joseph Goebbels, the Reich propaganda minister. The slogan became a popular one.

Hitler's orders were to defend 'Fortress Europe' to the last man, and throw the Allies back into the sea. But his policy of operating a 'divide and rule' approach to his generals was hampering the execution of his orders: Rundstedt's favourite, Geyr, and Rommel were still arguing. Rommel maintained that an Allied landing must be prevented at all costs, while Geyr countered that it would be impossible to prevent it and therefore the Panzers must be held in reserve to crush the Allied advance.

The Führer personally dictated a compromise that satisfied neither general. Hitler gave Rommel the 2nd, 21st and 116th Panzer Divisions to defend the coast, leaving Geyr with only four mobile divisions. The meddling Führer trusted none of his generals: in April 1944, he had ordered Runstedt not to move the reserve without his express permission and stripped him of authority over the Gestapo. Only the Prussian code of honour, duty and loyalty still ensured the commander-in-chief's reluctant and cynical obedience.

News of the invasion reached the Berghof in the early morning of 6 June 1944. But Hitler's staff dared not disobey his orders, and failed to wake him. At last, the drowsy Führer roused himself and dressed. It was mid-afternoon before he finally agreed to Rundstedt's frantic requests to deploy the Panzer reserve.

One day earlier, on a wet and windy Monday, General Dwight D. Eisenhower, Supreme Commander of the Allied Expeditionary Force (SHAEF), stood on South Parade Pier, Southsea, and stared out over the grey Solent. The spire of Ryde church on the Isle of

Wight was just visible through the mist: it was only a day's sail to Cherbourg from the island and, around the corner of the Cotentin Peninsula, lay the beckoning beaches of Normandy.

But Ike's attention was focused on the sea behind St Catherine's Point: 'Piccadilly Circus'. There bobbed a vast armada of 5,000 craft, awaiting the signal to slip anchor; the battleships had arrived from Scapa Flow in Orkney, the transport ships and landing craft were roped together in the choppy water, the minesweepers were waiting to lead the way.

Winston Churchill ordered his private train to be stopped at a station near Portsmouth in order to be as close to Eisenhower as possible. He was entertaining a difficult guest: General Charles de Gaulle, who had arrived from Algiers the previous morning in a towering rage.

Flown in from North Africa on the night of 3 June, de Gaulle was understandably furious at being given only forty-eight hours' notice of the liberation of France.

'We are outraged at the way France's Allies, particularly the English, have treated him,' Lieutenant Valois, head of Free French signals at Duke Street, told Leo Marks at Norgeby House.

The general had been excluded from all discussion about Overlord; he hadn't even been told the date of the invasion until Churchill sent for him on the night of 4 June. But the greatest of all insults, said Valois, 'was that his French troops in the 3rd SAS regiment had received their orders before he'd been allowed to know where they were.'

The general had also been ordered to communicate with his own followers in British codes that, said Valois accusingly, the British could read. It was unacceptable, now that the *Comité Français de Libération* in Algiers had proclaimed itself the provisional government of France on 3 June.

'It's SHAEF who've decided that only the British, Americans and Russians can use their own codes while the invasion is in progress,' replied Marks. 'General de Gaulle hasn't been singled out for special treatment.'

The Frenchman shook his head. The war leaders – 'especially

Mr Churchill' – had treated General de Gaulle as if he were . . . he struggled for the word.

Marks didn't know the French for 'outsider' and nearly said '*juif*', Jew, but bit his tongue.

'*Il est tout seul*,' finished Valois quietly. 'He is quite alone.'

It had been humiliating for de Gaulle to be summoned into Churchill's presence and informed that Operation Neptune was already taking place. French commandos were already at sea, SAS troops were briefed and sealed on a Gloucestershire airfield. But Churchill dared not risk blowing the D-Day secret. Haunted by memories of past failures – the Dardanelles, Dakar and Dieppe – he was far less confident than the Americans that the great amphibious assault would succeed.

Ever since Dunkirk, Churchill had been convinced that Germany could only be driven out of Europe by a cross-Channel landing. The British army had been driven back across the Channel in 1940 and, with the help of the Americans, it would return across the Channel to reverse that defeat. But now that day had arrived, the prime minister feared a bloodbath. As he kept vigil with his wife, Clementine, on the night before the invasion, he said: 'Do you realise that by the time you wake up in the morning, 20,000 men may have been killed?'

Churchill had strained every sinew to guard the D-Day secret. He had locked down the UK borders and placed a ban on all travel to Ireland after the Dublin government had refused a plea from Roosevelt to break ties with Berlin and Tokyo. He had banned access to huge areas of the English coast, tightened postal censorship, ordered ships' crews to be strictly vetted, forbidden diplomats to leave Great Britain. He had even been prepared to order the liquidation of a senior RAF officer who knew too much: Air Commodore Ronald Ivelaw-Chapman, commander of a squadron identifying German radar installations in north-west Europe, was shot down over France four weeks before D-Day. 'Recover him at all costs,' Churchill ordered Morton, 'or have him killed.'

There was simply too much at stake to risk entrusting the secret to the Free French. Their codes were leaky: Marks had been cracking them since 1942 and re-encoding the messages from RF agents in British codes in order to protect their lives. As a consequence, the security-conscious prime minister had ordered that no intelligence that could possibly compromise Overlord should be passed to the Free French.

Churchill had realised, however, that de Gaulle's co-operation was vital on D-Day. The Allies needed the Resistance to play a vital part in the invasion and, from August 1942, the War Cabinet's 'Most Secret' Directives to SOE had ordered it to conform to their plans by organising patriot action: preventing the arrival of enemy reinforcements by the interruption of road, rail and air transport, interrupting enemy signal communication in and behind the battle area generally, preventing demolitions by the enemy and attacking enemy aircraft and personnel.

There were four plans: Plan *Vert*, Green, sabotage of the railways; *Violet*, cutting telephone cables; *Tortue*, Tortoise, blocking the roads; and *Bleu*, Blue, sabotaging electric power lines. Such sabotage would contribute to victory by isolating Normandy from the rest of France. Nevertheless, Eisenhower expected the Allied air forces to be his principal weapon in preventing the Germans from sending up reinforcements; it was thought that the Resistance's efforts would be no more than a 'bonus', in the catchphrase of the time. Stewart Menzies – C – was even more scathing, opining that: 'SOE's odds and sods would merely have a nuisance value.'

Thanks to its *parachutages*, by this time SOE's 'odds and sods' were armed with 74,131 Sten submachine guns; 27,047 pistols; plus rifles, Brens (light machine guns), bazookas (anti-tank rocket launchers), PIATs (Projector Infantry Anti-Tank weapons) and mortars. But it was also clear that the *Forces Françaises de l'Intérieur* (FFI), in spite of SOE's efforts, were 'pitifully equipped' for modern war. Their fighting value depended entirely on their skill, discipline and enthusiasm, an unquantifiable commodity about which Allied high command was in the dark. But there were around 100,000 men with arms who would take orders from London – possibly 3 million men including the railwaymen and trade unionists – and

Churchill pleaded with Roosevelt: 'It is very difficult to cut the French out of the liberation of France.'

The US president, however, took the view that Allied armies were not invading France to put de Gaulle in power. Until elections were possible, he ordered that the liberated territories were to be administered by the Allied Military Government of Occupied Territories (AMGOT). American troops were to be issued with a special Allied currency, printed in the USA.

It was a red rag to a bull. De Gaulle was furious that the president refused to recognise him as head of the provisional government, or even to allow Eisenhower to give details of the invasion to General Pierre Koenig, his commander of the *Forces Françaises de l'Intérieur*.

Eisenhower wrote to Washington:

> General Koenig feels very keenly the fact that he is denied even the most general knowledge of forthcoming operations although French naval, air and airborne units are to be employed, and much is expected from [the] French resistance.'

Churchill again added his pleas to Eisenhower's, but Roosevelt refused to meet de Gaulle. As a result, when the general arrived for lunch on Churchill's train and was invited to broadcast to the French people on D-Day, he refused to do so. It seemed to the deeply patriotic but egocentric French leader that neither Anglo-Saxon understood his problems with the Resistance – a political tinderbox primed to explode after liberation. The threat of the Communists seizing power and scuppering de Gaulle's chance of becoming France's president was uppermost in his mind as he stood stiffly in the railway carriage, his head almost touching the ceiling. Furiously he rejected the new Allied currency – '*une fausse monnaie*'.

Churchill's temper flared in turn. He had laboured hard to bring the Americans round: he had persuaded them to send French General Philippe Leclerc's *2ème Division Blindée* to England, thus making possible its future triumphant advance on Paris; he had given de Gaulle succour in the dark days of 1940 – a London office, BBC airtime, aircraft and funds for the Resistance. In return, the French cockerel had crowed his disdain, pecking angrily at the Allied hands that fed him.

Churchill, a balding British bulldog, growled at the Frenchman towering over him:

> Don't ask me to choose between the Americans and you. We are going to liberate Europe, but it is because the Americans are with us. So get this quite clear. Every time we have to choose between Europe and the open sea, it is the open sea that we shall choose. Every time I have to decide between you and Roosevelt, I shall always choose Roosevelt.

Momentarily, de Gaulle backed down. Over lunch, the two leaders drank a huffy toast to each other.

'To de Gaulle,' said Churchill, raising his glass, 'who never accepted defeat.'

De Gaulle raised his in reply: 'To Britain, to victory in Europe.'

But when Churchill showed the general the proclamation he was asking him to make to the French people on D-Day, which still failed to recognise the authority of the provisional government, de Gaulle waved it angrily away. On 6 June, Eisenhower and the other leaders of the Occupied countries spoke to their people on the BBC; de Gaulle alone refused to go to the microphone and speak to the French.

Churchill exploded when he heard the news. 'Fly the traitor back to Algiers,' he raged to Morton. But de Gaulle was there to stay.

A quarter of an hour before the French SAS touched down on the soil of France, the RAF dropped two teams from the 1st SAS regiment, and 200 dummy parachutists, onto the Cherbourg Peninsula. This was Operation Titanic, a small but audacious part of Fortitude. Ten paratroopers, an officer and four men, and an army of straw puppets, floated down in the night sky, with Very pistols, and gramophones playing records of small arms fire and soldiers' voices in the background.

The *Explosivpuppen*, as the Germans were to call them, burst into flames on landing. At 3 a.m the German 915th infantry regiment was sent in hot pursuit of the straw army.

'The buggers have fallen for it,' radioed an SAS operator on his one-time pad, as the German troops spent the morning of 6 June chasing the 'invaders', thus allowing the Americans to establish themselves on the most difficult of the beaches: 'Omaha'.

A small operation had paid a big dividend: Hitler had swallowed Fortitude as surely as he had swallowed his sleeping draught.

Meanwhile, Resistance fighters on the Cotentin Peninsula executed Plan *Violet* and cut the underground telephone cables in order to disable German field telephones. In the middle of the night, desperate *Wehrmacht* officers screamed down their lines to their headquarters. The line was dead. They turned instead to their radios, and Ultra decoded their messages.

All over France, resisters at 137 wireless stations in over forty SOE circuits were doing likewise. It was fortuitous that Eisenhower had changed his mind at the last minute and had decided to throw the whole Resistance behind Neptune. Instead of an elaborate phasing system by which the Resistance would have been called out province by province into 'active guerrilla', the action messages that were broadcasted simultaneously from the BBC resulted in every circuit contributing to secure a maximum effort and thus ensure the success of Neptune.

All over the country, SOE agents responded, helping the sea god raise his trident and open a path through the waves to France.

On the morning of 6 June, the White Rabbit, in his punishment cell in Fresnes prison, where he was mourning the death of Brossolette heard a shout from the air vent: '*Allo, le camarade anglais*. Your comrades have landed. *Vive la France!*'

Yeo-Thomas listened as the other prisoners sang 'The Marseillaise'. To him it was like 'a heavenly choir'. Standing to attention, tears pouring down his face, he replied with 'God Save the King'.

23

The Battle of Les Souches

HENRI WAS the first to see the *mouchard*, spotter plane. It was a German Heinkel 46, buzzing over the château like a bluebottle. He watched as it circled three times, dipping over the cornfields and the woods, which were now in full leaf. Could the Boches see signs of movement, of the 'Wrestler' *maquisards* stowing armaments in the barn? 'We could use the PIATs on the plane,' thought Henri, if they were able to bring it down, 'but that would give away our position.' Turning on his heel, he ran to find Pearl.

Pearl had been expecting German attention. Three days after D-Day, her guards had stopped a man on a bicycle on the road outside Les Souches. They had escorted him down the drive, past the pink dog roses and honeysuckle towards the black iron gates of the château, and brought him to Pearl.

'Where have you come from?' she had asked.

'Paris,' replied the traveller, who was on his way to see his family.

'Paris?' repeated Pearl.

'Yes, that's right.'

'Have you been stopped on the way?'

'No,' said the cyclist, 'no, this is the first time I've been stopped.'

Pearl had felt a stab of irritation. Her men had felled trees across the roads, had cut the phone lines, had severed enemy communication, but London's orders to 'make havoc' had been ignored by other circuits. 'We were the only ones who'd done so by cutting down trees all over the *département*.'

'Oh God,' thought Pearl, 'now we're for it.'

Immediately after the landings, Henri had 'requisitioned' all the outbuildings at the chateau 'in the name of the Resistance', and the *maquisards* had begun using them as sleeping quarters and arms stores. Henri had also warned the Pétainist owners of the chateau, Monsieur and Madame Hay des Nétumières, to leave.

Thinking themselves safe from the Germans, they had refused. 'They completely failed to understand the situation,' said Pearl. Their refusal had fatal results: Monsieur Hay des Nétumières would be shot and his wife deported, dying in Ravensbrück. Vichy sympathies served as no protection against German wrath.

News of the landings, broadcast over the radio, swept through northern Indre and the Cher valley. In the streets, people whispered to each other, their lips barely moving but their eyes alight with excitement: '*Ils ont débarqué*. They've landed!'

The news produced the same crescendo of joy in south-west France as it did in Châteauroux. In the Lot, SOE agent George Hiller exulted at '. . . the beauty of life, the joys of spring, the stream of men and cars, the relief of being armed.' The *débarquement* triggered a tsunami of action. The years of *attentisme*, of sitting on the fence, were finally over. It was their time, said the French, time to rise up, an unstoppable movement. And, for the first time, the Germans felt a new emotion: a ripple of fear, which would become an ocean of dread as the despised French, who in 1940 had 'run like rabbits', in the words of Jean-Paul Sartre, now rediscovered their courage and honour.

For many men, 6 June was the day they rushed to enlist with the 'Wrestler' *maquis*: '*Je pars ce soir*. I'm leaving tonight,' was the cry in houses all over the area as husbands and sons, young and not so young, evaders from forced labour, escaped POWs, old soldiers, doctors, shopkeepers and peasants melted into the forests of the Indre. Pauline's band of irregulars swelled rapidly, and would soon number 500 men.

At last, the years of effort and sacrifice produced what Churchill and de Gaulle, Gubbins and Koenig, Colonel Passy and Buckmaster, all the scores of agents already dead, and the hundreds of agents still alive – in prison, or out of it – had been striving to achieve: a French national uprising. The mass *levée* was finally happening.

The Germans were initially taken by surprise by the popular insurrection, but as its size and scale became evident, their reaction was rapid and *rücksichlos*, ruthless. From Clermont-Ferrand, two columns of troops would set out to march against the Indre: the first, the Stenger column, advancing towards Argenton-sur-Creuse and Châteauroux; the second, the Burckhardt column, formed from three companies of the SD's 192nd Security Regiment, and the uniformed army *Feldgendarmerie* of Vierzon, Romorantin and Bourges. Both columns orders were to comb the northern sector of the *département* and stamp out the *maquisards* without delay.

As Pearl had realised, the Germans were on her tail. On 10 June, the day after the spotter plane had made its reconnaissance flight over Les Souches, one of her new volunteers, a former sailor named Raymond Billard, a.k.a. 'Gaspard', was driving along the winding road which ran through the pines between the château and the Sebassier guardhouse when, to his surprise, he found his way blocked by a German jeep.

'I was face to face with the Fritz.' Billard jammed on his brakes. The Germans were as astonished as the *maquisards*. 'We got out quick,' says Billard. But as he roared back down the drive to safety, machine gun fire followed him. From then on, it was only a matter of time.

At first light the next day, Sunday 11 June, the Burckhardt column marched out of their barracks in Bourges to clean up Pearl's patch at Les Souches, the 'Wrestler' HQ. The Gestapo was certain that the Englishwoman known as 'Pauline' was commanding a large force of 'terrorists' and hiding a stack of arms. The German battle group of 2,000 men, the feared Gestapo with the *Feldgendarmes* conspicuous in their gleaming brass breastplates, was tasked to destroy her and her force.

It was a warm summer's day, and the local Catholic priest, the Abbé Vaucluse, had arrived early to say Mass with the *maquisards*. Henri, who was far more devout than Pearl, had met him at the lodge and escorted him down the drive to a clearing in front of the château which served as an open-air church. Henri had set up a makeshift altar and Madame Sabassier had provided a white linen cloth to cover it; the abbé had brought a silver crucifix from his private chapel that he set upon the altar, and holy wafers for the service. The sun was rising and the early morning sunlight gleamed on the cross as the members of the *maquis* bent their heads and began murmuring the familiar Latin, their responses following the rise and fall of the priest's words as he led the service: '*Nomine patri et filio* . . .'

Henri drove back down the drive to Pearl who was waiting impatiently for him at the lodge. She was still in her nightclothes, and feeling uneasy. She had spent a restless night, tossing and turning, dreaming once again that the Germans were about to arrest her.

As Henri clattered up the stairs to the attic, she hushed him: 'Quiet, Henri. I need to hear if there's any trouble.'

'Trouble? *Pouf*, there won't be any trouble. It's Sunday. The Fritz won't attack on a Sunday.'

'Why not?'

'Sunday's a holy day, everyone knows that.'

'I wouldn't be so sure. It's the perfect opportunity.'

'*Le bon Dieu nous protège*. How many times have I've told you – God is looking after us. We are on the side of right, the Fritz is on the side of the Devil . . .'

'*Tais-toi*, Henri, shut up. I can hear something.'

Pearl leaned out of the window. The bugle call was faint, carried on the still morning air, but she heard it distinctly. There it was again, the notes of the bugle coming from the direction of the main road, where she had stationed her guards. They were sounding the alarm. She leapt upright and shouted: '*On est attaqués!* We're under attack!'

'*Non, non*,' protested Henri. 'It's Sunday, I told you – the Fritz won't attack on a Sunday.'

'I heard the bugle, Henri! *Vite, vite*, quick, go and look.'

'It's a waste of time . . .'

'Quick, Henri, please.'

Henri and René Sabassier peered along the drive and saw figures advancing towards them. Henri grabbed his gun and pointed it out of the window. 'I'll just shoot in the air,' he said, and fired.

Pearl turned on him in fury: 'Idiot! Are you off your head?'

'I think they are Germans,' said Henri. 'Look, they're running towards us.'

'Now you've done it.'

'I was an idiot, on reflection,' said Henri, later. 'I thought I'd let off my gun, fire a shot in the air to find out if they were Germans or *maquisards*. We found out pretty damn quick!'

Cursing under her breath, Pearl threw on her clothes, grabbed her leather handbag and the old cocoa tin in which she stored the 'Wrestler' funds, and ran to the ladder at the back of the house. It led from the attic down to the garden, and offered their only escape route. She had lost valuable moments: the Germans could see her climbing down the ladder and began shooting. Bullets whistled around Pearl's head as she slid down the last few rungs of the ladder and dropped to the ground.

Jumping on her bicycle, she pedalled furiously down the drive towards the outhouse in which she had stored the arms from their last parachute drop. She knew that the magazines would have to be filled and the hand grenades cleaned and primed before they could be used; she could see no sign of her little group of *maquisards* and hoped that they had heard the shots and taken cover.

'I was doing all this on my own, as fast as I could – I'd got no time to clean the guns.' It was too bad. Pearl was still loading bullets into the magazines and putting detonators into the grenades when Billard (Gaspard) her lieutenant, burst in.

'Move fast!' he ordered, 'The Germans are coming up the alleyway – you'd best get out of the way.'

Looking over her shoulder, Pearl saw that the burly sailor was right. A German soldier had come round the corner and was walking towards the château. Looking beyond him, she estimated that over fifty lorries were parked on the road, as hundreds of soldiers jumped down from them and advanced across the field. She could see them moving rapidly towards her, firing at random at anything that moved.

'Hurry, Pauline,' urged Gaspard.

Dropping the box of grenades, Pearl took her pistol from its holster and ran towards the white gate in the wall in front of her. Henri, who had followed her, crouched behind one of the barns and covered her escape with his American carbine.

Two Germans were now advancing up the drive towards him. Henri took careful aim, shot and killed the first one, and received fire from the second.

The shots brought more Germans running up the drive. 'That's brought them in, all right,' said Pearl to herself, as ever more soldiers came hurtling around the corner, 'but they're not going to catch me in the house, not on your life!' Determined not to die ignominiously, trapped in a shoot-out like the great Michael Trotobas, she ran like the wind into a field of wheat to the left of the château and threw herself to the ground. The standing corn hid her; but still she was not safe. The rapidly arriving Germans were holding flaming torches aloft and began setting fire to the nearest outbuildings.

Pearl glanced behind her and saw the flames leaping towards the roofs of the outbuildings, and heard the crackle of fire as she crawled forward, her heart thudding in her chest. She hoped that her khaki blouson battledress would blend into the ripening wheat and that the movement of the corn, rippling in the wind, would hide her progress. But as she wriggled towards a small copse, which she hoped would provide better cover, shots rang out: the Germans had seen her.

> . . . they started setting fire to everything, including this barn. And they were coming into the wheatfield. So I slowly crawled. They took a potshot, several potshots at me, because they could see where I was moving . . .

Pearl lay still: more shots. But they had missed, for the moment. She glanced down at her revolver. It was her favourite .32 Colt, but she knew that alone she was no match for the 2,000 Germans hunting her. She also knew that if she were arrested with the gun, it would incriminate her: without it, she might talk her way out of a situation. Pearl scratched a hole in the earth with her nails, and pushed her pistol into the soil. She pulled her beret down over her hair, and kept her head down in the stalks of wheat: 'I thought I was going to be able to get out of this wretched field at the end, to get into the wood. But I wasn't very far from a road, and there were lorries coming up and down all the time.'

If she moved a muscle, the waving corn betrayed her presence. Shots rang out again. She was trapped in the wheat, unable to go forward or backward, afraid for Henri. She imagined him being overpowered by the Germans as they came up the drive, shot, his body thrown into a lorry and driven away to Bourges, or being taken alive to Gestapo HQ like Mardon the mayor. She was helpless.

She could hear distant gunfire in the forest and the sound of running feet. She imagined the Germans overturning the altar as they attacked the *maquisards*, the old abbé tumbling to the ground, the cross falling into the dust, the men taking cover behind the farm buildings and trees, firing as they went. She heard the roar of mortars, and guessed that the Germans had brought up their heavy artillery. Her embryonic *maquis* numbered less than fifty, Alex's FTP barely double that. There was every chance that they would be annihilated.

Her heart sank into her boots. It seemed that her mission was about to end in ignominy. For so long she had escaped the Gestapo but now they had finally caught up with her and her men. It could only be a matter of hours before the 'Wrestler' circuit was stamped out and the flame of resistance, which had caught fire under her leadership, flickered and died. She buried her head in her hands as she waited for the soldiers to push their way through the crop, for eager hands to seize her.

But nobody came. The sounds of skirmishing in the woods continued during the hours that Pearl lay hidden under the burning sun, guarding the 'Wrestler' funds, and counting the fifty-six German lorries passing to and fro on the road beside the field; they were carrying away the weapons she had so carefully stored in arms dumps. Overhead, the *mouchards* buzzed as they patrolled the château grounds from the sky. Behind her, she could see the plumes of smoke from burning buildings rising in the air. Not until it grew dark and the Germans had driven away, did Pearl feel safe enough to emerge, scratched, thirsty and hungry. It was 10.30 p.m. The black skeletons of the barns were still burning, flames leaping into the sky, and the smell of smoke drifted through the trees. She returned to the lodge, which was still intact, hoping to find Henri. Madame Sebassier and Yvonne did not recognise the tall figure walking towards them and, mistaking Pearl for a German ran terrified into the house.

At the time of the initial German attack, the Sabassier family had decided to take shelter at a neighbouring farm, La Barraque, a kilometre away. Henri and René Sabassier had hidden in the fields like Pearl. Yvonne and her mother had not been so lucky. Just as they were about to leave the lodge, the Germans had burst into the courtyard, firing overhead.

'We wanted to join the others, but we would have got ourselves killed,' says Yvonne.

'Where are the terrorists?' demanded the Germans. The two women shrugged their shoulders. They hadn't seen any 'terrorists'. They knew nothing.

All day, the Germans mounted guard over them. Yvonne was afraid she was about to be raped. In Brittany, where on 18 June 1944, André Hue, organiser of the 'Hillbilly' circuit, fought a pitched battle with the *maquis* of Saint-Marcel against the Germans and Cossacks, terrible reprisals had ensued against the farmers and their families:

> Women were being raped then shot in front of their husbands, fathers and children; and if it was not that way round then fathers were shot in front of their women, but only after the women had been publicly raped.

Yvonne's father was also afraid his women would be violated in retaliation for harbouring Pearl and Henri. Anxiously the men – René, Henri and another *maquisard* – watched the soldiers from their hiding place in the field. 'If they do anything to the women, we attack,' René said to Henri. As they kept guard, they saw the Germans order the women into the house.

The German solders pushed the frightened women into the kitchen and told them to start cooking. '*Moi, je viens de Russie*,' a Russian private told Madame Sabassier, confessing that he was tired of war. The soldiers seemed to Yvonne no vengeful Cossacks or crack SS, but middle-aged men, and she began cooking omelettes with her mother.

Within the hour, however, the mood had changed. The Germans arrested the son of the neighbouring farmer and found a cache of grenades in a nearby copse. In fury, they torched more buildings, burning down the cowshed, ransacking the farm, chopping up the furniture. The Sabassier women were told they were going to be deported. Herded onto a lorry, they were abruptly ordered out again. That night, their attackers drove away, promising to return for them. It was at that point that the terrified women saw Pearl approaching in the gloom, and ran screaming into the house.

Madame Sabassier fried her last two eggs for Pearl before

leaving with her daughter to spend the night at another farm nearby. The two women returned to the lodge early the next morning to look for grandmother Sabassier – the Germans had left her, unharmed, sitting on a heap of manure – but on Tuesday, the Gestapo returned at 7 a.m. with the *Feldgendarmerie* to torch the Sabassiers' home and burn the château to the ground. They had found an arsenal of weapons and a wireless transmitter, and intended to deport the women but, warned by the *maquis*, Yvonne and her mother had hidden from their captors. The Germans shot their pigs and left.

On the night of the attack, Sunday 11 June, Pearl set out from Les Souches alone. It was nearly midnight. As she headed into the night she blinked back her tears as she thought of Henri: her last words to him had been angry ones, after he had given their presence away to the Germans by shooting into the air. And yet, he had saved her life. He had risked his own life to do so, and now she had no idea of his whereabouts or even whether he was still alive. Forcing herself not to weep, she began walking in the dark. She was unsure of her way, for she had decided to head for a nearby farm which she had visited only once before, with Henri, and now he was not there to guide her. She came to a crossroads, but when she looked at the names, they were the wrong ones. She shivered in the darkness. It was twelve kilometres along the deserted lanes.

She was looking for a crossroads with a stone cross beside it, which read: 'Doulçay.' There she hoped old father Trochet and his wife would take her in. It was not far, if only she could see the way. As she paused at the next crossroads, Pearl heard footsteps coming towards her. A party of *maquisards*? A guard at the Trochet farm? No, it was a man on his own.

'You're a woman, isn't that nice,' said the man. His breath smelt of alcohol.

'*Oui, je suis une femme.*'

'All on your own, are you?'

'No, I'm with my fiancé.'

'I don't see any fiancé.' The man lunged forward. 'Come here, I want to kiss you.'

Diagram of Resistance in the Northern Indre from 25 May 1944

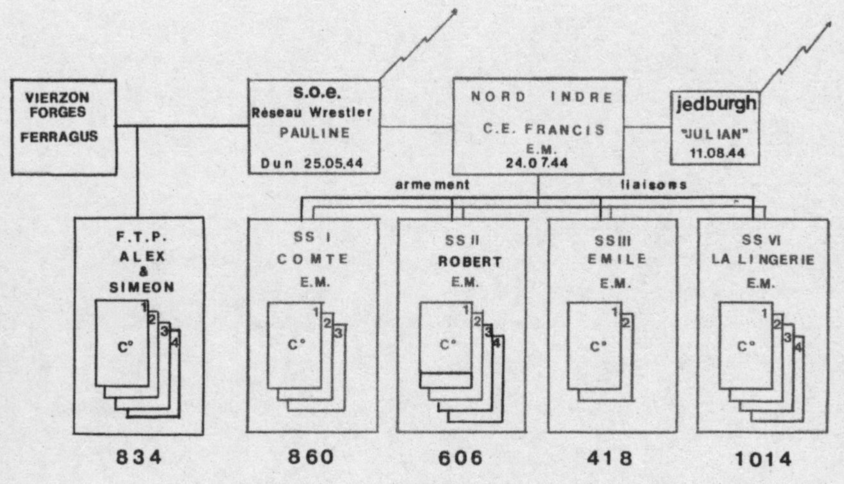

Effectifs 3732/3800 avec E.M. & S.

60 Avions 150 T. Armes

The Organisation of the Wrestler Maquis with Four Sub-Sectors, August 1944

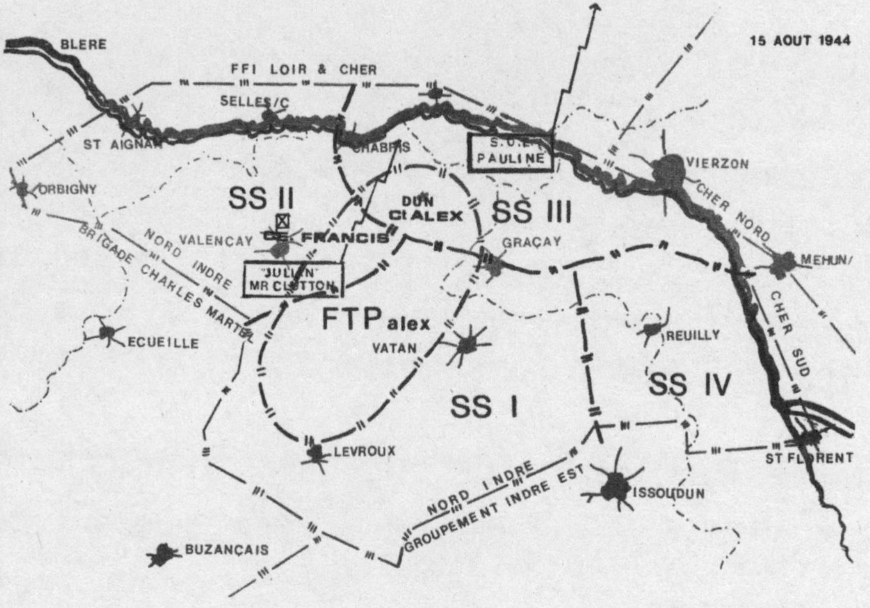

24

Lieutenant Pauline

PEARL DEFTLY side-stepped the drunkard's outstretched hand. Nine months in the field had hardened her muscles and sharpened her wits, and she was more than a match for the local lecher. She sped past him, jogging along the country lanes in the moonlight until she reached the Trochet family farm at Doulçay, near Maray, Loir-et-Cher.

Her cross-country flight to the east brought her to the south bank of the river Cher, away from the Burckhardt column, which would sweep on from Les Souches to bring 'death and ruin' to Alex's *maquis* at Les Tailles de Ruines and to the village of Dun-le-Poëlier and its neighbours. The struggle between the Nazis and the Resistance was to prove tragically unequal in the little villages of the Indre and Loir-et-Cher; at Dun, the Germans killed eleven resisters and six civilians and torched houses in revenge for the death of an officer. The slow rhythm of peasant life, bounded by the seasons and the beasts in the field, was shattered without warning as the Gestapo and *Feldgendarmes* burst into village squares and brave but poorly armed *maquis* groups fell before an onslaught of bullets.

At last, Pearl stumbled into the Trochets' farmyard. It was still dark, and she could not wake the farmer. Suddenly, she saw there was another man there. Pearl went up to him. Curiously, he was gardening in the middle of the night by the light of a little lamp.

'Can you give me somewhere to sleep?' asked Pearl.

'Yes,' replied the farm hand. 'You can come into my house.'

The earlier episode on the road still fresh in her mind, Pearl was reluctant to go inside. '*Non, merci.*'

'Come inside,' the man urged her.

'*Non, non, non, non*, I don't want to go into your house.'

Finally, the farmhand agreed to let her sleep in a barn, and Pearl lay down thankfully on a pile of hay. But, tired as she was, she was unable to sleep. In the stables beneath her was a horse that usually roamed the fields outside, but was tethered that night below her. All night the tinkling of the bell on the horse's collar kept her awake: '"Ding-a-ding." Oh! I didn't sleep at all.'

It was not simply the horse shifting in its stall that kept Pearl from sleeping, but her fears for the *maquisards* and, most of all, for Henri, whom she had not seen since midday.

'What on earth has happened to everybody?' She lay rigid in the hay, her mind reliving the events of the day: she had heard shots and groaning all around her. 'I thought I'd never see my chaps alive again.'

At ten o'clock in the morning, as Pearl anxiously scanned the fields: 'There was Henri!' He came striding around the corner, past the dunghill and the hissing geese, towards her. Pearl ran into his arms.

'Where've you been?' was her first question.

'Oh, thank heavens! Thank heavens, Pearl. I didn't know where you were.'

'I was here all night.'

'And I was with the Sabassiers, at the Barboux farm.'

'You're not hurt?'

'No.'

Pearl sighed with relief. 'Oh, Henri, I was so afraid that you'd been shot.'

Henri grinned, and gently stroked her anxious face. 'There's only one bullet that's dangerous,' he said. '*C'est celle qui porte votre nom!* The one that's got your name on it.'

They had only been parted for one night but, during the hours in which she feared for his life, Pearl had realised – with a degree of shock – her dependence on Henri. Sometimes his thoughtlessness and lack of guile irritated her but, as she let her head rest on his shoulder and felt his thudding heart through the stiff fabric of his army tunic, she was suddenly conscious of the extent to which she, fiery and driven, needed his solidity and unquestioning devotion. For the thousandth time she reproached herself for her sharp words to him the day before. There were times when Henri could be foolish, stupid even; when he acted without thinking; but when her life was in danger, when she was on the point of being killed or raped, he had calmly picked off the German soldiers and saved her.

'You were a hero yesterday,' she said.

'Rubbish!' Henri laughed, but she could see he was moved by her words.

'*Mon héro*,' she repeated. She had made him her second in command and he had proved his loyalty. 'Oh, Henri,' said Pearl. 'I don't know what I would have done if anything . . . I couldn't go on living, if the Germans . . .' Her voice faltered. She could not complete the sentence. Looking up at Henri, his dark hair flopping over his forehead, his face burnt a deep brown by the country sunshine which had chased away his urban pallor, she thought he had never looked more handsome.

Henri drew her closer. 'So you missed me last night, did you, Pearl?'

'Oh, so much.'

He pulled her roughly towards him, and kissed her hard. 'I love you, Pearl. I'm tired of waiting for you to say yes . . . We could all be dead tomorrow.'

'I love you too, Henri.'

'I want you, Pearl.' He stroked her hair. 'What is the point of it, this stupid virginity of yours, in wartime?'

She sighed as they slowly drew apart. This topic had lain unspoken between them like an invisible barrier for too long. 'Don't be cross, Henri. I thought you were dead last night.'

'I might have been. We may be killed before we can get married. Have you thought of that? And we would never have been together as man and wife . . . There's a war on, you know. Everything is different now.'

It was a long speech for Henri, and one he had clearly thought about deeply. Pearl respected him for it, as much as she respected him for the unhesitating courage he had shown the day before. She began to reconsider her principles. They were deeply held: but did they make sense any longer? All around them, people died; the blood that pumped through Henri's veins might spill out onto the green grass, and his heart might cease to beat. And he would never have made love to her, because she had always refused. Pearl shuddered. She thought of the regrets that she would carry with her to the end of her life if he was killed. At that moment, she vowed that next time she would not say '*non*' to Henri, and push him away. Instead, she would draw him closer; she would accept him totally. The battle of Les Souches had changed everything for her.

The *maquisards*, too, had noticed Henri's marksmanship. Michel Mockers, a volunteer in the 'Wrestler' *maquis*, remarked on 'Jean's coolness under fire: 'Jean was a calm, placid kind of guy who would coolly shoot his German at the battle of Les Souches.'

The men of the fields were impressed, too: Jean had risked his life to save Pauline, the Englishwoman, whom he clearly loved.

'Together they formed the most united and charming couple you could possibly find,' noted Mockers.

There was little doubt that with Henri, a native Frenchman, by her side, Pearl found acceptance as a *maquis* leader easier than she would have done as a lone foreign female. She had been using a false ID card as 'Madame Cornioley', and her status as one half of *le couple Cornioley*, an engaged couple, contributed to her acceptance by the community on whom she depended.

In the next fateful weeks, Henri would show his worth. Constantly by Pearl's side, he protected and encouraged her, his pistol in his pocket, and travelled hundreds of kilometres as her liaison between the different *maquis* groups all over the valley of the river Cher and north Indre.

When Pearl and Henri walked hand in hand into the stone farmhouse, Henri Trochet, his wife, and son, André, welcomed them without hesitation, despite knowing they risked their lives. The farmhouse was a large L-shaped building in front of which hens clucked happily and a posse of geese kept guard. Old *père* Trochet took great pride in his collection of ducks, which could also be seen quacking hungrily as the plump farmer waddled out to feed them. The manure heaps and haystacks were on the edge of the farmyard; over the fence in the next-door field the carthorses grazed on the hillside. Rusty machinery, old ploughs and carts decorated the barn. But the heart of the home was the kitchen, in which Madame Trochet could invariably be found. The farmyard door was propped open in the warm sunshine, and the hens wandered in and out. For Pearl, who had always wanted to live in the country or by the seaside, it was a sort of heaven, despite the circumstances. She could often be found sitting at the kitchen table – the Trochet farm became her new HQ – and, although she had few domestic skills, the *maquisards* remember finding her topping and tailing haricots verts with Madame Trochet, or shelling peas.

Madame Trochet gave Pearl and Henri a bedroom at the back of the farmhouse. It was private and, for the time being, safe. There was no hot and cold running water: Pearl washed with a jug and ewer on a marble washstand. Nor was there an inside lavatory: '*Le petit coin n'existait pas*,' so they used an outside privy. Madame Trochet stuffed fresh straw into a palliasse, and threw a clean cotton sheet over the mattress, and Pearl and Henri had never been more comfortable.

Pearl was intensely grateful to the Trochets, who became close friends, for 'the excellent help and reception' they gave her. 'There was an almost perpetual stream of people coming round, some staying with us, and quite apart from this they received and hid a considerable amount of arms.'

Pearl, like Ben Cowburn and Francis Cammaerts, knew that if a British agent was caught, only one life was sacrificed. The French, however, risked the deportation and death of a whole family, would see their farms ransacked and burnt, their homes and livelihood destroyed. But despite this threat, the women of France, like Madame Sabassier and Madame Trochet, let SOE agents into their homes, cooked for them and remained resolutely cheerful. 'I really met the cream of humanity, in all walks of life,' Pearl would say of the French resisters in 1944. 'I couldn't have done the job if they hadn't helped me.'

Nevertheless, the day after the battle of Les Souches was a sombre one. Henri wrote: 'The battle of Les Souches was no skirmish but an attack prepared by the Germans against what they believed to be a large force of *maquisards*.' Pearl's official report:

> We were attacked by two thousand Germans on the 11th June at 8 o'clock in the morning and the small *maquis* comprising approximately forty men, badly armed and untrained, put up a terrific fight, with the neighbouring communist *maquis* belonging to Alex, which numbered approximately one hundred men. The German attack was fairly violent, they had guns and artillery, but considering the large number and the length of the battle (it lasted until 10 o'clock at night), the *maquis'* losses were far less than those of the Germans, the latter having lost 86 and the *maquis* 24, including civilians who were shot and the injured, who were finished off [by the Germans].

Pearl took stock. Her men had fought like 'lions' according to her report, but now they were scattered and demoralised. Her arsenal of weapons had been seized, her HQ burnt to the ground. She had no wireless operator. The farmers around Dun-le-Poëlier, unlike the Trochets, had lost confidence in her after seeing the Sabassier lodge burnt to the ground by way of reprisal:

> This attack completely disorganised the set-up . . . the farming people were not very helpful, as they had seen the Germans setting fire to neighbouring farms. Several of the *maquis* returned home, and we had to move to another part of the country.

It would have been understandable if Pearl had decided to draw in her horns, even to give up. Such, indeed, was the tenor of the urgent message from General Koenig, the Free French head of the *Forces Françaises de l'Intérior*, to all Resistance forces after D-Day:

PUT MAXIMUM BRAKE ON GUERRILLA ACTIONS STOP CURRENTLY IMPOSSIBLE TO SUPPLY ARMS AND AMMUNITION IN SUFFICIENT QUANTITIES STOP WHEREVER POSSIBLE BREAK OFF ATTACKS TO ALLOW REORGANISATION STOP AVOID LARGE GROUPINGS FORM SMALL ISOLATED GROUPS.

The Germans had thought that there was a 'large grouping' at Les Souches, overestimating the size of the local *maquis*, and devastation had been the result. Pearl's *maquis* and Alex's had numbered just 140, the Germans 2,000. It had been a tragically unequal battle but, with the help of the Communists, the 'Wrestler' *maquis* had, nevertheless, survived. They were bleeding, but not broken.

Pearl's first priority was to re-establish contact with her brave lions, whom she had heard shooting at the Germans from her hiding place in the wheat field, but not seen since 11 June. Her second priority was to replace her stock of weapons, without which there could be no more fighting.

From the Germans' point of view, the actually understrength forces opposing them looked very threatening. The Nazi war machine roared into overdrive against the 'terrorists', in contrast to Koenig's order to the *maquis* to back-pedal.

At his HQ at Clermont-Ferrand, General Friedrich ('Fritz') von Brodowski, *Oberfeldkommandant* of *Südfrankreich* had made up his mind to crush the Resistance without mercy. As commander-in-chief of the German regional prefects in nine *départements*, his authority was far-reaching.

Two days after D-Day, Brodowski recorded in his *Kriegstagebuch*, war dairy, his order of 8 June to deploy a *Kampfgruppe*, a battlegroup generally consisting of 8,500 men, against Châteauroux 'to re-establish the situation in this region'. It was one of five *Kampfgruppen* sent on mopping-up exercises against the 'terrorists' of *Südfrankreich*.

Fifty-eight-year-old Brodowski had been Governor of *Südfrankreich* for under two months, having taken over the post on 15 April 1944 after seeing service in Hungary and Kiev, but he had quickly become alarmed at the concentrations of 'terrorist gangs' in the region, which ranged from the Loire to the Dordogne. In May, he had created a special division 'for the suppression and annihilation of the *maquis* of the Auvergne and Limousin'.

1 June 1944: Brodowski's war diary had reflected a relatively optimistic mood:

> Reliable reports from Vichy say that the German *Wehrmacht* should not allow itself to be fooled by the 10,000-strong *maquis*. Greater danger lies in the unhindered growth of the *Armée Secrète*, which is being organised across the whole country, but particularly in the Massif Central. There are plans for recruits to be drawn in to be armed by airdrops by the Anglo-Americans.

Brodowski had decided on a crushing blow. From Lyons on 3 June, his order had gone out to 're-establish the authority of the occupying forces in the Dept. of Cantal and neighbouring areas, to use all measures to combat the emerging groups and destroy them.' On D-Day itself, 6 June, the *Kommandant* of southern France had recorded his plans for an all-out assault on the 'terrorists . . . from all directions supported by *Luftwaffe* air strikes.'

It was this directive that had launched the Burckhardt and Stenger columns, which attacked in Châteauroux, and further north into the Nord Indre and the Sologne. The Germans were determined to stamp out the conflagration before it spread, even if it meant tying down the army in central France.

Buried at the bottom of the page in Brodowski's war diary entry for 6 June is some momentous news he had just received: 'Report comes in of the Anglo-American invasion in the area of Cherbourg.'

At the battle of Les Souches, Pearl must have felt like David facing Goliath, as she saw the extent of German might arrayed against her. But she was not deterred. She had faced many tests as a *clandestine* and the lesson of her childhood: '*faire face à la vie*', to face up to life, had never left her. She was 'task-orientated', in military parlance; and if she did not know the motto of her Witherington ancestors – 'I will not fail' – she nevertheless acted by it.

A week had gone by since the battle of Les Souches. Pearl was still out of contact with her *maquisards*.

One enthusiastic leader of a group of resisters that had responded to her call to arms was Paul Vannier (Henri chose his alias, 'La Lingerie', as Vannier kept a shop selling ladies' underwear in Reuilly). He and his men had fled north across the river Cher to the forest of Orsay in the Sologne, where they were hiding out, waiting desperately for news of Pauline. *Capitaine* Vannier, stocky and thickset in his boots, riding breeches and American jacket, usually exuded an air of impenetrable calm, but by the second week in June, his need was urgent. His lieutenant, Michel Mockers, wrote up the crisis in his journal: '*Le capitaine* still has no news of *le lieutenant Pauline*, and with every day that passes the situation is becoming dramatic because of the lack of arms . . .'

Restlessly, the *capitaine* paced the forest floor. Eventually, he decided to return home to the little town of Reuilly, situated between Vierzon and Issoudon, a strategically important location as it sat on the main Toulouse–Paris railway line. This line was vital to the Germans if they were to bring up troop reinforcements to Normandy, including the crack *Waffen* SS 2nd Panzer Division 'Das Reich', which had been stationed at Montauban, near Toulouse. Vannier's men had been cutting the line every day, but now they were running short of explosives for their demolition work.

Earlier, Pearl had supplied Vannier with *plastique*, the soft, buttery, almond-smelling putty which was used to blow up the line. She had showed the men how to become *plastiqueurs*, bombers. At first in the camp, they had practised with the time-delay fuses, inspecting the acetone capsules used in limpet mines, factory demolition or rail charges, designed to be simple and reliable in all climatic conditions. The men watched as Pearl showed them the glass capsules – the different yellow, orange and green colours denoting the different time delays they had – placed within the thumbscrew, which was turned to crush the capsule. They had followed Pearl down the embankment to the railway line itself, and watched her dexterously form the *plastique* and attach it to the points, or under a bridge. Then they had crouched behind trees and watched the line buckle and heave, the railway engines toppling sideways, and the cursing Germans. As fast as the enemy mended the line, they blew it up. Under her instruction, they had become adept at sabotage.

Vannier had been waiting for a new parachute drop from England. Everything depended on a word from Pauline that the aeroplanes were coming. The reception committee was ready. His friend, a vet, Jacques Bergeron, had gone on his motorbike to Vierzon to warn two other men to stand by with their lorry; the *capitaine* himself had planned the operation with another old friend, a farmer named Maurice Surtel, who, like Vannier himself, was one of the first resisters from Reuilly.

Vannier remembered the delirium that had swept through his little group on 6 June when they heard that the Alllies had landed. '*La grande nouvelle . . . Le moment est venu de prendre le maquis.* The great news . . . the moment had come to join the *maquis.*' They were all Reuilly men. At midnight on 6 June, a gendarme resister had opened the door of the barracks, he and his fellow gendarmes had filled their bags with arms and munitions, stowed them in their saddlebags, and bicycled with him to the d'Orsay forest. There, Vannier had met up with his old friend, Maurice Stag, and formed a *maquis*, but the constant German attacks had forced them to withdraw.

Now only three revolvers and three machine guns remained between Vannier's forty men. Even so, they had been cutting the railway line and telephone wires every day. Under the German occupation it was, said the despondent *capitaine*, 'the only distraction possible'. But if their struggle was to succeed, he must have tyre-bursters, Bren guns, Stens, grenades, PIATs and bazookas, as well as *plastique* to squeeze under the railway lines with such gratifying consequences.

For Pearl, the lack of arms is critical. She urgently needs to radio London to arrange a new *parachutage*, but she is still without her radio operator, Tutur. In this emergency, Pearl knows her only option is to turn for help to Baron Philippe de Vomécourt, organiser of the 'Ventriloquist' circuit and the nearest SOE agent. She has never met him, although his reputation is well known as a wily fox of an agent who has already escaped once from a German prison.

De Vomécourt is far away in the Sologne, on the north side of the river Cher, the former Demarcation Line between the Occupied and Free Zone, and there may be German soldiers patrolling it. But Pearl's journey is essential: the agent has a radio and will send a message for her to London.

De Vomécourt, widely known by his *nom de guerre* of 'St Paul', has made his *maquis* camp at Saint-Viâtre. Pearl's mission is to find him. She does not take Henri. He is too impulsive. She must do this alone, with the help of a local guide.

Three days after the battle of Les Souches, Pearl cycles out of the Trochet farm with Pierre Chassagne, a former member of Pierre Culioli's 'Adolphe' circuit. They cycle westwards, past the blue flowers of the hemp fields, towards Saint-Loup, where they have to cross the river. Pearl takes off her shoes, ties the laces together, hangs them around her neck and heaves her bicycle onto her back. Wading through the cold, fast flowing water, she keeps a sharp lookout for German soldiers. Green weeds twist around her skirt, sharp stones cut her feet, and she is afraid of losing her balance and slipping under the brown water, or losing her indispensable bicycle, which is growing heavier by the minute. Just as she reaches the middle of the river where the water is deepest, she hears a noise: a traction – a 4-wheel drive with a characteristic engine sound – comes around the corner, and she crouches down and hopes the shadows of the trees hide her from the passing soldiers.

At last, panting, Pearl reaches the bank on the other side and stumbles up it to safety. There is a hole in her skirt, which is soaking wet. Wringing out the wet material, she exchanges a quick glance with her guide, Chassagne: he smiles and gives her a thumbs up. They cycle on together, over the canal, where the barges full of hemp float slowly on their way towards Saint-Viâtre.

A few kilometres from their destination, Pearl and her guide are sitting on the grass verge beside the road, eating the sandwiches that Madame Trochet has prepared for them. It is lunchtime, and the sun is high in the sky when Pearl see another traction, coming along the road towards them in the distance.

'Quick, Pierre!' She runs behind a tree and crouches in the thick foliage, and Chassagne follows her. The noise of the vehicle grows louder. As the truck draws level, Pearl turns to Chassagne: 'I know that number plate.'

'Whose truck is it? '

'It belongs to the owners of the château Les Souches, the old *milicien* and his wife. Some people called Hay des Nétumières. Their château was burnt down and it looks like the Fritz have taken their truck as well.'

'That truck's full of German officers,' says Chassagne. 'They're on their way to Saint-Viâtre.'

'Now it's St Paul's turn to be attacked!' exclaims Pearl.

The Burckhardt column had also crossed the Cher. It had reached the Sologne and was on its way to attack the *maquis* of 'St Paul', which was based at de Vomécourt's estate of Bas Soleil, where he had received the first F Section parachute drops of 1941. But the agent, who habitually disguised himself as a gamekeeper, was too cunning to wait for the Germans. On 17 June, he and his men had dispersed, melting silently into the forest. The Germans were frightened of the dense acres of woodland, whose paths and glades were known only to the *maquis*, and had kept to the roads.

The Burckhardt column swept on through the Sologne to Souesmes, east of Salbris, where it attacked another *maquis*, led by Polish resister Captain Stanislaw Makowski. Despite being heavily outnumbered, Makowski decided to engage the Occupier in open combat. Some 700 Germans attacked around fifty *maquisards*, setting fire to the undergrowth and employing mortars and artillery. The little group of *maquis* was decimated. As it withdrew under cover of darkness, thirteen *maquisards* lay dead, and 121 Germans.

The next morning, St Paul visited the field of battle to watch the Germans and French reclaim their dead. 'As I watched the bodies dragged away,' he wrote later, 'I wondered: "Who would live to see the time when the last German had been driven out, and men, like those who now lay dead, could return to their homes and peaceful lives again?"'

Reprisals were swift and savage: the Germans seized the *maquisards*' women, deporting their wives and daughters to Ravensbrück.

It was an important lesson for the *maquis*. They could harass and needle the German forces; they could carry out audacious hit-and-run attacks on the mile-long column of lorries, horses and men – a *maquisard*, wearing the hat of a captured German major, would drive a car towards the column as his passengers fired machine guns from the window, killing scores of Germans – but it seemed that the Resistance's inferiority in manpower and firepower meant that they could never be a match for Nazi terror.

Chassagne has delivered Pearl's message for London to St Paul, hidden in the strap of his saddlebag. The next day, she receives a visit at the Trochet farm from a tall, mysterious figure in tweed cap and moleskins.

'*Vous ne me connaissez pas?*' the visitor asks Pearl. 'You don't recognise me?'

'Non.'

'*Je suis St Paul.*'

Pearl suddenly notices the game bag and gun slung over the stranger's shoulders, and realises who he is. 'Thank you for sending my message.'

'London has received it. Is there anything else I can do for you?'

De Vomécourt returns with new clothes for Pearl to replace the skirt with a hole in it. He brings her a pair of trousers, which are too short for her long legs, and a pair of old ski boots which formerly belonged to Muriel Byck, his young radio operator, who had died of meningitis in May. Pearl accepts them eagerly. Boots are much in demand, and the *maquisards* often remove them from German corpses or prisoners. 'I find the Germans always respect uniforms,' remarks de Vomécourt.

In her khaki battledress and beret, dropped in an earlier *parachutage*, Pearl at last looks like the military commander she is fast becoming. Her *maquisards* are now dressed in blue uniform, bought by a local supporter, and proudly wear their FFI blue, white and red *brassards*, armbands, bearing the cross of Lorraine.

After a week of silence, in late June, *Capitaine* Paul Vannier receives a coded message from Pearl. It is brought by one of her *agents de liaison* on a bicycle: perhaps Henri, or one of two young women whom Pearl has recruited.

'*La pêche est bonne*. The fishing is good.'

It was one of the 'mysterious messages', writes Mockers, which came through *la radio anglaise*. It meant that a *parachutage* was on its way. Chosen by Vannier, or maybe by Henri Cornioley, the message was perhaps intended to evoke memories of the 'superb "pêches de vigne",' the fruit of the vine, of which the locals were justly proud.

Capitaine La Lingerie and his men wait expectantly. All Pearl's 'Wrestler' dropping grounds accepted by Allied aviation in the Nord-Indre sector have been given the name of fish or crustaceans: *Langouste*, lobster, *Crevette*, prawn, *Congre*, Sole, *Baleine*, whale . . . That night, the drop will be made on a Reuilly ground: *Rouget*, Mullet.

At 11 p.m., fourteen men creep out of the farm that was their HQ. The landing ground is close by:

> Towards midnight, the noise of an engine. The lamps are lit. One light starts flashing the letter 'D', agreed by radio. The aircraft banks and descends, then rakes the landing ground with volleys of machine-gun fire and, a few seconds later, drops bombs which fall close to the village of la Ferté.

The men throw themselves to the ground: it isn't an Allied aircraft after all, but the Fritz. The operation is a total failure, although none of the *maquis* have been killed.

For another eight long days the men wait. Finally, Pearl sends the password a second time: '*La pêche est bonne*.'

On 24 June, Pearl's thirtieth birthday, an SOE *parachutage* at last takes place on *Baleine*, the landing ground close to the Trochet farm. 'This was the best birthday present I ever had,' says Pearl. Three aircraft drop seven tons of containers, enough to completely re-arm the 'Wrestler' *maquis*: 'It was the first big drop after the landings. I spent two days and a night distributing the material to the *maquis* leaders . . . two days without washing, because I didn't have time!'

News of the drop spreads fast. 'We got grenades, Stens, *plastique* . . .' Liaison is restored with the former *maquisards* in the surrounding villages: Pearl and Alex, the FTP chief, are again in touch. The numbers of volunteers soars to 1,000 then 1,500 men, who need not only guns but training, not only food but shelter and pay. Pearl notes:

> When they came to me, well, I kept on saying please get me a military commander. I was a courier, I wasn't trained for that sort of thing. Well, there were so many of them and I said to Henri, you know we must do something about this. They were all coming in and fiddling and there was no law and order about it. And you know what he said, oh, I was cross with him: 'You have bitten off more than you can chew.'

Pearl glowers at Henri: 'I am going to show you if I have bitten off more than I can chew!'

hand. 'This was the best birthday present I ever had,' says Pearl. 'They made a drop – seven tons of containers, enough to completely re-arm the "Wrestler" maquis. It was the first big drop after the landings. I spent two days and a night distributing the material to the maquis leaders – two days without washing because I didn't have time!'

News of the drop spreads fast. Wagner grenadier Stein, platform [illegible] is [illegible] with the rumour magnified in the surrounding villages. Pearl and Alex, the FTP chief, are again in touch. The numbers of volunteers soars to 1,000 then 1,500 men, who need not only guns but training, not only food but shelter and arms. Pearl notes:

> When they came to me, well, I kept on saying please put me a military commander. I was a courier. I wasn't trained for that sort of thing. Well, there were so many of them and I said to Henri, 'you know, we must do something about this.' They were all coming in and bidding and there was no law and order about it. And you know what he said, oh, I was cross with him! 'You have bitten off more than you can chew.'

Pearl glowered at Henri. 'I am going to show you if I have bitten off more than I can chew!'

25

Into the Fray: the 2nd SS Panzer Division 'Das Reich'

On 8 June, the same day on which Brodowski ordered his troops to crush the *maquis* of Châteauroux, the famous 2nd SS Panzer Division 'Das Reich' rumbled out of Montauban on a 450-mile journey northwards to Normandy, which would end seventeen days later.

Two days earlier the 'Das Reich' had received a signal:

SINCE THE EARLY HOURS OF THIS MORNING THE INVASION HAS BEEN TAKING PLACE ON THE CHANNEL COAST. PREPARATIONS ARE TO BE MADE FOR A MARCH.

The star division of the *Waffen* SS, the armoured wing of the *Schutzstaffel*, sworn to protect Hitler, was further away than Rommel would have liked – his instinct that the Panzers should have been kept close had proved correct. There were only three SS out of ten Panzer divisions in France on D-Day. It was imperative that the 'Das Reich', numbering 18,460 men and 209 tanks, hasten northwards to reinforce the weak infantry defending the Normandy beaches.

This did not seem an impossible task. British intelligence estimated that the 'Das Reich' would be available for a counter-thrust against the beachhead soon after 6 June: '2nd SS Panzer Division will . . . be concentrating in a forward area by D + 3.' The Allies expected that the terror squads of the 'Das Reich', whose armour amounted to one tenth of the entire German armoured strength in the west, would be in the thick of the Normandy battle by 9 or 10 June.

But the division received a strangely contradictory order. On 6 June, Brodowski had reported his troubles with the Resistance in the Corrèze: 'French mobilisation is progressing . . . There are reports of gunfights. Tulle is heavily threatened by gangs' and, the following day, Rommel's chief, Field Marshal Gerd von Rundstedt, ordered the 'Das Reich' to divert its march.

It was to prove a fatal mistake. Instead of making all speed to Normandy, the crack division was to go to Tulle to suppress the 'terrorist' gangs. Brodowski recorded the order in his war diary: 'With immediate effect 2 SS Panzer Division to make its way to Tulle . . .' where the German garrison had surrendered. Brodowski also planned to use 'Das Reich' in yet another mopping-up operation east of Tulle. 'For the Cantal operation,' he wrote, 'also available are 2 Battalions of the SS Panzer Division "Das Reich" . . . [although] all troops involved must as soon as possible be made available for other purposes.'

There was a puzzling lack of urgency in Brodowski's diary about the battle of Normandy; he was preoccupied with a private battle of his own with the Resistance. So also was the 'Der Führer' *Panzergrenadier* regiment of the 'Das Reich', one of the division's two armoured infantry brigades: they had been fighting the *maquis* bandits ever since returning from the Eastern Front on 6 April 1944. With the help of the *Milice* of Toulouse, the SS had spent May pillaging the villages of the Tarn-et-Garonne. SOE agent, George Hiller, and his *maquis* had blown up the Ratier airscrew factory at Figeac in January in one of F Section's most successful acts of sabotage, and the revengeful Panzers had arrested and deported more than a thousand townspeople. The terror had been ratcheted up still further when, on 5 June, a secret order from SS General Heinz Lammerding, a personal friend of Himmler and commanding officer of the 'Das Reich' division, decreed that in punitive sweeps against the Resistance: 'for each German killed, ten terrorists are to be hung.'

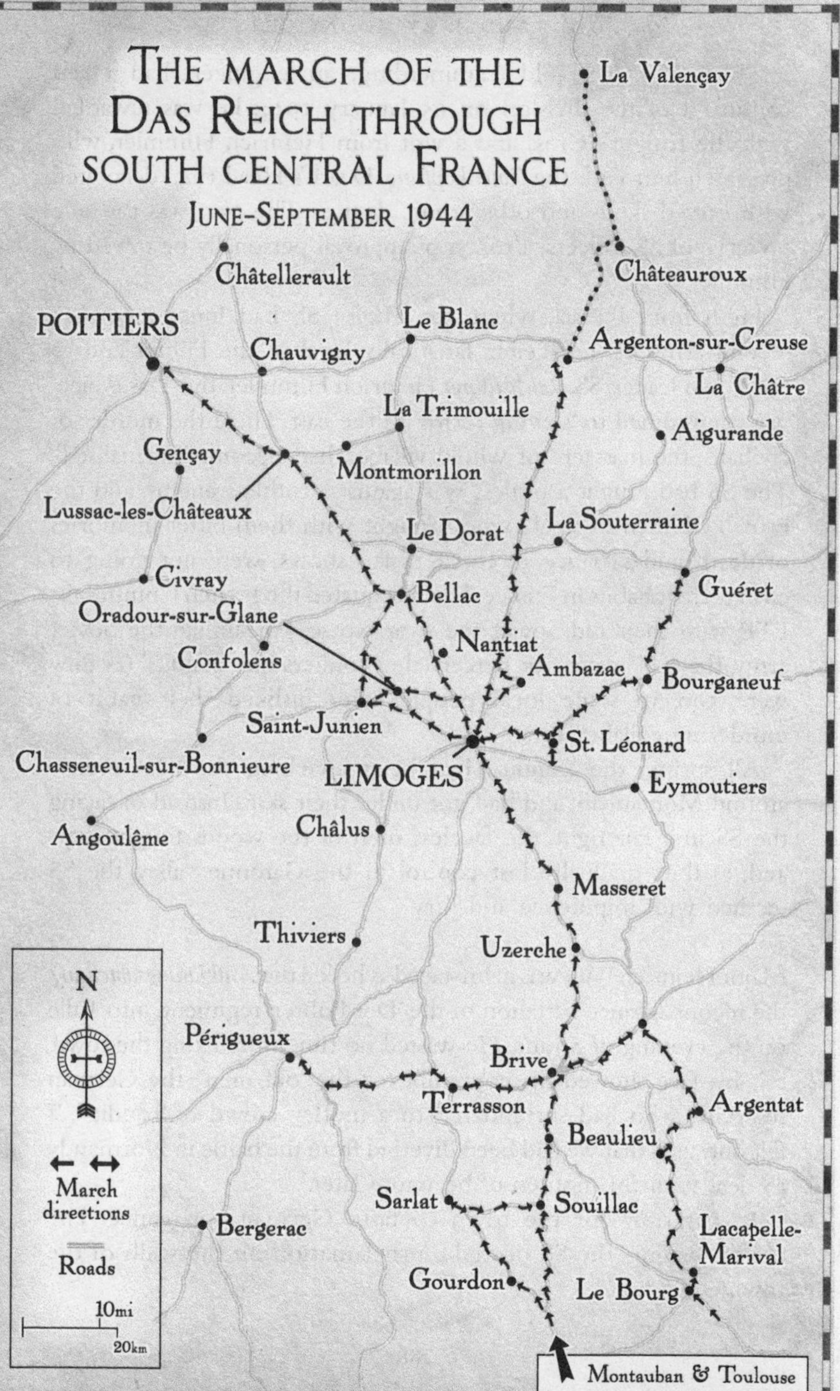
THE MARCH OF THE
DAS REICH THROUGH
SOUTH CENTRAL FRANCE
JUNE–SEPTEMBER 1944
La Valençay
Châteauroux
Châtellerault
POITIERS
Le Blanc
Chauvigny
Argenton-sur-Creuse
La Châtre
La Trimouille
Aigurande
Gençay
Montmorillon
Lussac-les-Châteaux
Le Dorat
La Souterraine
Civray
Guéret
Bellac
Oradour-sur-Glane
Nantiat
Confolens
Ambazac
Bourganeuf
Saint-Junien
St. Léonard
Chasseneuil-sur-Bonnieure
LIMOGES
Eymoutiers
Angoulême
Châlus
Masseret
Thiviers
Uzerche
N
Périgueux
Brive
Terrasson
Argentat
Beaulieu
March
directions
Sarlat
Souillac
Bergerac
Lacapelle-
Marival
Roads
Gourdon
Le Bourg
10mi
20km
Montauban & Toulouse

Thirty-eight-year-old Lammerding, an engineer, had taken command of the division on 25 January 1944: he was rewarded with the Knight's Cross and a visit from Heinrich Himmler, who presented him with the *Totenkopfring*, Death's Head ring, decorated with carved skulls and other runic devices. The ring was the sole preserve of SS officers, a token of approval personally bestowed by Himmler.

Fresh from Russia, where the *Waffen* SS had functioned as a second army of the Reich, fanatically loyal to the Führer and to their own leader, SS *Reichsführer* Heinrich Himmler, the 'Das Reich' was accustomed to 'sowing terror' in the east. There the murder of civilians, the massacre of whole villages, had become 'normalised'. The SS had fought a pitiless war against a ruthless enemy, and the brutalised 'men of steel', who brought with them bitter memories of death and sacrifice in the Russian snows, were not going to change their habits in France. The SS equated the French Communist FTP with their old Soviet foe – or worse. For, unlike the Soviet army, the FTP were not perceived as soldiers but 'bandits' (as they were, too, to some local people, who disliked their habit of murdering collaborators).

All spring, the 'bandits' had been attacking the 'Das Reich' around Montauban, and had got under their skin. Instead of facing the SS in a fair fight, the faceless men of the woods fought dirty and, as they gradually lost control in the Garonne valley, the SS seethed with impotence and fury.

Major Heinrich Wulf was grim-faced as he led the *Aufklärungsabteilung*, the reconnaissance battalion of the 'Der Führer' regiment, into Tulle on the evening of 8 June. He wasted no time in retaking the town, but his face showed his contempt for the 'old men', the German reservists who had surrendered to a motley crowd of 'bandits'. 'I felt outraged that we had been diverted from the battle in Normandy to deal with this nonsense,' he wrote later.

It was time for the town to taste German vengeance. The next morning, the SS posted a proclamation on the walls of the town:

CITIZENS OF TULLE!

> Forty German soldiers have been assassinated in the most abominable fashion by Communist gangs. The peaceful population has submitted to terror. The military authorities wish only for order and tranquillity . . . The appalling and cowardly fashion in which the German soldiers have been killed proves that the instruments of Communist destruction are at work . . .

For the Germans, the 'bandits', by not participating in open combat, had no noble feelings of honour. For the *maquis* and those that helped them, there was to be only one penalty: the hangman's noose.

As forty German soldiers had been murdered by the *maquis*, so 120 *maquis* – or their supposed accomplices – would be hanged, and their bodies thrown in the river. And, in a refinement of the earlier directive, for every German soldier wounded, three *maquis* would in future be hanged, while for every German soldier killed, ten *maquisards* or an equal number of their accomplices would be hanged.

According to German reports, forty of their dead had been horribly mutilated by the FTP: 'Their faces had been stoved in, and their testicles cut off and stuffed in their mouths.' It was for this reason, alleged the SS, that reprisals were taken.

After hanging ninety-nine civilians, the 'Der Führer' in their half-tracks and trucks roared out of town towards Limoges. They were not, however, to move forward to Normandy: they were still needed for 'clearance operations' against the *maquis*.

For the Occupying forces, the situation was deteriorating. North-east of Limoges, the town of Guéret had been in the hands of the *maquis* since 6 June, and was now completely cut off from Lammerding's HQ. Brodowski sent in a reserve battalion from Montluçon on 8 June, which 'had to retreat in the face of heavy opposition. 7 dead, 10 wounded.' His response was to intensify the crackdown. 'The situation in the Massif Central in the last few days requires immediate and ruthless attack by strong forces.'

The Germans, however, were also running out of fuel, so Brodowski took action:

> By the orders of HQ, fuel and oil are being seized from stores and private ownership. They may only be used by the *Wehrmacht*. All civilian motor vehicles are forbidden with immediate effect. From Friday 9 June, any civilian vehicle on the road will be shot at without warning . . . These measures apply particularly to departments of Puy de Dôme, Allier, Cantal, Haute-Loire.

New orders went out to advance on Châteauroux, 'to clean up the situation'. Lammerding transferred his divisional HQ to a villa on the road out of Tulle towards Clermont-Ferrand, and took stock of the situation. On 9 June, he decided to sweep the region, clear the vital road links and destroy all *maquis* concentrations. Summoning Major Wulf, he ordered him to prepare to advance eastwards at first light on 10 June.

Half an hour later, the order was cancelled. In Normandy, German reinforcements had been brought in but were failing to repulse the Allies. 'It was evident that these forces would not be sufficient to drive the enemy back into the sea,' reported the *Oberkommando des Wehrmacht* war diary on 9 June. Allied aviation was punishing the *Wehrmacht*, suffocating their tank attacks, 'So the Führer ordered the following units to be moved in – 2 SS Pz Div (which had been on clearance operations in southern France).'

Rundstedt swiftly ordered the 'Das Reich' to send its 'wheeled elements' overland direct to him in Normandy. The tanks and half-tracks were to be entrained 'immediately, regardless of present operations.' The need in Normandy was desperate.

But the 'Das Reich' was not easily diverted from its operations against the Resistance. Bogged down in southern France, encircled by 'gangs', short of petrol, the division found it impossible to execute Rundstedt's orders. Nor was it entirely minded to do so: Lammerding, based in his HQ outside Clermont-Ferrand, was fixated on the need to shore up the crumbling German local divisions. 'The paralysis of the German posts is quite disgraceful,' he wrote on 10

June. 'Without determined and ruthless action, the situation is this area will develop until a threat exists whose proportions have not yet been recognised. In this area a new Communist state is coming to life, a state which rules without opposition and carries out co-ordinated attacks.'

The barbarians were at the gates of the German empire. Lammerding knew that the task of eliminating them should have been accomplished by local divisions, and could be 'if only they would pull together sharply.' The general wrote with feeling: 'Panzer divisions in the fifth year of the war are too good for this.' But what was the alternative? His emotions were engaged and he felt that there was no one else to send but 'Das Reich'.

But by now his division was in turmoil, its heavy army shattered. Only the trucks could move northwards on schedule. Broken-down Tiger tanks were lying all over the roadside: 60 per cent of them out of service, having proved unfit to travel long distances by road. Lammerding was waiting for spare parts, promised for 11 June. In a long, despondent report of 10 June, he wrote:

> The tanks and towing vehicles require at least four days for repairs . . . the complete crippling of rail movement by the terrorists will anyway prevent an earlier entrainment . . . The lack of adequate transport, the substantial distances to be covered in unfavourable terrain, the dispersal of units over 300 kilometres . . . has weakened the strength of the division out of all proportion during the last eight days.

The utter folly of the Germans in sending Panzers on a wild-goose chase against guerrillas, rather than keeping them entrenched in Normandy as Rommel had wished, was evident in this report.

It was also a great tribute to the climate created by the Resistance after D-Day.

It was Lammerding's misfortune to be moving through circuits run by some of F Section's most successful agents. Tony Brooks ('Alphonse'), the youngest agent 'F' ever sent to the field, emerged from the shadows, stuck a Union Jack on his car, and set about cutting the railway line north of Montauban; his speciality was blowing up the flatcars on which tanks were transported. His circuit, 'Pimento', manned by the *cheminots*, ensured that only a single northbound train was able to pass through Montauban before it was liberated three months later.

This single train was useless to Lammerding. Hunting what reserves of petrol they could find, his men were forced to set out overland. But George Starr's 'Wheelwright' team had blown up most of the petrol dumps. The route of the 'Das Reich' took them through Philippe de Gunzbourg's territory, a subsector of 'Wheelwright', or, if they took a more easterly direction, through Jacques Poirier's 'Digger' and his daring ambushes around Brive and Tulle. Poirier had taken over Harry Peulevé's 'Author' circuit after his arrest, and was fighting to avenge his leader, imprisoned in Fresnes. 'We set out,' says Poirier, 'to make a mess.'

Pearl and Amédée Maingard's circuits, 'Wrestler' and 'Shipwright', cut the railway lines in the Indre 800 times. The main line from Paris to Toulouse via Châteauroux and Limoges, where 'Fireman' was operational, ran through the middle of the Indre, and 'it was of extraordinary importance to the main battle in Normandy to keep that main line closed to German traffic'.

> The extra fortnight's delay in what should have been a three-day journey may well have been of decisive importance for the successful securing of the Normandy bridgehead . . . Between them these circuits left the Germans so thoroughly mauled that when they did eventually crawl into their laagers close to the fighting line . . . their fighting quality was much below what it had been when they started. The division might be compared to a cobra which had been struck with its fangs at the head of a stick held out to tempt it; the amount of poison left in its bite was far less than it had been.

The marauding 'gangs' also succeeded in goading Lammerding into disobeying his orders: in yet another extraordinary development, as he waited in his villa for his tanks and half-trucks to be patched up, the general decided that instead of making straight for Normandy, he would send the 'Der Führer' regiment, which had finally crawled into Limoges, on further operations even deeper into *maquis* country: Major Helmut Kämpfe and the 3rd Battalion were to push north-north-east towards Argenton-sur-Creuse and to Guéret in a two-pronged strike – the Resistance had taken Argenton, and beleaguered German troops were begging for assistance.

On 9 June, the 15th Company of the regiment marched into Argenton and retook the town, killing fifty-four people in reprisals. Brodowski then sent the Stenger column into Argenton, and further troops were sent to Saint-Flour 'to clean up the Massif Central'. But his war diary was becoming a litany of despair: the Germans could no longer hold the line in southern France. The *Kommandant* reported: 'Anti-aircraft installation with 70 men plus guard troops reported surrounded by 3–4,000 insurrectionists. Only a few days munitions and food left.'

After retaking Argenton, Major Kämpfe with the 3rd Battalion advanced on Guéret, where the *Garde Mobile* training school had defected to the Resistance on 6 June. 'Renewed successful assault and relief of Guéret,' reported a relieved Brodowski on 9 June. But the reprieve was short-lived. Two days later, the Germans were forced to surrender: '2,000 terrorists entered Guéret overnight surrounding HQ and gendarmerie buildings. Surrender to terrorists at 13.30h as ammunition running low and buildings . . . set on fire.'

When the *maquis* of the Haute-Vienne had examined a truck stolen from the Germans, they had discovered the identity of their enemies: inside the vehicle was a crate, with a uniform with SS silver runes. There was also a wristband of 'Das Reich'.

It was at this point that the personal element in the SS's 'war on terror' became fatal to their behaviour and reputation.

On the night of 9 June, as Major Kämpfe drove back from Guéret in his open car, exhilarated at having retaken the town, the Communist *maquisards* ambushed and captured him. The disappearance of their battalion commander caused consternation among the men of 'Der Führer' regiment; they could not even telephone Lammerding with the news because the Resistance had cut the telephone lines. When at last the Panzers reached their commanding officer at Tulle, Lammerding ordered them to search for Kämpfe – a tall, popular thirty-four-year-old officer – with the utmost rigour.

At first light the next morning they began combing the area. South of Limoges, soldiers from the 'Deutschland' regiment set up a roadblock in the village of Salon-la-Tour, where by chance they stopped a black Citroën car, conspicuous at a time when most people travelled in charcoal-burning *gazogènes*. Inside were two SOE agents, Violette Szabo and Jacques Dufour. Violette, who had only been parachuted back into France two days earlier, was arrested and taken to the Gestapo at Limoges.

The day after hanging most of the male population of Tulle, Major Otto Diekmann led the 1st Battalion of the 'Der Führer' regiment into Limoges, where he learnt to his fury that his close friend and brother officer, Major Helmut Kämpfe, was missing. The Gestapo of Limoges informed him that a high-ranking German was being held by the *maquis* at a nearby village: Oradour-sur-Glane. Diekmann at once ordered his men to move against the village.

At the Hotel Milord in the sloping main street of Oradour, refugee families were eating lunch in the sunshine. Children played on the grass nearby. It was 10 June, four days since the landings, and news had come in that a beachhead had been established by the Allies: people were counting the days until their deliverance.

At 2.15 p.m., 120 SS led by *Hauptsturmbannführer* Kann roared into the village in a convoy of trucks and half-tracks and ordered the inhabitants to gather on the Champ de Mars, the fairground in the centre of the village. 'Some of the SS were chatting and laughing, and gave the impression that they were on a routine mission rather than getting ready for mass murder,' remembered one nineteen-year-old boy, Robert Hébras.

The villagers were divided into groups: the men and boys

separated from the women and children and babes-in-arms, who were led down the hill to the church.

Robert was driven into a barn with other young men. At 4 p.m. he heard an explosion. 'On this signal, the men behind the machine guns settled into position and fired . . . Every man fell, one on top of another.' As the SS covered the corpses with hay and wood and set them alight, Robert, surprised to find that he was still breathing, crawled out from under the pile of bodies, slipped through a wall and hid in a rabbit hutch.

From the church came another explosion. A box of explosives had been pushed into the building by the SS, and the fuses lit. As the women choked and screamed, one mother, Madame Rouffanche, climbed up to the window behind the altar and threw herself out. A woman behind her held out her baby to her but its cries alerted the Germans, who fired, killing both mother and child. Madame Rouffanche was the only female survivor of the 642 people murdered by the SS.

Brodowski wrote in his diary:

> *Bei Aktion der Truppe am 10.6 wurde Ort Oradour (31 km südw. Limoges) in Schutt u. Asche gelegt.* Troop action on 10/6 left Oradour in rubble and ashes.

Three days later he attempted to justify the massacre:

> 600 people are supposed to have died. An *Untersturmführer* of the SS Panz. Div. 'Das Reich' was taken prisoner in Nieul . . . and was taken to Oradour. He was able to escape. The body of a senior paymaster was found, which showed signs of mistreatment. The entire male population of Oradour was shot. Church caught fire. Explosives were being stored there. Women and children also perished.

The massacre delayed the division. It was not until 12 June that the 'Das Reich' moved out of Limoges towards Poitiers, lashing out on its way at the 'terrorists' at Bellac, before crawling wearily into Châtellerault.

Maddened by the *maquis*, the serpentine convoy of the 'Das Reich' spent its poison on its way north. Instead of the three days the Allies had expected the march to take, the very first *Kampfgruppe* did not trickle into Normandy until between 15 and 30 June; not until 30 July was the SS division able to combine as a fighting force, but by then it was too late to turn the tide of the battle. The precious hours and days had ticked away as the SS forgot all about driving the Allies back into the sea and pursued their own personal vendettas.

26

Warrior Queen

As men flocked to her standard, Pearl was conscious that commanding an army of Frenchmen was 'no job for foreigners'. With the appearance of eager partisans, France could, in theory, liberate herself. Resistance leaders such as 'Colonel' Georges Guingouin, Philippe de Gunzbourg or André Malraux were already leading their compatriots in the Corrèze and Dordogne. But in the Northern Indre, there was no one but Pearl to command all those who had answered her call for volunteers.

It was not for want of asking. From 10 June, noted Philippe de Vomécourt, 'Pearl Witherington, the SOE agent operating to the south of me, who found herself in charge . . . of more than 2,000 *maquisards*, asked and asked again for a Jed team to help her.'

The three-man 'Jedburgh' teams, the brainchild of Colin Gubbins, were made up of an American, a Briton and a Frenchman, dropped in uniform to assist the Secret Army after D-Day. But Pearl had to wait until August until a Jedburgh came to her aid. Nor did her pleas to London for a French military commandant bring any response:

> I wish to put on record that on a number of occasions I received no reply to various telegrams, notably to my request for a military mission at the beginning of June. There was a complete lack of directives from London except for the sabotage of the Tours–Vierzon line . . .

In the absence of a French commander, Pearl, a thirty-year-old Englishwoman, had no alternative but to fulfil the role herself. 'It wasn't my official mission to command the resistants,' she said, 'but, swept along by events, I had to make the most of my modest capabilities.'

Still smarting from Henri's comment that she had bitten off more than she could chew, Pearl resolved to show her mettle. There would be no more thieving and muddle: she would exercise her authority over the eager young men, many of whom had come straight from the harvest to volunteer at the Trochet farm. They were only nineteen or twenty: she was thirty, old enough to command respect. It was she who could offer them weapons and pay a wage from SOE funds. They must obey her if they were to become an effective fighting force.

Pearl's first act was to appoint four captains to command the *maquis*, which she divided into four subsectors. They were *Capitaine* 'Emile' Goumain, a regular army officer; *Capitaine* 'Robert' (Camille Boiziau), a Communist who had joined her from de Vomécourt's *maquis* after they were attacked at Souesmes; *Capitaine* 'Comte' (Perrot), a former adjutant in the French army; and the cheerful *Capitaine* 'La Lingerie' from Reuilly. Of the four *maquis* captains, Comte, 'an exceedingly capable officer with a great deal of drive,' had the best-equipped, trained and drilled troops, but Pearl found all her captains efficient, untiring and 'excellent'.

Her priority was to arm the flood of volunteers. After Pearl's 'birthday' parachute drop, arranged by de Vomécourt's radio, regular radio contact with London had been restored when her own 'pianist', Tutur, returned from Châteauroux, but transmission still presented many difficulties:

> My W/T operator has considerable trouble in keeping the batteries charged. The *peddle rechargeur* is quite out of the question, as also is the power plant, which needs thirty hours of heating and half a ton of wood. Compared with the Jedburgh battery, our system is positively shocking, and an infernal waste of time and money. There is no electric current in most of the farms, and when we take to the woods still less. Consequently we have to spend most of our time going backwards and forwards to towns

> to have the batteries charged, and that is not always possible owing to the lack of electric current, due to bombing or sabotage.

Despite these problems, Pearl successfully organised twenty-three parachute operations resulting in sixty aircraft dropping 150 tons of *matériel*, enough to arm her own *maquis*, as well as Communist Alex's FTP.

SOE's non-political stance was of vital importance in the weeks after D-Day, as circuit chiefs cut through political disagreements to arm any group who shared their aim of driving out the Germans. When Philippe Liewer of the 'Salesman' circuit in the Haute-Vienne met Georges Guingouin, the FTP leader, on 25 June, the Communist 'was very bold and outspoken in his desire to collaborate with me on the condition that I had no political motive; I was just as bold, and stated that I was only interested in winning the war, and that providing he undertook to attend to all targets which I might designate, I would arm his troops to the best of our ability.'

'We are soldiers of integrity who will carry out orders received from London,' Major Crawshay of Jedburgh 'Hugh', the first Jed to be dispatched to France on 5 June, told Colonel Martel – alias Colonel 'Chomel', Commandant of the Brigade Charles Martel and FFI departmental leader at Châteauroux – when, fearing a Communist takeover after liberation, the Resistance leader had protested bitterly at Crawshay's policy of arming FTP elements. 'We placed ourselves on a pedestal as direct representatives of General Eisenhower and General Koenig,' said Crawshay. When there was 'political trouble', he made a point of 'taking the bull by the horns' and pleading for a united French effort.

In this guerrilla phase of the war, Pearl faced increasing vigilance from the Germans as their panic and ferocity grew in line with the aggression of the *maquis*. The enemy was fearful of venturing far from main towns except in 'repression columns', but the area around the Loire and Cher rivers, owing to its strategic importance, was heavily garrisoned, and at Vierzon there was flak and searchlights. German planes also reconnoitred if they suspected any illegal activity.

> Our parachute operations were exceedingly difficult, owing to the presence of *Postes de Guet* [look-out posts] manned by Germans, the effectiveness of which were increased after D-Day, and the demarcation line, which ran along the whole of the north of the circuit. It was quite impossible to have daylight operations and also to light fires in non-moon periods.

The failure of a parachute drop on ground *Rouget* – four *maquisards* had been killed after searchlights spotted the aircraft and German search-parties followed the noise of exploding grenades from broken containers – was a wake-up call for Pearl. She was determined to be extra careful, and drew up strict rules for the reception committees. Before each drop, she briefed their chief as he waited for the BBC 'personal messages' in a farmhouse near the landing grounds. Once the drop was confirmed, she repeated her orders to the men as they waited in the dark on the edge of the meadow with their torches or bicycle lamps to light up the flare path for the aircraft with its precious cargo of agents and containers. There were to be no loud cries of 'A*ttention!*' said Pearl, as the containers descended, no noise, and certainly no smoking; no laughing, or letting off their pistols in the air from boredom. It was not like the old days, she said sternly, when excited parties received the agents, running off with the parachutes for their girlfriends to make into dresses. Pearl noted: 'It was absolutely essential to have everything cleared off the grounds before daybreak, as reconnaissance planes were always scouring the countryside from 5 o'clock onwards.' Containers were removed from the ground and stored in camouflaged hiding-places, prepared in advance. During receptions, roads in the surrounding areas were blocked.

As the number of drops increased, Pearl's tight discipline ensured that trained men were always sent to supervise the reception committees. Her security was equally strict: only the chief of the reception committee knew the BBC messages, and the remainder of the committee were called together by courier.

But when Pearl came to open the containers, she was often disappointed: 'I cannot help feeling that the armament sent to my circuit was poor compared with the armament received in other circuits.' The heaviest weapons she received were a Bren gun and bazooka, and there were not nearly enough bazookas. As for the Sten, '[it] is hardly a weapon for country fighting. Several accidents happened with the Sten going off on its own.' But Sten guns were cheap, and SOE sent them to her, and to the other circuits, 'in considerable numbers'.

Acting as an arms instructor with inadequate weapons made Pearl's task more difficult, especially as young men were still arriving daily at her door. She wrote tartly: 'It is difficult to train at short notice peasants who have never held a rifle or seen a machine gun.'

Pearl suspected that London HQ was discriminating against her because she was a woman. 'It was probably because I was a woman that, at first, London didn't send me much money.' She was simply getting less money, and fewer arms, than male organisers, despite the number of men under her command. Pearl's indignation grew:

> I have to arm the men, of course, but also to feed them. Many of the farmers feed them, but we also have to buy in provisions . . . I received Frs. 500.000 on the 24th June, and a further Frs. 500.000 on the 28th July. From then on, I received nothing until the sum of Frs. 2.000.000, half of which were in bonds, was sent through Jedburgh HUGH, at the beginning of September.

All through August, she was out of funds. 'I remained for approximately over a month without money, in spite of repeated requests for funds,' she reported. The silence from London – where Buckmaster's command of 'F' was being transferred to General Koenig, as COSSAC now had operational command of SOE – infuriated Pearl, especially as her 'army' was growing rapidly – she had had to recruit a cook to run a field kitchen. She wrote indignantly: 'The upkeep of 2,600 men is no cheap or easy matter.'

But Pearl was ever resourceful. People of substance, seeing the tide turning in the Allies' favour, became anxious to help the winning side. She went into Châteauroux and made some profitable visits: 'We had to collect money from collaborators,' she said. Her powers of persuasion enabled her to collect 1 million francs for her Châteauroux *cachette*, which kept her going until September.

She also kept meticulous accounts, something that was almost unique in SOE history, and revealed her care for her troops. Asked by SOE before she left 'to keep an account of the money you spend . . . if you spend a lot of money,' Pearl had turned to a young trainee accountant, Gaëtan Ravineau:

> I thought, well now, we have got all these chaps and money coming in and . . . some of them were married with children and we had to give them something. And in any case, if they had been in the army they would have received money . . . And I said would you take charge of the accounts of the four *maquis*, and he said yes . . . He had an awful time . . . trying to make them write down what we spent, what we received and making the figures tally.

When Pearl returned to London, Baker Street was astonished to be presented with her neat figures detailing every franc she had spent, on food, cigarettes, uniforms, boots, tyres and medical supplies. 'What's this then?' asked the SOE officer, when Pearl offered him a copy of her accounts.

'A record of my income and expenditure with the *maquis*,' she replied.

'Goodness me,' said the bureaucrat. 'It's the first time I've seen anything like this.'

Pearl had been surprised when it was all totalled together. 'I had spent a lot of money, it was six million altogether.' She also, to general astonishment, handed back what remained of the money she had received: 200,000 old francs. Other agents, like Violette Szabo, might have purchased a designer dress or two, but not Pearl – although she did buy herself a hat for 330 francs.

In the field, Pearl continued to be embarrassed by her lack of a proper uniform. Her third personal suitcase had been dropped to the wrong ground and never recovered, and she was still wearing a crumpled and mud-stained ATS khaki battledress. Despite de Vomécourt's efforts to help:

> My trousers are flying at half-mast because they are too short, my shoes are skiing boots which I'd inherited from Muriel [Byck] who'd died, and my cap is a beret because my uniform had been parachuted and is ATS. And so I just don't know what I am. I can't wear it, thank heavens, because it's too small, and so I pinched a beret off one of the chaps.'

She need not have worried. Pearl may not have had an officer's cap, nor indeed in any way resembled a conventional British officer in appearance, but she had the natural air of authority of a born commander: one which transcended any sartorial shortcomings. Tall, athletic, smiling, her blonde hair tucked under her beret, her appearance soon became legendary, as did her care for her troops. They called her '*Notre Mère*', and adored the woman whose concern for them seemed like that of her mother for her children. And, like a mother, she could also be strict, when necessary: a French radio operator who had been making up tall stories that he had been parachuted into France was reported to her. 'I really was cross. I said, give me your uniform and your revolver this minute and if ever I catch you doing this again, you really will be in trouble.' Defrocked, disarmed, the radio operator had slunk away in disgrace.

'Her troops venerated her,' said her citation for the *Legion d'honneur*. One of her lieutenants wrote simply: 'She was for us what de Gaulle was for France . . . She became our symbol.'

'I stood in admiration before her,' said another, 'because she approached us in a spirit of friendship. Everything that Pauline asked of us, we did very willingly . . . She was obeyed.'

Quietly, Pearl put a stop to the Communists' attempts to help themselves to FFI arms: 'There was an incident when twelve French machine guns were stolen from us, but Alex did not go so far as to steal arms from our depots, though he knew where some of them were,' she says. Concerned that the FTP, easily identified by the bright red star on their uniforms, were attacked several times by the Germans, 'due to their own mistakes, such as walking about fully armed in small villages,' she turned to de Vomécourt to help her. Pearl and he walked over to Alex's tent, but he refused to remove the badges. It was a small failure. From then on, 'the Communists kept themselves to themselves.'

In June and July, Pearl and her *maquis* not only blew up railway bridges, kept the railway lines cut, blocked roads, climbed electricity pylons to cut the lines and cut underground cables, they also supplied military intelligence to SHAEF. This task was initially refused by Gubbins: F Section's circuits 'were not "intelligence" circuits,' he said. 'They were there for action, and the passing of intelligence was a waste of time and . . . of wireless space. Besides, the collection of information was in other hands' – SIS's. But as the Normandy landings approached, Eisenhower had become alarmed at the paucity of intelligence and had asked SOE for help. Gubbins 'strongly resisted', aware that 'radio operators in the Field were already working almost beyond endurance', but in the end had agreed that organisers might report back on specified major types of intelligence.

Pearl herself provided vital military intelligence on enemy troop movements, clashes with German troops, and the location of petrol trains. Her signals to and from headquarters, decoded on squared paper, are rare survivors. One decoded telegram from Special Forces HQ to Marie after D-Day read:

> *POUR MARIE: POUVEZ-VOUS NOUS DIRE OÙ SE TROUVE LA 11E DIVISION BLINDÉE QUE NOUS CROYONS DANS LE VOISINAGE DE VOTRE REGION.* CAN YOU TELL US THE WHEREABOUTS OF THE 11TH ARMOURED DIVISION WHICH WE THINK IS IN THE NEIGHBOURHOOD OF YOUR REGION . . . TELL US HOW MANY BOGEYS (WHEELS) YOU CAN SEE ON ALL TANKS COMING THROUGH YOUR REGION.

Headquarters made this request because Allied commanders were anxious to know how many German Tiger tanks were hastening towards the Normandy front. Tigers were the new super-tanks, which outperformed Allied armour. Realising that enthusiastic *maquisards* might call any tank a Tiger, they wanted a 'bogey', wheel count, to be sure, as well as information on the signs and divisional marks on the tanks. Henri was indignant: 'Are we meant to capture a tank in order to crawl under it and count these bogies, whatever they are? Doesn't London understand the danger we're in?'

Pearl also pinpointed targets for precision bombing by the RAF, for example radioing information on the location of a petrol train on the Vierzon–Bourges line reported by Captain La Lingerie. She and Henri watched the firework display as the RAF bombed the sixty wagons. Afterwards, a message came through from Special Forces HQ:

> THANK YOU FOR INFORMATION IN YOUR 47 (THE NUMBER OF THE MESSAGE). HAPPY TO TELL YOU THAT FOLLOWING THIS THE RAF FOUND SIXTY PETROL WAGONS ON THE VIERZON–BOURGES LINE AND BOMBARDED THE TARGET THE NEXT MORNING WITH VERY GOOD RESULTS. THE SUPREME COMMANDER ASKS US TO CONGRATULATE YOU ON ALL THE INFORMATION GIVEN IN 47.

As the 'Wrestler' *maquis* took more casualties, Pearl recruited a Swiss doctor, Dr René Bertoly, to run a casualty clearing station for the wounded *maquisards*. She and Henri, Kneper, and two young women, Anne and Monique Bled, ran the liaison between the different *maquis* sectors. But security-conscious Pearl allowed no one but herself to liaise with Tutur, her 'radio', whose daily contact with London was vital. She realised that she had begun to worry over his safety. 'There's going to be an accident,' she thought. Once again, her antennae were twitching.

Pearl undoubtedly had some clairvoyant abilities; she also saw numbers in colour and could sense auras. This time, she felt a sudden premonition of danger, just as she had before the battle of Les Souches, and knew she must move Tutur from his hiding place at the nearby Trochet farm to a place of greater safety. But where?

Not for the first time, Pearl's luck held. She found a 'little' castle, the Château de Chêne, near Vatan in the Indre, from which Tutur could transmit. She breathed a sigh of relief. The château served as a field hospital, too, where Dr Bertoly also cared for a wounded English aviator who had a serious head injury, and performed plastic surgery on a *maquisard* who had been shot in the face by a machine gun.

Pearl's premonition proved correct. Once again it seemed to Henri, and to Pearl too, that a guiding spirit, perhaps *le bon Dieu*, was protecting them. Shortly after, the Germans renewed their hunt for the new 'Wrestler' HQ: an informer had sent a letter to the Gestapo denouncing Pearl. The Germans decided to raid the farm, which they had been told was in the vicinity of the village of Maray, Loir-et-Cher:

> When the Germans got to Maray village, they said: 'Where is the Trichet farm?' And it so happened there was a farm with that name. You see it was luck again. It was on the other side of Maray, we were on the east side and the cowherd who was in the village heard this and came crashing down to us saying, the Germans are looking for you. We all jumped out of the windows and went into the woods.

'We narrowly escaped the visit of forty-five German soldiers to the farm,' she reported to London, 'but fortunately the name given was not correct and the Germans went to the wrong farm.'

But Pearl was shaken at the thought that old father Trochet, a familiar, beloved figure in his hunting cap, with an immense flannel cummerbund around his waist, might be arrested and deported, as Auguste Chantraine had been after helping her. Nor could she bear to think that Madame Trochet and André might also be deported.

Pearl felt increasingly guilty. She brooded over the risks to the Trochets, which increased every day she and Henri lingered at the farm. She had grown fond of Madame Trochet, whom she sometimes helped with the butter-making in the dairy, where plenty of elbow grease was needed to churn the cream into yellow blocks, stamped with the local *marque* and left to rest on a marble slab. The rich Charolais milk had to provide butter and cheese for many visitors, and when she was not busy, Pearl liked to lend a hand.

'I did an awful lot of waiting, and Madame Trochet tried to make her butter and it was really hot, this was one of those hand [churns] . . .And she was going round and round with this wretched thing, and I said, let me do it for a bit.' But 'the butter just would not butter' in the warm weather. 'It was terrible! She was a hard-working woman, she had chickens and her Barbary ducks and her coots and cows, plus the house and the cooking.'

Pearl decided that she could no longer endanger her generous hosts. It was time to move into the woods and live *en maquis*.

On 25 July, Pearl's pleas for a French military commander were finally answered. François Perdriset, alias Commandant 'Francis', arrived from Châteauroux to take over command of the *maquis*, at the instigation of Commandant Surcouf, *Armée Secrète* chief of the *département*. His arrival sparked a quarrel between Pearl and Henri.

Henri distrusted Perdriset. In the 'hierarchy of resistance', those who had taken up the cudgels early felt a certain cynicism towards the johnny-come-latelys, the *résistants de la dernière heure*, who only rediscovered their patriotism after D-Day. Contempt was particularly reserved for the *Naphtalinés*, the former French army officers who had only recently taken their old uniforms out of mothballs.

Perdriset was a former officer who had been arrested by the Gestapo in January and later released. Another story still tarnished his reputation, however. At the beginning of February 1944, Robert Monestier, departmental head of the MUR, had been walking down the street towards the house of some Jewish resistants named Katz in Châteauroux when to his utter horror: 'Suddenly, I saw a German car slow down and I saw Francis Perdriset inside it.' What was Perdriset doing in a German car outside the Katz home?

The story took an even more sinister turn when it was told that on 11 February, a young girl, Denise, went to school in Châteauroux.

She was expecting to see her friend, Françoise Katz. But when the teacher took the register and called out: 'Françoise Katz,' there was complete silence.

'Our heads were bowed, crying,' wrote Denise.

'Why are you all crying? What's the matter?' asked the young teacher.

Denise's father had told her that the Germans had taken Françoise and her family away that night. The girl was deported to Auschwitz.

For Henri, too many question marks hung over Perdriset's head. It seemed to him, as it did to Monestier, that Perdriset was suspect. The volunteers in the *maquis* were equally hostile towards the poisonous *naphtaliné*, the 'arrogant, blinkered' career officer, taking over from their beloved Pauline.

The ever-intensifying feelings finally broke out between Pearl and Perdriset when he began tampering with her organisation of the *maquis*. 'There was an *engueulade*, a shouting match between us two . . . Commandant "Francis" wanted to make changes, to give the men [formal] military ranks.' Pearl replied: 'I've organised the *maquis* in a certain way, and in my opinion you'd better keep it that way, or else get out.'

The steely glint in Pauline's blue eyes told Perdriset that he was not going to win this argument. He backed down. 'He didn't change a thing,' noted Pearl with satisfaction. Perdriset might not have challenged Pearl, had he known her better. The warrior queen was accustomed to being obeyed.

Nevertheless, it was with a certain relief that on 27 July Pearl saw Perdriset take over formal command of the four 'Wrestler' batallions that she had been leading for two months. From then on, the two worked closely together.

There was another subject still weighing on Pearl's mind that summer. Her virgin status, which she had prized and preserved for so long: on 12 August 1944, it would be exactly eleven years since Henri had proposed to her. It seemed hardly possible that her engagement had lasted so long or that her hopes of marriage had been so constantly deferred by events. 'You have got to understand that I cannot marry you at present,' Henri had said to her in 1933, after she had accepted him. 'It is out of the question because I have to look after my mother and sisters, and you will have to wait.'

'Well, I didn't think he was going to wait eleven years!' said Pearl, later. She was frustrated by her long engagement. Ever since returning to France, she had dreamed of marrying, but it was impossible in Occupied France. How could she, Cécile Pearl Witherington, marry under her own name when she was living clandestinely with a false ID card? She reasoned that if Henri married her as 'Marie Vergès' as well as 'Witherington', he would be a bigamist.

Milestones had passed: their first wartime Christmas together in Paris under his father's roof; Henri's arrival in Montluçon on 31 April; Southgate's arrest; their moving in together at the Sabassier lodge; but nothing had brought home to her the depth of her love so much as the battle of Les Souches. Newly aware of the transience of life, she had listened to Henri when he asked, why wait for our wedding night? Perhaps that night would never come. Pearl's thirtieth birthday on 24 June had been the night she had finally yielded to him. 'I thought "I don't know what is going to happen" and so I gave way, and that was it,' wrote Pearl, later. 'I broke my engagement . . . Of course, [some] people just didn't think about it, they just did it like animals and jumped from one chap to another.' Such promiscuity held no attraction for Pearl, however; Henri was the only man for her. 'I didn't jump from him at all.'

In the privacy of the little stonewalled bedroom at the back of the Trochet farm, Pearl and Henri finally learnt to know each other's bodies. They were left alone. *Père* Trochet was busy with his hunting and trapping, his wife with her domestic tasks. Despite the lack of soap and water, the young couple enjoyed a new intimacy. They lived intensely in the moment, not caring what tomorrow might bring. They heard the drone of planes, the crackle of flak; outside, cocks crowed, dogs barked: they held each other tightly during those passionate nights. It was probably the happiest time in Pearl's life.

'Pearl had a soft centre,' says Tom Roberts, son of Nancy Fraser-Campbell. 'She was brusque on the surface, but underneath she was soft and loving.'

With the arrival of Perdriset and his adjutant, this intimacy had been interrupted, however. In order to protect the Trochet family, Pearl and Henri had left the farmhouse and moved into the nearby woods, where they set up camp with Perdriset. They erected tents of khaki parachute silk, which leaked at first until practical Pearl came up with the idea of a double skin to each tent, 20 centimetres apart, laid over oak branches. They slept in sleeping bags made of more parachutes, stuffed with Monsieur Trochet's best hay. SOE's 'silken bounty' also served to make tents for Perdriset and his adjutant, for an office with a table and typewriter, and one for visitors to sleep in.

Henri had been given a puppy by a farmer's wife. Pearl wrote: 'We picked him up and he went to sleep in our tent. But of course I had long hair then and as I can't stand hair round my neck, it was in plaits. My plaits were outside the bed and as soon as daylight started, there was my puppy . . . pulling my hair.'

Sam, the spaniel puppy, chewed Pearl's plaits, slept on their sleeping bag, and wagged his long tail over their faces, becoming a good hunting dog who worked the woods with them. He was 'wonderful', said Pearl.

It was at this time also that Pearl's pleas for more clothes were answered by one of the Baker Street secretaries. Opening a parcel addressed to 'Marie' in one of the containers, she was surprised to find several silk negligées and nightdresses in pink and peach satin. Pearl laughed as she stroked the lingerie; she was not in a hotel but a dripping tent, surrounded by soldiers. Instead, she asked *Capitaine* La Lingerie to run her up a pair of serviceable pyjamas.

On 11 August, Captain Comte, chief of subsector 3 of the *maquis*, came running into the Doueçay camp to report to Pearl and Perdriset that the previous night he had received a Jedburgh mission.

'What?' exclaimed Pearl. 'I don't know anything about this.'

'That's why I've come to tell you about it,' said Comte. 'We don't know what to do with them. There are three of them, in uniform.'

'It's imperative that I see them because I don't know what the heck's going on.'

The next day Comte brought in the Jeds. Pearl was surprised to see a '*monsieur d'un certain âge, un major anglais.*' He had been parachuted to a ground near Vatan with his radio, Sergeant James Menzies, and Lieutenant Brouillard, codename 'Vermont'.

Why was the tall Englishman still in uniform? It was dangerous because there were still plenty of Germans in the area.

Pearl extended a hand: '*Mais, qu'est-ce que vous faites ici?* What are you doing here?'

'*Et vous, donc?*' replied the major.

Pearl laughed sarcastically. 'I've been here quite a while. I'm SOE. I was parachuted in. We've got four *maquis* here.'

The major shook hands. 'Arthur Clutton, ma'm, OC Jedburgh "Julian". And you are?'

'Agent Marie, SOE.'

Pearl's attitude would remain critical of London for sending her a Jed so late in the day:

> I was never warned of the arrival of Jedburgh 'Julian' in spite of the fact that this team was dropped in my circuit. They arrived far too late to do any work of great importance and were never told of my existence . . . I have nothing against this Jedburgh but it is inconceivable to me that this state of affairs should have existed at that stage of *maquis* life . . .

Major Clutton was to prove more useful than Pearl at first realised. On 18 August, a courier came running into her camp gasping that portly Paul Vannier, *Capitaine* La Lingerie, and one of his units, was attacking a battalion of German soldiers at Reuilly. Of more import, the enemy was no longer wearing the grey uniform of the *Wehrmacht*, but the black tunics of the 'men of steel', the 'SS' blazoned in silver runes.

The crack *Waffen* SS 2nd Panzer division 'Das Reich' had arrived on Pearl's patch.

27

Jedburgh 'Julian'

MAJOR ARTHUR Henry Clutton, codename 'Stafford', turned to his wireless operator, Jim Menzies. He needed to know more about the mysterious woman described by his boss, Captain Crawshay, as 'Pauline alias Geneviève alias Marie in the region of Valençay'.

'Send an urgent message to headquarters,' he instructed the company quartermaster sergeant. Menzies coded the message:

> 15 AUGUST, FROM JULIAN:
> WHAT IS POSITION AGENT MARIE. STATES SHE WAS SENT SOE . . . HAS BEEN ORGANISING MAQUIS THIS AREA PAST MONTHS. IS SHE TO CONTINUE THIS CAPACITY. MAY BE USEFUL.

Minutes later he received a reply:

> FROM SPECIAL FORCES HQ TO JULIAN:
> WE UNDERSTAND GERMAN 159TH DIVISION IS MOVING NORTH TO BATTLE ZONE. DO ALL POSSIBLE TO DELAY OR STOP THEM. ANYTHING YOU CAN DO TO HELP MARIE APPRECIATED. BELONGS SAME ORGANISATION AND IN CHARGE NORTHERN PART INDRE. SUGGEST YOU WORK CLOSELY TOGETHER.

Clutton scanned the message. He knew he had got off on the wrong foot with Marie at his puzzling meeting with her in the forest of Graçay. He and team 'Julian' had been parachuted onto ground Mascara, ten kilometres west of Levroux, to work in the Indre and Loire under the direction of Jedburgh team 'Hugh', led by Captain W. R. Crawshay of the Royal Welsh Fusiliers. Crawshay, who was the Regional Military Delegate (DMR) in the area, had urgently needed assistance.

A team of SAS, 'Bullbasket', who had been dropped with him on 6 June to work with Amédée Maingard, had just been massacred by the Germans, who had executed their thirty-five prisoners in accordance with Hitler's 'Commando Order' on 7 July. The few survivors, including Maingard himself, had been airlifted back to England on 10 August.

Twenty-four-year-old Crawshay, son of a former British ambassador to France and a fluent French speaker, had been disillusioned with the SAS:

> We never considered that uniformed troops, foreign to the country and its language, could carry out sabotage in better conditions than the Resistance. On the contrary, they attract far more remarks, and consequently draw danger not only on themselves, but on all the *maquis* in the region . . .

Ambushed and executed by the Germans, the secret mass graves of the SAS would be discovered after the Liberation. Welsh Lieutenant Twm Stephens had been wounded, captured and tied to a tree; the Germans paraded the Verriers villagers past him, before clubbing him to death with their rifle butts. American Lieutenant Bundy was also executed. In all, of 100 SAS captured by the Germans in France during operations after D-Day, only six survived.

Calling for back-up, Crawshay had stipulated that he would only accept an 'outstanding' Jed. His request had resulted in the arrival of Clutton and team 'Julian'. Jeds 'Hamish' and 'Ivor' were already in the region.

Clutton saw that he had arrived late in the day. Met by *Capitaine* Comte and taken to Pearl's camp, he had been stunned to meet a woman apparently organising a *maquis*. It was a 'rum show'. Having checked with Special Forces HQ, he set himself to remedy the poor impression that he had made on Pearl. Forty-six-year-old Arthur Clutton may have appeared middle-aged to Pearl, but he had won the Military Cross for conspicuous gallantry in World War I, and was a lean, fit and urbane officer. He knew how to charm the proud and prickly young woman standing before him in her worn battledress. She had lost her precious RAF Eureka beacons and two S-phones in the battle of Les Souches; she was being short-changed by SFHQ in terms of armament; her radio was inefficient. He saw at once that her *maquis* had accomplished much, but she – and François Perdriset – could do with his help. This was especially so because the Indre was now designated 'high priority'.

In fact, the arrival of 'Julian' was more opportune than either Clutton or Pearl at first realised, and he was immediately sent by Crawshay to the Issoudon region with orders to intercept German traffic on the right bank of the Cher river. In the initial phase of guerrilla warfare after D-Day, Crawshay had thought that the Creuse was the important area on which to concentrate, but by the second phase, from 25 June–10 July, he had realised the strategic significance of the Indre. It had been:

> A period of intensive organisation where thanks to the parachute operations of Hamish, Edward [another Jed team], Pauline . . . the resistance in the Indre produced as first class troops five mobile battalions in addition to well organised *maquis* in every sector . . . There were five hundred rail cuts from 6 June to 6 July in Indre alone.

The Americans were also established in the Indre. OSS Jedburgh team 'Hamish', led by Lieutenant Robert M. Anstett (codename 'Alabama') was dug in at La Châtre, while on 8 July, as Crawshay's war diary recorded, the *maquis* of the Vienne, who had been attacked at the same time as the SAS group, withdrew to the Indre after the 'Bullbasket' fiasco. There was a lot of man-power in the area.

By now, something approaching outright panic was growing among the Germans in the central region, while a new note of paranoia had crept into *Kommandant* Brodowski's war diary by 10 July:

> Apart from the few towns which are still held by German troops, chaos reigns in the whole region. Transport is at a standstill. The

main roads, not to speak of the rest, are constantly under the control of the *maquis*. The train lines are crippled by daily increasing attacks. The communications networks, with the exception of the radio, are, despite the greatest efforts of the repair troops, only occasionally useable . . . In the open countryside, the red Terror rules, moving from village to village finishing off everyone that has the faintest smell of anything German.

Der rote Terror. The Red Terror. The French Communists were winning. The very words penned by Brodowski had the smell of defeat. However stoical, however committed to the Führer, it could only be a matter of time before the Germans began a lemming-like run back to the Fatherland: Operation Dragoon, the Allied landings on the Riviera on 15 August, would be the catalyst for a violent movement northwards as 200,000 Germans headed for home.

As July shaded into August, Crawshay noticed the first signs of a general retreat of German troops: they were flooding into the Indre in a race towards Germany. On 1 August, he wrote: 'The resistance in Indre et Loire were in the key position.' Special Forces HQ ordered 'the four BBC phrases calling for an intensification of guerrilla activity [to be] passed down to commanders of battalions . . .' and Crawshay noted that, 'Sabotage operations increased as regards the roads, for the railways in the Indre have long been out.'

But there was a worrying lack of intelligence over the repression columns coming towards the region. Despite having between 8,000–10,000 armed Resistance fighters in the region, Crawshay lamented that he could not plan for a policy of guerrilla action, as he was not sure of the enemy's future movements.

Crawshay would need all the fighters he could get. As early as 17 June, London had alerted the Military Delegate for the Indre that the 'Das Reich' division was moving into his region:

DAS REICH DIVISION BELIEVED MOVING NORTHWARD BY RAIL COUTRAS-POTIERS. ALERT SAS AND INFORM US IF ANY OF HIS TEAMS CAN ATTACK.

But the SAS could do nothing to stop the 'Das Reich'. In June they were deep in the forest of Verriers in the Vienne and unable to help. Only the *maquis* armed by SOE organisers, and the Jedburghs, were available to attack and delay the 'Das Reich'.

On 22 June, SFHQ ordered Crawshay to 'interfere with movement German infantry division moving northwards from Toulouse and report progress.' This signal probably referred to the 2 SS Panzer Division 'Das Reich', whose march had started at Montauban. By 12 July, Crawshay was requesting 'special bombing of HQ . . . Boche Colonel commanding repression columns Indre, Vienne, Creuse and Loire . . . tanks also present.'

The German columns were protecting the hated Limoges Gestapo as they withdrew with the SS – 'All enemy movements are towards the north.' Seven days later, Crawshay reported 'Boche armoured divisions' attacking the Creuse *maquis*, who were 'fighting magnificently' as they also withdrew to the north.

'Very interested your information Boche armoured divisions,' responded London on 21 July, anxious to know where the divisions were coming from and on which route. '2 Divisions now reported at Bellac,' radioed Crawshay. His prediction was that 'Boche will probably disperse from Bellac on roads Poitiers–Argenton–Le Blanc–La Châtre.'

The imminent arrival of the *Waffen* SS had become Crawshay's priority, however. He sent an urgent message: 'Reliable source states that SS column will occupy Le Blanc shortly, probably 31st.'

On 1 August, Crawshay requested RAF attacks 'on emergency sked'. Two German columns of over 100 vehicles each had left Châtellerault and Poitiers with an advance guard of seventeen vehicles, and were about to mount an operation against Le Blanc.

The 'Das Reich' is back. Panzer units are about to surface from the mêlée of German troops heading north and arrive on Pearl's doorstep, at the town of Valençay, which lay north-east of Le Blanc, and forty-three kilometres from Châteauroux, in the heart of northern Indre.

The SS are enraged by the weeks of ambushes and attacks

they have suffered at the hands of the *maquis*. Fanatical fighters, they are in no mood for surrender like the 'old men' of the reserve regiments who are fleeing now. Their minds are on reprisals, bloody reprisals, which will teach the 'terrorists' a well-deserved lesson. In particular, they are determined to have their revenge on a certain Lieutenant Louis Chauvier, a wounded *maquisard* hiding in Valençay, who has previously led an attack against them. Chauvier and the other casualties have been taken by Dr René Bertoly to a hospital, where they are being cared for by nuns.

At 3 p.m. on 16 August, the SS column advances on the ancient town of Valençay, famous for having one of the most beautiful châteaux of the Loire. The peace of the historic town is shattered as over 300 *Waffen* SS, with tanks, half-tracks and lorries, roar through the cobbled streets. The crack troops, in their black uniforms, pour from the lorries and fan out, shouting: '*Ici maquis, ici terroristes, Valençay terroriste!*'

The Germans run from house to house, yelling '*Raus! Raus!*' but they find only frightened townsfolk, women, children and old men. The *maquisards* have been forewarned and are hiding in the forest of Gâtine, which borders the town to the north.

'*Ces brutes à la tête de mort*,' wrote Georgette Guéguen Dreyfus, widow of FTP leader, *Capitaine* Dreyfus, who was killed at the end of August. 'These brutes wearing the death's head . . . emerge in a fury and kill eight innocents and burn forty-two houses.'

Part of Valençay is by now in flames, but the men of 'Das Reich' are still frustrated at not having found their quarry, Lieutenant Chauvier. They move on to the *Maison de Charité*, and hammer on the door. There is no sign of Chauvier there, so they set the convent on fire and advance to the hospital, which is also run by nuns of the religious order, '*La Puye*'.

The soldiers of the swastika march into the hall, and demand to see the doctor. They are received by Sister Claire-Saint-Alphonse, the mother superior. An officer demands: '*Ici vous soignez Chauvier?* Is Chauvier a patient here?'

'*Connais pas Chauvier*,' replies the nun. 'There is no one here of that name.'

By now the SS have reached the door of the ward in which the wounded *maquisards* are being nursed. There, two nuns, Sister Marguerite and Sister André-Hubert, attract the attention of the soldiers: Sister Marguerite picks up a new-born baby boy and, holding him in her arms, hurries forward, barring their way.

'*Ici maternité?*' asks the German soldier. '*Ah! Excusez! Excusez.*'

He turns on his heel, and the Germans troop noisily out, followed by the nuns, still holding the baby. Valençay hospital is spared, as well as fourteen *maquisards*, including Chauvier.

That night, Pearl's 'Wrestler' *maquisards* from subsector 2 emerge from the forest and spirit Chauvier away in the night to a nearby farm. They evacuate all the wounded under the noses of the SS, who have left Valençay burning as they move on towards Dun-le-Poëlier. Cheated of Chauvier, they are determined to find the Communist, Alex.

Major Clutton first reports the presence of 'Das Reich' to SFHQ on 16 August: 'Roads Châteauroux–Vierzon–Châteauroux–Bourges–Châteauroux–Valençay cut last night. 400 SS troops attacked section *maquis* yesterday. Our losses 10 killed.'

His war diary for 16 August, the day on which the '*les hordes Hitleriennes*' pillaged the town of Valençay reads: 'Ambush at Taille aux Ruines on Route Nationale 732.'

> 120 FFI commanded by army chaplain Father Valucri attacked a convoy of 360 German soldiers who had just burned forty houses at Valençay. They were part of SS Division 'Das Reich.' The battle lasted two hours and the losses inflicted on the enemy were 76 killed and 120 wounded. The losses of the FFI were 28 killed.

The *Waffen* SS also clash violently with the *maquis* at Saint-Aignan, before fighting *Capitaine* La Lingerie at Reuilly, torching the towns and killing the inhabitants as they go. Alex, their next target, is one step ahead of them, however. Georgette Dreyfus reports that the German column stop en route to Dun, asking villagers the whereabouts of the FTP leader and arresting and interrogating the mayor's secretary, who professes ignorance. 'The SS climb once more into the jeep at the head of the column – a jeep full of objects stolen from Valençay – and drive on to the château de la Roche, where they hope to surprise Alex and his men.'

The armoured column, the lorries bursting with soldiers, the trucks with sub-machine guns, driven by the SS dressed in black, are furious that they haven't found Alex's *maquis*. They roll up the drive to the château. The farm is deserted: no labourers, no animals, not even a dog. The château is empty, its doors bolted . . . *Un vaste silence.* Alex had warned everyone in advance.

The raids showed the personal nature of the vendetta that members of the 'Das Reich' division were pursuing against named 'terrorists'. As early as 12 June, recorded *Kommandant* Brodowski: 'SS Panzer Division "Das Reich" made it their business to rescue 23 missing men from the German garrison at Guéret and bring them to the Limoges Gestapo.'

It was remarkable that as late as 16 August, SS columns of 400 men were still mounting attacks on individual *maquisards* in the Indre. The sacking of Valençay was a waste of time, just as sacking Oradour had been. Of Valençay, Pearl said: 'It wasn't Oradour, but it wasn't very pretty.'

The story of resistance in the Indre supported the argument that SOE circuits delayed and 'mauled' the 'Das Reich' division badly: if it had arrived on D-Day + 3 as expected, the Allies would have had a far harder fight on their hands in Normandy. '[Pearl's] guerrillas encountered units of 2nd SS Panzer Division "Das Reich" and contributed to its slow march to the invasion area,' wrote historian Declan O'Reilly.

Along their route, the 'Das Reich' 'multiplied their massacres', in the words of Madame Dreyfus, at Tulle, at Oradour, at Argenton, at Valençay, circling their killing towns on the Michelin map in red. But, by striking again and again at the Resistance fighters, or by taking part in revenge attacks, the division was fatally weakening itself.

Many crack SS units were still 'bandit-hunting' through July and August with the help of the *Milice*, wreaking havoc wherever they went, abandoning any pretence at legal warfare, until the conflict in the Indre took on the tenor of a civil war. Otto Diekmann, who led the massacre at Oradour, was killed in action in Normandy on 29 June, possibly in a suicidal attack as he was facing a court martial for exceeding his orders. 'The Germans lost it,' wrote Defence Attaché Air Commodore Michael Brzezicki. 'They simply lost it.'

And, as the weeks ticked by, Montgomery broke through from Caen, and Patton began his race to the Rhine.

Anxious to make up for lost time, Major Clutton had made it his business to see that Agent Marie received the supplies she needed to stop the Germans crossing the Cher. He had signalled on 15 August:

AGENT MARIE . . . HAS LIST OF CODENAMES APPROVED DROPPING GROUNDS. STATED DELIVERY ARMS ALREADY PROMISED BUT NOT RECEIVED. CAN DELIVERY BE MADE THESE GROUND. ARMS, PLASTIC, TIRE BURSTERS, MEDICAL URGENT. TWO AND A HALF MILLION FRANCS REQUIRED FOR TROOPS' PAY.

The next day, he promised to 'do all to delay [159th] division' or stop them crossing to Normandy, but 'have no plastic, tire bursters'. When would the next two ops on ground Mascara take place? 'Include plane-load plastic. Serum anti-gangrene required for wounded.'

Their common aim drew Clutton and Pearl together. She had already transformed the Indre *maquis* into a potent fighting force by mid-August but, as the SOE containers dropped from the sky, each with 27 Sten submachine guns, 36 rifles, 6 Bren guns, 8 kilos of explosive, 40 grenades and 20,000 rounds of ammunition, it became even better armed. Soon Pearl prevailed on Clutton to lend her Sergeant Menzies and the Jedburgh radio to coordinate Allied bombing. On 2 August, she signalled:

FROM MARIE THROUGH JULIAN. REQUEST URGENT AIR RECONNAISSANCE AT SAINT-AIGNAN. 80 HUN LORRIES WITH ANTI-TANK GUNS STATIONED AT CROSS-ROADS. ANOTHER HUN COMPANY ARRIVING TODAY.

In late August, Colonel Chomel, departmental head of the FFI, ordered Perdriset and Pearl to regroup in the forest of Gâtine, north of Valençay. Pearl was annoyed that she was to leave Doulçay and station the troops in a place they didn't know: '*J'ai piqué une belle colère.* I flew into a temper.' It was nonsense, a grave strategic error, she expostulated. 'But I was no longer commandant.'

Pearl was worried. She was under orders to prevent the German exodus to the Fatherland, but 'Our greatest strength was to know our terrain.' *Maquisards* didn't fight like soldiers who fought to win ground, she protested, anxious that many of the *maquisards* would be fighting in areas with which they were unfamiliar. '*La guérilla ce n'est pas la guerre!*' The rules of Witherington's War: harass the enemy, then melt away; never hold ground nor seek confrontation.

After two and a half months with the Trochets – in their farmhouse or encamped on their land with Perdriset – she and Henri said a sad goodbye to the farmer and his wife, and moved the twenty-six kilometres west to the forest. All four 'Wrestler' *maquis* now pitched camp in the forest of Gâtine, more than 3,500 in number.

The number of Germans on the run had increased since Hitler's order of 17 August to evacuate southern France. Two days later, General Sachs, commander of the 64th Armoured Corps, had ordered all German troops to retreat to the east, camouflaging their withdrawal as an 'anti-terrorist' operation, and attacking and destroying the Resistance as they marched. The southern group was under the command of the small, wily but forceful General Elster. Sachs ordered his generals: 'Not a locomotive, not a train, not a power plant, not a factory must fall intact into the hands of the enemy.' Bridges had to be blown across the Garonne, the Dordogne and the Lot. Scorching the earth they had occupied for four years would be the Nazis' final farewell.

As the Germans fled, as in other parts of the region, growing number of atrocities took place. Clutton was horrified to discover on 17 August: 'Germans after action Monday chopped up 4 PWS alive. *Maquis* have treated their PWS decently to date.'

Under Hitler's 'Commando Order', the Germans did not take prisoners. All members of the SAS or paramilitaries captured operating behind the lines were shot, whether or not in uniform. But Pearl herself had seen the bodies of dead *maquisards*, and knew that they had not simply been shot – they had been tortured, too. The evening before the decision was taken to execute a German officer, she had seen the bodies of *maquisards* who had been blinded, their eyes smashed with rifle butts. They had then been crushed under the wheels of a lorry. Empty, bloody sockets had stared up at the sky. She wrote: 'Their treatment of *maquisards* they caught was appalling. After killing them they would proceed to atrocious mutilation beyond recognition . . . You couldn't have any illusions. If you were a prisoner, you were a dead man.'

It was François Perdriset who took the decision to avenge the comrades who had been killed in this barbarous fashion, giving the order to shoot the captured German officer. Pearl watched stony-faced as an Alsatian *maquisard* put two bullets in the German's head.

Commented Clutton:

> At the beginning of the conflict, the FFI did take prisoners and treated wounded and unwounded with consideration. As time went on and it became obvious that all FFI captured by the enemy were shot like rabbits and in some cases tortured, their attitude changed. Many Germans were shot in reprisal, and towards the end no prisoners were taken.

Pearl herself never shot a German. Of the 'awful day' at Valençay, she said: 'I didn't go out and fight with a gun. I don't think it's a woman's job. We're made to give life, not take it. I couldn't have stood up and coldly shot somebody.' But she was responsible for the deaths of many German soldiers. Whether she placed explosives on bridges and railways in person, or trained others to do so, the result was the same. And she admitted that if a German had attacked her physically, she would have killed him, using the silent killing methods taught her at Beaulieu.

Pearl's time in the camp at Gâtine was happier than she had anticipated. There was the joy of knowing that the enemy was fleeing and then, on 25 August, Paris was liberated.

'Paris martyred, but Paris liberated!' proclaimed de Gaulle. 'Liberated by herself, liberated by her people, with the help of the whole of France, that is to say of the France which fights, the true France, the eternal France.'

He made no reference to the sacrifice of the Resistance, although it was Georges Bidault and the National Council of the Resistance who welcomed him to the Hotel de Ville; nor was there any mention of the Anglo-Americans, who had only at the last minute agreed not to by-pass Paris in their dash to Germany: 'Well, what the hell, Brad,' Eisenhower had reportedly said to General Omar Bradley. 'I guess we'll have to go in.'

Montgomery, however, refused Eisenhower's invitation to send even a token British force.

South of the Loire, the battle continues. The old Non-occupied Zone is still not free. Deep in the Gâtine forest, Perdriset, Pearl and Clutton dig in. The late summer rain has come, and they struggle with damp and the mud.

The people all around them are impatient for liberation. They are tired of waiting. Great swathes of France are already free. It is their turn now. They believe that when the day of liberation finally comes, it will also be 'the day of retribution'.

Capitaine 'La Lingerie' obtains permission to 'occupy' his home town of Reuilly and, on 24 August 1944, the proud *capitaine* and his *maquisards* march into Reuilly to the roll of drums. They are welcomed with open arms. The FFI, as the *maquis* are now known, have come as liberators. *'Un air de fête règne dans le pays.* An air of celebration reigns in the country. People pour out into the streets.'

Madame Vannier is not only decking her own house with flags and bunting, but selling it from her *atelier* to an eager queue of her neighbours, when a *Waffen* SS soldier carrying an American carbine suddenly bursts out of an alleyway.

Bullets whistle past Madame Vannier's head as Germans pour into the streets. There are SS soldiers in black, but there are also many men of the Africa Korps, with their distinctive helmets, pouring from an armoured train, which has halted at Reuilly station.

Madame Vannier and her daughter hide in the pig-sty, and the *maquisards* flee. The Germans are turning the tables on the partisans, having learnt, too, *la guérilla*.

29 August is another long day of ambushes and skirmishes. But the Germans are afraid of the forest of 'Katine', as they call it, and never enter it.

That night, a measure of calm descends on the *maquis* HQ, where Pearl and Henri, Perdriset and Clutton are stationed at the *Belle Etoile* farm. It is time for dinner.

Around the big, scrubbed table, covered for this occasion by a snowy tablecloth and small bunches of flowers, sit *le commandant Francis, les lieutenants Pauline et Jean, le capitaine Bourguignon* [Perdriset's deputy], *le major Stafford, le lieutenant Brouillard,* James and two girl couriers, Hélène and Solange.

They have eaten and drunk well: sirloin steak and red wine. The room buzzes with conversation and is thick with smoke from German cigars. Eventually, the major rises, and the guests stream out into the night to a chorus of goodbyes.

As *Capitaine* La Lingerie returns to his billet, he hears the strains of a French song:

J'attendrai, le jour et la nuit,
J'attendrai toujours . . .

Poking his head round the door of a little Renault, hidden in a copse, he sees a pair of English shoes hanging over the front seat and a body on the back seat. It is James, Stafford's radio. His entire knowledge of French songs is encapsulated in these few words, which he repeats endlessly.

'Hello!' says the captain. '*Ca va?*'

'*Oui*. Very well.' There is a discreet hiccup.

Gently the *maquisard* closes the door and goes on his way. The melody pursues him:

J'attendrai, le jour et la nuit,
J'attendrai toujours . . .

They were a tight unit, the *Belle Etoile* HQ: one night, when their petrol had been stolen from their car and Pearl and Clutton, in a group of six or eight, were walking back to Valençay, they had begun to sing Joan of Arc's marching song, the song of Lorraine, '*Avec mes Sabots.*'

Pearl was astonished to discover that only one person knew all the words: '*C'était mon Anglais!*' It was her Englishman. Side by side, the 'proud children of Lorraine' had marched to the chant of: '*Oh! Oh! Oh! Avec mes sabots . . .*' and the miles disappeared.

It may have occurred to Arthur Clutton that Pearl, marching with her *maquis*, was a woman made in the mould of Joan of Arc. Young, visionary, dedicated to her army, Pearl shared many of Joan's qualities. When she returned to England, he presented her with a little cross of Lorraine, inscribed on the back: '*Avec mes sabots.*' She would cherish it for the rest of her life.

28
The Elster Column

RIVERS OF men continued to flow into the Indre, including German soldiers, defeated, desperate, armed and dangerous. They were caught in a trap: eastward lay Nevers, gateway to the Swiss frontier, to Germany and their waiting women and children; but ahead of them lay the river Loire, whose right bank was controlled by General Patton and the 3rd Army; while behind them, in the south, the 1st Army of French General de Lattre was chasing them with all the eagerness of a Jack Russell terrier let into a barn full of rats.

Three generals commanded the columns of Germans fleeing to the Fatherland. One, fifty-year-old General Botho Elster, led a column of nearly 20,000 men, comprising the greater part of the 159th Infantry Division. The column stretched for several kilometres, a motley collection of tanks, armour, foot soldiers, horsedrawn and motorised vehicles, customs officers and *Feldgendarmerie*. For Elster, an energetic general who had won his spurs in tanks, it was not an appealing command, but he brought his not inconsiderable talents to the task of leading his men to safety.

Ahead of him lay not only the ambushes of the *maquis*, but the threat of being strafed by Allied bombers. 'In the first stages of the retreat,' wrote Crawshay, 'the Germans feared air attack more than the *maquis*, and subsequently withdrew in driblets. They were soon forced to change their policy however, and withdrew in great convoys.' This permitted SOE circuits and Jedburgh teams to call down 'shattering bombardments' upon them. This necessary grouping into convoys as the result of SOE action was, in his opinion, 'probably the greatest service rendered by the *maquis* to the Allied command.'

As vital intelligence was conveyed to London, the arms of a pincer closed on the Elster column: they could neither escape to the north, nor retreat to the south. Their original escape plan had been to strike northwards towards Bourges but soon, to Crawshay's delight, 'they all converged on the Cher valley'. The column had been driven into the jaws of Pearl's 'Wrestler' *maquis*.

Intending to escape the Americans by crossing the river Cher into the Sologne and marching to the bridges of the Loire, at the Cher, Elster met his nemesis: Pearl Witherington a.k.a Agent Marie a.k.a Pauline and her army stopped the column dead.

Le capitaine Pauline, as she was now known all over the Indre and the Cher, was given her orders to halt the German advance to the Loire on 25 August. Charles Martel (Colonel Chomel) FFI departmental leader at Châteauroux, asked her to take up position in the north of the *département* on *routes nationales* 76, 17 and 156.

All four sectors of the 'Wrestler' *maquis* were to fight as one, and they intensified their sabotage. Captain Robert's subsector 2 blew up numerous bridges to stop the Germans reaching the Loire. Pearl reported:

> They destroyed the bridges at Peguets, Souverain, Sarey, Soubry, l'Arche, Gué Fesmont, Terverty, L'Allemandière, Gourdinerie, Vicq S/Nahon, Entraigues, Langé, two bridges near Châteauvieux, and the Grand Moulin bridge. To this list must be added over a hundred barrages blocking the roads, as well as the cutting of the Châteauvieux–Seigny road, effected by the use of mines.

The tyre-bursters, for which Pearl and Clutton had pressed so hard, were put to good use. The boxes containing plastic explosives and detonators were hidden in small holes in the road and covered with horse dung. Sitting fifty yards away behind a bank or a tree, the *maquisards* would watch gleefully as a German vehicle drove over the 'manure' and an explosion ripped away the tyre, perhaps turning over the car. Roads were also mined with piles of stones that covered a pound of plastic explosive, attached to a pull-switch. The first and second lorries in a convoy were allowed to pass, but when a lorry in the middle of the convoy was level with the pile, 'We tugged at the pull-switch.' Several hundredweight of sharp stones would then be blown into the air, stripping the lorry so completely that, even if it did not catch fire, all that remained of the vehicle and men was a skeleton chassis and dismembered bodies.

'Pearl's tiny army fought a larger and better equipped force . . . to a standstill, aided only by three special-forces officers.' There were many hard-fought battles in the last fortnight in August, when Pearl's partisans forced the convoys to do a dramatic about-turn: she was with Captain Robert's brave battalion when they blew up a lumbering convoy of German lorries and exchanged fire with the German infantry, who turned tail and ran in the opposite direction:

> On 25 August, the same section (Battalion Robert) attacks a convoy of 18 Hun lorries. The front two are put out of action and block the passage of the rest of the convoy. The Huns deploy skirmishers and advance . . . Our men take up position facing the enemy and open fire at a distance of 50 or 75 metres. The Huns lose 30 dead and 50 wounded. *Le convoi est obligé de faire demi-tour.*

The next day, an even more furious battle ensues on the N760, seven kilometres north of Valençay, after the *maquis* ambush and kill three German motorcylists: scouts for the approaching convoy.

> 128 Hun vehicles (half-tracks, tanks and lorries) arrive. *Les boches stoppent et se mettent en batterie.* The Huns halt and unlimber the guns.

The German guns engage and the battle lasts for five hours, only ending at 10 p.m. Once again, Pearl's army is victorious: teenage boys who only weeks earlier had finished their hay-making, left their horses in their fields, bade farewell to their mothers and left their peasant farms to answer Pearl's appeal for volunteers, have turned into soldiers, steady in the face of fire from an overwhelmingly superior enemy force. It is a tribute to Pearl's leadership and that of the battalion captains she has also trained. 'We only had one dead, two wounded,' she reports proudly.

One recurring phrase in her account of the achievements of 'Wrestler' sums up those weeks:

> *On attaque sans cesse le boche.* We continually attack the Huns . . . On the 28th [August] a company from Comte's Battalion kills 5 Huns who were trying to cross the Cher . . . The 29th, the same company, after a skirmish, kills 20 Huns. On the 31st the Huns completely encircle the 3rd Battalion.

Pearl's battalions were heavily outnumbered, however. By the end of August, there were: '4,000 Huns at Valençay, 6,000 at Saint-Aignan, but Comte's battalion of 800 men went into battle. The Huns had heavy artillery and tanks, the battle was extremely violent and losses were heavy . . .' Pearl's breathless account continued: 'We lost 120 dead and 1 missing . . . Hun losses approximately 180 dead and 300 wounded.'

She calculated that the Germans lost 1,000 men over five months, and their wounded ran into thousands.

Harried by the Resistance, bombed by Allied aviation, the Germans were repulsed. Returning the way they had come, they were forced to abandon their plan to cross the Loire. 'Frightened, disordered, counting their dead, they drew back from the Sologne district, from the Cher and the Sancerre district,' recounted Philippe de Vomécourt.

But they didn't go quietly. As the Germans huddled together in the triangle of ground between Châteauroux, Vierzon and Bourges, then began to fall back, they reacted ever more viciously, their revenge attacks on the 'bandits' escalating.

'The Germans were building up a huge debt,' added de Vomécourt, 'and we were determined that that debt should be paid.'

The Resistance leaders met at Romorantin, a few miles north of the German 'triangle', and decided to 'squeeze' the Germans. In this endgame, the enemy would be forced to surrender or to fight. It seemed that the Resistance was about to achieve the climax of its power, 'a victory which would repay the Germans for their crimes . . .' wrote de Vomécourt optimistically. 'The 18,000 Germans, dead or alive, will be the prize and the vindication of the Resistance.'

But payback was a long time coming. Hopes were raised and as quickly dashed. Valençay, already liberated by the FFI, in defiance of Crawshay's orders, was reoccupied; on 26 August, the townspeople awoke to find that 300 Germans were squatting in the Château de Valençay, seat of the Duc de Valençay. Their numbers were growing rapidly: 600, 800 then 1,000. The German officers presented themselves to the duke and informed him that they had pitched camp in his elegant park. Lorries and tanks poured through the gates. Terrified that there would be a repeat of the blood-letting of 16 August, and that their houses would be set on fire again, the townspeople fled.

Rats were leaving the sinking ship. The *Milice*, the French collaborationist paramilitaries, were running from the Germans. Yet from their hiding places behind the trees, the *maquisards* who watched them go reckoned they were making a mistake: 'The only hope for the *Miliciens*, the French traitors,' said one eye-witness, was to '*suivre les maîtres auxquels its se sont vendus*, to follow the masters to whom they have sold their souls.' Retribution after the war would be swift.

The Elster column had found temporary respite in the open plains around Châteauroux and Valençay, but the general knew he had to move on. But where to? If his men tried to push through the hills towards Nevers and the Swiss frontier, the *maquis* would destroy them. They had nowhere to go.

Pearl's battalions had regrouped in a triangle. At its base were the towns of Saint-Aignan (Battalion Comte) and Chabris (Battalion Emile), and at its head was Valençay (Battalions Robert and La Lingerie). The German retreat was about to become a débâcle.

Pearl was still based at a farm belonging to the Driand family in the forest of Gâtine: *La Belle Etoile* – now re-named *La Bonne Etoile*, the good star – had become the nerve-centre of her joint operations with Perdriset and Clutton. The four battalions of her *maquis* were camped in the forest around her, and all day messengers clattered into the courtyard with news from Valençay, which was only a kilometre or two from the 'Wrestler' camp. As Pearl waited for news of the latest skirmish or ambush, her heart swelled with pride. It seemed to her that SOE had come full circle: 'For us, SOE began and started there. It was next to Valençay that the French section made its first contact in France, with Max Hymans, on 6 May 1941, after a radio operator was parachuted there. And now we have ended up in the same place.'

The three-way collaboration of Pearl, Perdriset and Clutton had become a fruitful one. 'Major Clutton and I worked in close collaboration and got on exceedingly well,' she wrote. 'He was extremely popular with all the French people with whom he came into contact.'

At the beginning of September, the FFI – as she and Henri, de Vomécourt, Perdriset, Clutton and Charles Martel all recognised – had brought the Germans to the point of surrender. Elster's capitulation to them was expected any day.

On 4 September, the capture of Poitiers by the FFI hastened the end. On the same day, Lyons was liberated. French negotiators approached General Elster at his HQ, a château near Châteauneuf-sur-Cher, owned by the Comte Guillaume d'Ornano. '*La guerre est perdue pour l'Allemagne*. Germany has lost the war,' they said. 'The continuation of the struggle is devastating the region.'

Elster knew this was true. Germany had lost the war. But he was afraid of the consequences if he surrendered to the *maquis*. He replied: '*Je ne veux avoir affaire au* maquis. I don't want to deal with the *maquis*.'

Count d'Ornano responded that regular forces were close by.

'Then we need to act quickly,' said the German.

Major Crawshay had been observing events with a degree of frustration. His plan had partially succeeded: he had forced the enemy to retreat in convoys, bringing them up against 'a solid hedgehog' of the Resistance through which all the enemy from the west and southwest of France had to pass. 'Enemy columns . . . en route to the Cher valley or to direction Valençay were . . . caught in ambush and dreadfully punished, right up to the end of August.' But he needed back-up.

On 27 August, Crawshay and US Lieutenant Anstett from team 'Hamish' flew by Dakota to England. They informed London that between 60,000 and 100,000 Germans still remained west of the Indre, and asked for Allied air support as well as an American column from the north bank of the river Loire.

But Brittany was taking priority for *parachutages* in August; nor was there any sign of General Patton and the Americans. As a result, the German 16th Infantry Division managed to escape. Nevertheless, Crawshay was pleased with the FFI's 'impressive' results, most notably when intelligence reports came in that an SS party of 200 men was advancing from Poitiers to blow up the dam at Eguzon-Chantôme, the most important source of water power in France:

> We immediately surrounded the barrage with a thousand FTP and asked London for parachute troops. We could not actually occupy the barrage as it was garrisoned by 300 *Wehrmacht*.

On the night of 14 August, London sent thirty American parachutists under Captain John Cook, with Lieutenant Colonel Serge 'Butch' Obolensky. Their task was to take the dam and the Eguzon electric plant without the Germans destroying them. The Americans, with 200 *maquisards*, headed for the site and made contact with the French Vichy commander of a unit that was there to help the Germans protect the installation.

'My orders are to defend Eguzon against any assailant,' said the Vichy officer.

'Mine, delivered by General Koenig of the French Forces of the Interior,' replied the American, 'are to take Eguzon and keep it intact for France.'

Implying that he had a large number of forces under his command, the para commander added that he was ready to attack. The French officer agreeed to inform the German garrison that if they left without damaging the plant, they would not be shot. The Americans and the FFI were able to save the dam without any loss of life.

A message arrived from de Vomécourt that the requested American column could not arrive before 14 September. Clutton decided to take the initiative. He approached an American officer at Romorantin, a Lieutenant Magill of 329th Infantry regiment, and led him to Charles Martel at his HQ at the Château de Palluah.

Martel had offered to accept Elster's surrender but had been refused. Eager to deal the Germans a knockout blow, he asked Magill for American heavy armour to finish off the job. It looked as if there was going to be a bloodbath. Elster would not surrender to the Resistance: there were thousands of Germans and comparatively few FFI.

To avoid a last stand by the Germans, Clutton escorted Martel in his jeep to the HQ of American General Macon, GOC 83rd Division, where it was agreed to meet Elster at Issoudon on 10 September to discuss terms of surrender.

Clutton was present when the American and German generals met. It was immediately apparent to him that Elster was playing his weak hand with great skill:

> From the outset, General Elster showed himself to be a very skilled negotiator and he succeeded in converting the exceedingly unfavourable situation in which he found himself into one of relatively great advantage.

Elster repeatedly emphasised the 'irresponsible' nature of the FFI and the necessity of his men remaining fully armed; Clutton was further dismayed at Macon's reaction when Clutton offered him the services of a detachment of the French SAS for escort duties:

> He turned down the offer flatly, saying that he knew the SAS were good fighters but that they were not well enough disciplined

> and he feared the Germans would not agree . . . He spoke to me about saving the Germans from the bloodthirsty French.

Martel stressed that since Elster had been forced to surrender by the FFI, he expected arms and equipment to be handed over to the French. But, as the talks continued in English and German, he was increasingly excluded. The atmosphere was one of 'two great gentlemen making an agreement in circumstances only marred by the presence of some troublesome Frenchmen'.

On Sunday, 17 September, General Elster surrendered to General Macon at Beaugency, west of Orléans. The terms of the surrender outraged Pearl and the Resistance leaders. Elster's troops were to be allowed to retain their armour and to march 'with honour' through the sixty miles of country held by the FFI, before surrendering on the Loire to the Americans. Despite a last-minute dash by de Vomécourt to plead with General Patton at 3rd Army HQ, and a telephone call from Patton to Eisenhower, the supreme commander, who gave permission to stop the 'surrender march', the march went ahead.

> No one who watched them go past would have known they were defeated troops, about to surrender. They swaggered, they flaunted their standards and flags. They even sang German marching songs as they went through the villages where . . . only one week before, they had murdered local people . . .

As his men marched out of the Indre, leaving a devastated country behind them, Elster decided to make a gesture of contrition. '*Herr Präfect!*' he wrote on 15 September to the prefect of the Indre at Châteauroux. He apologised for the 'highly regrettable damage my men have caused in the Indre. I and my troops wish to offer in compensation the sum of 8 million francs.' History does not relate whether this sum was paid; but it is on record that the *maquisards* behaved with exemplary restraint as the enemy they had brought to its knees marched past them singing the '*Horst Wessel*' song, the anthem of the Nazi party.

It was also the day when all German arms were to be handed over to the FFI, but Clutton and Colonel Surcouf were suddenly informed that they lacked the right authority from General de Gaulle. Clutton jumped into his jeep and raced to Paris, but by the time he returned with the requisite authority, it was too late; the 83rd Division had already handed the German arms over to the 9th Army.

Clutton would not let the matter rest. He drove on to HQ Zone Communications Le Mans to plead the French case for the return of horses and vehicles not required by the Americans:

> I told General Collins, GOC, that I could not see why the French should have to buy back equipment that the Germans had stolen, quite apart from the fact that the stuff was theirs by right of capture . . . He replied that . . . he was convinced that some of the horses had never been French horses.

Clutton pressed for the welfare of the horses, and General Collins was sympathetic enough to take him to General Simpson, 9th Army. Both generals flew to Paris 'for instructions horses.' Meanwhile, 'horses dying', Clutton radioed SFHQ on 22 September: 'Am soldier not economist but cannot see why French should buy back equipment stolen by the Germans.'

But SFHQ was growing weary of his protests: 'Your mission being terminated,' they radioed on 25 September. 'Report Paris as already instructed.'

'*Le major Clutton a fait des cavalcades à tout casser pour essayer d'empêcher ça,*' wrote Pearl of the Elster surrender, '*mais ça n'a pas été possible.*' Clutton had pelted helter-skelter all over the country trying to stop the Elster surrender, but to no avail.

Neither Pearl nor the FFI leaders wanted a bloody retribution, but they had wanted justice. Pearl's instinct for fair play was hurt when she and the *maquis* leaders were cheated of receiving Elster's surrender. Her own comments on the affair were stinging:

> General Elster refused to negotiate with the FFI for obvious reasons. General Macon was completely ignorant of the fact that

> the capitulation of the Germans was due to the FFI. The latter were completely ignored at the meeting and the Huns were allowed to proceed to the Loire fully armed. The Americans went so far as to ask the *maquis* to lend lorries for the transportation of these 'gentlemen', which was promptly refused.

Pearl and the local population were horrified to learn that 'when the Germans arrived in the Loire they were received by the American Red Cross with cigarettes, chocolates and oranges [things unknown to French civilians for the past five years], and were seen to walk arm in arm in French towns.' The capitulation 'was a heavy blow to FFI pride, and totally undeserved, when it is considered that no Americans were anywhere near our circuit or further south.'

But, ultimately, Pearl understood: the Germans were regular soldiers who had wanted to surrender to soldiers. Her boys were not soldiers but freedom fighters. She knew, however, that they had done the one thing that mattered: 'We liberated France south of the Loire.'

the capitulation of the Germans was due to the FFI. The latter were completely ignored at the meeting and the Huns were allowed to proceed to the Loire fully armed. The Americans went so far as to ask the maquis to lend lorries for the transportation of these 'gentlemen', which was promptly refused.

Pearl and the local population were incensed to learn that, when the Germans arrived at the Loire they were received by the American Red Cross with cigarettes, chocolates and oranges, things unknown to French civilians for the past five years, and were sent to walk arm in arm in French towns. The capitulation was a heavy blow to FFI pride, and totally undeserved, when it is considered that no Americans were anywhere near our circuit or further south.

But, ultimately, Pearl understood: the Germans were regular soldiers who had wanted to surrender to soldiers. Her boys were not soldiers but freedom fighters. She knew, however, that they had done the one thing that mattered. We liberated France south of the Loire.

29

Liberation

As the Germans marched out, the Indre celebrated its liberation. There were victory parades in every town: in Valençay, Pearl and Clutton marched side by side with Perdriset, Jim Menzies, Henri and Lieutenant Brouillard, leading the battalions of the North Indre and Cher Valley *maquis*, flags flying, to the cheers of the townspeople. Children threw flowers; young women kissed the soldiers. But the expressions on the faces of the *maquis* chiefs and the Allied officers were sombre, exhausted. They spoke of victory but also of death, of comrades and families mutilated and killed, of mothers and children deported and of homes laid waste.

Despite grievous losses, France's greatest art had been preserved in the Château de Valençay, where the treasures of the Louvre had been moved for safe-keeping at the beginning of the war. When Elster's men moved out of the ducal park, Perdriset moved his in, exchanging camp life for unaccustomed luxury; Pearl and Henri slept in a ballroom in a bed that was, said Henri, 'larger than a battlefield'.

The men were billeted next to the Venus de Milo and *The Victory of Samothrace*, which coincidentally had once provided inspiration for the personal messages of 'Wrestler': the phrase '*La Victoire de Samothrace fait du vélo*. The Victory of Samothrace is riding a bike' announced an important arms drop on 9 August, while '*Le penseur de Rodin est constipé*' or 'The Venus de Milo is doing her knitting,' signalled other *parachutages*. However, when Clutton alerted the Louvre to the fact that the FFI were quartered beside the Venus de Milo, the curator, Monsieur van der Kemp, decided that: 'Weapons and cigarettes are not compatible with antique goddesses' and the *maquisards* were dislodged from the château.

'Fighting was over, politics began, "Hugh" left,' wrote Crawshay curtly in his war diary in September 1944.

In the Indre, it was a time for the settling of scores. The 'collabos', collaborators (or those suspected of being so), were arrested. 'We shaved the heads of women accused of "horizontal collaboration",' recalled historian Yves Chauveau-Veavy, 'but at the same time confirmed traitors, old torturers, got off the hook.'

In the aftermath of the fighting, old quarrels resurface. At the Lion d'Or hotel in Valençay, Pearl, Henri and Perdriset invite a *Bureau Central de Renseignements et d'Action* (BCRA) mission from the regional military delegation to join their 'mess' for dinner.

One of the Gaullist delegates begins addressing Henri in English, as he is wearing British uniform.

Henri laughs. 'Don't bother speaking English to me, mate. I can speak French as well as you.'

'*Ah bon?* What have we got here?' exclaims the Gaullist officer. 'A Frenchman in a foreign uniform! *Mon Dieu!* I regard you as a deserter from the French army!'

The whole table springs to its feet.

'I refuse to sit down with a traitor!' declares the Gaullist.

Uproar breaks out, with Henri making frantic signs to Pearl, who is sitting at the other end of the table, to stick up for him.

She is deeply upset. She frog-marches Henri's tormentor into another room and takes him to task. What does he mean by saying Henri is a traitor? Does he think that during the war she and Henri drove around with a notice saying: '"*Ici réseau britannique*, British circuit this way – join here"?'

'No,' says Pearl, her voice choking with emotion. 'People came to us Brits because we helped them, it made no difference whether we were English or French, we waged war together . . . my fiancé, Henri Cornioley,' she insists, ' is a patriotic Frenchman.'

But Pearl's words are lost in the mêlée. It is the first indication to her that SOE's contribution to the victory will quickly be forgotten.

De Gaulle's assumption of power was already a fait accompli: 'With the military defeat of the German army on French soil, the whole structure of Pétain's *Etat Français* was whirled away down the wind of history,' writes M.R.D Foot. 'It had rested on German bayonets and when they left, it collapsed.' As astute as he was visionary, de Gaulle outwitted and outflanked the Communists, before making short shrift of the foreign 'mercenaries' – in September 1944, SOE organisers received an order from de Gaulle to 'quit the soil of France', in some cases within two hours.

'*On nous avait "ordonné de quitter le sol français."* We were ordered to "leave the soil of France",' Pearl remembers, distressed at this pre-emptory dismissal – or, in her own words, '*coup de pied au derrière*, kick up the bum' – from the general.

All over France, SOE's British agents were having the same experience. In liberated Bordeaux, Major Roger Landes a.k.a 'Aristide' was received by General de Gaulle on 17 September.

'I was very badly received,' the agent recalled. 'The general says to me: "*Vous êtes anglais, votre place n'est pas ici.* You are English, your place isn't here." I am very surprised by this reception, I don't understand it.'

Major Landes was then warned of a change of programme: his invitation to a celebratory lunch with General de Gaulle was withdrawn. In the afternoon, he was called instead to the Prefecture and received by the minister of war, Monsieur Diethel, who informed him that, '. . . *que je dois quitter la France dans les deux heures*.' He, too, must get out of France within two hours.

The next day, Captain Peter Lake a.k.a 'Basil', who had parachuted into France with Robert Beauclerk a.k.a 'Casimir' as part of an inter-Allied mission to the Dordogne on 9 April 1944, also met de Gaulle.

'What are you doing here?' enquired the general.

'I am training special troops for special operations,' replied Lake.

'You have no business here.'

'I obey the orders of my superiors.'

'Our troops don't need training,' retorted de Gaulle. 'You have no business here, I say. You have no right to exercise a command.'

'*Mon général*, I exercise no command.'

'We don't need you here,' repeated the general. 'It only remains for you to leave. I have already told one, Aristide, who was indulging in politics, to get out. Another that I have despatched is Hilaire, in Toulouse. You, too, must go home. Return, return quickly . . . *Au revoir*.'

Bewildered by this ingratitude, Pearl and the other Britons left the country for whose freedom they had risked their lives. They had no way of knowing how deeply humiliated de Gaulle had felt by his treatment at the hands of Churchill; nor did the general, who had spent his war in exile in London or in Algiers, greatly comprehend the contribution made by Allied agents to the Resistance.

General Eisenhower, by contrast, was unstinting in his praise for SOE. On 31 May 1945, he wrote to Major General Gubbins:

> I must express my great admiration for the brave and often spectacular exploits of the agents and special groups under control of Special Forces Headquarters . . . While no final assessment of the operational value of resistance action has yet been completed, I consider that the disruption of enemy rail communications, the harassing of German road moves and the continual and increasing strain placed on the German war economy and internal security services throughout occupied Europe by the organised forces of resistance, played a very considerable part in our complete and final victory.

Even in January 1944, Churchill had expressed doubts about the outcome of the invasion. He knew that it would be a monumental undertaking, and that victory could by no means be guaranteed:

> It is to my mind very unwise to make plans on the basis of Hitler being defeated in 1944. The possibility of his gaining a victory in France cannot be excluded. The hazards of battle are very great.

> The reserves of the enemy are capable of being thrown from point to point with great facility.

But within days of D-Day that was no longer true. The Germans had lost control of their rear, their war diaries expressing their panic and paranoia as the Resistance harried and snapped at their heels. It was to emerge later that eight of the Germans' sixty-odd divisions were tied down to fighting in their rear while, in addition, a seventeen-day delay was imposed by SOE circuits on the 'Das Reich' so that a division that had raced from the Russian front to Strasbourg in a week and a day, had been unable to reach Normandy until after the beachhead had been established.

On tactical and strategic grounds, the Resistance had more than proved its worth.

For Pearl, the greatest reward was the memory of the close harmony that had existed between French resisters and British agents in the field.

'*Je tiens surtout à exprimer la très vive joie qu'ai éprouvée à collaborer avec des officiers britanniques*. I want to express the great joy I felt in working with British officers,' wrote Pierre Hirsch, one of Southgate's radio operators, to Buckmaster at the 'Home Station'. 'I wish that the profound fraternity which united us during the combat will continue in the future for the common good of our two countries.' The memory of comradeship, the respect of the *maquisards*, was important to Pearl. After the humiliation of 1940, the Resistance had saved the soul of France.

Memories of her humiliating treatment by General de Gaulle were not easily forgotten, however. Pearl had spent five years of her life in the war against Hitler, in the struggle against an ideology of manifest evil to whose defeat she committed herself, heart and soul. Like so many British agents, she loved two countries, and felt so deeply the rape of France by the invaders that she was prepared to die in the cause of its liberation. She was willing to make any sacrifice and, as she witnessed the arrest and deaths of those who were caught by the Gestapo, she came to understand the extent of that sacrifice. Agents she knew well, like Southgate, had been deported to Buchenwald. Farmers like Auguste Chantraine had followed him to the camps and never returned. Others she did not know, like the White Rabbit or Eileen Nearne, had been terribly tortured. Some, like Pierre Brossolette, had committed suicide, jumping to their deaths from the windows of 84 Avenue Foch rather than talk under torture and betray their comrades. The fear Pearl had felt as a *clandestine* was one that would never leave her: she would carry it with her to the end of her life, shaking with terror years after the war when she saw a German in uniform or heard the German language. Nor would she ever forget the other women agents of SOE, the young women whose lives were cut short so abruptly in 1943 and 1944, thanking *le bon Dieu* that she and Henri had been spared.

And now she and Henri faced an uncertain future. During her twelve months in the field, Pearl had lived more intensely than at any other period in her life. She had lived with passion and pain, revelling in open combat and demonstrating that a woman such as herself could fulfil a combat role as successfully as any male agent. Decisive, courageous, discreet and intelligent, she had radiated a charisma that had made her loved and adored by her men. But, even as Pearl marched through Valençay, acknowledging the cheers of the townspeople, and shared victory dinners with her comrades, she knew that nothing would ever be the same again. The certainty of knowing that she had 'a job to do' was over. Never again would she be Agent Marie, never again would she lead a group of *maquisards* down to a railway line, or hide behind the trees watching a German lorry thunder past. Ahead lay London and demob: for the last time, she would take off her battledress and beret and lay them in a drawer; that chapter in her life was about to close.

Major Clutton left the Indre acknowledging that team 'Julian' should have been sent 'at least six weeks earlier'. Had this been done, he believed that the enemy might have been brought to 'a complete standstill'. In his war diary, the last entry is 'An appreciation of the work carried out in the area since June 1944 by Miss P. Witherington alias Marie alias Pauline, an agent of the SOE. The excellent state of organisation of *maquis* troops in the area,' he wrote, 'was largely due to her efforts.'

On 21 September, a message arrived from SFHQ to 'Julian':

> PERSONAL FOR MARIE FROM COLONEL BUCKMASTER. WANT YOU TO RETURN UK SOONEST AS NO FURTHER WORK FOR YOU IN FRANCE . . . BRING WITH YOU ALL BRITISH COMMISSIONED PERSONNEL. THIS MEANS TUTUR, HENRI, MARC. BRING WITH YOU ALL CRYSTALS AND STORE IN SAFE PLACE . . .

Witherington's war was over.

30

Postwar

V2 ROCKETS were dropping over London as Pearl and Henri arrived in the capital on 10 October 1944. Major Mackenzie at F Section had warned Mrs Witherington on 19 September that her daughter would be home within two or three weeks.

'I may be in Cornwall for two weeks . . . on leave with my other 2 S/Os,' Pearl's mother responded, unaware of her daughter's exploits, adding that she wanted Miss Atkins to 'send along October allowance as soon as possible in case of change of address.' Although Gertrude professed to be 'thrilled' at the return of Pearl, whom she had not seen for over a year, telling Vera, 'I am sure you are all pleased with her efforts,' her main worry was whether the flying bombs would interrupt the arrival of the postal order for £9 that she received monthly from Pearl's pay. It was an example of the incomprehension that would face many agents on their return, bound as they were by the Official Secrets Act from talking about their wartime service.

Mingling with the London crowds left Pearl with a feeling of acute embarrassment. She was still in khaki, wearing her battered blouson battledress, trousers which were too short and scuffed ski boots. 'I had nothing else to put on my feet, and only an old mac without a belt.' Waiting outside a shop in Regent Street with her sisters, she heard three women remark, 'Look at her! What a funny uniform!' But at Block 2, Montagu Mansions, Special Forces HQ, memos had been flying back and forth regarding Pearl and Sonia Butt ('Blanche' – an SOE agent who had been dropped to the 'Headmaster' circuit on 28 May 1944):

> . . . women who hold honorary commissions in the WAAFs, have completed their missions abroad and will shortly be returning to

civilian life . . . They are extremely short of clothes . . . Treat this as urgent.'

A week later, Pearl and Sonia gratefully received 80 clothing coupons each with which to go shopping. But where to go in wartime London? Pearl made a cautious trip to Barkers in Kensington High Street, which she had heard was a cheap shop. 'I had £57. And so I went to Barkers . . . and I found myself a tartan skirt, cut on the cross.' The skirt, whose purchase she soon regretted as a poor imitation of a kilt, was a further source of embarrassment when Nancy Fraser-Campbell took Pearl to meet her father, a Scotsman.

'Do take your coat off,' said Fraser-Campbell.

'"I daren't,"' Pearl had replied. 'I was so embarrassed! It was all I could pay for – I got myself a coat, a navy coat and that skirt.'

At Montagu Mansions, Pearl had been upgraded to Section Officer in August. 'Since June she has been in complete charge of this circuit and has shown outstanding powers of leadership and organising ability,' read the citation. Her promotion to Flight Officer followed from 1 September 1944 in recognition of her 'complete control of a *maquis* region since D-Day.' Her pay was raised by £75 to £425 per annum and, on 17 October, she was finally given a kit allowance of £20.

In fresh uniform, there was no need to wait a moment longer. The day for which Pearl had waited eleven years had finally arrived: her wedding day. On 26 October, just over a fortnight after arriving in London, Pearl and Henri were married at Kensington Register Office, in the presence of her mother and two of her sisters. The couple were so eager to marry that they had booked the registry office for the day before, but as their papers were not ready the wedding was postponed for a day. It was a low-key, wartime wedding, but as Henri slipped the ring on her finger and her mother threw confetti, Pearl was overwhelmed with joy that, after all their adventures, she and her beloved Henri were finally man and wife. There was no need now for a fake ID card saying 'Madame Cornioley'. She had taken his name, she was Cécile

Pearl Cornioley, a married woman, and could have a real card that told the world so. She was also now *française de mariage*, a French citizen.

F Section was determined to mark Flt/O Witherington's wedding to Lieutenant Cornioley. 'The above two agents are being married tomorrow and we should be grateful for your approval to pay them from the F Rear Link Float £7 10s as a wedding present,' read a memo. 'Turned down by D/Fin by telephone,' was scrawled across the bottom. Money was tight, but nevertheless a wedding gift of a silver 'flapjack' (powder compact) and cigarette case at a cost of £6 was eventually approved and presented to the couple. And in November, a bonus of £50 was recommended for Witherington, who 'took charge of a *maquis* of 1,500 men and with colossal bravery, led it into action and generally arranged its organisation with extreme devotion.'

It mattered to both Henri and Pearl to have a religious ceremony in the presence of his family, too. The couple returned to Paris and set up home together in a small apartment at 4 rue de Buci, Paris 6e, a stone's throw from the church of Saint Germain des Prés. It was a fresh start on the left bank in a *quartier* of artists, a far cry from the luxury of the Faubourg-Saint-Honoré where Henri had grown up. The new flat did not even have a separate bathroom, but Pearl and Henri were happy simply to be together. They were not far from his parents, who had moved to 29 Avenue de la Bourdonnais, in the 7e, near the Eiffel Tower.

A church wedding ceremony followed in January 1945 at the Protestant Temple of the Oratory at the Louvre. Still poor as church mice, Pearl and Henri were again married in military uniform. As they walked along the Faubourg-Saint-Honoré afterwards, a leather-goods shop caught their eye and Henri bought Pearl a manicure set. It was their only souvenir of the day.

By now, Pearl's reputation was spreading. Her unique achievement as the only woman to run an SOE circuit in the summer of 1944 was recognised by Lord Portal, who invited her to a reception with the male SOE organisers.

He arrived with all the air commodores and wing commanders milling around having a look at the youngsters. We were feeling about this big. And then all of a sudden he came up and said, 'Ah, there you are!' . . . He was really ugly but absolutely charming. We arrived in a huge room with a long trestle table, and he said, 'Do sit down.' And he said to me, 'Since you've done a man's job, what do I have to do? Offer you a cigar, too!'

An even more 'important personage' than Lord Portal now wanted to meet Pearl. She was in Paris when a telegram arrived:

WE REQUIRE PEARL RPT PEARL IN LONDON SOONEST POSSIBLE FOR PRESENTATION TO SUPREMELY IMPORTANT PERSONAGE BRING UNIFORM WIRE ETA STOP THIS IS HIGHLY URGENT AND IMPORTANT.

'I thought it was Churchill,' said Pearl. 'I never expected it to be the Queen.' She was flustered at the thought of being presented to Her Majesty. 'And so I said, "What do we do in uniform, do we salute?" And the answer came, "You are military so you salute first, and you are a woman, so you curtsey."'

Pearl managed to both salute and curtsey and, formalities over, Queen Elizabeth led Pearl and Yvonne Cormeau, George Starr's radio operator, into a music room and spread out a 'tiny' map of France on the grand piano.

'Tell me where you operated.'

Pearl and Yvonne pointed out their circuits: 'Wrestler' and 'Wheelwright'.

'How many men did you say you had?' asked the Queen.

'We were over 3,000 towards the end,' replied Pearl.

'Did you have any trouble with them?'

'No, ma'am.'

Perhaps a little white lie for the Queen. Pearl was a loyal mother to her 'lions' to the end.

In November, Buckmaster asked Pearl to join the Judex Mission, which had left Southampton in a convoy of four vehicles on 28

September and was to spend seven months touring liberated France.

Ordered by Brigadier Mockler-Ferryman to 'proceed to Paris by military aircraft' to the Hotel Cecil in rue Saint-Didier, Pearl caught up with the group, which included Nancy Fraser-Campbell, George Donovan Jones a.k.a Isidore and Hector's former radio operator, and Jacqueline Nearne, as well Buckmaster, Henri and herself. They were to investigate any cases of victimisation of people who had worked with British officers, to draw up lists of citations for decorations and to collect wireless sets, which were needed in the Far East for the war with Japan.

For Pearl, however, the priority was to thank the families who had aided her personally. She and Henri went first to the Doulçay farm, to visit the Trochet family, and thence to the Sabassiers, to give them 20,000 francs in compensation for their losses. People were puzzled to see Pauline in WAAF light blue uniform, but in Châteauroux, Montluçon and Clermont-Ferrand she was received like a queen: '*Ah, voilà Pauline!* . . . As if I'd come down from the moon.' There were civic receptions and presentations, although in bombed-out France the Judex delegates had sometimes to spend the night in sleeping bags in bistros, as the Resistance had blown up hotels used by the Gestapo.

Pearl and Henri returned to the Hotel du Faisan in Châteauroux, which was still standing, and remembered their reunion in September 1943, when Maurice Southgate had brought Pearl to meet Henri. 'I was shaking with nerves,' laughed Henri. Sitting around the table with old friends, Pearl showed them her ring and toasts were drunk to the couple's happiness, to old friends, to France and freedom.

Pearl compiled lists of those in the 'Wrestler' *maquis* whom she recommended for decorations. But although she wrote fully about the Trochets, the Sabassiers, about Dr Bertoly, she was too modest to spell out Henri's achievements, 'as he is now my husband.' As a result, Henri did not receive a British decoration.

The mood of euphoria that had swept France in the early months of liberation persisted as Buckmaster and his party inspected demolished bridges, now being rebuilt by German prisoners of war. 'Wherever we went,' he wrote, 'we were met by evidence of the intense affection for and admiration of Great Britain during the war.' Meeting survivors of the early groups, there were no reproaches for the colonel from 'Buck's Boys'. The only bitterness they encountered, recorded Buckmaster, was towards 'the late-comers among the French – the "*Naphtalinés*" [whose uniform still smelt of mothballs].'

Pearl probably visited 'Le Cerisier' at Tendu, the farm of Auguste Chantraine a.k.a Octave, who had been deported first to Dachau and then to Mauthausen, where he died on 15 March 1945. The memory of Chantraine was indelibly imprinted on her memory.

In 1945, the British government rewarded its heroes. Pearl's colleagues were among their number. She may have felt a pang of envy as she scanned the *London Gazette*: Major Crawshay, Amédée Maingard, Philippe de Vomécourt, Robert Maloubier, Francis Cammaerts, George Starr and George Hiller all received the DSO. Major Clutton was awarded a second bar to his Military Cross; Roger Landes and G. D. Jones received a bar to their existing MCs.

But what of the women? For the War Office hierarchy, they presented a problem, since there was no precedent for recognising women's service in a combat role. As far as Major General Colin Gubbins was concerned, Pearl deserved equal recognition with the men. He put her forward for a Military Cross on 12 April, writing that after the battle of Les Souches:

> Witherington had to reorganise from the beginning. She organised 23 successful supply-dropping operations and her re-armed and re-constituted *maquis* then began guerrilla action on a large scale, causing havoc among German columns passing through the area to the battle front.
>
> Throughout her long tour of duty Flt/O Witherington showed outstanding devotion to duty and accomplished a most

> important task. Her control over the *maquis* group to which she was attached, complicated by political disagreements among the French, was accomplished through her remarkable personality, her courage, steadfastness and tact. It is strongly recommended that she be awarded the Military Cross.

An earlier citation, probably by Wing Commander Redding of the Air Ministry, gave a more personal view of Pearl. Commenting that she was 'not content with a sedentary job' in the Air Ministry, and 'wanted action,' he wrote:

> We always knew that Flt/O Witherington would be a success. Her sure way of dealing with problems, her clear brain, and her incisive determination left no doubt as to her competence and quick-wittedness . . . Long journeys by train and by road through continual Gestapo controls were her regular lot . . . Witherington never hesitated, and for twelve months succeeded in baffling the enemy, despite the fact that she was searched for and a reward offered for her arrest.

Praising her 'superb qualities of leadership, tactfulness and courage,' and pointing out that her commanding officer, Southgate, had received the DSO, he added: 'Miss Witherington was fortunate to find her fiancé in France . . . Her story is a true romance, and our pride and esteem for this gallant girl is very great.'

But Pearl was deemed ineligible for the MC. She was next proposed for the George Medal by Buckmaster, then the OBE (Military Division), with a note 'Original citation was for George Medal.'

'Is the OBE not possible?' Buckmaster had scribbled on the recommendation.

'D/Fin (Gubbins) prefers MC.'

'G.M?' was added below in a different hand.

In this context, Pearl's shock and surprise when Vera told her in October that she had been awarded the MBE (Civil) was understandable. In an icy letter to Flight Officer Atkins, she set out her reasons for refusing the award:

> The work which I undertook was of a purely military nature in enemy occupied country. When the time for open warfare came we planned and executed open attacks on the enemy. I spent a year in the field and had I been caught I would have been shot or, worse still, sent to a concentration camp . . . Our training, which we did with the men was purely military, and as women we were expected to replace them in the field . . . I personally was responsible for the training and organisation of three thousand men for sabotage and guerrilla warfare.
>
> The men have received military decorations, why this discrimination with the women when they put the best of themselves into the accomplishment of their duties? Precedence? If so, it should not come into consideration. When I undertook my duties in the field, I did not personally take into consideration the fact that the mission had no precedent.'

'There was nothing civil about what I did,' said Pearl.

An earlier letter Pearl had written to Vera in April 1944 indicated – if indication was needed – that a woman could excel in a combat role in the military, even as a guerrilla leader: 'We are all OK here and kicking like mad,' she wrote. 'I get a bit hot round the collar now and again but I must say I'd far sooner be here than sitting in an office.' To Maingard, who knew her worth, she was their circuit's 'angel angle' [angel Englishwoman].

It was because Pearl hated injustice that she felt compelled to decline a decoration which, if offered to a man, he would have deemed an insult. As she put it herself, 'In the face of Field Marshal Sir Bernard Montgomery and General Eisenhower's appreciation of the military value of our work behind the lines, I must say the M.B.E. looks puny . . . If I wear a decoration, I wish to be proud of it.'

Lise de Baissac also wrote to Vera protesting that 'the work which I volunteered to do in 1942 was of a military nature' and declined a civilian MBE, 'which does not give a true picture of my work or the spirit in which I undertook it.' When Yvonne Cormeau declined the civil MBE too, the press caught wind of the rumpus.

'Who are the WAAF officers who parachuted into France to join the *maquis* months before D-Day?' demanded *The Sunday Express* in March 1945, after Sir Archibald Sinclair had praised the WAAF parachutists in the House of Commons; only two were named in the press, Sonia Butt and Maureen O'Sullivan. The mystery deepened until it was reported in the *News Chronicle* that Flt/O Witherington had refused the civil MBE 'as a matter of principle as she felt it unjust that women engaged in work of military importance should not have equal treatment with male comrades.'

Prominent women wrote to congratulate the fiery agent on her stand. Viscountess Astor, vice-president of the Six Point Group; Vera Brittain; Violet Bonham Carter; and Megan Lloyd George all praised her action in the 'fight for equal citizenship':

> Numerous injustices are being perpetuated simply because many women will not trouble to insist upon their just rights . . . The Birthday and New Honours Lists would soon cease in their usual extraordinary anomalies of award between men and women for similar services if other women would display your strength of mind in refusing inadequate honours and decorations.

Despite having blotted her copybook, it was decided to send Pearl on an American lecture tour in February 1946, just as the fortune-teller in Oxford Street had foretold in 1943. Air Vice Marshal Douglas Colyer, who was in charge of the RAF mission in the US, had a sharp word with her when he saw Pearl arrive in WAAF uniform wearing the decorations which a grateful France had bestowed upon her: the *Légion d'Honneur*, *Croix de Guerre* with *Palme* and Resistance medal, but without the MBE.

'What's all this nonsense about the MBE?' he asked, in a tone she had never heard before.

Pearl explained her reasons.

'Never mind all that,' barked Colyer. 'You're not parading around

America with all these French gongs and not an English one. Put it on! That's an order!'

'Very well,' said Pearl, 'but I'm taking it off the minute I leave America, do you hear me, because I don't want it!'

On board the *Queen Mary*, as they re-crossed the Atlantic together, Pearl bearded Colyer in his cabin and asked him to raise the decorations issue with the authorities. She had by now discovered that it was because she and the other women agents had held only honorary commissions, not having progressed through the ranks to officer training, that they had been deemed ineligible for military honours.

'You have to change the rules,' Pearl told Colyer.

Colyer agreed, and in September 1946, Pearl and the other SOE female agents were awarded the military MBE.

It was a moment of victory, which crowned Pearl's triumphant tour of the US. 'Pearl the Waaf sure is sumpin'!' was the headline in a Washington newspaper as her 'goggle-eyed' audience learnt that the Nazis had put a price on her head.

Vera, who had put Pearl forward for the trip, offered her help 'should you be in any kind of flap or difficulty', writing, 'I am consumed with envy, and wish I could go with you.'

SOE's instincts in choosing Pearl as their ambassador were correct, for she was loyal and discreet, defending Buckmaster from emerging charges of incompetence, of sending women to their deaths and even of '*deliberately*' [Buckmaster's italics] dropping agents into enemy hands.

'Most of the casualties . . . emanated from the collapse of the "Prosper" circuit,' said Pearl. 'If you focus on that, you come away with the impression that SOE was a failure and Maurice Buckmaster couldn't organise breakfast for two woodpeckers in Sherwood Forest . . . In fact that is not correct.' Of 480 agents sent, 130 had died, the same casualty rate as in a battalion in the field.

For others, however, Maurice's prolonged failure to detect the German radio game that led to the deaths of great agents like France Antelme, remained proof of his incompetence: 'Almost unforgiveable' mistakes were made, admitted one SOE expert.

Pearl knew this, and questioned whether Buckmaster had 'turned out to be the best person for the job. The agents didn't think so, but I have to assume that Gubbins back in London was satisfied . . . We were just doing a job of work.'

And in the end, the job was done.

It was hard to return to the trappings of normality and peace. After the excitement of wartime, postwar France felt flat and dull. For Pearl, by 1946, not only was life an anti-climax as she swept and dusted and created disasters in the kitchen in her and Henri's new little flat in the rue de Buci, but money worries beset them.

'We had lost everything,' Pearl says. Monsieur Cornioley's beauty business had folded: the glamorous *Laboratoire Cornioley* was no more. Henri lacked qualifications; it was also possible that he was suffering from post-traumatic stress disorder after the war. Other ventures that he tried – dealing in army surplus clothing, working in a garage – also failed. She and Henri were virtually destitute after Pearl resigned her WAAF commission in 1945, while her hopes that SOE would find her a new job were dashed.

There was no denying that Buckmaster tried his best to help Pearl. 'Most heartily recommend,' he wrote in his reference for her, but SOE was itself reduced to a skeleton staff by March 1945. 'As you know, we have drastically reduced our staff within the last three months, and suffered no less than four moves,' wrote Vera Atkins to Wing Commander Redding on 10 March, excusing herself over the disappearance of 103 clothing coupons due to Flt/O Witherington, which had gone missing.

On 4 April, Nancy Fraser-Campbell wrote to Colonel Buckmaster saying that she had spoken to Robin Brook, SOE head of the French and Low Countries department, 'with regard to Pearl's future employment' and he stated that 'in view of the present state of military affairs' the application for an administrative job for her would probably not go through. Nancy, however, had seen Philippe de Vomécourt, who had said that he could offer her a civilian job. 'Your fourth good idea for Pearl to work with Antoine STOP wire particulars of job,' responded Buckmaster. But in the end, these ideas all came to nought.

'The simplest action would appear to be to dispose of her in Paris,' wrote Major Mackenzie eventually to Nancy. But the bleak winds of austerity were blowing through postwar France just as they were in England. SOE was itself closed down in January 1946.

There were moments of great happiness, however. In 1948, when she was thirty-four, Pearl gave birth to her daughter, Claire. 'I wanted a little girl and it was a little girl, and I was quite enchanted . . . The happiest day of my life [was] the day my child was born.'

After working since she was seventeen, and after the trauma of war, Pearl longed to be a mother and to stay at home with her baby. But, four months after Claire was born, a financial crisis forced Pearl back into the workplace: she had made the mistake of leaving Henri in charge of finances.

'I had put aside 6,000 francs, and when I went to fetch it, it was gone. "Where are the 6,000 francs that were in the gramophone?"' I asked Henri.

'There was a chap that was with us in the *maquis* who had a terrific story, he said he needed 6,000 francs . . .' Henri shrugged. 'So I gave it to him.'

Worse was to follow. Pearl had taken baby Claire to stay with Monsieur and Madame Trochet at their farm in the country when Henri arrived, distraught. 'Everything has gone,' he said. Pearl discovered that they had lost all the money they had accumulated during the war. A firm in which Henri had invested had failed. As one of their friends said, 'Henri had an ungift for making money.'

In this crisis, Pearl turned once again to the one man she knew she could rely upon: her old mentor, Douglas Colyer. He found her a job at the Canadian Embassy, and she went on to work as a secretary for many years at the World Bank. It may have occurred to Pearl that in marrying Henri, she had picked a man who was, in some respects, as unfitted as her father to support a family. Was history repeating itself? Had she chosen a husband as feckless as Wallace Witherington? Like Wallace, Henri had grown up as a poor little rich boy, unaccustomed to working for his living. But Pearl was determined that her daughter Claire would never suffer as she had suffered as a child. She would do what she had always done as a girl: shoulder the burden of responsibility and provide for her family.

There were difficult times. One day, Pearl turned on Henri: 'If you want to go down the ladder, you will go down the ladder on your own,' she snapped. 'I am not going down the ladder, I refuse.'

Henri regarded his strong wife: 'If I hadn't met you, Pearl,' he said, 'I would have been a hobo.'

Sometimes Pearl asked herself why her life had turned out to be so hard: 'I take life as it comes,' she said, 'but I have had so many difficulties and such a fight for everything.' She knew the answer: '*La vie est dur.* Life is hard.' It was something she had learnt by the age of twelve and now, as then, she resolved to step up to the challenge.

Henri remained in her shadow, deferring to his more masculine and resourceful wife. As one agent's widow said, 'There was only space for one bombshell in the room.' All the same, 'they adored one another'.

In Paris, typing and daydreaming, Pearl's thoughts returned continuously to the agents with whom she had served. She wanted to see Maurice Southgate (Hector) again. He had been liberated from Buchenwald, in May 1945, by the Americans.

A few days before VE Day – 8 May 1945 – Buckmaster went to Euston station to meet the RAF van that was bringing Hector, and other recently released camp inmates, from a British aerodrome to London.

> Skeleton hands parted the back-flap curtain and five caricatures of British officers gingerly lowered themselves to the pavement, on to legs that seemed like match sticks. They sketched salutes to their shaven heads. The most gaunt of the five men advanced a pace. With a shock I recognised this apparition as Hector. He stiffened to attention and said, without expression: 'Sorry I made such a muck of my mission, sir.'

Buckmaster heard Vera, who had come with him to meet Hector, 'give a distressed gulp'. Pearl was also distressed when she met Hector again: the light had gone out of his eyes. It had been beaten out of them; they were dark and expressionless.

'Some of them [the agents] came back,' said Pearl. 'They were in such a state I thought, "No, it just isn't possible that a human being can put another human being in such a state." . . . When Maurice came back from Buchenwald, he was just like an animal. The eyes were the eyes of a cow . . . He never really came back to normal.'

Leo Marks was equally shocked to meet Yeo-Thomas, the White Rabbit, after his escape from Buchenwald.

> An old man was watching me from the doorway. I was about to ask if he had an appointment when I realised that he'd never needed one.
>
> I knew that sixteen of Tommy's friends had been suspended from hooks in the Buchenwald crematorium, and had been killed by slow strangulation. They were hanging from his eyes.
>
> 'Fuck 'em,' I said.
>
> 'I did my best . . .' His voice was a quaver . . . We shook hands in silence.
>
> I waited until his footsteps had shuffled away and was then violently sick on behalf of mankind.

The cost of war was all too plain to see. Many of the 'survivors' were damaged, their personalities and bodies irrevocably marked by suffering.

Epilogue

It is 1953. Pearl and Henri have returned to the bench on the Champs-Élysées on which they used to sit as love-sick teenagers, and they are holding hands. Pearl is humming the song which they have made their own: a *chanson* of Georges Brassens about young lovers kissing on a public bench, '*Les Amoureux des Bancs Publics*':

Les amoureux qui se bécotent sur les bancs publics,
Bancs publics, bancs publics,
Et se fouettant pas mal du regard oblique
Des passants honnêtes

Like the lovers in the song, Pearl and Henri used to smooch on the public benches without caring a fig for the sideways looks of passers-by. They used to whisper, '*Je t'aime*,' to each other, and kiss and cuddle. Pearl leans her head on Henri's shoulder; he bends to kiss her and they smile at their shared memories

The years have passed, but their love story has endured. Claire is five now, and Pearl often takes her to spend her summer holidays with the Trochet family at the old farm, or to stay with Mimi who has married her RAF sweetheart and is living by the sea in Sussex. Their mother died in 1951, but Pearl and Mimi are still close; Suzie has five children now, and Doudou is also married.

Pearl and Henri have moved to a larger flat at 12 rue Pergolèse, down the road from Henri Déricourt's old apartment. They often entertain old comrades from SOE, including Nancy. Pearl has never really learnt to cook, but she and Henri take their friends to a restaurant around the corner.

When Pearl retired, and Henri's health declined, they moved together to a retirement home at Châteauvieux, near Romorantin. They returned to the area that was most significant in Pearl and Henri's life, to the Sologne, the Nord Indre and the Cher Valley.

Determined that the sacrifice of the SOE agents should not be forgotten, Pearl decided to campaign for a memorial to be built at Valençay to commemorate the lost agents of F Section. Inaugurated on 6 May 1991, the fiftieth anniversary of the despatch of F Section's first agent to France, by Monsieur André Méric Minister for Veteran Affairs, in the presence of HM Queen Elizabeth the Queen Mother, the monument stands at the entrance to Valençay, not far from the famous forest of Gâtine. It is in two columns, the black column representing the night and the essential secrecy of Resistance operations; the white column representing 'the shining spirit which ultimately triumphed'. The two columns are linked by the moon, by whose light the agents and the Resistance met in the meadows of France in the *parachutages* that turned the tide of war. Not until she saw inscribed on the memorial the names of the ninety-one men and thirteen women who died, mostly in concentration camps, could Pearl finally rest.

Henri died in 1999, and so did not see the centenary of the *Entente Cordiale* in 2004, when Pearl was presented with a CBE at the Elysée Palace in Paris by HM The Queen, who declared: 'We should have done this a long time ago.'

There was one honour Pearl still coveted, however: her parachute wings, which she had not received during the war due to training restrictions.

'When I got to England,' said Pearl, 'I said: "Well, what about my wings?" and they said, "You can't have them."'

'We've won the war, but I can't have my wings!' Pearl had exploded with rage. 'As time went on I got madder and madder about this because I thought it was so unjust. One thing with me I can't stand is injustice . . .'

Finally, a senior RAF parachute instructor, who had heard Pearl's story, visited her in her *maison de retraite* and presented her with her wings. It was one of her proudest moments.

Pearl lived to see her daughter Claire marry. She died, aged ninety-three, on 24 February 2008: an old lioness, nodding by the fire, dreaming of her 'lions', her brave *maquisards* and the battles of 1944.

Dramatis Personae

British

Witherington, Cécile Pearl. WAAF Assistant Section Officer. SOE agent. Codename: 'Marie'. Nom de guerre: *le lieutenant/capitaine Pauline*. False ID names: Geneviève Touzalin/Marie Jeanne Marthe Vergès. Courier to Maurice Southgate ('Hector'), organiser of the 'Stationer' circuit. From May 1944 Organiser of the 'Wrestler' circuit.

Agazarian, Jack. SOE agent. One of Prosper's radio operators.
Antelme, Major France. SOE agent. Codenames: 'Bricklayer', 'Renaud'.
Atkins, Vera. SOE intelligence officer.
Bégué, Georges. SOE agent, alias 'George Noble'. Radio operator and first F Section agent to be parachuted behind enemy lines into Occupied France, nicknamed 'George I'. Inventor of system of '*messages personnels*'.
Bloch, André. SOE agent, radio operator, nicknamed 'George IX'. Radio operators were known as 'George' after Bégué, or 'pianists' in SOE slang.
Bodington, Major Nicholas. Buckmaster's deputy.
Borrel, Andrée. SOE agent. Codename: 'Denise'. Courier for Prosper.
Bourne-Paterson, Colonel. Deputy head of F Section.
Buckmaster, Colonel Maurice. F Section's information officer, promoted to its head in October 1941.
Cammaerts, Francis. SOE agent. Codename: 'Roger', organiser of the Jockey circuit and a former conscientious objector.

Clutton, Major Arthur. Codename: 'Stafford'. OC of Jedburgh team Julian.

Colyer, Air Commodore Douglas. Air Attaché at the British Embassy, Paris in 1940. Pearl's boss and mentor.

Cowburn, Major Benjamin. SOE agent. Codename: 'Benoit'.

Crawshay, Major W. R. OC of Jedburgh team Hugh.

Culioli, Pierre. A lieutenant of Prosper in the Sologne.

Dalton, Hugh. Minister of economic warfare.

Dansey, Claude. Deputy to Sir Stewart Menzies of SIS.

Déricourt, Henri. F Section's air movements officer. A former French Air Force pilot.

Fraser-Campbell, Captain Nancy. Worked in F Section with Vera Atkins, captain in the First Aid Nursing Yeomanry (FANY).

Gubbins, Major General Colin. SOE's director of training, director of SOE ('CD') September 1943–June 1946.

Hambro, Sir Charles. CD May 1942–September 1943.

Hiller, George. SOE agent. Organiser of 'Footman' circuit.

Jones, Captain George Donovan. Codenames: 'Isidore/Claude'. Radio operator, 'Stationer' circuit.

Khan, Noor Inayat. SOE agent and radio operator, codename: 'Madeleine'.

Koenig, General Pierre. Head of the *Forces Françaises de l'Intérior* (FFI).

Maingard, Amédée. SOE agent, codename: 'Samuel'. Radio operator in 'Stationer', head of 'Shipwright' circuit from May 1944.

Marks, Leo. SOE's head of codes, cryptographer.

Menzies, Sergeant James. Radio operator, Jedburgh Julian.

Menzies, Sir Stewart. 'C' (director) of the Secret Intelligence Service (SIS/MI6).

Nearne, Jacqueline. SOE agent. Hector's first courier.

Nelson, Sir Frank. 'CD' (director) of SOE July 1940–May 1942.

Norman, Gilbert. SOE agent, codename: 'Archambaud'. Radio operator for Prosper.

Portal, Sir Charles. Chief of the air staff.

Rudellat, Yvonne. SOE agent. Courier for Prosper.

Selborne, Lord. Minister of Economic Warfare.

Southgate, Major Maurice. Codename: 'Hector', organiser of 'Stationer' circuit.

Sporborg, Harry. SOE's regional controller of Northern Europe and a former solicitor in Slaughter & May.

Suttill, Major Francis. SOE agent. Codename: 'Prosper'. Organiser 'Physician' circuit.

Trotobas, Michael. Codename: 'Sylvestre', *nom de guerre, le capitaine Michel*, organiser of the 'Farmer' circuit.

Yeo-Thomas, F.F.E ('Tommy'). Wing Commander, SOE agent and deputy head of Free French RF Section. Alias 'Shelley'. Nickname: 'The White Rabbit'.

French

Briand, Théogène. Field name, 'Alex'. Leader of the Communist FTP in the Nord Indre.

Brossolette, Pierre. Founder member of the CNR.

Brouillard, Lieutenant. French member of Jedburgh team Julian. Codename: 'Vermont'.

Carré, Mathilde. Codenames: 'Lily, Victoire', double agent, radio operator.

Chantraine, Auguste. Codename: 'Octave'. Mayor of Tendu.

Comte, Capitaine. (Perrot). Leader in Wrestler *maquis* and former adjutant in the French army.

Cornioley, Henri. *Nom de guerre, le lieutenant Jean*. Pearl's fiancé, and former machine-gunner in the *19e Train hippomobile*.

de Vomécourt, Philippe. Codename: 'Gauthier'. Nom de guerre: 'St Paul'. Organiser of 'Ventriloquist' circuit.

de Vomécourt, Pierre. Codename: 'Lucas'. The first SOE F Section circuit organiser of the 'Autogiro' circuit.

Dewavrin, André. Codename: 'Colonel Passy'. Head of Free French intelligence service, the BCRA. Formerly an agent of the French Intelligence Service, the Deuxième Bureau.

Dufour, Jacques. Codename: 'Anastasie'. *Maquisard*.

Emile, *Capitaine* (Goumain). Leader in Wrestler maquis.

Guerne, Armel. Prosper's second in command.

Hirsch, Jacques. Son of a Jewish *résistant* family. Deputy to Maingard.

Hirsch, Pierre. One of Hector's radio operators.

Kneper, Robert. An escaped prisoner of war. *Maquisard*.

La Lingerie, *Capitaine* (Paul Vannier). Leader in Wrestler maquis. A shopkeeper from Reuilly.

Mardon, Mayor of Dun-le-Poëlier. Local chief of the AS.

Martel, Charles. *Nom de guerre*, 'Colonel Chomel'. FFI departmental leader at Châteauroux.

Moulin, Jean. Codenames 'Max', 'Rex', founder of the CNR.

Perdriset, François. *Nom de guerre*: Commandant 'Francis', Wrestler maquis.

Robert, Capitaine. (Camille Boiziau.) Leader in Wrestler maquis.

Surcouf, Commandant. AS chief of the *département* of the Indre.

Villiers, Colonel. Head of the 'Gaspard' *maquis* in the Auvergne.

German

Bleicher, Sergeant Hugo. 'Ace of the *Abwehr*' (Germany's counter-espionage organisation).

Boemelburg, *Obersturmbannführer* (Lt. Col) Karl. Head of the SD (Gestapo) at 84 Avenue Foch.

Diekmann, *Sturmbannführer* (Major) Otto. Leader of the assault on Oradour-sur-Glane.

Elster, General Botho. Commanding officer of the Elster column.

Geyr, General Leo von Schweppenburg. Commander of Panzer Group West.

Goetz, *Oberleutenant* Josef. Radio mastermind in SD HQ, 84 Avenue Foch, Paris.

Kieffer, Hans Josef. Counter-intelligence chief in Avenue Foch.

Lammerding, *Reichsführer* (SS General) Heinz. Commanding officer of the 2SS Panzer Division 'Das Reich'

Stenger, Lieutenant Colonel. Security Regiment 196, part of the SD.

von Brodowski, General Friedrich ('Fritz'). *Oberfeldkommandant* (Governor) of Süd-Frankreich, Southern France.
von Rundstedt, Field Marshal Gerd. Commander-in-Chief West.

Glossary

AS *Armée Secrète* (the Secret Army).
BCRA *Bureau Central de Renseignements et d'Action*, Free French intelligence service.
COSSAC Chief of Staff to the Supreme Allied Commander.
CNR *Conseil National de la Résistance*. Leadership of the Resistance set up by Jean Moulin in May 1943.
FFI *Forces Françaises de l'Intérior*. Umbrella term for all armed forces inside France, from 1944.
FTP *Francs-Tireurs et Partisans*: Communist-led armed Resistance group.
Milice Ultra-violent group created by Vichy.
MUR *Mouvements Unis de la Résistance*. Umbrella term for Resistance groups in the Non-Occupied or Southern Zone after 1943.
Non-Occupied or 'Free Zone', area of France to the south of the demarcation line.
OSS Office of Strategic Services, US intelligence services, forerunner of the CIA.
SD *Sicherheitsdienst* (Gestapo): SS intelligence service.
SHAEF Supreme Headquarters Allied Expeditionary Force.
SIS Secret Intelligence Service.
SOE Special Operations Executive. British military and intelligence organisation set up by Winston Churchill in July 1940. Its circuits in France were run by three sections, French Section (F), Gaullist French Section (RF), and D/F escape lines.

Acknowledgements

I should like to thank my inspirational editor at Hodder & Stoughton, Hannah Black, whose advocacy for Pearl's story has made this book possible, Rupert Lancaster, for also believing in it, and my agent, Elizabeth Sheinkman, formerly of Curtis Brown, for her help and advice. Thank you also to the team at Hodder: Assistant Editor Kate Miles, picture researcher Juliet Brightmore, copy editor Belinda Jones, and everyone else who worked with such dedication during the editorial process.

I owe a great debt to those historians who generously made available to me their own research material on Pearl Witherington, in particular those friends of Pearl's whom she asked to write her biography many years ago: the late Professor M.R.D. Foot and Colonel John Sainsbury. The 'physical research' on Pearl and her *maquis* became a pleasure in the company of Michael Foot, John and his wife, Gill, with whom I followed in Pearl's footsteps as we traversed the Indre and the Sologne, searching for the site of her landing drop, visiting the Trochet farm, and attending the 20th anniversary of the inauguration of the F Section Memorial at Valençay in 2011. John also hunted indefatigably in the archives at Blois and Bourges. I am also much indebted to Professor Mirjam Foot, Michael's widow, for making private papers available, and to the novelist Gillian Tindall, with whom I trod the streets of La Châtre in search of the spot where Pearl was nearly strangled as a *milicienne*. In Châteauroux we found the Hotel du Faisan, where Pearl and Henri were reunited in 1943. The generous hospitality of the Sainsburys at Cour-Cheverny, and of Gillian and her husband

Richard Lansdown, helped me immeasurably. Thank you also to Sir Peter Westmacott, former British Ambassador, Paris; to Beth Tibble for her tales of the history of the Residence, and to Defence Attaché Air Commodore Michael Brzezicki and Wing Commander Graham August, for information on Douglas Colyer and showing me Pearl's place of work in the 1930s.

Thank you to Pearl's relatives, in particular her sister, Hélène (Mimi) Oddie, for her vivid recollections and unpublished account of the Witheringtons' escape from France; to Mimi's sons, Vincent and Peter, and daughter in law, Annie Oddie, for loaning precious photograph albums. My thanks are due also to many other people who gave me interviews, including Pearl's nephew Tony Thompson and his wife; Tim Buckmaster, Maurice Buckmaster's son, who allowed me to see his father's private diaries; Francis J. Suttill, son of 'Prosper'; Dr Henry Sanford and Isobel Willis at Wanborough Manor; journalist Hervé Larroque, for his kind permission to quote from his conversations with Pearl and Henri Cornioley transcribed in *Pauline*; Tom Roberts, son of Nancy Fraser-Campbell; oral historian Martyn Cox for providing transcripts and photographs; David Harrison for photographs; Dr Declan O'Reilly for sharing his unpublished research on Pearl; Duncan Stuart, former SOE FCO advisor; Julie Wheelwright for material on Eileen Nearne; Elisabeth Amherst; Elspeth Forbes-Robertson; Judith Hiller; Nicholas Neve; Noreen Riols; Willie Beauclerk; Bob Maloubier, President of Libre Résistance; Paul Marshall and Caroline Griffith at the Special Forces Club; Alexandra Martens; Marc du Pouget; Bob Body and Steve Harris for information on Tempsford; Trevor Mostyn; Pat Grayburn; Rina Gill; Robert Jones; Deirdre Lay; Elaine Freed; Moris Farhi; Ann Salter; Moira Williams; Dawn Firth; Cherry Clarke; Mary Sebag-Montefiore; Sylvia Whitman; Laurence Nguyen; Gerard Coutin and Mary Duncan in Paris; Martyn Bell; Sam Jordison; Ros Schwartz and any others whom I have inadvertently omitted.

I am deeply grateful to my fellow biographer Neil McKenna, who had been a wise and insightful editorial advisor and friend, unstintingly generous with his time in reading and criticising the manuscript, and to David Smith, for his German translation and research in the German War Diaries in the Nuremburg archives and elsewhere.

Thank you to the staff of the National Archives at Kew, the British Library, the London Library, the Imperial War Museum Sound Archive and Collections, the Special Forces Club, Valençay library, Châteauroux Municipal Archives, Tangmere RAF Museum, and to the local historians and eye-witnesses of the Resistance in the Indre, the Cher Valley and the Sologne, Yves Chauveau-Veauvy, Georgette Guéguen Dreyfus, Gilles Groussin, Paul Guillaume, Michel Mockers, Maurice Nicault, without whom it would not have been possible to tell Pearl's story. I am also grateful to scholars such as David Stafford, Matthew Cobb and Max Hastings, on whose work I have depended.

I wish to thank my infinitely long-suffering husband, Geoffrey, for his patience and good humour while listening to the manuscript being read aloud to him, and discussing Pearl night and day; my son, Edward, for help with the illustrations, and my two daughters, Emma and Lucy, and their families, for always being there.

Carole Seymour-Jones
Peaslake
April 2013

Picture Acknowledgements

Corbis/E.O. Hoppé: 3 above left. Getty Images: 3 above right. Courtesy of Hélène Oddie: 1, 7 above left and right. Press Association Images: 8 above. RAF/© Crown Copyright: 8 below left. Rex Features: 2 below right, 4 above left. Courtesy of Colonel John Sainsbury: 6 above left and below. Carole Seymour-Jones: 5 below, 8 below right. Special Forces Club: 2 above right and below left, 3 below left. Courtesy of Francis J. Suttill: 3 below right. TopFoto: 6 above right. Private Collections: 2 above left, 4 above right and below, 5 above left and right, 7 below.

Every reasonable effort has been made to trace the copyright holders, but if there are any errors or omissions, Hodder & Stoughton will be pleased to insert the appropriate acknowledgement in any subsequent printings or editions.

Maps and Diagrams

Page ix: 'Former F section circuits active under EMFFI August 1944' first appeared in M.R.D. Foot's official history *SOE In France: An Account of the Work of the British Special Operations Executive in France 1940*, 1966. © Crown Copyright.

Pages viii and 287: Clifford Webb.

Pages 266 and 267: Courtesy of Colonel John Sainsbury.

Notes

1. Into the Field

1. 'Harvest moon', Hugh Verity, *We Landed by Moonlight: Secret RAF Landings in France 1940–1944* (Manchester: Crecy Publishing, 2000), p. 125.
2. 'Fought to the last ditch', Bickham Sweet-Escott, *Baker Street Irregular* (Methuen, 1965).
3. Nancy Fraser-Campbell, interview with her son, Tom Roberts, September 2012.
4. 'Well, I asked to be his courier', Pearl Witherington, interview 16 with Tom Roberts, 25 November 2006.
5. 'Very intelligent, straightforward', Cécile Pearl Witherington, training report, 17 July 1943, Pearl Witherington Personal File (PW PF).
6. 'What's happening?', Pearl Cornioley (Witherington), *Pauline: la vie d'une agent du SOE, Témoignage recueilli par Hervé Larroque* (Editions Par Exemple, 1995), p. 10.
7. 'Flight Sergeant Cole', Operation Report, 22–23 September 1943, and F/Sgt Cole debriefing report, Bob Body, www.tempsford-squadrons.info.

2. Darkest Hour

1. '*Les Anglais!*' Bruce Marshall, *The White Rabbit* (London: Evans Bros, 1952), pp. 6-8.
2. 'We spent the time', Cornioley, *Pauline*, pp. 58–59.
3. 'Gigantic guerrilla', Max Hastings, *Finest Years: Churchill as Warlord 1940–45* (HarperPress, 2009), p. 43.
4. 'We have to go', Mimi Oddie, 'My Family's Escape from the Germans, Normandie 1940', unpublished, 1989, Oddie family archive.
5. 'Only 22 miles', John (Paddy) Moffitt, 'My Escape', unpublished, undated, Oddie family archive.
6. 'With eyes like glacier lakes', Jean-Paul Sartre, *Iron in the Soul*.
7. 'I thought, Crikey . . .', Mimi Oddie, 'My Family's Escape'.
8. 'One of the Germans', Philippe de Vomécourt, *Who Lived to See the Day: France in Arms 1940–1945* (Hutchinson, 1963), p. 26.

9. 'I was furious', Eric Taylor, *Heroines of World War II* (Robert Hale, 1991), pp. 147–8.
10. 'Churchill took a keen', David Stafford, *Churchill and the Secret Service* (John Murray, 1997), p. 6.
11. 'To set up a new section organisation', M.R.D. Foot, *SOE in France: An Account of the Work of the British Special Operations Executive in France 1940–1944* (London: Whitehall History Publishing in association with Frank Cass, first published 1966, revised edition 2004), pp. 8–10.
12. 'I felt as if I were walking', Winston Churchill, *The Second World War. Vol 1: The Gathering* Storm (Cassell and Co., 1949), p. 596.

3. The Longest Winter

1. 'To refuse to collaborate', De Vomécourt, *Who Lived to See the Day*, p. 37.
2. 'Pearl put all our eggs', Mimi Oddie, 'My Family's Escape'.
3. '"Run!" cried the passeur', conversation with Mimi Oddie, 30 March 2011.
4. 'The lights in wine sauce', Taylor, *Heroines of World War II*, p. 146.
5. 'Miss Witherington!', Paddy Moffitt, 'My Escape'.
6. 'I have never been so ashamed', Nancy Wake, *The White Mouse* (Australia: Macmillan, 1986), p. 41.
7. 'We have been beaten everywhere', Charles d'Aragon, *La Résistance sans Héroïsme* (Paris: Editions du Seuil, 1977), p. 12.

4. Escape

1. '*Tu viens de la part*', Maurice Buckmaster, *They Fought Alone: The Story of British Agents in France* (Odhams Press, 1958), pp. 34–35; Foot, *SOE in France*, pp. 155–6. After escaping from prison, Morel was passed by SOE agent Virginia Hall onto an escape line over the Pyrénées, and became F's operations officer in March 1943.
2. 'My first winter', Cornioley, *Pauline*, p. 61.

5. Pearl

1. 'We were born in Paris', Mimi Oddie, 'My Family's Escape'.
2. 'For Witherington', 'The Ballad of Chevy Chase', no 128, Arthur Quiller-Couch, ed, *The Oxford Book of Ballads*, 1910.
3. HMS *Witherington* served as part of the escort for an Atlantic convoy that came under sustained attack by U-boats in 1943, marking a turning point in the Battle of the Atlantic in favour of the Allies.
4. 'Enjoyed the bottle', interview with Tony Thomson, 3 December 2009. Wallace's grandparents were both shopkeepers in Worcester: his father, Walter, was the son of a 'druggist' or chemist and his mother, Henrietta

Martha Allies, was the daughter of Frederick Allies, whose shop sold fishing tackle. They married in 1865, and moved to London, where Walter's architectural practice flourished. By the time of Wallace's birth, the family were living in 'The Hollies' in Highbury Park. Wallace was the only surviving boy, having seven sisters.

5. 'I can't stand sticky things', Cornioley, *Pauline*, p. 31.
6. '*Tu faire face a la vie*', ibid. p. 103.
7. '*Tu veux un verre?*', ibid. p. 103.
8. 'You're a tough one', ibid. p. 101.
9. 'As for my childhood', ibid. p. 32.
10. 'I had terrible gaps', ibid. p. 101.
11. 'It was the best room', interview with Mimi Oddie, 30 March 2011.
12. 'Well, I'd taken his place . . . *Je ne pige pas!*', Cornioley, *Pauline*, p. 33.
13. 'You, you great big elephant', ibid. p. 113.
14. 'We knew few people . . . *on vivait en vase clos*', ibid, p. 107.
15. 'None', interview with Mimi Oddie, 30 March 2011.
16. 'Can I borrow', Cornioley, *Pauline*, p. 107.
17. 'Wallace returns to England': the certificate of death for Wallace Seckham Witherington, 29 August 1932, gives the cause of death as pulmonary tuberculosis, and his occupation as 'architect'. Apparently of no fixed abode in London, he gives his address as 33 rue Vignon, Paris. His brother-in-law, F. M. Jeremy of Bromley, Kent, was in attendance at his death.
18. '*Pas de problème*', Cornioley, *Pauline*, p. 116.
19. 'Oddly scented', Valentine Lawford, *Bound for Diplomacy* (John Murray, 1963), p. 299.

6. A Forbidden Romance

1. 'The purchase is a remarkably cheap one', Duke of Wellington, quoted in Jean Nérée Ronfort and Jean-Dominique Augarde, *À l'ombre de Pauline: La Résidence de l'Ambassadeur de Grande-Bretagne à Paris, avec la collaboration de Sir Michael Llewellyn Smith* (Paris: Éditions du Centre de Recherches Historiques, 2001), p. 21.
2. The full-length study of the Duke of Wellington is by the Comte d'Orsay.
3. 'Here I was', Lawford, *Bound for Diplomacy*, p. 297.
4. Lord William Tyrrell (1866–1947) was British ambassador to France 1928–1934. He later regretted not having realised the threat posed by Hitler. Ronfort and Augarde, *À l'ombre de Pauline*, p. 95.
5. 'I have no armies', Pauline Bonaparte Borghese quoted in Ronfort and Augarde, *À l'ombre de Pauline*, p. 2. The sculpture of Pauline is a copy of the original by Canova.
6. 'Chosen by destiny', '*Le sentiment justifié d'avoir été choisie par le destin*', ibid.
7. 'The garden gate', conversation with Beth Tibble at the British Embassy in Paris, 5 May 2011.

8. '*Ce n'est pas moi qui suis dure, c'est la vie!*', Cornioley, *Pauline*, p. 101.
9. Georges Brassens, 'Les Amoureux des Bancs Publics', CD, *Chanson pour L'Auvergnat* (Master Serie, Polygram, 1991).
10. 'My family', Cornioley, *Pauline*, p. 116.
11. 'One fine day', Pearl Witherington, interview 7 with Tom Roberts, 24 November 2006.
12. 'Mummy didn't like him', conversation with Mimi Oddie, 30 March 2011.
13. 'I took her out for a Welsh rarebit', Pearl Witherington, interview 7 with Tom Roberts, 24 November 2006.
14. 'That marked a turning point', Cornioley, *Pauline*, p. 158.
15. 'He had a flashing smile', press release on the appointment of Air Vice Marshall Douglas Colyer as head of RAF Delegation to the United States, British Information Services, 4 January 1945, Colyer Papers, Imperial War Museum (IWM) 79/6/1.
16. '*J'ai beaucoup aimé Duggie*', Cornioley, *Pauline*, p. 163.
17. 'French Air Officers', Air Commodore Douglas Colyer DFC, CH, Report of Air Attaché, France, May–June 1940, on the last six weeks of French participation in the war as it affected the office of the Air Attaché, Paris, to Director of Intelligence, Air Ministry, 2 July 1940, Colyer Papers, IMW 79/6/1.
18. '13 ladies . . .', Report by Sqn Ldr Eaton to Air Commodore Colyer, 17/6140, Colyer Papers, IMW 79/6/1.
19. 'Unquenchable cheerfulness', Sir Ronald Campbell to the Rt Hon Viscount Halifax, 22 July 1940, Colyer Papers.

7. London at Last

1. 'She thought we'd died', conversation with Mimi Oddie, 30 March 2011.
2. 'YWCA hostel', Pearl Witherington, interview 2 with Tom Roberts, 24 November 2006.
3. 'Walked a thousand miles', press cutting, May 1941, Mimi Oddie archive.
4. 'An intense and indiscriminate attack', *The Times*, 12 May 1941.
5. 'England was determined', Cornioley, *Pauline*, p. 19.
6. 'A black day', Dorothy Sheridan, ed, *Wartime Women: An Anthology of Women's Wartime Writing for Mass-Observation 1937–45* (Heinemann, 1990), p. 115.
7. 'After two or three minutes', Martin Gilbert, *Finest Hour: Winston S Churchill 1940–41* (Heinemann, 1983), p. 358.
8. 'We're only interested', quoted in David Stafford, *Churchill and Secret Service* (John Murray, 1997), p. 198.
9. '*L'homme du destin*', Max Hastings, *Finest Years: Churchill as Warlord 1940–45* (HarperPress, 2009), p. 49.
10. 'Today, as a year ago', *The Times*, 14 July 1941.
11. 'Looked forward to the day', ibid.
12. 'Crackpot', Matthew Cobb, *The Resistance: The French Fight against the Nazis*

(Simon & Schuster, 2009), p 34. This was the reaction of a military friend of Agnès Humbert in Limoges, when she told him of de Gaulle's speech, which was widely reproduced in the press.

13. 'We could not admit', De Vomécourt, *Who Lived to See the Day*, p. 24.
14. '*Salut aux Morts!*', R. J. Minney, *Carve Her Name with Pride: The Story of Violette Szabo* (Pen and Sword Books Ltd, 2006), p. 276.
15. 'My idea in volunteering', Cornioley, *Pauline*, pp. 21, 26.
16. 'It was something I really felt deep down', Pearl Witherington, interview, *For Valour: Pearl Witherington MBE*, BBC TV programme, 14 May 1995.
17. 'And he, knowing my ex-boss', Darlow Smithson, 'The Real Charlotte Greys', Pearl Cornioley interview transcript, 2 January 2002.
18. 'Your work is a gamble', quoted in Foot, *SOE in France*, p. 15.
19. 'Returned to unit', Foot, *SOE in France*, p. 138; Nigel West, *Secret War: The Story of SOE, Britain's Wartime Sabotage Organisation* (Hodder & Stoughton, 1992), p. 30.
20. 'I think that the dropping of men', Foot, *SOE in France*, p. 140.
21. 'A female "assassin"', Sweet-Escott, *Baker Street Irregular*, p. 53, notes that in autumn 1940 Whitehall told SOE that 'a body such as ours was supposed to be able to arrange for the disappearance of Middle Eastern politicians who were actively working against our allies,' but although preparations were made in Cairo, 'Whitehall's consent was never forthcoming, and we had to infer that after all cold-blooded murder was not part of our code. 007 had not yet been invented.'

8. The Baker Street Irregulars

1. 'Detonator summer', David Stafford, *Britain and European Resistance 1940–1945: A Survey of the Special Operations Executive, with Documents* (Macmillan, 1980), pp. 29–48.
2. SOE's Charter, 19 July 1940, in West, *Secret War*, pp. 20–21.
3. 'To co-ordinate all action', Foot, *SOE in France*, pp. 8–10.
4. 'A secret organisation', Maurice Buckmaster, *Specially Employed: The Story of British Aid to French Patriots of the Resistance* (The Batchworth Press, 1952), p. 15.
5. 'Fifth Columns', Hugh Dalton, *The Fateful Years: Memoirs 1931–1945* (Frederick Muller Ltd, 1957), p. 288.
6. 'The battle', Sweet-Escott, *Baker Street Irregular*, p. 13.
7. 'For security reasons', ibid. p. 17.
8. 'Subsequent behaviour', Stafford, *Britain and European Resistance*, p. 209.
9. 'The thought went through my mind', Buckmaster, *Specially Employed*, p. 9.
10. 'Spotted by Dalton', Dalton, *The Fateful Years*, p. 288.
11. 'At the best SOE', Major General Sir Colin Gubbins, 'SOE and Regular and Irregular Warfare' in *The Fourth Dimension of Warfare*, ed M.

Elliott-Bateman, p. 85, cited Stafford, *Britain and European Resistance*, p. 209; Gubbins had come from MI(R), a War Office research unit on the development of guerrilla warfare under the command of Major Joe Holland, which evolved at the same time as Section D in SIS, and was a building block of SOE, together with Electra House, the black propaganda organisation. SOE at this time was known as SO(2), as SO(1) was responsible for propaganda.

12. 'It came as a source of surprise', Foot, *SOE in France*, p. 65.
13. 'Passy had somewhat naturally', Sweet-Escott, *Baker Street Irregular*, p. 66; West, *Secret War*, p. 30.
14. 'We had practically no means', Colonel Passy, *Deuxième Bureau Londres* (Editions Solar, 1954), p. 146.
15. 'There was, and still is', Colonel Bourne-Paterson, British Circuits in France, 30 June 1946, quoted in West, *Secret War*, p. 104.
16. 'Pearl's ring inscribed', Maurice Buckmaster diary, 11 November 1941, unpublished, Michael Buckmaster archive and conversation with Michael Buckmaster, 5 April 2011.
17. 'The general idea', Buckmaster, *They Fought Alone*, p. 11.
18. 'Good God, Buckmaster', conversation with Michael Foot, 6 May 2011.
19. 'These are to be sent', Desmond Morton to 'C', 27 September 1940, in Stafford, *Churchill and Secret Service*, p. 192.
20. 'Fourth arm', Hugh Dalton, 'The Fourth Arm', Secret Paper of 19 August 1940, in Foot, *SOE in France*, p. 11.
21. 'Toasts were drunk', *The Times*, 14 July 1941.

9. First Flames

1. 'True point of departure', '*le véritable point de depart de la resistance active en France*', *Rapport de Georges Bégué (George I) sur la participation de l'Indre à la resistance organisée par le réseau Buckmaster en 1941*, undated, John Sainsbury archive.
2. Citation for Max Hymans' OBE, undated.
3. 'George was at 28 de la rue des Pavillons', Nouvelle République du Centre-Ouest, 23 January 1991, celebration of the 30th anniversary of the death of Max Hymans, who was Finance Minister in 1938, before serving as a Captain in the 31st Artillery Regiment. At the end of 1941 his clandestine work was discovered by Vichy Police and he returned to London, where he became director of air transport for the Free French.
4. '*Roger les cheveux blancs*', De Vomécourt, *Who Lived to See the Day*, p. 38.
5. '*G. Bégué fut le premier*', anonymous account of Bégué's arrival in the Indre, undated, John Sainsbury archive.

10. Enter 'Hector'

1. 'A childhood friend, Maurice Southgate,' Squadron Leader Maurice Southgate Personal File, PRO HS 6/579.
2. 'You know, Maurice,' *Pauline*, p. 26.
3. 'The sergeant said,' Joan Arkwright, 'Joining the WAAF: the first three months, 1943, Wednesday 10th March 1943', Dorothy Sheridan ed, *Wartime Women*, p. 187.
4. 'He hadn't understood,' *Pauline*, p. 27.

11. Heroes and Traitors

1. 'Short-wave morse transmitter', Foot, p. 95. The B Mark II transceiver used by most SOE agents had a fairly wide frequency range of 3.5–16 megacycles a second, but its signal was weak, not more than 20 watts.
2. 'I was very lucky', Georges Bégué, *Rapport de Georges Bégué*, c1942, John Sainsbury archive.
3. 'Le Capitaine anglais', Brigade de Surveillance de Limoges secret report, *Affaire contre Morel, les époux Fleuret, Langelaan, Trotobas, Bourguennec, Le Havel, Dunais Georgette, Roche, Jumeau, Bégué, Hayes, Lyons, les époux Bloch, Abel et Liewer inculpés à la sûreté extérieure de l'Etat, 1941*, John Sainsbury archive.
4. '*J'étais sur mes gardes*', Max Hymans, *Rapport sur les Arrestations qui ont debuts a Châteauroux en Octobre 1941*, signed 'Frederic', 11 August 1942, John Sainsbury archive.
5. 'George I was "blown"', Benjamin Cowburn, *No Cloak No Dagger: Allied Spycraft in Occupied France* (Frontline Books, 2009, first published 1960 by the Adventurers Club), p. 25; amazingly, Bégué managed to cobble together a radio in prison and let Buckmaster know that he was still alive.
6. 'It was a cheerful reunion', ibid. p. 67.
7. 'Where did you get all those?', E. H. Cookridge, *Inside SOE: The Story of Special Operations in Western Europe 1940–1945* (Arthur Barker Ltd, 1966), p. 138; Foot, *SOE in France*, pp. 171–9.
8. 'The wretched truth', Cowburn, *No Cloak No Dagger*, p. 72.
9. 'The casualty rate,' ibid. p. 99.

12. Churchill and SOE

1. 'I went to bed', quoted in Stafford, *Churchill and Secret Service*, p. 232.
2. 'As my department works', ibid. p. 238.
3. 'Dalton was sacked', conversation with M.R.D. Foot, 5 May 2011.
4. 'There was no hitch', William MacKenzie, *The Secret History of SOE*
5. 'When I reflect', in Stafford, *Churchill and Secret Service*, p. 236.
6. 'A sort of Penelope's web', Foot, *SOE in France*, p. 178.
7. 'We had begun to use', Cowburn, *No Cloak No Dagger*, p. 81.
8. 'Thanks. Is there anything', ibid. pp. 148–9.

9. 'Don't worry', Madeleine Currall interview, *Pearl Witherington: For Valour*, BBC Timewatch 1995.
10. 'Did business with the service', Cornioley, *Pauline*, p. 26.
11. 'It was all very secret', Nancy Roberts, *Pearl Witherington: For Valour*, BBC Timewatch 1995.
12. 'Strip, lad', Lieutenant Tony Brooks, in Roderick Bailey ed, *Forgotten Voices of the Secret War: An Inside History of Special Operations during the Second World War*, in association with the Imperial War Museum (Ebury Press, 2009), p. 99.
13. 'Spirit people from room to room', Buckmaster, *They Fought Alone*, p. 57.
14. 'I said, she has been at it', Pearl Witherington, interview 16 with Tom Roberts, November 2006.
15. 'I know PW well', Pearl Witherington reference with handwritten note written by Buckmaster, 14 September 1943, PW PF, HS/9/355/2, NA.

13. Offering Death

1. 'With a raspberry pip', Buckmaster, *Specially Employed*, p. 30.
2. 'Disguised as a FANY', conversation with Colonel John Sainsbury, 11 December 2009.
3. 'One of those terribly secret cars', Lieutenant Tony Brooks, SOE Circuit organiser, in Bailey, *Forgotten Voices*, p. 99.
4. 'Heated discussions', Irene Ward, *F.A.N.Y. Invicta* (Hutchinson, 1955), p. 208.
5. 'SOE recognised', Pearl Witherington, interview 5, Tom Roberts Archive, 25 November 2006.
6. 'In my view women', Captain Selwyn Jepson, Recruiting Officer, French Section SOE, in Bailey, *Forgotten Voices*, pp. 39–40; the story of Churchill's intervention is corroborated by Foot, to whom it was related by Jepson when he was ninety. Interview, 8 January 2011.
7. 'I did my best', Commandant Marian Gamwell, in Bailey, *Forgotten Voices*, p. 40.
8. 'After my husband was killed', Flight Officer Yvonne Cormeau, in Bailey, *Forgotten Voices*, p. 40.
9. 'Fury against the Germans', interview with Michael Buckmaster, 5 April 2011.
10. 'The sort of person', Vera Atkins, in Bailey, *Forgotten Voices*, p. 42.
11. 'I sense the web', George Millar, *Maquis* (William Heinemann, 1945), p. 1.
12. 'F Section in all sent 393 officers', Bourne-Paterson quoted in West, *Secret War*, p. 106.
13. 'From top to bottom', William MacKenzie, *The Secret History of SOE* (St Ermin's Press, 2000), p. 337.
14. 'The chance of his coming back', conversation with Tom Roberts, son of FANY Captain Nancy Fraser-Campbell, 6 October 2011.
15. 'I always felt terrible', Brigadier Sir Douglas Dodds-Parker, in Tom Roberts' interview 5 with Pearl Witherington, 25 November 2006, p. 8.

16. 'They were in no way conspicuous', Buckmaster, *Specially Employed*, p. 30.
17. 'The public schools', Foot, *SOE in France*, pp. 48–49.
18. 'How can we trust', conversation with M.R.D. Foot, 4 May 2011.
19. 'Buck's boys', Noreen Riols, 'Churchill's Secret Army of the Shadows', Guildford Book Festival, 16 October 2011.
20. 'When I saw him', Vera Atkins, quoted in Robert Marshall, *All the King's Men: The Truth Behind SOE's Greatest Wartime Disaster* (Collins, 1988), p. 98.
21. 'Not quick', Patrick Yarnold, *Wanborough Manor School for Secret Agents* (Hopfield Publications, 2009), p. 100.
22. 'Looked like a vicar's wife', Verity, *We Landed by Moonlight*, p. 99.
23. 'We shall be firing', Peter Churchill, *Of Their Own Choice* (Hodder & Stoughton, 1952), p. 17.
24. 'Outstanding, probably the best shot', Pearl PF, Preliminary Report, School No 20 Party 27AA, 12 July 1943, HS/9/355/2 NA.
25. '*C'est épouvantable*. It's dreadful', Cornioley, *Pauline*, p. 29.
26. 'I cannot sufficiently', Peter Churchill, *Of Their Own Choice*, p. 9.
27. 'They were offered strong drink', Buckmaster, *Specially Employed*, p. 30.
28. 'Why are you in FANY uniform?', Pearl Witherington, interview 5 with Tom Roberts.
29. 'Are you by any chance?', Churchill, *Of Their Own Choice*, pp. 25–26.
30. 'I held myself responsible', Pearl Witherington, interview 5 with Tom Roberts.
31. 'We'd become the first', Leo Marks, *From Silk to Cyanide* (HarperCollins, 1998), p. 277.
32. 'SOE Collaboration in Operations', Invasion Directive from the Chiefs of Staff, 12 May 1942, William MacKenzie, *The Secret History of SOE*, Appendix G, pp. 766–9.
33. 'The immense value to the war effort', Winston Churchill in MacKenzie, *The Secret History of SOE*, p. 413.
34. 'Mounted in too much of a hurry', Francis J. Suttill and M.R.D. Foot, 'SOE's "Prosper" Disaster of 1943', *Intelligence and National Security*, vol 26 No 1 February 2011; (Sir) Michael Howard, *Strategic Deception* (London: HMSO, 1990), p. 75.
35. 'Strategic deception scheme'; Churchill's interest in deception can be dated to a telegram from General Wavell, 'I have always had considerable belief,' Wavell telegram to Winston Churchill, 21 May 1942, quoted in Sir Michael Howard, *Strategic Deception in World War II*, first published as Vol V of *The Official History of British Intelligence in World War II* (Pimlico, 1990), p. 25.
36. 'Snatched at every crumb', Howard, *Strategic Deception*, pp. 57–8.
37. 'We have pulled in our horns', CAB 80/65 COS (42)399(o), Minute from Churchill dated 18 November 1942 (CAB – Cabinet Papers, COS – COSSAC), in the Public Record Office.

38. 'Such limited offensive operations', Howard, op cit, p. 72.
39. 'An invasion of Europe', press reports of the Casablanca Conference, quoted in Charles Weighton, *The Pin-stripe Saboteur* (Odhams, 1959) and Marshall, *All the King's Men*, p. 125.
40. 'Prepare an amphibious feint', Howard, *Strategic Deception*, p. 74.
41. 'An elaborate camouflage and deception scheme', Howard, *Strategic Deception*, p. 75.
42. 'They were regarded as horribly insecure', Marshall, *All the King's Men*, p. 128, quotes Roger Hesketh, 'Fortitude: The History of Strategic Deception in North Western Europe, April 1943 to May 1944', p. 20; Hesketh, posted to Section Ops (B) COSSAC and put in charge of the 'Special Means' subsection, was requested by the Ministry of Defence to write this history, but in 1986 the MOD withdrew permission to publish.
43. 'Clearly, if deception is involved', Harry Sporborg, interview with Robert Marshall, 21 March 1983, in Marshall, *All the King's Men*, p. 295, n. 18.

14. The Prosper Disaster

1. 'Hideous muddles', private diary of Maurice Buckmaster, 9 May 1943, Michael Buckmaster Papers.
2. 'In May 1943 a message came from Churchill', Maurice Buckmaster, BBC Interview, 1983, Special Operations Executive Sound Archive, IWM.
3. I certainly think that we should make all plans', Max Hastings, *Finest Years*, pp. 349–50.
4. A major operation to seize a bridgehead', ibid. p. 358.
5. 'Both men assumed', Suttill and Foot, 'SOE's "Prosper" Disaster of 1943'.
6. 'Amount of *matériel*', Marshall, *All the King's Men*, p. 292, cites figures for all *reseaux*, archives of the Ministère de la Guerre at the Château de Vincennes, Paris (ref. 13P68, *Matériel sur parachute et déportation*).
7. 'A massive increase in *parachutages*', interview with Francis J. Suttill, 1 November 2011. The records for the number of July drops to Suttill's DZs are missing from the RAF file.
8. 'F Section was doing exactly', interview with Francis J. Suttill, 1 November 2011.
9. 'Your conception of a letterbox', quoted in Sarah Helm, *A Life in Secrets* (Little, Brown, 2005), p. 28.
10. 'Madeleine was given the Monet letterbox', Francis J. Suttill, 'Report Prosper 19 June 1943', HS 9/911/1, PF of PHA Lejeune, NA.
11. 'Gilbert Norman sitting at a table', statement by Maud Laurent, 1950, Francis J. Suttill papers. She had opened the door to the Germans.
12. 'He had taken room 15', Paul Guillaume, *La Sologne au temps de l'héroisme et de la trahison* (Orléans: Imprimerie Nouvelle, 1950), p. 75.

15. Radio Games, and 16. Agent Marie

1. 'Serious breach of security', Leo Marks, *Between Silk and Cyanide: The Story of SOE's Code War* (HarperCollins, 1998), p. 326.
2. 'Tell him the samovar', conversation with M.R.D. Foot, 5 May 2011.
3. 'Prosper is tortured', deposition of Renée Guépin, courier for George Darling and *liquidateur* of the Prosper/Physician circuit, 17 March 1948, Foot, p. 281 and note. Guépin goes on to say that Prosper was sent to Fresnes prison for a year, which is untrue. Francis J. Suttill questions the reliability of Guépin's evidence, since Prosper arrived at Sachsenshausen Concentration Camp on 3 September 1943, according to the witness statement of a former boilerman at the camp; interview with Francis J. Suttill, 1 November 2011.
4. 'Would have shot himself', Foot, *SOE in France*, p. 292.
5. 'He wrote Darling a letter', deposition of Joseph Placke, 1 April 1946, quoted in Jean Overton Fuller, *Déricourt, The Chequered Spy* (Michael Russell, 1989), p. 41. Darling was admitted to the Hopital de Gisors with the gunshot wounds of which he died on 25 June 1943. A party of Germans had arrested Suttill at Hotel Mazagran at 11am on 24 June. It was, therefore 'after not forty-eight but only about twenty-four hours that "Prosper" concluded his pact with Kieffer . . . [After] an interrogation through the night, it was probably around the breakfast hours of the 25th that the pact was concluded and "Prosper" wrote the letter to Darling . . . Prosper had concluded the pact and written the letter to Darling pretty quickly' (p. 358).
6. 'The betrayal came from London', Armel Guerne, interview with Fuller, 16 May 1957, Déricourt, p. 96. Jacques Bureau and Pierre Culioli also claim that when Prosper returned he said that the invasion would take place on 9 September, the date of the phantom invasion.
7. 'The legend has persisted', Dansey was featured as 'Sir Henry Ridley', the villain behind the Prosper disaster, in a novel by Larry Collins, *A Fall from Grace* (Granada, 1954) and a BBC Timewatch film in May 1986, which claimed that Déricourt was an MI6 agent who betrayed the Prosper network on the orders of Dansey 'in furtherance of a deception plan, Cockade Starkey'. These allegations are detailed in *All the King's Men* (Collins, 1988), by the programme's producer, Robert Marshall.
8. 'The Timewatch programme can only', letter from M.R.D. Foot, *Observer*, 11 May 1986, quoted in J. Fuller, *Déricourt: The Chequered Spy*, pp. 340–1. 'The "Timewatch" programme', he said, 'can only be characterized as imaginative fiction; an ingenious story, but not a true one.' Commander Kenneth Cohen, the head (under Dansey's supervision) of SIS's French section, had assured him that Déricourt had never been one of their spooks.
9. '*Tu es venu pour moi*', Fuller, *Déricourt: The Chequered Spy*, p. 115.

10. 'My father was threatened', conversation with Francis J. Suttill, 1 November 2011.
11. 'He was very disquiet', Fuller, *Déricourt: The Chequered Spy*, p. 99; in *Specially Employed* (1952), the first volume of his autobiography, Buckmaster states that Prosper was recalled because 'the Allies were not ready to return to the Continent in the summer of 1943, as so many Frenchmen confidently hoped. The fires of enthusiasm would have to be damped down, without, however, being extinguished. Only a first-class man like Prosper could convey that message . . .' (p. 187). But by the time the second volume was published, *They Fought Alone* (1958), he had changed his story to something closer to the truth: 'In the middle of 1943 we had a top secret message telling us that D-Day might be closer than we thought. This message had been tied up with international politics on a level far above our knowledge . . . The necessary re-thinking was so sweeping that we decided . . . to bring Prosper over to England for his new briefing . . . We had many conferences with Allied high-ups' (pp. 207–9).
12. 'One of the most trustworthy', Buckmaster, *They Fought Alone*, p. 208.
13. '"Robin" (Worms) me glissa. Worms sidled up to me', deposition of Maurice Braun, 11 October 1950, fichier 72AJ 39J, *Archives nationales de Paris*, quoted in Francis J. Suttill, 'Le Réseau "Prosper-Physician" et ses Activités dans la Région Centre', *Resistances en Touraine et en Région Centre, Bulletin de l'Association ERIL*, April 2010, p. 52. Gilbert Norman has on occasion been confused with Déricourt, one of whose aliases was 'Gilbert'.
14. 'Your brooch has brought me luck', Sarah Helm, *A Life in Secrets*, p. 44.
15. 'Pearl and Antelme came in', Maurice Buckmaster private diary, 9 September 1943.
16. 'Most officers dressed every night', Noreen Riols' talk, Guildford Book Festival, 16 October 2011.
17. 'The blade was two-sided', George Millar, *Maquis*, p. 109.
18. 'Wimsey's approach to Bluck', Pearl Witherington PF, HS/9/355/2 NA.
19. 'I just sat there on the edge', Captain Oliver Brown, in Bailey, *Forgotten Voices*, p. 53.
20. 'What was really rather clever', Lieutenant Robert Ferrier, ibid. p. 52.
21. 'How much?', Cornioley, *Pauline*, pp. 165–6.
22. 'The clairvoyant had divined correctly', Pearl Witherington, interview with Tom Roberts, 24 November 2006. Pearl confessed to her interviewer that she was still a virgin in 1943.
23. 'Dear Miss Atkins', Pearl Witherington to Vera Atkins, 16 September 1943, PW PF, HS/9/355/2.

17. Henri

1. '*Ça ne risque rien*', Millar, *Maquis*.
2. 'Wedding dresses', André Hue, *The Next Moon* (Penguin, 2004), notes that

a wedding dress made of parachute silk is on display at Le Musée de la Résistance at Saint-Marcel, p. 317.

3. '*Ah, c'était le choc*', Cornioley, *Pauline*, p. 17.
4. 'He was terrified', Marcus Binney, *The Women Who Lived for Danger: The Women Agents of SOE in the Second World War* (Hodder & Stoughton, 2002), p. 189.
5. 'M and Madame Dezandes took a terrible risk', Cornioley, *Pauline*, p. 37.
6. '*Il attendait un bonhomme*', ibid. p. 36.
7. 'Through Hector', Pearl's PF.
8. 'Yes, it's a fine moonlight night', Foot, *SOE in France*, p. 25.
9. 'Prosper's circuit and its sub-circuits', ibid. p. 252.
10. '*Des bottilons en tissu . . . C'était mieux*', Cornioley, *Pauline*, p. 18.
11. 'Prosper's dropping zones', map compiled by Prosper's son, Francis J. Suttill, in 'SOE's Prosper Disaster of 1943', *Intelligence and National Security*, Vol 26, No 1, February 2011, pp. 99–105.
12. '*Pourquoi les Allemands ont-ils cerné cette région de la Sologne?* Why did the Germans', Paul Guillaume, *Au Temps de la Heroisme et de la Trahison* (Orléans: Librairie Loddé, 1978), p. 82.
13. 'A steady flow of greatly increased deliveries', Sir Charles Hambro quoted in Stafford, *Britain and European Resistance*, p. 108.
14. 'Bevan was "deeply unhappy"', letter from Sir Michael Howard to Francis J. Suttill, 5 February 2004; Bevan also confirmed to M.R.D. Foot that 'Cockade Starkey' was one of the three occasions on which he used SOE: the others were to reinforce Operation 'Fortitude', the grand deception that covered 'Overlord' in June 1944, and Operation 'Animals' which, like 'Mincemeat', provided cover for 'Husky', the invasion of Sicily; conversation with the late Professor M.R.D. Foot, 2011.
15. 'He gave his life as ordered', Buckmaster, *They Fought Alone*, p. 207.
16. '*Il avait reconnu Rex*', Colonel Passy [André Dewavrin], *Mission Secrètes en France (Novembre 1942–Juin 1943): Souvenirs du B.C.R.A.* (Paris: Librairie Plon, 1951), p. 254.
17. 'Let me have your proposals', Churchill to Selborne, PREM 3/184/6 June–July 1943, in Stafford, *Churchill and Secret Service*, p. 268.
18. 'They have gone hunting a very big tiger', Selborne to Churchill, in Stafford, *Britain and European Resistance*, p. 110.
19. The Secret Army (*Armée Secrète*) was the brainchild of a former French infantry captain, Henri Frenay. It can be defined as 'the embryonic armed wing of the Resistance in the Non-Occupied Zone' (Matthew Cobb, *The Resistance*, p. 150, see Bibliography). Frenay wanted to lead the AS, but this was opposed by d'Astier. In 1942 Frenay proposed General Delestraint as leader; de Gaulle agreed, but forbade any large-scale military activity except in conjunction with an Allied invasion – the reason why SOE circuits and FTP were the only ones actually resisting for a long time. In June 1944, the AS finally merged with other *maquis* to become the FFI.

20. 'Do not touch Gaullist organisations', Pearl Cornioley, interview transcript, Darlow Smithson, 'The Real Charlotte Grays', 2 January 2002, Martyn Cox archive.
21. '*Oui, c'est bien gentil*', Cornioley, *Pauline*, p. 42.

18. Explosions Arranged

1. 'Blow up the Michelin factory', Cornioley, *Pauline*, p. 37.
2. 'Operation completed', Cookridge, *Inside SOE*, pp. 277–9. The safe house is in a street today renamed rue du Capitaine Michel, Foot, *SOE in France*, p. 239.
3. 'Olivier was arrested', see West, *Secret War*, p. 129 n 4, quotes Bourne-Paterson, *British Circuits in France 1941–5*, p. 50: Lt Reeves 'is strongly suspected of having betrayed his commanding officer (Michael Trotobas) although he has been officially cleared in England of the charge of having wilfully done so.' Forty-five people were arrested when Trotobas was shot.
4. Ernest Floege escaped and returned to England to volunteer again, West, *Secret War*, p. 127.
5. 'Irish charm', Sweet-Escott, *Baker Street Irregular*, pp. 127, 137–44, 153. Col William Donovan, adviser to President Roosevelt on matters concerned with intelligence, propaganda and SOE activities from spring 1941, was an Irish-American and Catholic who had distinguished himself as commander of the 'Fighting 69th', earning the nickname of 'Wild Bill Donovan'. The OSS was the forerunner of the CIA.
6. 'Energy', see also Foot, *SOE in France*, p. 30.
7. 'We want to blow up', Buckmaster, *They Fought Alone*, p. 153.
8. 'Solely due to the lack of sabotage', Binney, *The Women Who Lived for Danger*, p. 190.
9. 'From Marie', Pearl Witherington Report, 11 March 1944, Pearl's PF, HS/9/355/2.
10. 'We were discussing', David Stafford, *Secret Agent: The True Story of the Special Operations Executive* (BBC Worldwide Ltd, 2000), p. 202 (book to accompany the TV series *Secret Agent*, produced for the BBC by Darlow Smithson Productions Ltd); Roger Landes' story has also been told in *Aristide: Warlord of the Resistance*, a biography by David Nicolson, and in E. H. Cookridge, *They Came from the Sky*, pp. 81–160.
11. 'Hitler's Commando Order', Foot, p. 169.
12. 'Jacques was in a blue funk (*Jacques avait une trouille intense*)', *Pauline*, p. 48; Jewish resistants, see Cookridge, *They Came from the Sky*, p. 332.
13. 'Plenty to do, and how!', report of Sqn Ldr M. Southgate, Southgate's PF, HS6/579, PRO. Hector's suspicions were in fact unfounded; Gaëtan was arrested in February 1944, West, *Secret War*, p. 128.
14. 'Dubito, ergo sum', Foot, p. 276.

15. '*Où allez-vous, madame?*', Cornioley, *Pauline*, p. 45.
16. '[Marie] returned very excited', Southgate's PF.
17. 'Go to La Châtre', Cornioley, *Pauline*, p. 56.
18. Langlois family: there is a plaque in La Châtre paying tribute to Gaston Langlois: '*Ici a débuté en 1942 la Résistance Libération M.U.R. organisée par Langlois Gaston and Langlois Ginette.*'
19. 'When I arrived in France', Pearl Witherington, interview 7 with Tom Roberts, 23 November 2006.
20. 'If it is decided to destroy Michelin', Pearl Witherington Report, 11 March 1944, PW PF.

19. Churchill to the Rescue

1. 'Radio signalmaster', two bright FANYs at Grendon first spotted the mistakes in the Dutch traffic, Mrs Denman and Mrs Brewis.
2. '*Prijs/preis*', Marks, *Between Silk & Cyanide*, pp. 336–4.
3. 'Sister service', ibid. p. 431.
4. 'Do you accept?', ibid. p. 443.
5. 'Ever-jealous mandarins', David Stafford, *Britain and European Resistance, 1940–45* (Macmillan, 1980), p. 103.
6. 'Any dramatic change', ibid. p. 136.
7. 'I have always held the view', Desmond Morton in Stafford, *Churchill and Secret Service*, p. 276.
8. 'To learn and devise', DO (44)2, in CAB 69/6 PRO, in Stafford, *Britain and European Resistance*, p. 141.
9. 'We have been called amateurs', statement by Colonel Maurice J. Buckmaster, OBE, Appendix A, in Cookridge, *Inside SOE*, p. 602.
10. 'Without Churchill', '*D'Astier, Les Dieux et les homines*', 20-21, tr. Foot, *SOE in France*, p. 311.
11. '*Nous mangeons toujours de la purée de pois.* We are still eating mashed peas, but there's dessert on the menu . . . *Le cheval n'oublie jamais ses amis.* Cheval never forgets his friends', Yeo-Thomas (Cheval) signalled to Polydor (Brossolette), Marshall, *The White Rabbit*, p. 195.
12. 'At last we had moved', Gubbins in Stafford, *Britain and European Resistance*, p. 117.
13. '*Stressant, fatigant*', Cornioley, *Pauline*, p. 43.
14. 'It is essential', PW Report, 'Escape Route' (USA Pilots), 26 April 1944, PF.
15. 'London had twigged', Foot, *SOE in France*, p. 302.
16. 'There existed', PW Report, 10 April 1944, PF.
17. '*Que'est-ce que vous faites?*', Cornioley, *Pauline*, p. 54.
18. 'I trust you have satisfactory', Mrs G. Witherington to Vera Atkains, 3 January 1944, PW PF.

19. 'I have made all possible', Capt E. G. Bissett to Mrs Witherington, 24 March 1944, PW PF.
20. 'My other two S/O WAAFs', Mrs Witherington to Capt Bissett, 28 March 1944.
21. 'If they turn up at 11', memo 'Thursday' from Vera Atkins, HS/9/355/2, undated.
22. 'I understand Miss Pearl Witherington', Air Commodore F. Beaumont to Capt Bissett, 29 May 1944, PW PF.

20. The Fall of Hector

1. 'How was Chantraine?', Maurice Nicault, *Résistance et Libération de l'Indre les insurgés* (CCB Royer, 2003), p. 126.
2. 'To indicate a landing-ground', report by Sqn Ldr M. Southgate, 9 May 1945, Southgate PF, NA130, HS 6/579.
3. '"British" circuits were purely paramilitary', Duff Cooper, Top Secret Circular to British Consuls, 29 November 1946, attached to Major Bourne-Paterson, 'The "British" Circuits in France 1941–44', Confidential Report, 30 June 1946, NA HS 6/469.
4. 'The B.C.R.A, under the leadership of Colonel "Passy"', Bourne-Paterson introduction to 'The "British" Circuits,' p. iii.
5. 'If Alex needs some money', Nicault, *Résistance et Libération*, p. 131.
6. 'The sending of about twenty agents to SOUTHGATE's circuit in one month. This was done in order to comply with SHAEF directives to strengthen the Northern zone, as we could not parachute direct to the North and North-West owing to blown circuits, RAF restrictions, etc. This operational decision, bad as it was for SOUTHGATE's circuit, was fully justified by subsequent events.' Top Secret Letter from Colonel Buckmaster to AD/E, 9 May 1945, attached to Southgate's PF.
7. 'We've got to receive', Nicault, *Résistance et Libération*, p. 135.
8. 'That April', Southgate PF.
9. 'To Mr Eden and Selborne', Bourne-Patterson, 'The "British" Circuits'.
10. 'Highly suspect', Marks, *Between Silk & Cyanide*, p. 511.
11. 'Three redoubts', Cookridge, *Inside SOE*, p. 354.
12. 'Where is Phono?', ibid. pp. 300–3.
13. 'I have been betrayed', ibid. p. 303. Vogt cannot, however, be considered a reliable witness.
14. 'Ah well', Buckmaster in Marks, *Between Silk & Cyanide*, p. 514.
15. 'Died in hospital'. In fact, France Antelme was executed at Gross Rosen, August–September 1944. Madeleine Damerment was shot in the neck at Dachau, 13 September 1944. Lionel Lee was executed at Gross Rosen, August–September 1944, as was R. B. Byerley, Canadian General List. John Sainsbury, *The F Section Memorial* (Welwyn: Hart Books, 1992).

16. '*Tu vas chercher*', Cornioley, *Pauline*, p. 46.
17. 'At about 8 am Samuel', Southgate Report, PF.
18. 'Picked up in a double Lysander operation', Verity, *We Landed by Moonlight*, p. 219; Philippe de Vomécourt returned to France on this flight.

21. Countdown to D-Day

1. 'Why did I insist?', Cornioley, *Pauline*, p. 40.
2. '*Ça m'est arrivé deux fois*. It happened to me twice', ibid. pp. 172–3. Pearl believed that there were very fine, immaterial [electro-magnetic] waves beyond our control which explain the mystery of her *sensibilité* or sensitivity.
3. '*Southgate était tombé*', Nicault, *Résistance et Libération*, p. 144.
4. 'The gardien, René Sabassier', Yves Chauveau-Veauvy, *L'Eté 44, Indre Nord, Loir-et-Cher Sud* (Sologne Graphic, 2004), p. 38.
5. 'A further conclusive demonstration of the truth', Bourne-Patterson, 'The "British" Circuits', p. 4.
6. 'Be near me when my light is low', from 'In Memoriam', Tennyson, quoted by Leo Marks, to whom it seemed 'a personal appeal', *Between Silk & Cyanide*, p. 36.
7. 'It's a long way to Tipperary', Sqn Ldr Southgate Report, 9 May 1945, NA HS 6/579.
8. 'Oh, this is Southgate', ibid. On his journey from Fresnes prison to Buchenwald, in a party of 36 men, Southgate met Lt Steele (Laurent), the agent who confirmed that he had recognised Southgate's photo and ID card at HQ, Paris; it was not, as Pearl thought, Bob Starr.
9. 'These telegrams were sent', ibid.
10. 'An operational necessity', Col Buckmaster, Top Secret letter to AD/E, 9 May 1945, NA HS 6/579.
11. 'The effect on the prisoner', ibid.
12. '*On mange l'orange*', quoted by Fuller, *Déricourt: The Chequered Spy*, p. 102.
13. 'Large sums of money', Table IV, Sums of Money sent to Circuits in Northern France under Enemy Control, 1943–1944, Foot, p. 304. A total of 8,572,000 francs was sent but, as Foot and William Mackenzie point out, SOE could easily afford this sum.
14. 'Escapist . . . people said he lived in his own world', conversation with Michael Buckmaster, 21 April 2011.
15. 'It was certainly never any part', Foot, *SOE in France*, p. 291; '*mit der Dummheit . . .*', Schiller, quoted by Foot, *SOE in France*, p. 258.
16. 'MRD Foot once asked General Gubbins', conversation with M.R.D. Foot, 6 May 2011.
17. 'MESSRS BLUNT, BINGHAM', Marks, *Between Silk & Cyanide*, p. 499. 'Blunt' was a pseudonym used by Major Blizzard when he was head of N Section.

18. 'Quantities of British food', Southgate Report, p. 9. In early June the Gestapo took Southgate on a tour of all the places and grounds found in the Montlucon documents: at first Chateauroux and Limoges, where he was escorted by 150 armed men, as the Gestapo were afraid that the Chateauneuf *maquis* would rescue him. He reached Tarbes, still under heavy guard, and was allowed to collect a suitcase and some personal possessions from his house there. He also learnt of the arrest of Lt Charles Rechenmann, alias Julien, who subsequently walked into Southgate's cell in Paris and shook his hand. On 20 June 1944 Southgate was sent to Fresnes prison, and in August to Buchenwald. He was awarded the DSO while in the concentration camp.
19. 'Up to ten organisations,' ibid. p. 10. Southgate was horrified that agents already captured, tortured and sent to Poland, such as Pickersgill, Macalister, Max and Leopold, were brought back in a hurry by air to Paris by the SD in order to extract fresh information from them in order to prolong German control of the penetrated circuits; had F realised earlier the significance of the lack of true checks in their agent transmissions, captured agents would have been spared further torture.
20. 'Which both they and we knew to be crucial', Bourne-Paterson, 'The "British" Circuits', p. 9.
21. 'A sound piece of deceptive activity', Foot, *SOE in France*, p. 291.
22. 'The Battle area was by D-Day', Bourne-Paterson, 'The "British" Circuits', p. 9. He lists the following new organisers who began working in early 1944:
Captain Benoist in the region of Nantes and Rambouillet
Major Hudson, Le Mans
Capt Wilkinson, Orléans
Lt Dedieu, Chartres-Dreux
Lt Henquet, Blois and Vendome
Major Dumont-Duillemet, Paris and Meaux
Major de Baissac, Normandy
Capt Mulsant, Nangis
Lt Bassett, Creil
Major Bodington, Epernay and St Dizier
23. 'Swarms into', Nicault, *Résistance et Libération*, p. 146.
24. '*Un étranger, et une femme*', Témoignage de 'Gaspard', Raymond Billard, in Cornioley, *Pauline*, p. 176.
25. 'After the arrest of Philippe', Nicault, *Résistance et Libération*, pp. 146–7.
26. 'From the time of our arrival', report by F/O Pearl Cornioley (Witherington), 23 November 1944, p. 2, Pearl's PF.
27. 'Towards 6.30 pm. *Vers 6 h 30*', Chauveau-Veauvy, *L'Eté 44*, p. 66.
28. 'We thank you', Marks, *Between Silk & Cyanide*, pp. 522–5.

22. Neptune's Trident

1. '*Devant le refus*. In the face of the refusal', report by F/O Pearl Cornioley, 23 November 1944, Pearl's PF.
2. 'Ah, Pearl', Henri Diacono, in Cornioley, *Pauline*, p. 188.
3. '*Quasimodo est une fete*', Cornioley, *Pauline*, p. 91.
4. 'Neptune's trident', Marks, *Between Silk & Cyanide*, p. 521.
5. '*Les sanglots longs*', De Vomécourt, *Who Lived to See the Day*, p. 218.
6. 'In wartime, truth is so precious', Winston Churchill, in F. H. Hinsley, *British Intelligence in the Second World War* (Stationery Office Books, 1993), p. 97.
7. 'They are supposed to be coming', Goebbels quoted in Antony Beevor, *D-Day: The Battle for Normandy* (Penguin, 2010), p. 31.
8. 'A serious turning point', Foot, *SOE in France*, p. 209.
9. 'Young men screamed', De Vomécourt, *Who Lived to See the Day*, p. 217. Estimates of the number of resisters before D-Day vary widely; the British estimated some 35,000 active *maquisards* in the field, though De Gaulle claimed 175,000 in the Secret Army. SOE believed the *parachutages* provided weapons for 50,000. Max Hastings, *Finest Years: Churchill as Warlord, 1940–45* (HarperPress, 2009), p. 459.
10. 'We are outraged', Marks, *Between Silk & Cyanide*, pp. 523–5.
11. 'The commandos were already at sea', Foot, *SOE in France*, p. 340.
12. 'Do you realize', Churchill in Martin Gilbert, *Road to Victory*, vol 7 of *Winston S. Churchill, 1942–1945* (Heinemann, 1986).
13. Air Commodore Ronald Ivelaw-Chapman, in Stafford, *Churchill and Secret Service*, p. 290; M.R.D. Foot and J. M. Langley, *M19: Escape and Evasion 1939–1945* (Bodley Head, 1979), p. 214. Overlord made Churchill's instruction redundant.
14. 'Marks went round to Duke Street', Marks, *Between Silk & Cyanide*, p. 384.
15. 'Conform with the general plan', directive to SOE, 9 August 1942, Mackenzie, *The Secret History of SOE*, pp. 766–9.
16. '*Plan Vert*', quoted in Beevor, *D-Day*, p. 46.
17. 'SOE had dropped', Mackenzie, *Secret History of SOE*, p. 602.
18. 'I am unable at this time', Roosevelt to Churchill, 13 May, quoted in Beevor, *D-Day*, p. 17.
19. 'General Koenig', ibid. p. 17.
20. 'Muddle, political ambition', Mackenzie, *Secret History of SOE*, p. 601.
21. 'An insurrectional government', quoted in Jean Lacouture, *De Gaulle: The Rebel 1890–1944* (New York: Harvill Press, 1990), p. 511.
22. 'We are going to liberate Europe', and 'to de Gaulle', quoted ibid. p. 522.
23. 'There is no room in war', Churchill, *Second World War*, p. 550.
24. 'Operation Titanic', Foot, *SOE in France*, p. 341.
25. 'The buggers have fallen', Marks, *Between Silk & Cyanide*, p. 527.

26. '137 wireless stations', Mackenzie, *Secret History of SOE*, p. 602.
27. 'It was judged', Foot, *SOE in France*, p. 341.
28. '*Allo, le camarade anglais*', Marshall, *The White Rabbit*, pp. 158–9.

23. The Battle of Les Souches

1. 'I said, "Where have you come from?"', Smithson, 'The Real Charlotte Greys', p. 22.
2. 'We were the only ones', Cornioley, *Pauline*, p. 65.
3. '*Ils ont débarqué*', Nicault, *Résistance et Libération*, pp. 256–9.
4. '500 men', *témoignage de Madame Pearl Cornioley*, Paris, 13 January 1973 in Michel Jouanneau, *L'Organisation de la Résistance dans L'Indre, Juin 1940–Juin 1944* (1975).
5. '*On est attaqués!*', Cornioley, *Pauline*, p. 66; today the bullet holes in the rusty gates of the chateau bear witness to Pearl's narrow escape.
6. 'The Germans are coming', Smithson, 'The Real Charlotte Greys', p. 23.
7. 'Women were being raped', André Hue, *The Next Moon* (Viking, 2004), p. 164.
8. '*Moi, je viens de Russie*', *témoignage d'Yvonne Marseille, née Sabassier*, in Cornioley, *Pauline*, p. 68.
9. '*Oui, je suis une femme*', ibid.

24. Lieutenant Pauline

1. 'Death and ruin, *la colonne dite Buckhardt . . . qui allait porter la mort et la ruine dans tout le nord de notre départment*', Nicault, *Résistance et Libération*, p. 45.
2. 'Killed 11 resisters', Jean Grazon, preface, *Combats des Maquisards Indre été 1944, à le mémoire des résistants tués, fusillés ou déportés* (Chateauroux: L'Imprimerie George Sand), pp. 142–3.
3. 'A tragically unequal struggle', Matthew Cobb, *The Resistance: The French Fight Against the Nazis* (Simon & Schuster, 2009), p. 254.
4. 'Ding-a-ding', Smithson, 'The Real Charlotte Greys', p. 44; conversation with John Sainsbury, 5 May 2011, who remembers that after the war Pearl used to keep the bell from the horse collar on the mantelpiece of her and Henri's flat at 12, rue Pergolèse, Paris.
5. '*Jean, lui, est le garçon calme et tranquille qui tuera placidement son boche à la bataille des Souches*', Sous-Lieutenant Michel Mockers, '*Maquis* SS4, Font-Moreau et Gatine', unpublished memoir of the *maquis* of Commandant Vannier, (ex Capitaine 'La Lingerie'), Bibliothèque de Valençay, undated, p. 16.
6. '*Le petit coin*', Cornioley, *Pauline*, p. 70.
7. 'The excellent help', report of F/O Pearl Cornioley (Witherington), 23 November 1944, Pearl's PF.
8. 'Put maximum brake', Jean-Louis Crémieux-Brilhac, *La France Libre: De*

l'appel du 18 juin à la liberation (Paris: Gallimard, 2001), quoted in Cobb, *The Resistance*, p. 250.

9. 'To re-establish the situation in this region', 8 June 1944, vol 37, Kriegstagebuch of Oberfeldkmommandant General Friedrich ('Fritz') von Brodowski, Archive of the Nurembourg Trials; the *departements* governed by Brodowski were the Corrèze, Haute-Vienne, Allier, Dordogne, Haute-Loire, Puy de Dome, Cantal and the Indre.
10. 'Stenger Column', the Security Regiments were part of the Sicherheitsdienst or SD organisation, and included Security Regiment 196, motorised detachment 960, reinforced by the 3rd Security Regt, 194. Karl Buckhardt's column was made up of men from Security Regt 192.
11. 'Acetone Time delay apparatus', see Tangmere RAF Museum display.
12. 'As I watched the bodies', De Vomécourt, *Who Lived to See the Day*, p. 230.
13. '*Vous ne me connaissez pas?*', Cornioley, *Pauline*, p. 70.
14. Muriel Byck, Hon. Assistant Officer MT, Women's Auxiliary Air Force. Dropped April 1944 with Makowski (leader of the Sousmes *maquis*) as a member of the VENTRILOQUIST circuit. Died on active service near Romorantin (Loire et Cher), 23 May 1944. Mentioned in Despatches. J. Sainsbury, *F Section Memorial*.
15. 'La Lingerie', Nicault, *Résistance et Libération*, p. 41. Maurice Nicault, cousin of the author, was a member of the reception committee for the failed *parachutage* described by Mockers.
16. '*Vers minuit*. Towards midnight', Michel Mockers memoir, p. 25.
17. 'It was the best birthday present', interview with Col. John Sainsbury, 6 May 2011.
18. 'When they came to me', Pearl Witherington, interview 3 with Tom Roberts, 23 November 2006.

25. Into the Fray: the 2nd SS Panzer Division 'Das Reich.'

1. 'Since the early hours,' quoted in Max Hastings, *Das Reich: Resistance and the march of the 2nd SS Panzer Division through France June 1944*, Michael Joseph, 1981, p. 8.
2. '2nd SS Panzer Division,' ibid, p. 12.
3. 'Knight's Cross'; this was awarded to Heinrich Lammerding on 11 April 1944.
4. '*Totenkopfring,*' Martin Davidson, *The Perfect Nazi*, Viking 2010, p. 23.
5. 'I felt outraged,' quoted in Hastings, p. 115.
6. 'Citizens of Tulle', proclamation in French, *Centre de la Mémoire,* Oradour-sur-Glane; English translation in Hastings, p. 118, who believes that the allegations of mutilation of German corpses by the FTP were probably true, p. 120; the mass reprisals were, it seems, personally ordered by Lammerding.
7. 'Since no communication,' Brodowski *Kriegstagebuch*, 8 June 1944.
8. 'It was evident,' OKW War Diary, 9 June, quoted in Hastings, p. 127.

9. 'The paralysis of the German posts,' Report of General Lammerding, 10 June 1944, in Hastings, p. 145.
10. 'A great tribute,' Max Hastings, p. 144.
11. 'We set out,' Jacques Poirier, quoted in Hastings, p. 218.
12. 'It was of extraordinary importance,' MRD Foot, *SOE in France*, p. 342.
13. 'The extra fortnight's delay,' Foot, pp. 349–351; Peulevé was at this point attempting to escape from Fresnes after interrogation by the Gestapo at Avenue Foch; mingling with French visitors to the prison, he handed the prison guard a blank scrap of paper instead of a visitor's pass and ran. The sentry raised the alarm and Peulevé was wounded and recaptured in a garden nearby. Deprived of medical attention, he dug the bullet out of his thigh with a spoon.
14. 'When I left London,' Report by Philippe Liewer, quoted in Susan Ottaway, *Violette Szabo: The Life That I Have,* Pen & Sword 2002, p. 102.
15. 'Nearing the village of Salon' Report by Philippe Liewer, based on account by Jacques Dufour, in Ottaway, *Violette Szabo*, pp. 106–7.
16. 'Some of the SS,' Robert Hébras, *Oradour-sur-Glane, The Tragedy, Hour by Hour,* translated by David Denton, Les Chemins de la Mémoire, Honfleur-Saintes, p. 18.
17. Madame Rouffanche testimony, ibid, p. 25.
18. '*Bei Aktion der Truppe,*' Brodowski *Kriegstagebuch*, 11 June 1944.

26. Warrior Queen

1. 'No job for foreigners', Foot, *SOE in France*, p. 343.
2. 'Pearl Witherington', De Vomécourt, *Who Lived to See the Day*, p. 223.
3. 'I wish to put on record', Pearl Witherington, 'Report by F/O Witherington,' 23 November 1944, NA.
4. '*Ce n'était pas ma mission officielle*', *témoignage de Pauline le 24 janvier 2003*, Gilles Groussin, *La Résistance dans le Canton de Valençay (Les maquis de Gâtine)* (Villedieu/Indre: Imprimerie Color 36, 2006), p. 130.
5. 'Was very bold', Liewer report.
6. 'We are soldiers of integrity', report of Team Hugh (106a), April through June 1944 Operations, vol 4 Jeburghs, J. Sainsbury archive.
7. 'Our parachute operations', Witherington, 'Report by F/O Witherington'.
8. 'Panic', Nicault, *Résistance et Libération*, p. 47.
9. 'To keep an account', Pearl Witherington, interview 7 with Tom Roberts, 25 November 2006, p. 5.
10. 'No longer wear the red star', Cornioley, *Pauline*, p. 93.
11. 'Were not "Intelligence" circuits', Bourne-Paterson, 'The "British" Circuits', p. iii.
12. '*Pour Marie*', decoded signal in French, SFHQ, Pearl Witherington archive, Imperial War Museum; Marcus Binney, *The Women Who Lived for Danger* (Hodder & Stoughton, 2002), p. 198.

13. 'Thank you for information in your 47', decoded signal in French, SFHQ to Marie, 1944, PW archives, IWM; Cornioley, *Pauline*, p. 90.
14. 'There's going to be an accident. *Il va nous arriver un accident, il y a trop de va-et-vient*', Cornioley, *Pauline*, p. 82.
15. 'Saw numbers in colour', Pearl Witherington, interview 15 with Tom Roberts, 2006.
16. 'When the Germans got to Maray village', Pearl Witherington, interview 15 with Tom Roberts, 2006.
17. 'We narrowly escaped', Witherington, 'Report by F/O Witherington'.
18. 'And she was going round and round', Pearl Witherington, interview 15 with Tom Roberts, 2006.
19. '*Soudain j'aperçus une voiture*. Suddenly I saw a German car slow down, and I saw Francis Perdriset in it', Robert Monestier in Groussin, *La Résistance*, p. 136; Georges Charreau, responsible for the Western sector of the AS, described Perdriset as a '*resistant de la derniere heure* who did not answer the call of 6 June 1944 until obliged to do so by "Robert" (Boiziau),' captain of sub-sector 2, a liar who falsified his record when he joined the FFI.
20. 'Our heads were bowed, *toutes les têtes sont baissées, en larmes*', witness statement of Madame Denise Blanc, 26 November 2002, in Groussin, *La Résistance*, p. 137; a primary school in Châteauroux has been named l'école Françoise Katz in her memory.
21. 'Arrogant, *c'était un militaire orgueilleux qui avait des œillères*', Madame Lucienne Roux du Bataillon 'Comte', 16 July 2003, in Groussin, *La Résistance*, p. 134.
22. 'SOE Marie-Wrestler 43–44: She Who Must Be Obeyed', written in English, translated by Martine Jarnevic-Béguet, quoted in Groussin, *La Résistance*, pp. 125–132.
23. 'You have got to understand', Pearl Witherington, interview 8 with Tom Roberts, p. 2.
24. 'I thought I don't know', ibid. p. 3.
25. 'Pearl had a soft centre', interview with Tom Roberts, son of Nancy Roberts, née Fraser-Campbell, September 2012.
26. 'We picked him up', Pearl Witherington, interview 15 with Tom Roberts, p. 9.
27. 'What? Comment?', Cornioley, *Pauline*, pp. 79–80.
28. 'I was never warned . . .', Witherington, 'Report by F/O Witherington'.

27. Jedburgh 'Julian'

1. 'What is position', signal from Julian to SHQ, 15 August 1944, Operations Team Julian, Jedburghs Vol 4, July–September 1944.
2. 'As regards the SAS', Major W. R. Crawshay, Operations Team Hugh, April–September 1944, Operations, Jedburghs 18 Vol 4.
3. Jedburgh Hamish was led by 1st Lt Robert M. Anstett with Frenchman

Lt L. Blanchere, and radio ISG L. J. Watters. Jedburgh Ivor's team was Capt. J. H. Cox (British), Lt Y. M. Dantel (French) and Sgt Loosmore (British).

4. 'Apart from the few towns', Brodowski, *Kriegstagebuch*, 10 July 1944, Nuremberg archive.
5. 'The resistance in Indre et Loire', Crawshay war diary, 1 August 1944, Operations Team Hugh.
6. Lieutenant Twm Stephens, in Max Hastings, 'The SAS: Bulbasket', *Das Reich: Resistance and the march of the 2nd SS Panzer Division through France June 1944* (Michael Joseph, 1981), pp. 206–7.
7. '*Ici maquis, ici terroristes!*', Georgette Gueguen-Dreyfus, *Resistance Indre et Vallée du Cher, tome II* (Paris: Editions Sociales, 1970), pp. 151–7.
8. '*Ces brutes*', draft chapter, '*Les Agents du SOE dans le Nord-Indre au mois d'août 1944*', in manuscript of a 'History of the Resistance in the Nord-Indre', by G. Gueguen-Dreyfus, annotated by Pearl Witherington and sent to Prof. M.R.D. Foot, undated, IWM.
9. 'The soldiers of the swastika', ibid.
10. '*Les hordes Hitleriennes*', plaque Façade de la Mairie, Valençay, which reads: '*Le 16 Aout 1944, les hordes Hitleriennes ont pillé la ville. Incendié 42 immeubles, assassin 8 innocents. SOUVENEZ-VOUS* [remember].' The injunction to remember is identical to that at the entrance to the 'martyred village' of Oradour-sur-Glane.
11. 'It wasn't Oradour. *Ce n'était pas comme à Oradour, mais ce n'était pas très joli*', Cornioley, *Pauline*, p. 85.
12. 'Mauled', Foot, *SOE in France*.
13. 'In the west [Pearl's] guerrillas', Dr Declan O'Reilly, 'Pearl Witherington's War: Resistance and Military Effectiveness in the Indre June–September 1944', essay, 2011. The use of the term '*Banden-bekamfung*' or bandit-hunting marks a qualitative change in the way the Germans reacted to guerrilla or partisan operations, argues O'Reilly. Before the invasion of Russia the Nazis had classified insurrection as guerrilla warfare, but in 1942 Himmler redefined anti-guerrilla military action by labelling the partisans 'bandits' and so excluding large areas of territory from any semblance of legal warfare.
14. 'The Germans lost it', conversation with Defence Attaché Air Commodore Michael Brzezicki, British Embassy, Paris, May 2011.
15. 'Otto Diekmann was killed in action', Diekmann, the battalion commander at Oradour-sur-Glane on 10 June 1944, was reported by his commanding officer, Sylvester Stadler, to Brigadeführer Heinz Lammerding for exceeding his orders, and was court martialled. He was never brought to trial because he was killed in action on 29 June. Fellow officers believed he committed suicide by deliberately getting himself killed in battle, according to Otto Weidinger, the last commander of the Der Führer regiment of Das Reich, and the division's historian. Otto Weidinger, *Comrades to the End: The 4th SS Panzer-grenadier Regiment "Der Führer" 1938–1945* (Schiffer Publishing, 2004).

16. 'From Marie through Julian', signal 1566, 28 August 1944, Operations Team Julian, July–September 1944.
17. '*Herbstzeitlose* order', Michel Jouanneau, *La Fin des Illusions: La Capitulation de la Colonne Elster, Septembre 1944, présentation Paul Mirguet (Surcouf)*, p. 26.
18. 'You couldn't have any illusions', Cornioley, *Pauline*, p. 86.
19. 'Our mission', Groussin, *La Résistance*, p. 131.
20. 'I didn't go out and fight with a gun', Pearl Witherington, BBC interview, 1983, cat no 8689, Sound Archive, IWM.
21. 'Paris martyred', quoted by Beevor, *D-Day*, p. 512.
22. 'What the hell, Brad', ibid. p. 494.
23. '*Un air de fête*', Mockers, '*Maquis* SS-4', p. 78.
24. '*Le commandant Francis*', ibid. p. 115.
25. '*Avec mes sabots*', '*La Marche Lorraine*' by Louis Ganne; Cornioley, *Pauline*, p. 97.

28. The Elster Column

1. 'The Resistance must be broken', Paul Gaujac, *Special Forces in the Invasion of France*, translated by Janice Lert (Paris: Histoire & Collections, 1999), p. 375.
2. 'General Botho Elster', Jouanneau, *La Fin des Illusions*.
3. 'They were soon forced', Major William Crawshay, alias Crown (Hugh), 'Operations Team Hugh, Jedburghs vol 4, July–September 1944,' 97; Team Hugh (No 4) comprised: Crawshay of the Royal Welsh Fusiliers, arriving from the Yugoslavia section of SOE in Cairo; Capitaine then Commandant L'Helgouach, alias Louis Legrand (Franck alias Scipion) from the Infanterie; Sous-Lieutenant R. Meyer alias Mersiol (Yonne), the W/T operator, from BCRA. The unusual presence of two Frenchmen shows the lack of available personnel in the OSS on 5–6 June 1944. Two SAS officers were also dropped with Team Hugh. The original German escape plan was Poitiers–Chatellerault–Tours–Bourges.
4. 'Pearl's *maquis*', Declan O'Reilly, 'Pearl Witherington's War: Resistance and Military Effectiveness in the Indre, June–Sept 1944', podcast, 5 [see bibliography].
5. 'Destroyed the bridges', Pearl Witherington, 'Wrestler Circuit: Organization of Flying Officer Pearl Witherington, WAAF (Marie), History of Organization, Sept 22/23,1943–4 Sept 1944 and Record of Achievements of Wrestler Circuit', appendix in French, sheet 27, 23 November 1944.
6. 'Frightened, disordered', De Vomécourt, *Who Lived to See the Day*, p. 17.
7. 'For us, SOE began', Cornioley, *Pauline*, p. 84.
8. 'La guerre est perdue', Jouanneau, *La Fin des Illusions*, p. 74; Elster made his HQ successively at the châteaux of the comte d'Ornano and the duc de Maillé.

9. 'My orders are to defend Eguzon', Gaujac, *Special Forces in the Invasion of France*, p. 240.
10. 'Blood-bath', conversation with Colonel John Sainsbury, 25 February 2010.
11. 'He turned down the offer', Major Arthur Clutton, Operations, Team Julian, pp. 732–3.
12. 'No-one who watched', De Vomécourt, *Who Lived to See the Day*, p. 271.
13. '*Herrn Präfekt! . . . Ich und meine Truppen*', 'Generalmajor Elster, der Führer der Marschgruppe Süd, an den Herrn Präfekten des Departement Indre, 15 September 1944', *Combats des maquisards Indre*, Été 1944, p. 161.
14. 'I told General Collins', Clutton, Operations, Team Julian, p. 736.
15. 'Le major Clutton', Cornioley, *Pauline*, p. 81.
16. 'General Elster', F/O Pearl Cornioley Report, 23 November 1944, p. 7.

29. Liberation

1. 'Fighting was over', Crawshay, Operations Team Hugh, p. 105.
2. 'We shaved. *On tond la chevelure*', Chauveau-Veauvy, *L'Eté 44*, p. 230.
3. 'Don't bother speaking English', conversation with John Sainsbury, 31 December 2009; Cornioley, *Pauline*, p. 136.
4. 'With the military defeat', Foot, *SOE in France*, p. 367.
5. '*On nous avait ordonné*', Cornioley, *Pauline*, p. 140.
6. '*Je suis très mal reçu*', report of Major Roger Landes ('Aristide'), 17 September 1944, HS6/579, NA.
7. 'What are you doing here?', report of Captain Peter Lake, nom de guerre Basil, circuit Digger, led by Hestor in the Dordogne, 18 September 1944, HS6/579, NA.
8. 'I must express', Eisenhower to Gubbins, 31 May 1945, Foot, *SOE in France*, p. 387.
9. 'Je tiens surtout', letter from Pierre Hirsch, nom de guerre Popaul, Stationer circuit, to Colonel Buckmaster, 7 October 1944, HS6/583, NA.
10. 'An appreciation', Clutton, Operations, Team Julian, War Diary vol 3, p. 741.
11. 'She was for us. *Elle était pour nous ce que De Gaulle était pour la France . . . elle était devenue notre symbole*', Gaspard (Raymond Billard), one of Pearl's lieutenants, quoted in Cornioley, *Pauline*, p. 177.

30. Postwar

1. 'I may be in Cornwall', Mrs G Witherington to Major I. K. Mackenzie, 23 September 1944, PW PF.
2. 'I am sure you are', Mrs G Witherington to Vera Atkins, 9 September 1944. In a further letter of 30 September to Vera Atkins Pearl's mother writes that she, Dudu and Mimi have put off their trip to Cornwall in order to welcome Pearl home.

3. 'Women who hold honorary commissions', memo from F/ADM to D/Fin, 9 October 1944, PW PF.
4. 'I had £57', Pearl Witherington, interview 11 with Tom Roberts, 24 November 2006.
5. 'He arrived', Pearl Witherington, interview 16 with Tom Roberts; PW BBC interview 1983, IWM sound archive.
6. 'To proceed to Paris', Brigadier E. Mockler-Ferryman to F/O Cornioley, 22 November 1944.
7. 'The Judex mission', Buckmaster, *Specially Employed*, p. 193.
8. 'Major Crawshay', *The London Gazette*, 21 June 1945.
9. 'Witherington had to re-organise', Major General C. Mc. V. Gubbins, Recommendation for the Military Cross for Flight Officer C. P. Witherington WAAF, 12 April 1945, PW PF.
10. 'Not content with a sedentary job', citation for F/O Witherington, signed 'Wing Commander Redding', 1945, PW PF.
11. 'Proposed for the George Medal', Col. Maurice Buckmaster, L'Officier liquidateur Regional, La France Combattante, Proposal for the George Medal for C. P. Cornioley, 14 April 1945, PW PF.
12. 'Original citation was for the George Medal', 'Recommendation for the award of the OBE (Military Division), Flt Of. C. P. Witherington, 9904, WAAF', undated. 'Is the OBE not possible?' is written in Buckmaster's hand and signed 'MB'.
13. 'The work which I undertook', Pearl Witherington to Vera Atkins, 20 October 1945.
14. 'We are all OK here', Pearl Witherington to Vera Atkins, 26 April 1944, PW PF.
15. 'Angel angle', Major Amédée Maingard (Samuel) report, 10 April 1944, PW PF. Maingard was referring to 'Angel' as in 'English' – a reference to Caesar's remark, 'Not Angles but angels', when he saw fair-haired prisoner children from Britain, home of the Angles.
16. 'The work which I volunteered to do', Lise de Baissac to Vera Atkins, 20 October 1945.
17. 'Who are the WAAF officers', Sqn Ldr William Simpson, DFC, 'WAAF girls parachuted into France', *Sunday Express*, 11 March 1945.
18. 'Numerous injustices', letter from the Six Point Group to Pearl Witherington, 30 September 1946, F/O C. P. Cornioley papers, 08/105/1 IWM.
19. 'What's all this nonsense?', Cornioley, *Pauline*, p. 98.
20. 'Should you be', Vera Atkins to Pearl Witherington, undated, 1946.
21. 'Deliberately', statement by Col. Maurice J. Buckmaster, OBE, i/c French Section 'F' of the Special Operations Executive from September 1941 to June 1943, Appendix A in E. H. Cookridge, *Inside SOE*, p. 603; Buckmaster strenuously denied 'the most appalling accusation' that 'we deliberately sent our agents into enemy hands . . . to distract the attentions of the

Germans from the operations of other "more important" organizations' and that this 'was deliberately concealed by us from the public'. These questions were raised in parliament in a motion tabled by Dame Irene Ward MP in November 1958, following the publication of books by Jean Overton Fuller and Elizabeth Nicholas. Subsequently Professor M.R.D. Foot was commissioned to write the official history of SOE in France.

22. 'Most of the casualties', Pearl Witherington, interview 13 with Tom Roberts.
23. 'Second rate mind', conversation with Duncan Stuart, SOE Advisor to the FCO, 1996–2002, 20 October 2012.
24. 'Turned out to be the right person', Pearl Witherington, interview 5 with Tom Roberts.
25. 'We were just doing a job of work', Pearl Witherington, BBC Interview 1983, Sound Archive, IWM.
26. 'Most heartily recommend', telegram from Buckmaster to Colonel Brook, 'reference conversation Saturday Pearl Cornioley nee Witherington alias Wrestler now available excellent practical operational experience', Chantilly, undated, PW PF.
27. 'As you know', Vera Atkins to Wing Cdr Redding, 10 March 1945, PW PF.
28. 'With regard to Pearl's employment', Capt. N. Fraser-Campbell to Col. M. Buckmaster, 4 April 1945, PW PF.
29. 'The simplest action', Major Mackenzie to Capt. N. Fraser-Campbell, Paris, 25 January 1945, PW PF.
30. 'I wanted a little girl', Pearl Witherington, interview 8 with Tom Roberts.
31. 'Henri had an ungift', conversation with M.R.D. Foot, 2011.
32. 'If you want to go down the ladder', Pearl Witherington, interview 8 with Tom Roberts.
33. 'Skeleton hands', Buckmaster, *Specially Employed*, p. 147.
34. 'Some of them', Pearl Cornioley, Smithson, 'The Real Charlotte Grays', 2 January 2002, p. 48.
35. 'An old man', Marks, *Between Silk & Cyanide*, p. 580.

Epilogue

1. Georges Brassens, 'Les Amoureux des Bancs Publics', CD, *Chanson pour L'Auvergnat* (Master Serie, Polygram, 1991).
2. 'The shining spirit', Sainsbury, *The F Section Memorial*, p. 7; the sculpture is the work of Elizabeth Lucas Harrison, entitled 'Spirit of Partnership'. Funded by contributions from all over France, including those from the *associations d'anciens combattants*, and also by a sum from the Gerry Holdsworth Special Forces Charitable Trust, the F Section Memorial is meticulously maintained by the town of Valençay. The 20th anniversary

of the inauguration of the Memorial was commemorated in the presence of HRH Princess Anne, The Princess Royal, on Friday 6 May 2011.

3. 'When I got to England', Pearl Witherington, interview 5 with Tom Roberts.
4. Monsieur André Méric, the Secretary of State for Veteran Affairs.
5. Squadron Leader Rhys Cowsill presented Pearl with her parachute wings, having first met her in 2005 when researching a book on leadership for the Royal Air Force: 'We were short of good stories about women leaders and she more than filled the void' (Leadership: An Anthology, ed John Jupp, crown copyright 2005, produced by the Royal Air Force Leadership Centre. Pearl is featured on pp. 119–20: 'The sabotage carried out by the Maquis under Pearl's control had an enormous impact on the ability of the Germans to reinforce to the Normandy area . . . It is also a remarkable example of bravery, of determination and of the importance of trust in leadership in bringing about success in the most extreme circumstances, against overwhelming odds. In return Pearl presented the No 1 Parachute Training School, of which Cowsill was Officer Commanding, with a portrait of herself. It was painted in the style of Whistler's Mother, 'perhaps fitting, for Pearl was Wrestler's Mother.'

Select Bibliography

Amoureux, Henri, *La Vie des Français sous L'Occupation*, Paris: Librairie Arthème Fayard, 1961

Astley, Joan Bright and Wilkinson, Peter, *Gubbins and SOE,* Leo Cooper, 1993

Bailey, Roderick and the Imperial War Museum, *Forgotten Voices of the Secret War: An Inside History of Special Operations during the Second World War,* Ebury Press, 2009

Beevor, Antony, *D-Day: The Battle for Normandy*, Viking, 2009

Bertram, Barbara, *French Resistance in Sussex,* Chichester: Barnworks Publishing, 1995

Binney, Marcus, *The Women Who Lived for Danger: The Women Agents of SOE in the Second World War,* Coronet, Hodder and Stoughton, 2001

Buckmaster, M. J., *Special Employed: The Story of British Aid to French Patriots of the Resistance,* London: The Batchworth Press, 1952

They Fought Alone: The Story of British Agents in France, Odhams Press, 1958

Chauveau-Veauvy, Yves, *L'Eté 44: Indre nord Loir-et-Cher sud,* Sologne Graphic, 2004

Churchill, Peter, *Of Their Own Choice,* Hodder and Stoughton, 1952

Churchill, Winston, *The Second World War six vols,* Cassell 1948–54

Cobb, Matthew, *The Resistance: The French Fight Against the Nazis,* Simon & Schuster, 2009

Colville, John, *The Fringes of Power: Downing Street Diaries 1939–1945,* Hodder & Stoughton, 1985

Cookridge, E. H. *Inside SOE: The Story of Special Operations in Western Europe 1940–45,* Arthur Barker Ltd, 1966

Cowburn, Benjamin, *No Cloak No Dagger: Allied Spycraft in Occupied France*, Frontline Books, 2009

Cremieux-Brilhac, Jean-Louis, *La France Libre: De l'appel du 18 juin à la liberation,* Paris: Gallimard, 2001

Dalton, Hugh, *The Fateful Years: Memoirs 1931–1945*, Frederick Muller Ltd, 1957

D'Aragon, Charles, *La Résistance sans Héroïsme,* Paris: Editions du Seuil, 1977

Davidson, Martin, *The Perfect Nazi,* Viking, 2010

De Vomécourt, Philippe, *Who Lived to See the Day: France in Arms 1940–1944,* Hutchinson, 1961

Faulks, Sebastian, *Charlotte Gray*, Vintage, 1999

Foot, M.R.D., *SOE in France: An Account of the Work of the British Special Operations Executive in France 1940–1944*, Whitehall History Publishing in association with Frank Cass, 2004

Fuller, Jean Overton, *Déricourt: The Chequered Spy,* Michael Russell, 1989

Gaujac, Paul, *Special Forces in the Invasion of France,* translated by Janice Lert, Paris: Histoire et Collections Special Operations Series, 1999

Gilbert, Martin, *Finest Hour: Winston S Churchill 1940–41*, Heinemann, 1983

Road to Victory: Winston S Churchill 1942–45, Heinemann, 1986

Churchill: A Life, Macmillan, 1991

Gildea, Robert, *Marianne in Chains: In Search of the German Occupation of France 1940–4*, Pan Macmillan, 2003

Grazon, Jean, ed, *Combats des Maquisards Indre été 1944, à le mémoire des résistants tués, fusillés ou déportés,* Châteauroux: L'Imprimerie George Sand

Groussin, Gilles, *La Résistance dans le Canton de Valençay (les Maquis de Gâtine)*, Châteauroux: Imprimerie Color 36

Guéguen-Dreyfus, G., *Résistance Indre et Vallée du Cher, tomes I et II,* Paris: Editions sociales, 1970

Guillaume, Paul, *Au Temps de l'Héroïsme et de la Trahison,* Orleans: Librairie Loddé, 1978

Hastings, Max, *Das Reich: Resistance and the March of the 2nd SS Panzer Division through France June 1944*, Michael Joseph, 1981

Finest Years: Churchill as Warlord 1940–45, HarperPress, 2009

Hébras, Robert, *Oradour-sur-Glane, The Tragedy Hour by Hour,* translated by David Denton, Honfleur-Saintes: Les Chemins de la Mémoire

Helm, Sarah, *A Life in Secrets: The Story of Vera Atkins and the Lost Agents of SOE,* Little, Brown, 2005

Howard, Michael (Sir), *Strategic Deception in World War II,* HMSO, 1990

Howarth, Patrick, ed, *Special Operations,* Routledge and Kegan Paul, 1955

Hue, André and Ewen Southby-Tailyour, *The Next Moon: the remarkable true story of a British agent behind the lines in wartime France,* Viking, 2004

Humbert, Agnès, *Résistance: Memoirs of Occupied France,* translated by Barbara Mellor, Bloomsbury, 2008

Ingersoll, Ralph, *Top Secret,* Partridge Publications, 1946

Jouanneau, Michel, *La Fin des Illusions: La Capitulation de la Colonne Elster Septembre 1944, Présentation Paul Mirguet (Surcouf)*

Kedward, H. R. *In Search of the Maquis: Rural Resistance in Southern France 1942–1944,* Oxford: Clarendon, 1993

Larroque, Hervé, *Pauline: Pearl Cornioley, parachutée en 1943, la vie d'un agent du SOE, Témoignage recueilli par Hervé Larroque,* Editions par exemple, 1995

Lawford, Valentine, *Bound for Diplomacy,* John Murray, 1963

Lee, Celia and Paul Edward Strong, eds, *Women in War, from Home Front to Front Line,* Pen & Sword Military, 2012

MacKay, Francis, *Overture to Overlord: Special Operations in Preparations for D-Day,* Pen & Sword, 2005

MacKenzie, William, *The Secret History of SOE: The Special Operations Executive 1940–1945,* St Ermin's Press, 2000

Marks, Leo, *Between Silk & Cyanide: The Story of SOE's Code War,* HarperCollins, 1998

Marshall, Bruce, *The White Rabbit,* Evans Bros, 1952

Marshall, Robert, *All The King's Men: The Truth Behind SOE's Greatest Wartime Disaster,* Collins, 1988

Millar, George, *Maquis,* Heinemann, 1945

Minney, R. J., *Carve Her Name With Pride: The Story of Violette Szabo,* Pen & Sword, 2008

Mulley, Clare, *The Spy Who Loved: The Secrets and Lives of Christine Granville, Britain's First Female Special Agent of World War II,* Macmillan, 2012

Nicault, Maurice, *Résistance et Libération de l'Indre les Insurgés*, CCB Royer, 2003

Ottaway, Susan, *Violette Szabo: The Life that I Have*, Pen & Sword, 2002

Passy, Colonel, *Missions Secrètes en France* (Novembre 1942–Juin 1943): *Souvenirs du B.C.R.A*, Paris: Librairie Plon, 1951

Ronfort, Jean Nérée & Augarde, Jean-Dominique, *A l'ombre de Pauline: La Résidence de l'Ambassadeur de Grande-Bretagne à Paris, avec la collaboration de Sir Michael Llewellyn Smith*, Paris: Éditions du Centre de Recherches Historiques, 2001

Sainsbury, John, *The F Section Memorial*, Hart Books, Welwyn, 1992

Sartre, Jean-Paul, *Iron in the Soul*, first published as *La Mort dans l'âme*, 1949, translated by Gerard Hopkins, Penguin, 1963

Seaman, Mark, ed, *Special Operations Executive: A New Instrument of War*, Routledge, 2006

Sheridan, Dorothy, ed, *Wartime Women: An Anthology of Women's Wartime Writing for Mass-Observation 1937–45*, Heinemann

Stafford, David, *Churchill and Secret Service*, John Murray, 1997

Secret Agent: The True Story of the Special Operations Executive, BBC Worldwide, 2000

Steinbeck, John, *The Moon is Down*, Viking Press, 1942

Sweet-Escott, Bickham, *Baker Street Irregular*, Methuen, 1965

Taylor, Eric, *Heroines of World War II*, Robert Hale, 1991

Tindall, Gillian, *Footprints in Paris: A few streets, a few lives*, Pimlico, 2010

Verity, Hugh, *We Landed by Moonlight: Secret RAF Landings in France 1940–1944*, Manchester: Crécy Publishing Ltd, 2005

Wake, Nancy, *The autobiography of the woman the Gestapo called The White Mouse*, Sun Books, 1986

Walters, Anne-Marie, *Moondrop to Gascony*, Bodmin: Moho Books, 2009

Ward, Irene (Dame), *F.A.N.Y Invicta*, Hutchinson, 1955

West, Nigel, *Secret War: The Story of SOE, Britain's Wartime Sabotage Organisation*, Hodder and Stoughton, 1992

Yarnold, Patrick, *Wanborough Manor School for Secret Agents*, Hopfield Publications, 2009

Primary Sources

Bégué, Georges, *Rapport de Georges Bégué,* John Sainsbury Archive

R, Bourne-Patterson, 'The "British" Circuits in France 1941–44, Confidential Report,' 30 June 1946, National Archives at Kew (formerly PRO), NA HS 6/469

Brodowski, General Fritz von, *Kriesgtagebuch,* Archive of the Nurembourg Trials

Buckmaster, Sybil and Michael, 'Échanges avec le public sur Maurice Buckmaster et ses actions.'

Ciret, Chantal, 'Bilan de la section F et des réseaux Buckmaster'

Ciret, Chantal, 'Le SOE, La section F et les réseaux Buckmaster en Région Centre', *Résistances en Touraine et en Région Centre,* Actes de Colloque Tours Avril 2010, Hors Série 3, Saint-Pierre-Des-Corps: Laurent Caureau, 2010

Cooper, Duff, 'Top Secret Circular to British Consuls', 29 November 1946, NA HS 6/469

Lheureux, Daniele, 'Le capitaine Michael Trotobas et son parcours'

Mockers, Michel, 'Maquis SS-4, Font-Moreau et Gatine,' illustrations de Roger Decaux, Peintre Officiel de l'Armée, nd

Moffit, John (Paddy), 'My Escape', unpublished, nd, Oddie Papers

Oddie, Hélène (Mimi) 'My Family's Escape from the Germans, Normandie 1940', unpublished, 1989, Oddie Papers

O'Reilly, Declan 'Pearl Witherington's War: Resistance and Military Effectiveness in the Indre, June–Sept 1944', Military History Seminars podcast, 9 November 2010, Institute of Historical Research

Roberts, Tom, Transcripts of 16 interviews with Pearl Cornioley, November 2006

Smithson, Darlow, 'The Real Charlotte Grays', I/V Pearl Cornioley, 2 January 2002, transcript, Martyn Cox Oral History archive

Stuart, Duncan, 'Of Historical Interest Only', in Mark Seaman (ed), *Special Operations Executive,* Routledge 2006

Suttill, Francis, 'Le réseau "Prosper-Physician" et ses activités dans le region Centre'

Suttill, Francis J. and Foot, M.R.D., 'SOE's "Prosper" Disaster of 1943', *Intelligence and National Security,* Vol 26, No 1 99-105, February 2011

Thiault, Benoit, 'La Ligne de Demarcation dans le Cher 1940–1943', Musée de la Résistance et de la Déportation de Bourges et du Cher

Douglas Colyer Papers, Imperial War Museum, IMW 79/6/1

Jedburgh Reports, Arthur Clutton, 'Report of Team Julian', Crawshay, 'Report of Team Hugh', Sainsbury Archive

Maurice Buckmaster, Diary, 1943, Tim Buckmaster Archive

Maurice Southgate PF, NA HS 6/579, including letters from Maurice Buckmaster

Max Hymans Reports, John Sainsbury Archive and Special Forces Club

M.R.D. Foot Personal Archive, letters from Pearl Cornioley

'Pauline' papers, Bibliothèque de Valençay

Pearl Cornioley Papers, Imperial War Museum

Pearl Cornioley Personal Papers, John Sainsbury Archive

'Pearl Witherington: For Valour', BBC Timewatch Programme, 1995

Pearl Witherington file, including Recommendation for the George Medal, FANY (Princess Royal's Voluntary Corps) Archives

Pearl Witherington PF, 3 vols, NA HS/9/355/2; HS 6/587

RAF Museum, Tangmere, displays

Index

Figures in italics indicate captions.

INDEX